WITH THE RUSSIAN ARMY,
1914-1917

May, 1916. A Council of War at G.H.Q.

A. General Shuvaiev, Minister of War.
B. The Grand Duke Serge, Inspector of Artillery.
C. General Alexyeev, Chief of Staff at G.H.Q.
D. General Ewarth, Commander-in-Chief, Western Front.
E. General Kryetsinski, General Ewarth's Chief of Staff.
    At end of table. General Pustovoitenko, G.Q.M. at G.H.Q.
F. General Sievers, Acting Chief of Staff to General Kuropatkin.
G. General Kuropatkin, Commander-in-Chief, Northern Front.
H. The Emperor, Supreme Commander-in-Chief.
I. General Brusilov, Commander-in-Chief, South-Western Front.
J. General Klembovski, Chief of Staff to General Brusilov.
K. General Ivanov, att. to G.H.Q., late Commander-in-Chief South-Western Front.

Frontispiece Vol. II.

WITH THE RUSSIAN ARMY
1914-1917

BEING CHIEFLY EXTRACTS FROM THE DIARY OF A MILITARY ATTACHÉ

BY

**MAJOR-GENERAL SIR ALFRED KNOX,
K.C.B., C.M.G.**

WITH 58 ILLUSTRATIONS, CHIEFLY FROM PHOTOGRAPHS TAKEN BY THE AUTHOR, AND 19 MAPS

VOL. II

The Naval & Military Press Ltd

Published by

The Naval & Military Press Ltd
Unit 10 Ridgewood Industrial Park,
Uckfield, East Sussex,
TN22 5QE England

Tel: +44 (0) 1825 749494
Fax: +44 (0) 1825 765701

www.naval-military-press.com
www.military-genealogy.com

In reprinting in facsimile from the original, any imperfections are inevitably reproduced and the quality may fall short of modern type and cartographic standards.

CONTENTS OF VOLUME II

CHAPTER XI

THE NORTHERN AND SOUTH-WESTERN FRONTS AND PETROGRAD
JANUARY-MARCH, 1916

PAGE

Changes in the distribution of the armies during the winter—The offensive on the South-West Front in December, 1915, and January, 1916—The raid on Nevel in November, 1915—The internal situation—The Rasputin scandal—Improvement at the front—Lack of officers—Quality of divisions of various categories—Faults of organisation in the replacement of casualties—Visit to the Northern Front in February, 1916—General Plehve's retirement—His character and services—Succeeded by General Kuropatkin—Opinion of General Bonch-Bruevich regarding Russian strategy—Great improvement in Russian position on the Northern Front—Defective communications—Intelligence system—Conversations with General Radko Dimitriev—His opinion of allied strategy, of Ferdinand of Coburg, of shell and S.A.A. supply, of "side-shows," of the Rumanian army—The Rumanian military attaché on the position of his country—The Russian policy towards Rumania—General Gurko—The South-West Front—The Chief of Staff, General Klembovski—The General Quartermaster, General Dietrikhs—Conversation with General Ivanov—His retirement   383

CHAPTER XII

THE RUSSIAN OFFENSIVE ON THE NORTHERN AND WESTERN FRONTS IN MARCH, 1916. THE SUPPLY OF MUNITIONS. THE RAILWAYS, APRIL-JULY, 1916

Grouping of the Russian army in the spring of 1916—Plans for the year—The offensive of March on the Northern and Western Fronts—Its failure—Faults in tactics—Folly of launching an offensive at such a season—Complaints at Staffs of the Front, of the Army and of Groups—Difficulty regarding American contracts—Attitude of the Russian Artillery Department—Dismissal of General Polivanov—His enemies—Stories—Engineer Bratolyubov—Conversation with General Polivanov—The new Minister of War, General Shuvaiev—Interview with General Shuvaiev—Visits of Allied missions—M.M. Viviani and Albert Thomas—M. Thomas's conclusions—Proposed visit of Lord Kitchener—The loss of the *Hampshire*—Russia's munition effort in the first seventeen and a half months of war—Summary of armament on March 20th, 1916—Rifles supplied by the Allies—Strength and weaknesses at the front—Influence of the lack of railways and of rolling-stock on the output of munitions and on the price of necessities—Application to Great Britain for large credits for railway material refused—Natural causes of strain on the railways—System of administration of railways in June, 1916—Visit to G.H.Q.—Conversation with the Emperor—Conversation with the Grand Duke Serge—General Shuvaiev's opinion regarding the supply of meat—An "unpleasant incident" 404

CHAPTER XIII

OPERATIONS ON THE SOUTH-WEST FRONT FROM THE COMMENCEMENT OF BRUSILOV'S OFFENSIVE (JUNE 4TH, 1916) TILL THE FORMATION OF THE GUARD ARMY (JULY 25TH, 1916)

The main Russian offensive of the year projected from Krevo on Vilna—The preliminary concentration and preparations—Fifty-eight Russian divisions on the Western Front and only thirty-eight each on the Northern and South-Western Fronts—Only two Austrian divisions north of the Pripyat and only two German divisions south of that river—Enemy armies opposing the South-West Front—Composition of the armies of the Russian South-West Front—Russian forces superior to the enemy in number of rifles, but inferior in guns, machine-guns and in air power—Promotion of General Brusilov to be Commander-in-Chief of the South-West Front—His career—Brusilov's offensive launched as a demonstration to help Italy—The Army Commanders—The attack of the 8th Army—Its brilliant success—The 11th Army fails—Careful preparation of the offensive in the 7th Army—Its success—Details of the dispositions for the attack in the 9th Army—The enemy routed—Czernowitz captured, June 17th—Reasons for the success of the 9th Army in contrast to the failure in December, 1915—Summary of the success achieved by the middle of June—Prompt German assistance sent to the defeated Austrian armies—Von Linsingen's enveloping attack against the 8th Army—The Russian 3rd Army is added to Brusilov's command and drives von Linsingen back to the Stokhod, July 4th-7th—The 9th Army completes the conquest of Bukovina, June 24th—Occupies Kolomea, June 29th, and Delatyn, July 10th—The 11th Army captures Brody, July 28th 432

CHAPTER XIV

THE TRANSFER TO THE SOUTH. EVENTS ON THE NORTHERN AND WESTERN FRONTS IN JUNE AND JULY, 1916

Brusilov's success causes the Russian Supreme Command to change its plans—The race to the south—Abandonment of the Krevo offensive—The offensive of the 4th Army north of Baranovichi—Its failure—General Abram Dragomirov's opinion regarding the cause of failure—General Ragoza's opinions regarding the Russian officer and the Russian soldier—His own repeated transfer—The lack of initiative in the Russian army and of character in the Supreme Command—Opinion of the General Quartermaster of the Western Front

Contents

on the abandonment of the offensive from Krevo and on the attempt north of Baranovichi—Abortive offensive from Riga bridgehead, July 16th-21st—Radko Dimitriev's suggestion of a surprise attack—Projected combined operation from the Riga bridgehead on August 21st—Abandonment of further attempts to prevent enemy transfers to the south—Dissatisfaction with the Allies—Prince Dolgoruki—General Fidotov—Actual transfers from the Western theatre to the Eastern theatre—The Staff of the 1st Army in October, 1916 .. 449

CHAPTER XV

The Operations of the Guard Army on the Stokhod, July 21st-August 12th, 1916. A Visit to the 9th Army

Formation of the Guard Army on July 21st—Its staff and composition—Interview with General Brusilov on July 30th—His plans—Opinion of General Quartermaster regarding lack of technical equipment—Russian and enemy losses—Deployment of the Guard Army—Successful attack on July 28th—Failure to cross the Stokhod—Heavy losses—Gloomy prospects—Atmosphere of mistrust in the Staff—Visit to the 8th Army on August 4th—Censorship—Anecdote of a visit to a Russian Staff in the Carpathians—The attack of the Guard Rifle Division on Vitonej—The infantry sacrificed owing to poor support of the artillery, the result of lack of training in combined manœuvre—A conference at Lutsk on August 4th decides on a new offensive—An anti-aircraft battery sent to the front to practise—Visit to the Staff of the 1st Guard Corps—The Grand Dukes Paul and Dimitri Pavlovich—Attack on the Kukhari Wood on August 8th—Dispositions—With the Staff of the 2nd Guard Infantry Division during the attack—The failure—Opinions regarding the cause of failure—Losses of the Guard Army up till August 9th—Abandonment of all attempts to advance direct on Kovel—Intrigue, the race to G.H.Q. to report—General Bezobrazov and the Grand Duke Paul removed from their command—The Guard Army rechristened "the Special Army," and the command given to General Gurko—Brusilov's opinion of the Staff of the Guard Army and of the direction of the artillery—Opinion of the General Quartermaster regarding the intervention of Rumania—Hindenburg takes control of the Eastern Front from the Baltic to Tarnopol—The 9th Army occupies Stanislau, August 10th, and Nadworna, August 12th—The 7th Army occupies Monasterzyska, August 12th—Bothmer retreats to the Zlota Lipa—Trophies of the 8th, 11th, 7th and 9th Armies, June 4th to August 11th—The flow of reinforcements to and against the 9th Army—The 9th Army ordered to force the Carpathian Passes, with the object of protecting the right flank of the Rumanian army—Character of the Carpathians—The Staff of the 9th Army, a happy family—An officer's opinion of certain Russian generals—Anecdotes of General Pavlov 459

CHAPTER XVI

Events on the South-West Front from the Middle of August till the Middle of November, 1916

Vladimir-Volinski becomes the immediate objective of Brusilov instead of Kovel—Despatch of the Russian detachment to the Dobrudja—Error of sending Serbs—General Zaionchkovski's conversation with General Alexyeev—Failure of the attempt of the 9th Army to force the Carpathians—The retreat of the Rumanian Army in October necessitates the transfer of forces to the south and so deprives the Russian Command of the initiative—Failure of the attempts of the 8th and Special Armies to advance on Vladimir-Volinski—The cause—General Dukhonin's opinion of the Rumanian army—Visit to the Special Army in October, 1916—Conversation with General Gurko—Brusilov's mistake in sending the Guard to the Stokhod—Concealed artillery positions—Depression of the infantry—General Kornilov tells the story of his escape from Austria—Opinion of General Gerois regarding the general Allied direction of the war—Visit to the 11th Army—To the 7th Army—Its staff—Devices to deceive the enemy—Stories of deserters—The 8th Army at Czernowitz—General Stogov's opinion of the cause of the check in the Russian offensive—Opinion of junior officers of Generals Shcherbachev and Kaledin—Lunch with General Trepov—Admiration for British determination—Army snobbery—Various opinions regarding the intervention of Rumania and the failure of the Russian Command to make the most of it—Proposed offensive of the 9th Army—A drive in the Carpathians—Composition of the Russian armies on the South-West Front in the middle of November, 1916—Twenty infantry and seven cavalry divisions transferred to territory formerly neutral as a result of the intervention of Rumania—General Brusilov's complaints—General Dukhonin's optimism—The Russian cavalry—General Brusilov's opinion of its work in the recent offensive and previously in the war—Generals Kaledin and Abram Dragomirov are stronger believers in the use of cavalry 483

CHAPTER XVII

THE THREE MONTHS PRECEDING THE REVOLUTION

Northern communications—The Skibotten sledge route and the Murman railway—Changes in the Ministry of War—The murder of Rasputin—The reactionary tendencies of the Government—The Allied delegations—Visit to Riga, Minsk and Moscow—The offensive from Riga in January, 1917—Proposed Russian offensive in the spring—Crisis on the railways—Conversations with Generals Polivanov and Byelyaev, with the Rumanian Minister and with M. Guchkov—Conversation with the President of the Duma, M. Rodzianko, and with Captain Markozov on the eve of the Revolution 509

CHAPTER XVIII

THE RUSSIAN ARMY ON THE EVE OF THE REVOLUTION

Reorganisation—Distribution—Analysis of infantry and cavalry units—Comparison with peace strength—Progress in the organisation of technical troops—Russia's effort in man-power—Wastage—Progress in armament and in technical equipment—Actual armament on the eve of the Revolution—The chivalrous strategy of the Russian Command—Prospects of the campaign of 1917 532

Contents

CHAPTER XIX

THE REVOLUTION IN PETROGRAD

PAGE

The mutiny on the morning of March 12th—At the Artillery Department —M. Rodzianko's telegrams to the Emperor—The Duma tries to take control—Visit to the Commander of the District at the Prefecture— The Liteini Prospekt in the evening—The beginning of the Sovyets— Danger owing to the officers holding aloof—First visit to the Duma —Ideas of the men of the Preobrajenski Regiment—A social-democratic proclamation—Scene of disorder in the Duma—Arrest of M. Sturmer and others—Arrest of M. Protopopov—The growth of disorder—The Revolution caused by the stupidity of the old Government—It degenerates into a class movement, because the natural leaders of the people were too loyal to their Allies to initiate a revolution during the war—General Polivanov is optimistic, but is not taking any risks—Order No. 1—History of the Order—A printed licence for cowardice and anarchy—Tragic position of the officers—M. Rodzianko's confidence—The Sovyet forces the deposition of the Emperor—The Emperor's abdication—Reception of the news by the Empress—The Grand Duke Mikhail renounces the throne—The first Provisional Government—Conversation with a labour leader on March 16th—Pessimism of officers—The brutality of the mob—Idleness and anarchy—The passion for speech—M. Guchkov realises the situation—Martyrdom of the officers—Kerenski the only man who can save the country—First interview with Kerenski on March 19th—His confidence—Arrival of General Kornilov—Visits to depot units of the Guard in Petrograd in March and April—Experiences in various units—The Government tries to save the situation by rhetoric, avoiding the application of force—Official optimism—Bad news from the front—The soldiers really children—Ceremony of recognition of the Provisional Government by the Allies on March 25th—The scene —General Polivanov's committee to frame regulations for the new " discipline "—General Kornilov's courage—Kerenski with the Ambassador on April 9th—Still optimistic—Guchkov shows greater common sense—Prince Lvov's reply to the Ambassador's warning .. 553

CHAPTER XX

THE NORTHERN FRONT IN APRIL, AND PETROGRAD IN MAY, 1917

Changes in the command—Move of the 1st Army—Expulsion of the best officers for futile reasons—Reasoning with the men—Pollution of the army by political agitation—Fraternisation—German proclamations in Russian and Russian proclamations in German—The 109th Division —The committees—Pretended optimism of the command—Pessimistic conclusions—Return to Petrograd—Kerenski at the St. George's benefit —Progress of Bolshevik propaganda—Rivalry between the Provisional Government and the Sovyet—Disturbances of May 4th—Liberation of prisoners of war—Wave of extravagant humanitarianism—Pacifist propaganda—Question of stopping the supply of munitions—Suggested removal of Kornilov, Guchkov and Milyukov—General Lechitski tells of the scandalous treatment of General Miller—Guchkov resigns—Letter to the Ambassador on the military situation—The Executive Committee of the Sovyet to co-operate in the formation

378   Contents

                                                                    PAGE
of a Coalition Government—The composition of the Executive Committee—Proclamations issued by the Sovyet—British labour delegation—Formation of the Coalition Government—Kerenski Minister of War—No improvement to be hoped from his programme—The Ambassador's interview with Kerenski on May 21st—Colonel Balabin's admiration for Kerenski—The ex-convict Lieutenant Kuzmin as Assistant to the Commander-in-Chief of the Petrograd Military District—Mr. Henderson's mission—The new Commander-in-Chief, General Polovtsev—Attitude of the Executive Committee of the Sovyet towards extremists—Cowardice of the 1st Army—Continued anti-war propaganda—Publication of the Declaration of Soldiers' Rights and of the Order for the Offensive—Pessimism of the Assistant Minister of War—Fall of output in mines, furnaces and workshops   593

CHAPTER XXI

THE SOUTH-WEST FRONT IN JUNE. KERENSKI'S OFFENSIVE IN JULY, 1917

Journey to Kamenets-Podolsk—General Brusilov's promotion to be Supreme Commander-in-Chief—His "political gymnastics"—General Gutor, Commander-in-Chief of the South-West Front—The 8th Army in June—Fewer agitators but harmful newspapers—A revolutionary doctor—An anecdote—General Gurko degraded—Talk with General Kornilov—Growing disorganisation—Poisonous propaganda and stupid catchwords—General Selivachev—General Notbek—The XLIXth and VIth Corps—Ensign Kirilenko—Army commissaries—Chief anxiety of the Command to restore order without bloodshed—Vacillating treatment of the mutineers of the VIIth Siberian Corps—Kerenski's arrival with proclamations—His failure to convince the 2nd Guard Infantry Division—The plan for the offensive of July 1st—The Russian Staffs—Russian superiority in numbers and in technique—The attack on July 1st—Its failure through cowardice of most of the infantry—Kerenski's folly and blindness—The success of the Czechs on July 2nd of no avail owing to the disaffection of the 1st Guard Corps—Conversation with the Commander of the 1st Guard Infantry Division on July 4th—Peace necessary for Russia—The South-West Front demands the restoration of the death penalty—Changes in command—The war in Russia now a secondary matter   627

CHAPTER XXII

PETROGRAD IN JULY AND AUGUST, 1917

State of Petrograd outwardly as in May—Conversation with the Assistant Minister of War—The Bolshevik rising on July 16th—Critical position on the 17th—The situation saved by disclosure of the tainted source of Bolshevik funds—An ambush—Scene from the Embassy windows—The Preobrajenski want to arrest the Bolshevik Kamenev—The revolt subsides, but the Government fails to take strong measures to prevent its recurrence—Kerenski to be Prime Minister—His vacillation—Dismissal of General Polovtsev—Funeral of the Cossacks—The first success followed by the retreat of the 8th Army—Enemy offensive

Contents 379

against the 11th Army—Disorderly retreat of the 11th, 7th and 8th Armies—The pillage and massacre at Kalusz—General Kornilov replaces General Gutor in command of the South-West Front—The death penalty re-established in the theatre of war on July 25th—Conference at G.H.Q. on July 29th—General Kornilov's Order of August 1st stigmatises the treachery of "certain units" and the heroism of the officers—Retirement of Generals Brusilov and Radko Dimitriev—General Kornilov appointed Supreme Commander in Chief, July 31st—Economic chaos—Prince Tumanov on the "wonderful Russian spirit"—Formation of the "Save the Revolution" Government, August 6th—Savinkov as Assistant Minister of War—Kerenski as Alexander IV.—The one hope that Kerenski and Kornilov may work together—Talk with M. Tereshchenko—With M. Savinkov—Dinner with M. Tereshchenko to meet Kerenski .. 653

CHAPTER XXIII
Kerenski Loses His Last Chance. September, 1917

The idea of sending a joint Allied note to the Russian Government—British attitude towards Russian policy—The conflict between Kornilov and Kerenski inevitable—The character and career of the two men—The State Conference at Moscow accentuates the differences—Russian military opinion—Savinkov's *rôle*—Evil influence on either side—Lvov's *rôle*—Kerenski refuses compromise—Kornilov's Order and the Appeal of the Sovyets on September 11th—General Polovtsev's experience on September 9th—The meeting of the Caucasian Native Division with the Government troops—Suicide of General Krimov—Tragic result of the disagreement for the officers—The murders at Helsingfors and Viborg—Arrest of prominent Russian officers—Savinkov resigns—Verkhovski is appointed Minister of War—His career—Opinions of Savinkov and Filonenko concerning the "Affair Kornilov"—Kerenski most to blame—His narrowness .. 677

CHAPTER XXIV
The Bolshevik Coup D'Etat. October-December, 1917

The position recognised as hopeless—The suggestions of a G.S. officer—Dinner with the American Military Attaché—Conversation with General Verkhovski—His project to raise the *morale* of the army—The death penalty—Conversation with Tereshchenko—His baseless fears regarding an advance on Petrograd—Five commanders-in-chief in two months—Savinkov's opinion of Chernov—Fighting-men engaged in talk—The "Equipment Market"—Police to be formed at last—Pessimism of Russian officers—Number of men at the front—Enormous accumulation of shell—Savinkov's account of his examination by three Jews—Verkhovski resigns—The Bolshevik *coup d'etat*—Formation of a Military Revolutionary Committee—The Government's decision to arrest Trotski—The Cossacks refuse to support Kerenski—The situation on November 8th—The whole capital, with the exception of the Palace Square, in the hands of the Bolsheviks—The storming of the Winter Palace—Its farcical defence—Attitude of aloofness of the General Staff—Confidence of the opposition socialists—Release of the women prisoners—Murder of Prince Tumanov—Bolshevik proclamation to the troops at the front

—Formation of a Bolshevik Government—Savinkov's adventures with the " relieving force "—The rising of the yunkers on November 11th—Liquidation of the relieving force, and escape of Kerenski—Murders in Petrograd—Verkhovski visits the Ambassador—Appeal of a patriotic Russian naval officer—New Declaration of the Rights of Soldiers—Idleness in the trenches—Anecdote of a pious robber—The revolt in Moscow 694

CHAPTER XXV

The Preparation of the Separate Peace

Reasons for the Bolshevik success—General Dukhonin dismissed and Ensign Kirilenko appointed Supreme Commander-in-Chief—His Order No. 1—The despatch of *parlementaires* from the 5th Army on November 26th—The Allied attitude—Trotski blusters—The Ambassador's even mind—Murder of General Dukhonin—Arrest of Generals Manikovski and Marushevski—The Armistice Delegation—Its composition—Its arrival at Brest Litovsk on December 3rd—A temporary truce arranged till December 17th—Events at Brest Litovsk—The Bolsheviks' indecent haste—Its object—General Skalon's suicide—An armistice signed to continue till January 14th, 1918—Degradation of non-elected officers—A deputation of officers' wives—The garrison of Petrograd specialises in the looting of wine-cellars—The army at the front engages in trade and fraternisation—Trotski's insults—General Boldirev's trial—A hitch in the peace negotiations—Trotski rattles the sabre—Departure from Petrograd.. 723

APPENDICES

A. Some Data Regarding Russian Field Guns in use in 1916 741
B. Letter addressed by the Military Attaché to the Ambassador on July 30th, 1917 742

LIST OF MAPS

MAP
XI. The Russian Front in 1916-1917.
XII. The Operations of the Armies of the South-West Front in the Summer of 1916.
XIII. Russia's Northern Communications during the War.

SKETCH D. The Cossack Raid on Nevel, November 25th-28th, 1915.
SKETCH E. The Operations of the Guard Army on the Stokhod in July and August, 1916.
SKETCH F. Plan of Petrograd.

LIST OF ILLUSTRATIONS

A Council of War at G.H.Q.	*Frontispiece*
	Facing page
Type of Causeway, S. of Riga	400
General Radko-Dimitriev, Commander of 12th Army	400
Starting to drive back after visiting the XXIXth Corps	401
The Emperor and Staff on South-West Front, 1916	401
Corner of Lake Naroch	406
The Russian Munitions Delegation, 1915	406
German wire entanglements, Lake Naroch, 1916	407
Road in village of Krivichi	410
Krivichi-Naroch road	410
Ural Cossacks	411
Group after Conference at Army Headquarters, 1916	411
View in the Carpathians	450
Bivouack of the 43rd Division in the Carpathians	450
Bridge on the Upper Pruth	451
Prince Radzivill's house at Nesvij	451
The Woodman's Hut south of Yanovka	500
River Stir at Sokal	500
Group of Military Members of the British Delegation in Riga bridgehead, 1917	501
Infantry in trenches awaiting attack, Riga bridgehead	501
Temporary Executive Committee of the Imperial Duma, 1917	600
Soldiers posing in the Liteini Prospekt, 1917	600
Methods of travelling, 1917	601
Trooper of the Tekinski Turkoman Volunteer Regiment	601

CHAPTER XI

THE NORTHERN AND SOUTH-WESTERN FRONTS AND PETROGRAD. JANUARY—MARCH, 1916

REFERENCE MAP No. XI.

I RETURNED to Petrograd in the third week of January, 1916. During the following months my chief work lay in the capital, where I acted as General Ellershaw's representative in questions of armament, but time was found to visit G.H.Q. and all three fronts on the Western Frontier.

Throughout the winter the Russian armies of the Northern and Western Fronts remained relatively in the position they had taken up at the end of the retreat from Poland in the preceding October. On the South-West Front there were a few changes. General Shcherbachev handed over command of the 11th Army to General Sakharov, and, with General Golovin as his Chief of Staff, took charge of the 7th Army, then forming as an active army at Odessa in the hope of a declaration of war by Rumania. After waiting in vain for this declaration, the army was moved north in December, 1915, and took up a line between the 11th and 9th Armies. In the neighbourhood of Volochisk a new Guard Army was formed under command of General Bezobrazov, with Count Ignatiev, late Commander of the Preobrajenski Regiment, as Chief of Staff, and Colonel Domanevski as General Quartermaster. The grouping of the armies of the South-West Front was therefore at the beginning of the year from right to left: 8th, 11th, 7th, 9th, with the Guard in rear of the 7th.

In late December the Russian 9th Army launched an offensive which ended in complete failure, but was spoken of later as having provided valuable, if dearly-bought, experience, to be made full use of in the following June.

The plan was for the 9th Army to attack and to occupy the Czernowitz heights on December 27th in the hope that the enemy reserves further north would be drawn south, and that the 7th Army, which struck on December 29th, would find little opposition.

The enemy, however, had ample warning during the slow concentration of the 7th Army from Bessarabia. Further, the commencement of the operation is said to have been delayed three weeks as the Emperor wished to review the Guard before handing it over to the Commander-in-Chief of the South-West Front. The enemy reserves were moved south from the front of the 8th and 11th Russian Armies, which had been told to stand fast, while those in front of the 7th Army remained where they were. The infantry of the XIIth and XIth Corps of the 9th Army suffered severely owing to the lack of heavy artillery and the failure of the field artillery to support their attack. They were forced to move forward to the attack from too great a distance, one commander actually ordering his infantry for the assault " to remain concealed in trenches not closer than 1,000 yards to the enemy's line." The whole operation was insufficiently thought out and badly prepared. For instance, the Commander of the 7th Army, who had just arrived from Bessarabia, complained that the 11th and 9th Armies, part of whose line he took over, gave him no sketches or photographs, and only the vaguest information of the enemy position that he was called upon to carry.

The Russian supply and transport broke down utterly. The 11th Army was supposed to draw its supplies from railhead at Tarnopol, the 7th Army from the station of Yermolintsi on the Proskurov-Kamenets branch, and the 9th Army from Kamenets. Thus three armies were dependent on two single lines of rail, which G.H.Q. expected to give sixteen pairs of trains a day, but which actually only ran four pairs. A thaw made the roads impassable, and the 7th Army in particular was reduced to a state of starvation.

Most of the fighting was over by January 3rd.

This short offensive was the only considerable operation during the winter, but raids on either side relieved the tedium of trench warfare.

In the month of March I heard an account of the raid on Nevel that had been carried out in the previous November. I was at the Headquarters of the South-West Front at the time, and was supping in the train with the Commander-in-Chief's personal staff—an aristocratic assembly of four princes, of whom one was rheumatic and another asthmatic, and three commoners.

Thursday, March 23rd, 1916.   BERDICHEV.

We supped at the fashionable hour of 10 p.m. Obolenski produced a friend, an officer from his Terek Cossack Regiment, who had taken part as leader of one of the nine detachments in the well-known Nevel raid in November, an operation which wiped out a German battalion and captured a whole divisional staff. He was a hard, self-reliant man, probably without much education, but with enough to recognise that he was a savage. I have never heard anyone tell a story with less " bounce."

The nine detachments, each about 100 strong, started from Mutvitsa on the Gnilaya Pripyat on the night of November 25th, and reached Komora, due north, before dawn.[1] There they lay hidden all day. After dark on the 26th they threw a bridge over the Strumets, but it broke after two detachments had passed, and further advance had to be postponed till the following night. The raiders then crossed the river on a bridge of goat bladders. Four detachments were left to guard the line of retreat, and the remaining five, led by local guides, moved on by a path across the marsh.

The Germans were known to have only a single piquet on a front of seven to eight versts; they relied on the difficulty of the marsh in their front and on their knowledge that this section of the Russian line was held by Opolchenie. The piquet of thirty men, only half a dozen yards from the path, was fast asleep, and 500 of the raiders had passed before a single man awoke. The Germans were surrounded and bayoneted, with the exception of one man, who was kept as a prisoner for intelligence purposes.

---

[1] See Sketch D.

The cold was intense—fourteen degrees of frost (Réaumur)—and there were no sentries at the divisional headquarters. The farmhouse was quietly surrounded. An ensign crept into a room full of sleeping officers, then turned out the light and "got to work" with his sword. Bombs were thrown into another room where officers were sleeping in armchairs, and the place was instantly in a blaze. The Germans who ran out were hoisted on bayonet and kinjal.[1] Here a woman volunteer, from Saratov on the Volga, betrayed her sex, for the sight of the blood and the butchery was too much for her, and she cried out : " What are you doing, soldiers ? You are blackguards ! " (*razboiniki*), and fainted.

The Divisional Commander came to the door, shading his eyes with his hand, and was instantly taken prisoner. Leontiev, the leader of one of the detachments, called on sixty Germans to surrender. Forty or fifty stood up, but one of the others shot him in the stomach, whereupon the lot were destroyed.

The Germans were gathering, and the raiders had to get back by daylight. They started with several prisoners, but had to kill most of them by the way. First the doctor fired two revolver-shots and was " stuck." Then a brigade commander shared his fate. Only the Divisional Commander and seven rank and file " went peaceably."

One of the Cossacks, who had been hit in the retreat, begged to be left behind, as in any case he was mortally wounded. Some Germans were seen to rush forward to bayonet him, and these were in turn attacked by some Cossacks who had remained behind searching for brandy.

The General spoke a little Russian and tried repeatedly to describe the appearance of a German lieutenant-colonel of the General Staff, and to ask if anything had been seen of him. At last a Terek Cossack officer pointed to the stains on his kinjal, and said : " There is your lieutenant-colonel's blood." The old man collapsed after this,

---
[1] Cossack daggers.

for the dead officer had been his son. Three days later, when left alone for a minute, he took a revolver from the table and shot himself. Here more than one kind-hearted Russian in the audience ejaculated "Hard lines!" (*tyajelo*).

The Russians got back with a loss of eleven killed and forty-three wounded. They had covered thirty-seven versts. In the morning the Germans sent seven aeroplanes "to look for their General."

War has still a spice of adventure when there is no barbed wire.

As Odishelidze and others had predicted, the rest of the winter months restored the *morale* of the troops.

Sunday, February 6th, 1916.　　　　　　　　PETROGRAD.

K—— told me that Prince Lvov, President of the Zemstvo Union, had visited G.H.Q. with Chelnikov, the Mayor of Moscow, ten days ago, and had had an interview with Alexyeev. They found him in much better spirits than in November, when he was terribly depressed. He said that the *morale* of the troops, which was bad in November, had much improved. He maintained, however, that, owing to the lack of technical equipment on the Russian front, the decision would have to be fought out elsewhere. The Galician offensive had failed because of many mistakes. The army, he said, lacked proper leaders. There was hardly a single man of ability above the rank of regiment commander. The Emperor never interfered in matters of military direction. Alexyeev is also said to have remarked that the Emperor had not a single honest man about him except Count Friedrichs, who was stupid, deaf and blind (*glup, glukh i slyep*).

In Petrograd and the large towns the burden of the war was being felt more and more. The cost of necessaries had risen enormously, and it was a mystery how the smaller officials managed to live. Of course there was abundance of everything in the country, if only the railways had been able to distribute it.

Foreign observers had grown accustomed to the long queues of poor people waiting for hours in the cold for their turn at the bread-shops and to the dreadfully crowded tramways. These inconveniences had continued so long that they had begun to think the people were too docile to make an organised attempt against the Government.

I went to see M. Rodzianko, the President of the Duma, to talk of the internal situation. I told him that officers' wives in Petrograd existed on supplies of flour and sugar that their husbands sent them from the front, and he replied that his own son, who was serving in the Guard, brought him presents of sugar whenever he came on leave. I spoke of the preventable sufferings of the people and of my astonishment at their patience under conditions that would have very soon driven me to break windows. He only laughed and said that I had a hot head.

M. Rodzianko, indeed, was emphatically of opinion that Russia would fight to the end. He said: " There may be some people in favour of peace, but they do not dare to speak. Rasputin will never work for peace, for he is run by a ring of banks who are making too much money out of the war for them to wish it to stop. Russia is all right if England would only give her more heavy guns and more money."

In spite of the optimism of the President of the Duma, the situation was dangerous, for the Rasputin scandal continually undermined respect for authority. It was said that Junkovski, the Assistant Minister of the Interior, had been dismissed from his post in the autumn because he had arrested Rasputin for disgraceful conduct at a night restaurant in Moscow, and Prince Orlov, the Chief of the Emperor's Military Cabinet, also lost his appointment for venturing to remonstrate with his Imperial master on the same scandal. In February Rasputin again made a disturbance in a night restaurant, this time in Petrograd, and, as he was breaking windows, a police inspector was called in to arrest him. The Pristav, however, was a man of common sense, and refused to act when he heard who the delinquent was. He said : " He got Junkovski dismissed, and would make short work of so small a man as me ! "

In this matter of Rasputin the Emperor was not to be moved, and it was soon realised that it was hopeless to remonstrate with him. It was the duty of our Ambassador to press as far as possible on the Emperor the necessity for liberal reforms in order to meet the public demand, and in this matter he always had the sympathy of M. Sazonov, the liberally-minded Minister of Foreign Affairs, but M. Sazonov specially asked him, when speaking to the Emperor on the internal situation, to avoid all mention of Rasputin.

During a visit to the Northern Front in February I was struck by the enthusiasm with which officers spoke of the spirit of the rank and file. The censors in the 12th Army (on the extreme right) read all letters and classified them according to their general spirit, as (*a*) " Good," (*b*) " Discontented or depressed," (*c*) " Complaining of officers," (*d*) " Complaining of food," etc. In all units 80 per cent. of the letters were said to show a good spirit, and in some units 100 per cent. The enemy had remained passive throughout the winter, and casualties on the whole front had averaged only 60 to 100 a day. There had been no sickness.

This, at all events, was what I was told at the Staff. When I visited the trenches it was difficult to believe that there was no sickness. For instance, in the 13th Siberian Division in the Riga bridgehead on February 26th, I found the men living under terrible conditions, in trenches full of water and in very damp huts, and many of the men certainly looked ill.

Again, a few days later a temporary officer told me that he was quite certain that there would be a revolution after the war, since the attitude of the army had completely changed owing to the death of so many officers of the old " cut-and-dried reactionary type."

It was all a matter of officers. Russia had abundance of men, but was commencing to feel the shortage of experienced officers and non-commissioned officers, as well as of armament and equipment. The rank and file of most regiments at the front were generally good, and regiments had about seventy " officers " out of their establishment of seventy-eight, but the fighting value of divisions varied in direct ratio to the number of officers they possessed who had served before the war and in accordance with the number of guns.

The divisions at this time might have been graded according to value as follows:

1. The regular divisions which existed as such in peace: three Guard, four Grenadier, fifty-two Line, eleven Siberian. These had sixteen battalions and thirty-six guns, and regiments averaged ten to twenty regular officers.

2. The rifle divisions which had expanded during the war from rifle brigades: one Guard Rifle, five European Rifle, four Finland Rifle, two Caucasian Rifle, six Turkistan Rifle. These had twelve battalions and eighteen field guns, and six to eight regular officers per regiment. They were of greater fighting value than the units of the next category on account of their traditions.

3. The second-line divisions formed on mobilisation on cadres detached from regular regiments: Numbers 53-84 Line, 12-14 Siberian and 3-4 Caucasian Rifle. These divisions had most of them their full complement of sixteen battalions and thirty-six guns, but few of the regiments had many of their original establishment of twenty-four regular officers left.

4. Divisions formed from Opolchenie: Numbers 101-127. These divisions had so far not distinguished themselves, and it was hardly to be expected that they would, for they had no proper officers to train them.

Friday, February 25th, 1916. RIGA.

We drove through Shlok to the advanced line of trenches. There were at least four lines of defence, each furnished with barbed wire, and as well constructed as is possible in ground in which it is impossible to dig deep without striking water. The country is everywhere thickly wooded and covered with marsh. In two or three weeks, when the snow melts, it will be impassable.

I saw something of the 440th Regiment of the 110th

January-March, 1916

Division. The men seemed excellent, as usual, but the officers were boys, with the exception of some half a dozen " dug-out " officers, who had no longer the energy to teach the youngsters their work. I talked for some time with a company commander, who told me he was over fifty and had retired twenty-five years ago after three years' service. He was a cultivated man, but confessed frankly that he hated soldiering. The officer in charge of the machine-gun section had eight guns, but only four that would fire. He was a mining engineer of about fifty, who had never served previously as an officer. I gathered that the Chief of Staff and his assistant were the only serving regular officers in the division. The officers all seemed so willing and so touched by the interest taken in them, but so thoroughly unhappy and so completely at variance with their surroundings! I cannot imagine this division being of much use in an offensive.

This division spent the whole of the next eighteen months in trenches on the same sector of the Riga front, with no fighting and with no relaxations. It is not surprising that when the rot set in in the army, it behaved almost more disgracefully than any other.

Saturday, February 26th, 1916. RIGA.
General Kolyankovski, the Commander of the 120th Division, complains of the difficulty of forming a new division from nothing. He has been given neither officers nor N.C.O.'s. He has telephones and part of his transport, but no guns, and he has no idea when he will get any. He has managed to capture two regular officers per regiment by—as he expresses it—" fishing " for them. He argues that each new regiment should be formed from a parent regiment, so that it might start with a certain tradition.

The vital importance of *esprit de corps* was, however, never realised by the Russian administration. For instance, the original idea of feeding each regiment at the front with drafts from an affiliated depot battalion in the interior was very soon abandoned, owing to difficulties arising from the defective communications and the frequent transfer of divisions from north to south and *vice versa*. Only the Guard regiments continued to receive drafts from sixteen depot battalions in which the men had been trained by officers of the unit they eventually joined at the front. Other regiments received drafts from the nearest depot battalion, and even men wounded seldom rejoined their original regiment.

In March, 1916, an attempt was made to improve matters in the infantry of the Line. One hundred and thirty-six four-battalion depot regiments were formed, each to feed with drafts exclusively a single infantry division serving on the Western Frontier. In addition, eighty-seven general service depot regiments were made available to supplement the affiliated depot regiments by supplying drafts to any division at the front in which the casualties had been too great for the affiliated units to replace. This scheme was excellent on paper, but was not generally translated into practice. It was left to the army or corps commander to decide to which regiments drafts should be allotted, and too often immediately the bewildered recruits arrived they were hurried into action. The gradual decline in the fighting efficiency of the Russian infantry, even before the Revolution, may be ascribed in large measure to the men being treated merely as cannon-fodder. The difficulties were great, but more effort should have been made to fill up regiments before they had been reduced by casualties to mere skeletons, and to fill them with men that had been taught from the moment they donned uniform that they were to serve in one particular regiment, and that that regiment was the best in the army.

My first visit in 1916 was to the Northern Front, as there was some anxiety lest the enemy should attack on the Dvina before sufficient rifles had been collected to arm the Russian units up to war strength. General Plehve from the 5th Army was acting in command at Pskov *vice* General Ruzski, who had gone to Kislovodsk for a " cure."

Sunday, February 20th, 1916.   PSKOV.
    I called on Plehve at 11.30 a.m. He received me very

January-March, 1916

kindly and asked me to lunch, at which his wife—a nice old lady—presided. The old man looked more fragile than when I saw him last at Dvinsk, in September, but his intellect was as keen as ever. He and his Staff are fully alive to the danger of the two to four weeks from March 15th, when the ice melts in the southern part of the Gulf of Riga, while the Mohun Sound and Reval are still frozen fast, rendering it impossible for the Russian destroyers to get round to lay new mines to replace those destroyed by the floating ice. The old man expressed confidence in being able, " with God's help, to hold his own."

Two days later General Plehve was removed from his temporary command on account of ill-health, and was replaced by General Kuropatkin from the Grenadier Corps. He left by train on the night of the 27th, and was much affected at the parting. Someone ventured to say, "Au revoir," but he replied: "No, gentlemen, it is finally good-bye." He died at Moscow a few weeks later.

Some description of Plehve's character has been given in a previous chapter. His methods were sometimes singular, and he had consequently many enemies. Dolgov, whom he removed from the command of the XIXth Corps, said that in the Dvinsk bridgehead in the autumn of 1915 Plehve posted a Cossack piquet in rear of one of his divisions with orders to report on any movement of the Staff to the front or to the rear. Indeed, it was said that he posted Cossack piquets on all the bridges to see that none of the Corps Staffs retired to the right bank. Dolgov complained that he had been forced to live with his Staff in a stable on the brink of the left bank, where field shrapnel flew over his head while he supped!

Whatever means Plehve employed, they attained the required object, and even his enemies allowed that no other general could have saved Dvinsk. He was, with the exception of the first two months of the war, continually employed against the Germans. His rescue of the 2nd Army at Lodz in 1914 and his defence of Dvinsk in 1915 were two performances that no Russian general surpassed in the course of the war.

His successor, Kuropatkin, had been in retirement from 1905 till he was appointed to the command of the Grenadier Corps in September, 1915. He was now sixty-eight years of age, two years older than Plehve, but was much more active. Everyone allowed that he possessed exceptional ability, and he had great charm of manner. The ablest officers, however, mistrusted his strength of will. The Minister of War, General Polivanov, had previously described him when discussing the Russo-Japanese war as a man "absolutely wanting in force of character." Novitski, the able commander of the 73rd Division, spoke of the appointment as of the "resurrection" of a man who had been fully tried and found wanting. He said: "It is as if the French were to recall Bazaine from the grave, or the Austrians Benedek." Bonch-Bruevich, the Chief of Staff of the Front, confessed that his "spirit was heavy within him" when he heard the name of Plehve's successor.

Continuation of Diary:

> Bonch-Bruevich as an adherent of Ruzski is a convinced believer in the East Prussian line of offence. He is of opinion that at the commencement of the war Samsonov's movement should have been delayed till it could have been carried out in overwhelming strength. The 3rd and 8th Armies should have occupied the line of the river San, and the whole of the remaining forces should have been sent north to cut in west of the Masurian Lakes. Samsonov's movement was made prematurely solely in order to help France.
>
> He points out that the whole Russian conduct of the campaign is too much influenced by the promptings of history and diplomacy. At one moment there is the cry that "the oppressed Russians in Eastern Galicia are calling for help"; at another, "Let us lend a hand to Serbia!" or "Let us impress Rumania!" He spoke of the futile offensive in the Carpathians in March, 1915, and then asked what possible good the recent offensive in Bukovina and Galicia could have done, even if it had been successful. "It could not have ended the war."

Bonch-Bruevich, of course, advocated an offensive in Kurland, and he was convinced that wherever Alexyeev might then be contemplating an offensive, the final decisive battle of the war in the Eastern theatre would be fought in the north. He dismissed as absurd the idea that the Germans might break through the Northern Front on the Dvina as they had penetrated Radko Dimitriev's lines on the Dunajec in May, 1915. The strength of the Russian works, and their arrangement in several lines some distance apart, made, in his opinion, such a rapid hostile advance impossible.

This was comforting, and the General's optimism was justified. The Russians had on the Northern Front 372 battalions opposed to from 176 to 189 German battalions. They had at least four defensive lines, and the Dvina was a much bigger obstacle than the Dunajec. As they had many guns of position, they were superior to the enemy in gun-power as long as they sat still. The rifle situation had improved enormously, the proportion of men without rifles, including such " employed men " as cooks, etc., on the whole front having dropped to 27 per cent. of the total strength of the rank and file. The stock of S.A.A. amounted to 325 rounds per rifle. It was only in the building of railways that the Russians had done little or nothing, and, though I reported on March 9th that the Russian position on this front was three times as strong in men, armament and defensive works as it had been in September, 1915, I was inclined to agree with a pessimistic staff officer who thought that the Russian army, owing to lack of communications, would take a year to fight its way back to the Nyeman.

The defective lateral communications, in addition, enormously increased the difficulty of the Command in concentrating sufficient force rapidly to meet a sudden unexpected thrust. It was therefore of primary importance for the Russian Intelligence to obtain early and accurate information of any enemy concentration. At Pskov the Intelligence service of the Northern Front was directed by Colonel Ryabikov, who had long specialised in the subject.

Monday, February 21st, 1916. PSKOV.
I asked Ryabikov how long before the launching of a

hostile offensive he could obtain information of the enemy's intentions. He said that his great object was to obtain immediate information of the arrival of a large body of reinforcements, say three corps, without which it was thought that the Germans were unlikely to risk a decisive attack. For this purpose he considers prisoners' testimony to be of little use, for they seldom know what is going on in rear. On the other hand, agents cannot always get back. He has agents in every town in Kurland, and these have instructions in ordinary times to pass their information on to messengers. In case of important information, such as of the arrival of three new corps, the agents have been told to risk everything to bring the news through themselves. They cannot, however, always get through.

Information of the projected attack on the Bzura in January, 1915, was brought by a Russian agent, who had been arrested and kept by the Germans for three months at Lodz, and had then been released on condition that he should work for Germany. He reached Russian headquarters with his vital information the night before the attack.

Air reconnaissance helps, but Ryabikov explained that he could only do his best, and could not guarantee timely warning.

An agent earns from Rs.100 (£10) to Rs.300 (£30) a month, in addition to travelling allowance. Ryabikov's men are chiefly Esthonians, but he has three Jews, whom he trusts little. The German agents are mostly Jews, with a few Esthonians.

It is increasingly difficult to pass men backwards and forwards through the German lines, so agents are encouraged to offer their services to the German Intelligence in order to secure freedom of movement.

The Germans move all local inhabitants to a distance of five versts back from their front line.

On the other hand, a few days later, at Dvinsk, Captain

Gullenbegel, an enormously fat but energetic Finn, who was in charge of the Intelligence of the 5th Army, expressed his confidence in being able to foretell any German offensive several days in advance. He claimed that he foretold the German cavalry raid on Svyentsyani in September, 1915, a whole month before it was launched. He gets his best information from prisoners, whom he divides into three classes: Alsatian deserters, whom he characterised as generally unobservant; Polish deserters, who were generally "stupid"; and Prussian prisoners, who, when properly "manipulated," took a "pride in showing the extent of their knowledge."

During this visit to the Northern Front I had several long conversations with General Radko Dimitriev, whose views were always of interest owing to his wide experience as Chief of the Bulgarian General Staff in the Balkan War and as Bulgarian Minister at Petrograd prior to the World-War. He had been transferred from the command of the IInd Siberian corps to take over that of the VIIth Siberian, as the latter corps was in the Riga bridgehead and its command involved responsibility for the whole system of defence.

Thursday, February 24th, 1916. RIGA.

Radko talked for two hours. He is clamouring to assume the offensive, but realises that we have superior gun-power to the Germans only so long as we occupy our present lines, for our heavy guns are not mobile. He realises, too, the difficulty of the communications, and thinks that, if we did advance, we should have to do so in dashes of five marches at a time to admit of the repair of the railways. He considers that he could advance if given three more corps.

He spoke scathingly of the want of co-operation among the Allies, especially in April last, when all the world knew that the best German troops were being withdrawn from the Western theatre and were being concentrated against him on the Dunajec, and yet the Allies in the West remained passive. He says that should the enemy now attack in the West, the whole Russian army should move forward to pin the enemy's reserves down, cost what it might.

He became the picture of vitality when he spoke of the iniquities of Ferdinand of Coburg. He knew him thoroughly, for he was Chief of the Bulgarian General Staff when the Balkan alliance was being arranged. Ferdinand pretended that the alliance was to be under Russian protection, but was all the time secretly informing Vienna. He constantly fooled the French and English by talking of his " French blood " and of his " cousin of England." When he came to Russia he was more Orthodox than any Russian archbishop. Radko said: " I knew him all the time as my own fingers! He was simply an Austrian lieutenant sent to Sofia to do what he was told, and he carried out his instructions to the letter."

He spoke bitterly of how his country had been drawn into the war on the side of Germany contrary to the wish of the mass of the people. He is convinced that Bulgarian troops will never fight against Russians, and that consequently no Bulgarian ministry will ever dare to send troops to the Russian front.

Radko considers that a sufficient supply of shell is of far greater importance than S.A.A. Before the war against Turkey Bulgaria had 800 rounds S.A.A. per rifle and 1,200 shell per gun. He took part in a conference at Sofia, at which it was agreed, in spite of his opposition, to purchase more S.A.A. The S.A.A. purchased was never used, for in the whole Balkan War the Bulgarian army only fired 300 rounds per rifle and 900 shell per gun. In 1904-5 the Russians only fired 486 rounds per rifle.

Radko is entirely opposed to " side-shows." He considers the capture of Erzerum " good," but he regrets it, as it may lead the Russian Command to increase its force in the Caucasus and so weaken it in the only decisive theatre.

He places the end of the war in November, but he is an optimist!

January-March, 1916

Sunday, February 27th, 1916.   PSKOV.

I dined last night with Radko's Staff at Riga, and after dinner went in to say good-bye to the little man, who looked more Napoleonic than ever with a lock of hair tumbling forward over his forehead.

He spoke a lot about the Rumanian army, which he thinks is not much good owing to the cleavage between the classes. I suggested that the Rumanian Corps had fought well at Plevna. He said that its work had been over-advertised. The Turks had no opinion of them. Osman, when he surrendered, was given a Rumanian cavalry escort, and he exclaimed: " For Heaven's sake, anything but that! Give me rather a couple of Russian Cossacks ! "

The boyars in Rumania funk the annexation of Transylvania, as it would bring in a troublesome population unaccustomed to the Rumanian feudal system. Bulgaria offered Rumania an alliance when Bratiano's father was in power, and Radko remembers that when it was explained that it would be to Rumania's advantage to possess Transylvania, Bratiano said : " Yes, without the Transylvanians ! "

Radko thinks that we should not trouble to bring Rumania in. " As long as she is neutral, our left flank is safe, and perhaps it is better so."

The Staff at Riga told me that yesterday the Conservative Deputy Purishkevich telegraphed congratulations to Radko on his birthday, adding : " If Russia had a few more generals like you, our armies would long ago have marched through the Brandenburger Thor."

The Rumanian Military Attaché at Petrograd had much to say regarding the mistrust of the Russian Government. His country was in urgent need of certain munitions that could only be obtained through Russian territory. It wanted Russian horses and Russian steel, but delivery was constantly postponed on various pretexts. He said that 85 per cent. of the Rumanian population was in full sympathy with France and England, but that they mistrusted Russia, " and with good reason." Russia asked Rumania to come in at once, but Rumania had no intention of coming in till she knew that the Russian army was in a position to protect her flanks. When Italy joined the Entente, she reproached Rumania with her neutrality, but nothing had done more injury to the cause of the Entente in Rumania than the strategy of the Italian Command. It had been expected that Italy would land troops in Bosnia and Herzogovina, but she had tried to scale the Alps with a third of her army and had done nothing with the remainder.

This was the Rumanian point of view. The Russian policy, as explained to me by the Chief of the General Staff at Petrograd, was not to trust Rumania too far for the present, as the time had not come for her co-operation to be of value. No grain would therefore be sent to Rumania lest it should replace Rumanian grain now being sold to the enemy, and munitions of war would be held up near the Rumanian frontier on some pretext or other till the country finally declared its policy.

It was interesting to find General Gurko in command of the 5th Army at Dvinsk, with General Kuropatkin as his Group Commander, for Gurko had been the president of the committee which compiled the official history of the Russo-Japanese War, and in that work the Commander-in-Chief was criticised, perhaps justly, but with a freedom that it is unusual for a rising officer to indulge in regarding a chief unless he is certain that that chief had been definitely " shelved." However, Kuropatkin bore no ill-will, and one of his first acts was to recommend that Gurko's appointment be made permanent.

Gurko at this time was fifty-three—a dapper little man who dressed neatly and wore a small imperial. He came of an old Voronej family, being the eldest of the four sons of the Gurko of 1877-8. He had had an interesting career. He was in the Pamirs in the troublous times of 1892, and in 1899-1900 acted as military attaché with the Boers, when he was captured by the

Type of Causeway, of which many miles were constructed S. of Riga.

[See page 397

General Radko-Dimitriev, Commander of the 12th Army, on trenches south of Riga.

[See page 397

Starting to drive back after visit to the XXIXth Corps S.W. of Dvinsk.

[See page 400

South-West Front. Spring of 1916. Principal figures left to right: General Ivanov, Commander-in-Chief S.W. Front (holding the map), General Shcherbachev, Commander 7th Army, Prince Bariatinski, the Emperor, Count Friedrikhs, Minister of the Court, the Tsarevich, Count Grabbe (in fur cap), Count Sheremeticv.

[See page 402

British, owing, as he told me, to his cape cart having broken down. Lord Roberts had passed him back to the Boers *via* Lorenzo Marques. He distinguished himself in the Russo-Japanese war, and in the subsequent years acted as military adviser to the Octobrists, who were active in forcing military reforms on the over-conservative Ministry of War. In August, 1914, he took the 1st Cavalry Division to the 1st Army in East Prussia, and watched Rennenkampf's left flank during the advance. When touch was lost with Samsonov he was sent with his division as far west as Allenstein to clear up the situation, and it required the exercise of all his war-craft to bring his command safely back by a long détour to the north. He was promoted to the command of the VIth Corps, which bore the brunt of the German attack on the Bzura, west of Warsaw, at the end of January, 1915, Gurko, in the stress of battle, directing no less than eleven divisions.

Officers had a high opinion of their new chief, who, being much the youngest of the army commanders, was very active and constantly visited the trenches.

In March I spent a few days at the Headquarters of the South-West Front in the Jewish town of Berdichev. This town was Ivanov's headquarters for the second time, for he had spent a week there at the beginning of the war, then moving forward to Rovno and later to Kholm. The working staff lived in the barracks outside the town, while the personal staff lived in a train at the station.

I met there for the first time General Klembovski, who had replaced Savich as Chief of Staff during the winter. He had commanded a regiment in the Russo-Japanese War, and in the World-War the 9th Division and later the XVIth Corps. He was evidently capable, but was unpopular with officers, who said he had renounced his original religion of Roman Catholicism in order to enter the Military Academy, which was debarred to Roman Catholics.

The General Quartermaster, Dietrikhs, had made his name when in the same capacity in the 3rd Army under Radko

Dimitriev, and gave the impression of a thoroughly active and intelligent staff officer. In the three general quartermasters at this time, Bredov of the Northern Front (forty-two years), Lebedev of the Western Front (forty-four years), and Dietrikhs of the South-West Front (forty-one years), the Russian army had three young men who had been advanced on their merits and whose selection it would have been difficult to better.

At Berdichev I saw once more dear old General Ivanov, whom I had not met since 1914.

Friday, March 22nd, 1916. BERDICHEV.

The furniture in the little room in the barracks which was occupied by the General was of the simplest. There were neither curtains, blinds, nor carpets. The old man has slept the whole campaign on a broken camp-bed, which his aide-de-camp complains he will never allow him to get mended.

The Commander-in-Chief works hard. He looks tired, and complained that he finds it difficult to get his proper share of sleep. He starts work at 6 a.m., rests from two till five, and goes to bed at 10.30 p.m., if operations are not in progress. He does not feed in the mess, as he is on diet.

I could not get him to talk of military matters, and yet I don't think he avoided them intentionally. He was only delighted that he had found a foreigner that he could talk Russian to and be understood, and so his tongue ran away with him. He talked for over half an hour on all subjects except the South-West Front. His chief theme was the growth of luxury and the extravagance of people nowadays. Pointing to his writing-table, a piece of furniture that a British artisan would scorn, he said : " Fifty years ago we had nothing like this, everything was rough and ready and without finish." When he was young—fifty years ago—ladies wore no hats as a rule, but one lady he knew—a rich landowner's wife—wore a hat, and he remembered her in the same one from the time he was twelve till he reached

Corner of Lake Naroch. March, 1916.

[See page 404

December, 1915. The Russian Munitions Delegation, taken after lunch at the Russian Embassy in Paris. Left to right: M. Tarné, Lieut.-Com. Romanov, Col. Federov, Col. Kelchevski, Gen. Savrimovich, Admiral Russin, Col. Knox, Lieut Lyubomirov.

[See page 362

Lake Naroch. March, 1916. German wire entanglements after attack of 21st March, 1916.

[See page 406

Lake Naroch. March, 1916. German wire entanglements after attack of the 21st March

[See page 406

January-March, 1916

the age of seventeen. " Nowadays women are not content unless they have a new hat every year " !

Ivanov was the most thoroughly Russian in appearance and character of all the Russian leaders. He was much liked by his immediate *entourage* on account of his kindly thoughtfulness. As a leader, he belonged to a past generation, and had to make way for younger men. A few days later he was appointed to the Council of Empire, handing over charge of the South-West Front to General Brusilov, who had commanded the 8th Army since the beginning of the war.

Appointment to the Council of Empire was for a Russian officer equivalent to compulsory retirement, but the Emperor, who was fond of the old man, called him to G.H.Q., and there he remained till the Revolution, an honoured guest, but unhappy in his idleness.

My visit to the South-West Front was cut short by news of the commencement of a Russian offensive on the Western Front and of severe fighting in the neighbourhood of Lake Naroch. Generals Ivanov, Klembovski and Dietrikhs all thought that the attack had been launched at the worst possible time, as the thaw might come at any moment and make advance impossible. However, as it was evident that no immediate operations were in preparation on the South-West Front, I hurried north through Minsk to see what might be possible of the fighting.

I heard afterwards that General Klembovski thought it necessary to ask G.H.Q. whether the British Military Attaché had permission to move from one front to another without in each case special authorisation !

CHAPTER XII

THE OFFENSIVE ON THE NORTHERN AND WESTERN FRONTS IN MARCH. THE SUPPLY OF MUNITIONS. THE RAILWAYS. APRIL—JULY, 1916

REFERENCE MAP XI.

IN the spring of 1916 the Russian Northern Group on the Dvina contained the 12th and the 5th Armies; the Western Front, with Headquarters at Minsk, contained from right to left the 1st, 2nd, 10th, 4th and 3rd Armies reaching to south of the Pinsk marshes, while the South-West Front from Berdichev directed the 8th, 11th, 7th and 9th Armies, the left of the last-named touching the Rumanian frontier.

It had been decided during the winter that the effort of the year should be made by the Northern and Western Groups. With this view a concentration towards the north was commenced in February. The two Guard Corps commenced entraining at Volochisk on February 26th, and the South-West Front also despatched the XXIVth Corps to reinforce the 10th Army. The Western Front in turn sent three divisions to the Northern Front.

The general idea was for the 2nd Army to move its two wings forward north and south of Lake Naroch in order to concentrate in the neighbourhood of Svyentsyani. The right of the 5th Army was simultaneously to take the offensive from the Jacobstadt bridgehead, and the Jacobstadt and Svyentsyani groups were eventually to join near Ponevyej. The 12th Army on the Lower Dvina, the Dvinsk Group of the 5th Army and the 1st Army were to demonstrate.

On the Western Front no less than ten infantry and one cavalry corps were concentrated on the front of the 2nd Army where it was intended to make the main thrust. The 3rd Army

April-July, 1916

was left to hold 175 miles of marshy front with seven infantry and six cavalry divisions.

The 2nd Army covered a front of sixty miles, including seventeen of lake. Smirnov, its Commander, accommodatingly " went sick " just before the operation commenced, and his place was taken temporarily by Ragoza, the energetic Commander of the 4th Army.

The Army was divided into three groups :

1. On the right under General Plyeshkov (Ist Siberian Corps). Ist, XXVIIth, Ist Siberian and VIIth Cavalry Corps.

2. In the centre under General Sirelius (IVth Siberian Corps), XXXIVth and IVth Siberian Corps.

3. On the left under General Baluev (Vth Corps), Vth, XXXVIth and IIIrd Siberian Corps.

The flank groups, whose commanders were considered capable and resolute, were to make the real attack. Sirelius, who had been already *stellenbosched* more than once during the present war, was to remain passive. With a view to the development of any success, there were held in reserve at the disposal of the Commander-in-Chief of the Front the XVth Corps in rear of the Right Group and the XXXVth Corps in rear of the Left Group. Two other corps were also close at hand and available—the IIIrd Caucasian on the right and the XXIVth on the left.

Heavy guns were distributed among the three groups as follows :

Guns.	Group 1.	Group 2.	Group 3.
4·2″ guns, Q.F.	—	—	8
,, ,, 1877	12	—	12
4·8″ howitzers	60	24	48
6″ howitzers	32	12	27
6″ guns	12	—	24

The Staff of the Western Front at the beginning of March worked out the quantity of shell necessary—not to destroy the enemy's obstacles and trenches—but on the artificial basis that some units would be in action ten days, and others from two to five days, and that the daily expenditure of ammunition would be:

3" guns	.. ..	200 shell.
4·2" guns	.. ..	50 ,,
4·8" howitzers	..	100 ,,
6" howitzers ..	..	50 ,,
·3 rifle	.. ..	20 to 25 S.A.A.

The event proved that this estimate was exaggerated as regards the 3" shell and the S.A.A., but too modest as regards the heavier calibres.

The Germans had warning. As evidenced by captured prisoners, they moved forty-five battalions to the front of the 2nd Army between March 14th and 28th. Of these, twelve came from reserve on the Northern Front and the remainder from the Minsk front.

The thaw set in on the 17th.

The offensive commenced on the 18th.

Neither at Jacobstadt nor anywhere on the front of the 2nd Army was ground permanently gained. One and, in places, three lines of enemy trench were carried, but had to be evacuated under the concentrated fire of the enemy's artillery and machine-guns. On the tenth day (March 27th), General Plyeshkov had to desist, as his front had become a lake. By that date the 2nd Army had lost 70,000 men, while the losses of the Northern Front were estimated at 30,000, and of the 1st Army at 10,000.

General Baluev commenced the bombardment at 8 a.m. on the 18th, and attacked at 4 p.m. The Vth Corps on his right occupied the enemy's first line of trench, but was held up by the blockhouses in the second line. After two days' further preparation the corps retook the first line, which had been abandoned, and rushed the enemy's second and third lines in an attack which commenced at 3.30 a.m. and was crowned with success by daylight. The ground thus gained measured about 2,000 yards in depth on a front of 4,000 yards. Baluev's subsequent efforts were concentrated on an attempt to capture a German salient, which had been nicknamed, like all salients on the Russian Front,

"Ferdinand's Nose." In this he had no success, though he attacked on March 25th, 27th and 31st, and on April 7th and 14th. Finally a German counterstroke re-established the front on its original line.

The operation was a complete failure. The Russians lost heavily and gained nothing, in spite of a greater concentration of heavy artillery on a narrow front than had been attempted in any previous action in the war. The expenditure of shell, in view of their slender resources, could only be considered extravagant, and the mismanagement of the whole enterprise could not fail to have a disastrous influence on the *morale* of the infantry, who as usual had to pay the price.

Meanwhile, on the Northern Front, the 12th Army had demonstrated south of Riga with a single division, and the XXIXth and XXIIIrd Corps had made a half-hearted attempt west of Dvinsk, losing 8,000 men and gaining nothing. The main effort was made on the Jacobstadt bridgehead, under the personal direction of General Gurko, the Commander of the 5th Army. Three hundred guns were concentrated, eighty of them of heavy calibre. The chief *rôle* was played by the IInd Siberian Corps on the right, under General Gondurin, and by the XXVIIIth Corps in the centre under General Slyusarenko. Of the eight divisions concentrated, less than half were engaged, for the original reserve of 16,000 H.E. shell of all calibres was soon exhausted, and the supplies promised were diverted to the Western Front. The attack commenced on March 21st and dwindled to an end on the 26th. The Russians gained a stretch of marshy ground about 1,000 yards in depth. The artillery failed entirely to support the infantry, who lost 28,000 men. The artillery had only a single casualty—an officer of the Horse Artillery who had come as a spectator from a neighbouring cavalry division!

Secret pamphlets [1] printed at G.H.Q. dealt scathingly with the local mistakes in this offensive.

---

[1] *Notes on the Operations on the South-West Front in December, 1915, and on the Western and Northern Fronts in March, 1916.*
Notes on the Employment of Artillery during the Offensive of March on the Western Front.

The failure was ascribed largely to lack of confidence in the Higher Command. It was stated that the operations were not thought out properly beforehand. Orders were written in the study without proper previous reconnaissance of the ground. The G.O.C. 2nd Army should not have handed over the immediate direction of the operations to three improvised groups, who were without proper staffs. The artillery served the infantry badly, often sitting inactive, while the infantry, who had occupied enemy trenches, was slaughtered. In the 2nd Army the heavy guns came up late—on the evening of the 16th and the morning of the 17th. Telephone communication was only established on the morning of the 18th—the day the operation commenced—so that officers and men had no time to get accustomed to their surroundings and to range their guns. After the 18th the heavy guns were constantly short of shell. Artillery orders lacked precision: for instance, the order, " The success of the attack must be assured by timely and careful preparation of the hostile section selected for assault." Often the task set the guns was beyond their power to accomplish: for instance, a battery of four light howitzers was told to destroy 2,800 feet of wire entanglement. The guns were kept too far back: for instance, light field batteries at 4,500 yards. The target was changed too often: for instance, one group of guns was asked to fire at 237 targets in three days.

Shrapnel must in future be used only at living targets. Experience proved that the proportion of H.E. shell should be increased to 50 per cent. in the case of 3" and 4·2" guns, to 75 per cent. in the case of 4·8" howitzers and to 90 per cent. in the case of 6" howitzers.

The training of the infantry had been affected by long sitting in trenches, and individual training was necessary to teach them to hold a position once gained against counter-attacks when most of their officers were out of action. Attention must be paid to the moral education (*vospitanie*) of the rank and file: for instance, in General

Plyeshkov's Group over 300 deserters were arrested in a single canteen in rear.

"Against a line defended by fire and by obstacles infantry of itself has no power of offence." The Russian batteries, anchored on their several islands in the midst of the general morass, remained idle spectators of the slaughter of their infantry.

So wrote the experts after the event. They naturally did not touch on the greatest folly of all—the launching of an offensive at such a season.

It thawed every day from the 17th till the 22nd. On the night of the 22nd there were five degrees of frost (Réaumur), and in the morning 300 men of a division of the Vth Corps had to be hacked out of the ice where they lay. The marsh in the centre of Baluev's front soon became impassable. There were no metalled roads from the railway, and it took the writer seven hours to cover the twenty miles from the railway to Baluev's Headquarters on the 31st. Continual fog prevented artillery observation, and in any case only one of Baluev's aeroplanes was fitted with wireless.

I asked at Minsk why the movement had not been made a month earlier or else postponed till a month later. Junior officers of the Staff said that the plan had been worked out some time previously, but that its execution was delayed by lack of rifles; that later it was hoped to commence on March 1st, but the concentration took longer than had been anticipated. The Commander-in-Chief, General Ewarth, and his Chief of Staff, General Kvyetsinski, told me separately that they thought the object was "to help the French."[1] Another officer said that "it was all Alexyeev's fault for giving way." An officer who had been at G.H.Q. during the operation gathered the impression that Alexyeev had been forced into action against his better judgment. He added: "We Russians are so noble-minded that we attack at once if anyone asks us for help, but no one has ever helped us when we were in difficulties!"

---

[1] The German attack on Verdun had commenced on February 21st.

The next stage of command, that of the Army, complained of interference from above. General Ragoza told me that in the height of the operation he received and sent 3,000 telegrams per day. He thought the staff of the Front was too large and that its many officers in the impatience of their curiosity made work for themselves and incidentally for others. If he could have satisfied their curiosity from his own knowledge, he said it would not have so much mattered, but unfortunately he had to worry continually subordinate commanders nearer the enemy to obtain the necessary detail.

General Baluev, the Left Group Commander, had his own complaints. He said that after five months spent in the same sector and exhaustive study of the ground, he had urged that the decisive attack should be made by his right wing. The Chief of Staff of the Front insisted that he should make the main assault with his left, in the belief that such a move would yield greater strategical results. He forgot that there could be no strategical results whatsoever, either great or small, without the preliminary tactical success, which Baluev asserted would be difficult to obtain in the open ground on his left. A compromise was agreed to. The Vth Corps attacked the right section, the XXXVIth Corps the left and the IIIrd Siberian Corps was held in reserve on the left. Baluev, on March 31st, maintained that if he had been able to follow up at once the success of the Vth Corps on his right with the IIIrd Siberian Corps, he would have driven the whole enemy front back.

Baluev I had met in 1915—a short, thickset man with a birthmark half across his face, but of a pleasant kind of ugliness. To his energy and to the brain of his Chief of Staff, General Walther, a man of English descent, who spoke English like an Englishman, the success of the Left Group, such as it was, was ascribed.

Of course he complained of the lack of technical equipment, and roared at me with a voice that shook the little cottage where his headquarters were, that he was fighting technique with flesh and blood (*jivoi sil*). As a matter of fact, the inferiority of the Russians in material had less to do with this failure than with any

Road in Village of Krivichi. March, 1916

[See page 409

Krivichi–Naroch road. March, 1916.

[See page 409

Ural Cossacks. Near Lake Naroch. March, 1916.

[See page 409]

Group after Conference at Army Headquarters, 1916. Six principal figures (left to right): General Polivanov, Minister of War; General Ewarth, Commander-in-Chief, Western Front; General Alexyeev, Chief of Staff at G.H.Q.; H.I.M. The Emperor, General Kuropatkin, Commander-in-Chief, Northern Front; General Ivanov, Commander-in-Chief, S.W. Front.

[See page 412]

of their disasters in the preceding eighteen months. On a front of nine and a third miles Baluev had 256 guns, of which 119 were heavy. He had more guns than the enemy. During the eight hours' bombardment of the 18th his guns fired 30,000 3″ and 9,000 shell of heavier calibre—an expenditure which would no doubt have been considered trifling in France, but which for Russia was extravagant. The operation failed because of the impossible weather conditions and the faulty co-operation of the arms, far more than owing to lack of technical equipment.

I was ordered by telegram to return to Petrograd, and arrived there on Sunday night, April 2nd. My instructions were to induce, if possible, the Russian Artillery Department to instruct its inspectors in America to abandon their pedantic methods of inspection, which were driving the contractors desperate and seemed likely to result in the wholesale abandonment of contracts.

Ellershaw had sent me out an imposing batch of contractors' letters as evidence. These I had translated and distributed. Before their contents had been fully grasped, he telegraphed out Lord Kitchener's proposal that a British arbitrator should be appointed to settle disputes between American contractors and Russian inspectors. I took this proposal to a very able general of the Artillery Department, whom junior officers had nicknamed " the Rasputin of the Department," partly owing to his appearance and partly because he enjoyed the unlimited confidence of the Chief of the Department. He was very unsympathetic and asked what qualifications Ellershaw, for instance, could have for such an appointment. Another general, who had much to say on the matter, was worse. He talked childishly. He said that Russia had enough shell and if the American contractors were to throw up their contracts he would be sorry, but that it could not be helped. It was " time that the British Government, which had rushed Russia into the orders, applied some pressure to the contractors. The latter had got enormous prices on the understanding that they complied with Russian technical conditions. They now continually asked for the easing of these conditions, but did not suggest a corresponding reduction in price."

Lord Kitchener's proposal had only been made in Russia's best interests, and considering that the British Government had assumed responsibility for the payment, it was most natural and proper. It, however, touched the *amour-propre* of the Russian Artillery experts, who were rather men of science than practical gunners, and who after two years of war had not yet understood the necessity for unlimited supplies of shell.

It was necessary to lay the matter before the higher officials.

Unfortunately, General Polivanov, who had succeeded Sukhomlinov as Minister of War in the summer of 1915, had been dismissed from his post on March 20th. He was informed by Imperial letter that the Emperor felt that in serious times like the present he must have as Minister of War a man whom he could trust to work in less close co-operation with non-official organisations that were openly hostile to the Government.

Polivanov was undoubtedly the ablest military organiser in Russia, and his dismissal was a disaster. The Emperor had always personally disliked him, but it is also true that the ex-Minister had magnified the work of the Military Industrial Committee beyond its due. This Committee, though a non-official organisation, worked entirely on Government funds, and its enemies affirmed that it was largely a shelter for men who wished to avoid service at the front. The following riddles were current at the front: "What is an army? An army is an assembly of people who have failed to evade military service. What are non-official organisations? Non-official organisations are large assemblies of people who have succeeded in evading military service." The leading spirit of the Committee was the Octobrist, M. Guchkov, who since his public exposure a few years previously of the Rasputin scandal had been a declared enemy of the court. It contained many politicians who necessarily talked, and talked naturally, against the Government. Apart from this, many impartial persons considered that the money the organisation spent on the development of small factories might have been

April-July, 1916

more usefully devoted to the extension of existing Government establishments. The Artillery Department, which of course hated the Committee, claimed that the only local committee that had produced anything worth talking about was that of Odessa, where the work was directed by an Artillery General.

Protopopov, the Vice-President of the Duma, with whom I dined on the eve of his departure with the parliamentary delegates to visit the Allied capitals, naturally as a capitalist, professed to regard the Military Industrial Committee under the guidance of Guchkov and Konovalov as a dangerous syndicalist society. He pointed out that there were " actually " working men on many of the sixty-eight sub-committees, and " even " on the central committee. He considered that the organisation had directly caused the late strike at the Putilov Works, for its members had a habit of going to the Works to ask the men if they were contented, " as if any workmen ever were contented." He held that Polivanov's dismissal was " a political necessity."

There was, of course, the usual crop of stories. It was said that soon after his appointment as Minister it came to Polivanov's knowledge that the Baltic Shipbuilding and Engineering Works were paying a commission of 2 per cent. on all orders. Much of this money was traced to one G——, the protector of the sister of a dancer who moved in high circles. A search in G——'s flat implicated the dancer and a certain Grand Duke not ordinarily connected with the Artillery Department.

Then there was the astounding story of the engineer, Bratolyubov, which would seem incredible, but was told me by a member of the Duma who vouched for its accuracy. The engineer arrived at G.H.Q. and announced that he had discovered a fire that could not be extinguished. Everybody was interested; it was thought that it would be such an excellent thing for Berlin. The Emperor commissioned his brother, the Grand Duke Michael, to see that the inventor was provided with everything needed for further experiments.

Bratolyubov arrived in Petrograd with an order signed by the

Grand Duke directing General Miliant,[1] the Chief of the Military Technical Department, to provide him with an automobile. Other signed requisitions followed for workmen, for ground for experiments, for the advance of funds. They were all complied with till one fine day a signed order was handed in for 14,000,000 roubles in gold (about £1,500,000), as well as large houses and vacant sites on the Kammenostrovski Prospekt and near the Baltic Railway Station.

Miliant reported to Polivanov, who sent his Chief of Staff to G.H.Q. to explain matters. Bratolyubov was arrested, but was released, it is said, at the intercession of Rasputin. The swindler had cleared over Rs.100,000!

Whatever the truth of these stories, it was evident that Polivanov had enemies in high quarters, who strongly objected to his interference with their personal schemes.

I called on him by appointment on the afternoon of April 26th. Diary:

> He was much depressed. He told me that Count Friedrichs, the Minister of the Court, when discussing the change of ministers one night in the Yacht Club, had said of him: "El est très intelligent, mais très dangereux, parcequ'il est trop parlementaire," and he suggested that perhaps in England or France he would not have lost his post for such a reason.
>
> Polivanov claimed to have accomplished the three tasks he had set himself when called to office in 1915:
>
> 1. The provision of a reserve of 800,000 men in the neighbourhood of the front, and of a further reserve of 1,000,000 men in the interior of the Empire.
>
> 2. The provision of rifles and shell.
>
> 3. The inauguration of a permanent system, under which men would only go to the front after three months' training.

Probably the Minister had had as much to do with the improved

---
[1] Chief of Staff of 1st Army in 1914.

situation of the army at the beginning of the summer of 1916 as any other Russian, but the main factor had been the inactivity of the enemy during the winter.

Getting little satisfaction from the Artillery Department, I saw the Chief of the General Staff, General Byelyaev, on April 17th. He took the British point of view and was indignant that any Russian general should have stated that the army had a sufficiency of shell. He said that the Japanese had made similar complaints regarding the pedantry of the Russian inspectors, and he pointed out that certain prominent officials of the Artillery Department had sons serving in America as junior inspectors. He said he would speak to the new Minister of War, General Shuvaiev, on the subject. I gathered later that he had had little success. He said that the new Minister " poor man, is simply overwhelmed with the details of his office." He found him " sitting at a table covered with papers that he was unable to tackle." The Grand Duke Serge said that Shuvaiev " knew nothing."

The new Minister was certainly of a very different type to his predecessor. During the twenty-four and a half years previous to 1905 he filled continuously posts as instructor or commandant of military schools. He then commanded an infantry division for three years and a corps for one year, and was selected in 1909 as Chief Intendant. His father had served in the ranks and his son was now an officer of the Guard. It was said he had told the latter to remember he was the son of a general, while not forgetting that his grandfather was a private.

Wednesday, April 27th, 1916. PETROGRAD.

On Monday at 11 a.m. I saw General Shuvaiev—a nice old man and quite straight and honest—but it was easy to see, as Byelyaev had said, that he had a narrow outlook.

I stated our case regarding the inspectors—that if the Russian inspectors continued their present methods in America we should get no shell, for the contractors would throw up their contracts, and, moreover, their influence and that of their employés would be thrown into the scale against the Entente in the coming elections, and might possibly result in the placing of an embargo on the export of material of war.

The Minister did not reply directly, but commenced with a little speech about himself. "He had served in all three arms, commencing as an infantry officer, serving in the artillery for two and a half years and commanding a Cossack cavalry school for fifteen years. He had commanded a division and a corps, when the Emperor suddenly called him to be Chief Intendant. He had no knowledge of the work, but his devotion to the Emperor was such that if the door were to open and His Majesty were to come into the room and to ask him to throw himself out of the window, he would do so at once." This with slow gesture and with tears of exalted self-pity in his eyes. "He had done his best as Chief Intendant and was supposed to have made a success of it, especially in the suppression of corruption." I said politely and truly that I had heard as much from members of the Duma.

He continued: "Now I am called upon again, unexpectedly, to administer the army in relief of General Polivanov."

He asked to what arm I belonged, and said that his experience had been such that he could take command of any arm in action at a moment's notice. (As a matter of fact his only previous war service had been in Central Asia in 1873 and 1875).

After all this he reached the point. He agreed that what was required was shell to kill Germans, but obviously the shell would have to be safe in transport and at the time of firing. "Shell that burst at the muzzle of the gun made a dreadful impression." He promised finally to see the new Inspector in Chief who had been detailed to go to America, and to give him instructions in the sense required.

The Western Allies had now arrived at the conclusion that influential missions might prevail on the Russian Government to set its house in order and to increase its war effort to force the decision which seemed difficult to obtain in France.

The French ministers, MM. Viviani and Albert Thomas, arrived in May. Their real object, according to the Russians, was to induce the Russian Government to send larger contingents of Russian troops to the Western theatre. It was said that they asked for 40,000 men a month, but only succeeded in extracting a promise for five brigades in addition to the brigade already in France and a second brigade then about to start for Salonika. These five brigades were to be despatched monthly from Arkhangel, commencing in August. In return the French Ministers promised to send some heavy guns for the Russian army.

The French visit undoubtedly did good. M. Viviani stirred his audience by his splendid eloquence at a banquet on May 16th to celebrate the twenty-fifth anniversary of the Franco-Russian alliance, and M. Thomas in his blunter way spoke many home truths.

I first met M. Thomas at 9 a.m. the day after his arrival, when he sent for me, as he said, at the suggestion of Mr. Lloyd George, to put many searching questions regarding the Russian situation. I sat next him at a farewell luncheon at the French Embassy on May 18th, the day before his departure, and tried to ascertain his conclusions.

> He said that the Russians had everything in the country that they needed, but did not make use of it owing to their slackness. Their shortage of steel arose from lack of labour in the coal-mines and from the fewness of the railways and the congestion on those that existed. No pay will induce the Russian worker to work underground in the summer, and M. Thomas thinks compulsion is necessary. He has no patience with the lack of energy which hesitates about laying a line thirty versts long that is urgently required to link coal-fields with steel works; he would admit the difficulty if it were a question of laying a line of 3,000 versts. He ascribes the whole congestion

on the railways to bad management. He had been to lunch with M. Trepov, the Minister of Ways and Communications, and had found him busy working out a big programme of railway construction that would require years to complete, instead of attending to the needs of the moment.

At Moscow M. Thomas told an assembly of the Municipal Council and of the Representatives of industrial interests that previous to the war France had had more strikes than any other country, but that since the war she had had none. He said: " You in Russia have had your strikes, and when the workmen are not on strike they have a habit of leaving their work for three or four days at a time as if there was no war. Everywhere I go I see numbers of men doing nothing, and yet Russia complains of shortage of labour."

At Petrograd on May 16th, at an official meeting presided over by the Minister of War and attended by many officers of the Artillery Department, M. Thomas was told that there were no railways to carry coal to the steel works. He replied vigorously that France, with the greater part of her industrial territory in enemy hands, had solved the problem of national defence in another spirit, that the factory of Neuve Maison, fifteen kilometres from the front, near Nancy, was fed by a daily train which carried coke from Galais, 450 kilometres distant, and was kept at work under heavy shell-fire in order to provide an additional shell factory.

A Minister of the type of M. Thomas was something entirely new to Russian experience. They laughed at his shaggy appearance, which they said was that of the typical Moscow merchant. The higher officials had looked forward to his coming with undisguised dread. General Byelyaev, the gentlemanly Conservative, slow-thinking and formal, positively trembled when he told me he had been detailed by the Minister of War to deal exclusively with the invader. Afterwards he told me that he was much struck by the power possessed by M. Thomas, who said: " I will give you that "; " I will arrange that when I get home,"

April-July, 1916

etc., etc. Byelyaev said: "Though a Socialist, he can do anything he likes; no one in Russia has such power. We are without a leader (*U nas nyet khozaina*), and yet Russia is an autocracy." The Grand Duke Serge said to M. Thomas: "You are an autocrat and I am an anarchist!"

Early in May Lord Kitchener told Count Benkendorf that he would like to visit Russia if given an official invitation. The Emperor, when informed by M. Sazonov, said he could receive him after June 10th, but remarked that he did not understand how Lord Kitchener could leave his own work for so long.

In a letter written on May 6th, but only received on the 18th, Ellershaw wrote:

> I have little doubt that shortly after you get this Lord Kitchener and I will be on our way to you. Of course you will be informed officially as soon as it is finally settled. I have been working for this for some time. Don't swear! I think it is really necessary and hope you will agree. The main thing is about the financial situation, but there are a thousand and one other things that I think he should talk about and get cleared up.

I did not agree with Ellershaw. I thought that the Russians required a rest and time to digest the many plain and unpalatable truths with which M. Thomas had fed them. I thought Lord Kitchener's visit would irritate rather than stimulate them. They had never regarded Great Britain as a big military power, but they knew we were rich, and they fancied inexhaustibly rich. They wanted our money and not our military advice. The Russian idea of Allied assistance was years afterwards very tersely described to me in Siberia by Engineer Stevens, the Chief of the American Railway Mission, when he said: "They want us to put a big bag of money on their door-step and then to run away."

I telegraphed confidentially to Ellershaw suggesting that if possible the visit should be postponed, and pointing out that the Russians wanted a big financial expert like Mr. McKenna much more than a military man.

On May 26th Ellershaw wrote:

    I am afraid that in spite of your cable it is quite impossible now for me to stop the visit. I am always ready to take your opinion of anything in Russia, and had I known your opinion in time I would not have worked like a slave and pulled every string to bring off what I believe to be intensely valuable. I had set great store by a visit of " K." to Russia. There his name is all-powerful and his personality undiminished in lustre. I had hoped that his influence might greatly improve cordial relations, that he might have a good effect on the future strategy, on politics and on the financial difficulties, and that under cover of his shadow I might be able to clear up all misunderstandings and to explain things strongly and clearly from the British as well as from the Russian point of view, without mincing matters. . . .

    We are to start on Monday week, June 5th, so should be with you on the 12th. One week is all " K." will spend. This gives us till the 19th, and we will be back here, I hope, by the 26th. I shall be most intensely thankful when the visit is done with, if only all goes well. . . .

    By the way, remember no cable from you to me is confidential, no matter how much you may mark it so. It goes to the D.M.O., M.G.O., Agar and " K.," and nothing can stop that.

On Tuesday, June 6th, at 7 p.m., I was working in the Military Attaché's room on the ground floor at the Embassy, when one of the secretaries came down from the Chancery with the dreadful news of the loss of the *Hampshire* with all hands. It was difficult to realise it, and, apart from the loss of Lord " K.," Fitzgerald and O'Beirne, impossible to imagine who could be found to take poor Ellershaw's place and to serve Russia as he did.

    I saw General Byelyaev a few days later. He was much affected when he spoke of Lord Kitchener, and quite overcome when he mentioned Ellershaw. He said with an expressive gesture that he now regarded the American contracts as " a washout."

Though M. Thomas's opinion of Russian administration is that generally held by the Western observer, our Ally should be given credit for what she had accomplished. In the first seventeen and a half months of war, *i.e.*, up till the end of 1915, Russia had sent forward to her armies 1,920 field guns, 355 mountain guns, 12 4·2" guns, 43 4·8" howitzers and 60 6" howitzers.

On January 13th, 1916, the number of guns on all Russian fronts, Northern, Western, South-Western and Caucasian, was 3,973 3" field, 245 3" mountain, 420 4·8" howitzers, 50 4·2" guns and 210 6" howitzers. There were in round numbers 4,500,000 3" shell, 250,000 4·8" shell and 165,000 heavy shell.

The great lack was that of rifles.

Saturday, January 29th, 1916.   PETROGRAD.

Federov showed me a paper he has drawn up advocating an idea that could only have suggested itself in the extraordinary conditions now existing in Russia. The Russian lateral railways are few and they work slowly. The German system of espionage is efficient and reports all moves of Russian forces immediately. The slowness of these moves allows the enemy ample time to concentrate and defeat any attempt at the offensive. The Russians have unlimited men but few rifles. Federov proposes to hold at a distance of a march in rear of the front fifty or more unarmed men for every 200 armed men in each company in the trenches. These fifty men would take turns of relieving their comrades in front. When it was desired to reinforce any particular sector, automobiles would be used to transport rifles in order to arm the reserve and enable it to reinforce the front. The idea was considered at G.H.Q. and rejected.

The armament situation improved rapidly. The following is

a summary of the strength and armament in the Eastern theatre about March 20th:

	NORTHERN FRONT.	MOVING NORTH.	WESTERN FRONT.	SOUTH-WESTERN FRONT.	TOTAL
Corps	13	3½	25	17	58
Divisions	27½	7	59	37	130½
Cavalry Divisions	8¼	2	17	11½	39
Battalions	396	108	927	585	2,016
Squadrons	202	72	553½	404	1,231½
Officers	6,700	1,800	17,461	11,309	37,270
Rifles	299,000	110,000	725,401	536,527	1,670,928
Sabres	41,000	15,000	70,283	51,840	178,123
Machine guns	1,079	250	2,736	2,159	6,224
3" guns	915	252	2,359	1,487	5,013
4·8" hows.	116	24	311	171	622
"Heavy guns"	179	16	242	108	545

The improvement in the situation as regards rifles and guns is to be ascribed largely to the lull at the front, which diminished the daily waste and permitted of the repair in rear of large numbers of damaged weapons.

The Allies had assisted in the re-armament in many ways, but especially in the provision of rifles. During the winter of 1915-1916, there were landed in Russia in round numbers from America 120,000 Winchesters; from France 445,000 Gras, 95,000 Kropatschek and 39,000 Lebels; from Japan and England 140,000 Japanese rifles; and from Italy 300,000 Vetterlis. The Lebel rifles were sent to the Caucasus and the Winchester and Japanese rifles to the Western Frontier, while the other rifles were distributed to railway troops and to Line of Communication and depot units to release an equal number of Russian rifles for use at the front.

Meanwhile the home output of Russian rifles had reached a figure averaging over 100,000 a month.

Generally speaking, the Russian military position had improved by the commencement of the summer of 1916 far beyond the expectations of any foreign observer who had taken part in the retreat of the previous year. The fighting of 1915 had taught the value of defences, and the autumn of that year and the succeeding winter had seen the construction of several defensive lines. All units at the front by the middle of May possessed their full complement of rifles. The output of small arms ammunition had increased. The number of machine guns had increased to an average of ten to twelve per four-battalion regiment. Most of the infantry divisions had now thirty-six field guns, and there was a reserve of some 8,000,000 of 3" shell. Most of the corps had a division of eight 4·8" howitzers. A considerable number of trench mortars and hand grenades had been provided.

The troops at the front had benefited by their long rest, and their spirit was good. Units were generally in excess of war strength. There were reserves of over 800,000 men in the immediate neighbourhood of the front, and considerably over a million in the interior of the country. Depot units were as well organised as the immense distances and the limited housing accommodation allowed to secure with the least possible delay a constant stream of trained men to replace casualties. The chief lacks in armament were 4·8" shell and a respectable quantity of heavy guns and shell.

Unfortunately the combination of the arms was still weak. Divisions had been allowed to stagnate indefinitely in a sector of trench at the front, and had not been drawn back, as they were constantly in France, for some weeks' hard training in manœuvre.

The transport, owing to lack of automobiles, was still archaic, and very little had been done to improve the railways. The difficulties of communication consequent on the abandonment of the Polish salient were foreseen, but scarcely any construction work was carried out in the winter, and the poorness of the Russian system in the immediate rear of the front now occupied was the chief cause of the failure of the offensive in January on the South-West Front and a contributory cause of the failure on the Northern and Western Fronts in March.

The official excuse was the shortage of rails. It is true that before the war Russia used to export rails to England, but factories formerly engaged in their production had been given up to the manufacture of shell, and the monthly output of rails had fallen from 600 to 300 versts. It is curious that in spite of this shortage of rails, the Russian Government had found it possible to complete during the war the laying of the line from Samarkand to Termez, a project that had been viewed for many years with alarm by the Government of India. This is, however, no evidence of deep political cunning, but merely an instance of the result of the habit of working in watertight compartments.

It was not only on the front that the insufficiency of the railways was felt. Progress in armament was hindered as much by the failure of the railways to transport raw material and fuel to the works in sufficient quantities as by the difficulty in obtaining machinery from abroad. Out of sixty-eight blast-furnaces which Russia possessed, only thirty-eight were working in May, owing to want of coal and metal.

The accumulation of private goods at Vladivostok increased at the rate of over 10,000 tons a week. Only 280 wagons moved west daily—100 with rails from America, 140 with Government stores and 40 with private goods. So great were the requirements of the Intendance Department for grain from Western Siberia that the limited transporting capacity of the lines there and in Eastern Russia in Europe made it impossible to allot a greater number of wagons to the Far East.

At Tornea, on the Swedish frontier, 600 tons arrived daily from abroad and only 500 tons went forward to Petrograd. The Arkhangel line was unable to work up to a steady 300 wagons a day, and imported goods accumulated for transport in the winter.

On June 20th I reported :

> The greatest danger of all is the danger of discontent in the large towns in the winter owing to the dearness of the necessities of life. The rise in prices is caused partly by speculation and partly by the fewness of the railways and the inefficiency of their working. In Moscow bread has risen 47 per cent. in price, in Odessa 80 per cent. Firewood has risen from 100 to 125 per cent. ; sugar, when obtainable, by from 65 to 70 per cent. Meat is unobtainable by the general public, though there are abundant supplies in Siberia. The country folk are contented enough, for they have grown rich through the high price of grain and the closing of the wine-shops, but the more

dangerous town population may give trouble in the winter.

The provisioning of the town population requires thought, for there are limits to the patience of even the Russian people.

A debate in the Duma on June 6th had thrown a strong light on the shortage of supplies. It was stated that the army had used over 14,000,000 head of cattle in the first year of war and that over 5,000,000 more had been lost in the evacuation of Poland. The " Left " ascribed the whole chaos to the wastefulness and want of foresight of the Ministries of War and Agriculture. The " Right " ascribed it to speculation, especially by Jews. One speaker said : " The supply of food and the cheapening of living are the problems on which success in the war depends." A priest suggested that all the fasts of the Church should be enforced by law. He pointed out that this plan would give 250 meatless days in the year, and he argued that the prohibition of meat on days when its use was permitted by the Church would lead to " temptation " and to " confusion." '

Letters to the Ambassador from the Minister of Finance on April 6th and May 2nd asked our Government to finance orders for railway material in America for 163,884,680 dollars, in England for £6,309,400 and in Italy for 165,000 lire. I visited M. Trepov, the Minister of Ways and Communications, on June 10th, and found him very bitter regarding " the hesitation " of the British Government to sanction the proposal. He had already in November asked for a credit of £39,000,000 to enable him to order material from America, but had been refused. He said that only a loan was required and not a gift, and that it would be impossible for us to lay out a similar sum to greater advantage with a view to the winning of the war !

The British Government, however, remained unsympathetic, and rightly so. If we had provided the money and the shipping to carry the material to Vladivostok, the Russian railways would never have been able to carry it forward, and it would have lain useless on the shore of the Amur Bay.

Apart from dishonesty, slackness and incapacity in the

administration, there were sufficient natural causes for the strain on the Russian railways.

First the country suffered from Peter the Great's choice of Petrograd as his capital. The supply of Petrograd, at the furthest possible point in the Empire, from the food-producing area was becoming increasingly difficult, as the population was swollen by over half a million refugees from the occupied territories and by the additional workmen in the enlarged munition factories. A far-seeing administration would have in the summer used the inland waterways to lay up stores of provisions for the winter months. Some attempt was made to do this, but the scheme, to be successful, required the intelligent co-operation of two Ministries—that of Ways and Communications and that of Agriculture—and so was foredoomed to failure.

Secondly, the transport of coal proved as difficult as had been foreseen before the war. In peace-time Poland and much of Western Russia were supplied from the Dombrova mines in South-Western Poland. These had been in enemy occupation since the first days of the war. Northern and Central Russia were supplied by British or German coal imported through the Baltic; South-East Russia was fed from the Donets coal-mines. The English coal that now came through Arkhangel was, of course, only a small part of the amount necessary to supply the munition factories of the north, and the necessary balance had to be transported 2,000 to 3,000 miles by rail from the Donets basin or from Siberia.

Thirdly, the supply of the army, with its millions of men and horses eating far more than they were accustomed to consume in peace, caused a far more intense traffic west of the general line Petrograd-Moscow-Kiev than had been known before the war. Again, in peace-time the principal ports of entry had been Petrograd, Riga and Odessa—all within a short distance of the most densely-populated region. Now all these ports were closed and over-sea supplies could only be obtained from Arkhangel in the far north, or from Vladivostok in the far east, and the long journeys to and fro locked up rolling stock.

Lastly, Finland, which in peace-time received most of its

foodstuffs from Germany, had now to be fed from Southern Russia or from Siberia.

The administration of the railways of the Empire was at this time divided into two directorates. The Western Rayon, comprising all the lines west of Petrograd-Kiev-Odessa, was under a General at G.H.Q., while the Eastern Rayon, including all the other lines, was controlled by the Minister of Ways and Communications at Petrograd.

Of the railways not occupied by the enemy, there remained 46,466 miles open for traffic and 3,704 miles open for temporary traffic. The rolling stock was divided between the Western and Eastern Rayons as follows : Western Rayon : 5,337 engines and 130,198 wagons ; Eastern Rayon : 14,829 engines and 363,731 wagons. Many of the engines were old, some dating from 1860, and they were mostly of small power. The proportion constantly laid up for repair had increased from 15·8 per cent. in 1914 to 17·3 per cent.

The directorates did not work tactfully together. M. Trepov told me that General Ronjin, the Director of the Western Rayon, had 20,000 wagons that rightfully belonged to the Eastern Rayon. The next day General Ronjin said that, on the contrary, the Minister had 8,000 wagons of his !

As there was difficulty in getting all the information required at Petrograd, I visited G.H.Q. early in June.

Sunday, June 11th, 1916.   MOGILEV.

I lunched at the Emperor's table. After lunch he talked very kindly to me. I told him that people had been very good to me since he had given me his pass for the front, and he said he was very glad to hear it. I then said that I had come to ask for a similar pass to enable me to get information at Petrograd and he said : " Certainly. Tell General Alexyeev so."

I spoke of the railway difficulty, but he did not seem to know much about it.

He was evidently in good spirits on account of Brusilov's success, and he remarked on the fact that Bethmann-Holweg continually prated of peace when no one of the Allies ever mentioned the word as a sign of Germany's declining *morale*.

I ventured to point out the necessity in Russia for anti-enemy propaganda, especially regarding the ill-treatment of prisoners by the enemy, and I quoted some instances of such ill-treatment that I had heard at the front. He agreed, adding that no one but Germans could do such things and that he could not imagine any of his people being so cruel.[1]

Then the Grand Duke Serge talked to me. He said that the Russian artillery had worked splendidly in Brusilov's offensive. He added with a twinkle in his eye that it always struck him what a difference there was in the method of waging war in France and in Russia. "In the Western theatre the enemy attacked and the French went back slowly, but still went back, and all the world exclaimed: 'What a wonderful army is the French army!' In Russia we take 106,000 prisoners in one week and no one thinks anything of it." I said that it was just the difference between being opposed by Germans and Austrians, and that the Russians had been lucky since the beginning of the war in having Austrians to keep their spirits up (*dlya podema dukha*).

Monday, June 12th, 1916.　　　　　　　　　　MOGILEV.

I went to see the Grand Duke Serge to talk of the railways. He sees the difficulty and the danger, but could only suggest that the Ambassador should go, together with M. Paleologue, the French Ambassador, to see M. Sturmer, the Prime Minister. He asked me if I knew Sturmer. I said I did not, but I did not like his name. He then told me the story of two men who persisted in talking German in a shop in spite of the manager's remonstrances. The police were called in, but when they arrived the two men were

---

[1] I recalled these words when twenty-eight months later I visited the house in Ekaterinburg, where the Emperor and his family had been foully murdered by some of his people a few weeks before.

simply repeating over and over again, " Hofmeister Sturmer, Hofmeister Sturmer," and it was impossible to arrest them for simply quoting the name of the Russian Premier.

The Grand Duke said that M. Trepov is " no good," and that all new ministers are the same. Immediately they are appointed they sack everyone. Within three days they change all their views, and they have the officials they had sacked back, only in higher posts; for instance, Borisov, formerly Director of Railways, is now Assistant Minister, and Ivanovski, formerly Chief of the Nikolas Railway, is now Director of Railways.

In the opinion of the Grand Duke nothing will put down prices in the big towns but the appointment of a dictator, who alone could co-ordinate the work of the various ministries.

A few days later I spoke to General Shuvaiev of the danger of disorder in the large towns owing to the lack of supplies, and instanced the shortage of meat as one of the evils that an improved organisation and the prevention of speculation in railway wagons might mend. He replied : " A man is better without meat. I have all my life kept all the fasts of the Church, and look at me now. Some animals eat meat and others do not. The lion is a meat-eater and the elephant is not. When we want an animal to do our work, we choose the elephant and not the lion. Petrograd is safer without meat." This sort of simple peasant philosophy did not help much.

There was an " unpleasant incident " in June.

Saturday, June 24th, 1916.   PETROGRAD.

Thornhill (Chief of the Intelligence Section) told me that he and two other British officers dined last night at Tsarskoe Selo at the mess of the Depot Battalion of the 1st Rifle Regiment of the Guard. About 1 a.m. the Grand Duke Boris, who was also a guest, made some astonishing statements. He said he was sure that the very next war would be between England and Russia, owing to the greed of our Government, that our attempt at the Dardanelles had all been bluff, that he knew for a fact that Russia had offered to take Baghdad, but that the British Foreign Office had declined, "because England wanted to take it herself."

We went to tell the Ambassador, and met him on the Quay. He was, I think, especially hurt that Boris, who had received so much hospitality at the Embassy, should have said such things. He agreed that Thornhill and I should go to Boris to tell him officially, as Thornhill had told him last night unofficially, that his statements are quite untrue, but he will first telegraph home to ascertain if there is any possible foundation for the stories.

Statements like these, coming from such a quarter, make one very sick of life. One works all one possibly can to keep the Entente going, and this is the result. Boris is Inspecting Officer of the Cossack Troops, and has thus unlimited opportunities for spreading poisonous lies like this right through the Russian Army.

Thursday, June 29th, 1916   PETROGRAD.

The reply came from the Foreign Office yesterday. There is no truth in the statement that we told the Russians that we wanted to take Baghdad, and we are to ask the Grand Duke the origin of his information.

I telephoned to the Grand Duke to ask if Thornhill and I could see him, and we arranged to arrive at Tsarskoe by the 4.7 train.

We went in uniform. The Grand Duke's car met us at the station and took us to his villa, which is quite English in style. He, of course, knew what we had come about. I gave him an *Aide Mêmoire* that had been drawn up in the Chancery, and said I had been told to give it to him with reference to the conversation that took place in the mess the other night. He read the paper, and the reading seemed to make his mouth dry. He said that it was very interesting. I then asked where he had heard such a statement, and he said someone had told him at the Stavka (G.H.Q.). I asked if it had been made by Pustovoitenko (the General Quartermaster) or by Alexyeev (the Chief of Staff), and he said: " No one so highly placed, but all the junior officers said it." I told him that the repetition of the ideas of junior officers by a man in his position was particularly harmful, as people thought he had access to secret documents and founded his statements on them. I pointed out that our alliance was much more difficult to maintain than that of the Central Powers, for there Germany was top dog, while we were all more or less equal, and that therefore we were constantly on the look-out for such statements as he had made in order to contradict them. I said that we had suspected at one time a Jewish banker, at another a German spy, but never a Grand Duke. Boris said that he had not made the statement anywhere else, that it was the first time he had made it, and he would not do it again. I asked him to inform the colonel of the Depot Battalion of the 1st Rifle Regiment that the statement he had made was untrue, and he said he would send the paper I had given him to the colonel to see.

We then had whiskies-and-sodas, and took the 4.43 train back to Petrograd. Quick diplomacy of the military type!

Later the Emperor spoke severely to the Grand Duke on the subject.

CHAPTER XIII

OPERATIONS ON THE SOUTH-WEST FRONT FROM THE COMMENCEMENT OF BRUSILOV'S OFFENSIVE (JUNE 4TH, 1916) TILL THE FORMATION OF THE GUARD ARMY (JULY 25TH, 1916)[1]

REFERENCE MAPS NOS. XI. AND XII.

IN April and May the Russian Supreme Command had made every preparation for the main advance of the year on a front of forty versts north and south of the village of Krevo, west of Molodechno.

It was intended that the main stroke should be delivered by the 4th Army on the right, and General Ragoza, who had moved with his Staff across the rear of the 10th Army to Molodechno, had twenty-two divisions concentrated under his command by the beginning of June. His advance was to be supported on the front south of Krevo by General Radkevich, with fifteen infantry and three cavalry divisions, and to be backed by the new Guard Army under General Bezobrazov, which contained four infantry and three cavalry divisions, and completed its concentration in rear by June 2nd. The Guard Army had commenced its entrainment for the north at Volochisk in April. The time required to complete its transfer may be partly explained by the large number of non-combatants and horses, a state of things unfortunately

---

[1] The so-called "Brusilov's offensive" on the South-West Front commenced on June 4th. I was in Petrograd all June, so saw nothing of the actual fighting that month. In July I visited the Western Front and gathered details of the Baranovichi offensive. In July and August I was with the Guard Army in the fighting on the Stokhod, and visited the 8th and 9th Armies, collecting some account of their work in June. In September and early October I visited the Northern Front. In October I returned once more to the South-West Front, and in that month and November visited all its five armies, the Special, 11th, 7th, 8th and 9th.

Operations on the South-West Front 433

typical of the Russian army, owing to the absence of motor transport.[1]

Careful and, for the Russian theatre, elaborate preparation had been made for the Krevo offensive. Twenty-six divisions were allotted for the actual attack. Positions for batteries had been chosen within 1,800 yards of the front line. Batteries had been connected with observation posts by three lines of underground wire. Ammunition dumps had been made at suitable intervals, and roads had been constructed for the bringing up of extra supplies. The routes to be followed by ambulances had been carefully selected and marked. It was thought that sufficient heavy guns had been concentrated: for instance, 138 heavy guns on a front of nine versts in the 4th Army. General Aga Khan Shiklinski, reputed to be the best scientific gunner in the Russian army, was given command of four divisions of heavy artillery in rear of the point of junction of the two armies in order to be in a position to assist in the co-ordination of the advance by supporting either army as might be necessary.

The main attention of the Supreme Command was directed to the Western Front, and it is calculated that on June 1st the five [2] armies of that Front—2nd, 4th, Guard, 10th and 3rd—contained fifty-eight infantry divisions, while the four armies of the Northern Front—the 6th at Petrograd and along the east coast of the Gulf of Riga, the 12th at Wenden, the 1st temporarily at Kreutzburg and the 5th at Dvinsk—and the four armies of the South-West Front—the 8th at Rovno, the 11th at Volochisk, the 7th at Gusyatin and the 9th at Kamenets-Podolsk—had each only thirty-eight divisions.

The enemy Command, who had, of course, ample information

---

[1] The strength of the Guard Army was:
   Battalions - 61
   Squadrons - 79
   Officers - 1,200
   Guns - 202 (168 3", 12 4·8" and 22 " heavy ").
   Machine-guns - 186 (162 with Infantry and 24 with cavalry)
   Aeroplanes - 12
   Rifles - 55,016
   Sabres - 10,491
The feeding strength of the army was: men, 127,660; horses, 52,425.

[2] The 1st Army had been transferred from the Western to the Northern Front.

of every Russian move, was fully aware of the Russian preparations, and probably regarded them with an even mind, as its best troops were all echeloned in the northern half of the Russian front. The Austrian army had been left to defend Galicia, in the reconquest of which in 1915 German forces had so powerfully co-operated. On the front from the Baltic to the river Pripyat there were only two Austrian divisions, while from the Pripyat to the Rumanian frontier only two German infantry divisions remained, the 82nd just south of the river, and the 48th opposite Tarnopol.

Five enemy armies held the front from north of the Pripyat to the Rumanian frontier.[1] On the left Von Linsingen's Army, containing two German infantry and two German cavalry divisions and two Austrian infantry and three Austrian cavalry divisions, astride the river Pripyat, opposed Lesh's 3rd Russian Army in the marshes of Polyesie. Further south the 4th Austrian Army, under the Archduke Joseph Ferdinand, with Headquarters at Lutsk, held with ten and a half infantry and one cavalry division the front from Rafalovka to Dubno. On its right the 2nd Austrian Army of Boehm-Ermolli, with Headquarters at Brody, occupied the front from Dubno to the south-west of Kremenets with eight infantry and two cavalry divisions. On Boehm-Ermolli's right the former "Southern German Army" of the Bavarian, von Bothmer, now containing only a single German infantry division and nine Austrian infantry and two Austrian cavalry divisions, with Headquarters at Brzesany, held the long front from south-west of Kremenets to south-west of Gzortkow. In the extreme south Pflanzer-Baltin's 7th Austrian Army, with Headquarters at Kolomea, and eight and a half infantry and four cavalry divisions, carried the line to the Rumanian frontier.

The four last-named armies stood opposed to the four Russian armies of the South-West Front, the distribution of which was as follows:

SOUTH-WEST FRONT.—*Headquarters*: Berdichev. *Commander-in-Chief*: General Brusilov. *Chief of*

---
[1] See Map No. XII.

Operations on the South-West Front 435

Staff: General Klembovski. *General Quartermaster*: General Dukhonin.

8TH ARMY: *Headquarters*: Rovno. *Front*: Kovel-Sarni railway to south-west of Kremenets. *Commander*: General Kaledin. *Chief of Staff*: General Sukhomlin.
Vth Cavalry Corps, Veliarshev, Orenburg Cossack Cavalry Division, 11th Cavalry Division.
XXXth Corps, Zaionchkovski, 71, 80, 100.
XXXIXth Corps, Stelnitski, 125, 102.
XLth Corps, Kashtalinski, 2nd Rifle, 4th Rifle.
VIIIth Corps, Vladimir Dragomirov, 14, 15.
XXXIInd Corps, Federov, 101, 105.
7th and 12th Cavalry Divisions.

11TH ARMY: *Headquarters*: Volochisk. *Front*: Southwest of Kremenets to south-west of Tarnopol. *Commander*: General Sakharev. *Chief of Staff*: General Shishkevich.
XVIIth Corps, Yakovlev, 3, 35.
Trans-Amur Cavalry Division.
VIIth Corps, Ekk, 10, 34.
VIth Corps, Gutor, 16, 4.
XVIIIth Corps, Kruzenstern, 37, 23.

7TH ARMY: *Headquarters*: Gusyatin. *Front*: Southwest of Tarnopol to east of Potok. *Commander*: General Shcherbachev. *Chief of Staff*: General Golovin.
XXIInd Corps, Von der Brincken, 1st Finland, 3rd Finland.
XVIth Corps, Savich, 47, 41.
IInd Corps, Pflug, 26, 43.
3rd Turkistan Division.
IInd Cavalry Corps, Composite Cossack Cavalry Division, 2nd Don Cossack Cavalry Brigade, Composite Cavalry Brigade, 9th Cavalry Division.

1st Independent Cavalry Brigade.
Reserve of Front: Vth Caucasian Corps, 2nd Finland, 4th Finland.

9TH ARMY.—*Headquarters*: Kamenets-Podolsk. *Front*: East of Potok to the Rumanian frontier. *Commander*: General Lechitski. *Chief of Staff*: General Sanikov.
XXXIIIrd Corps, Krilov, 1st Trans-Amur, 2nd Trans-Amur.
XLIst Corps, Belkovich, 74, 3rd Trans-Amur.
XIth Corps, Barantsev, 11, 32.
XIIth Corps, Kaznakov, 19, 12.
Composite Corps, 82, 103.
IIIrd Cavalry Corps, Count Keller, 1st Don Cossack Cavalry, Terek Cossack Cavalry, 10th Cavalry.

As Kaledin's right coincided roughly with the left of the Army of the Archduke Joseph Ferdinand, and both the armies of Lechitski and Pflanzer-Baltin touched the Rumanian frontier on the south, the Russians had thirty-eight infantry and twelve and a half cavalry divisions opposed to thirty-seven enemy infantry and nine enemy cavalry divisions. Moreover, as the Russian infantry divisions were practically all of sixteen battalions, they were individually superior to those of the enemy in rifle-power; for instance, the 9th Army counted 160 battalions and 108 squadrons against the 131 battalions and 92 squadrons of the opposing 7th Austrian Army. On the other hand, in guns, machine-guns and air-power the enemy had the advantage. He was, too, in occupation of a line which he had fortified during eight months, and his communications by road and rail were infinitely superior to those of the Russians.

In March General Brusilov was promoted to be Commander-in-Chief of the South-West Front in succession to General Ivanov. He was at this time sixty-three years of age. He had been educated at the Corps des Pages, but, passing out low, had only obtained a commission in the Cavalry of the Line. After spending no less than sixteen consecutive years in various appointments at

Operations on the South-West Front

the Officers' Cavalry School, he had commanded in succession the 2nd Guard Cavalry Division and the XIIth Corps. In the present war he had been consistently successful in command of the 8th Army, but had been perhaps lucky in having had only Austrians to contend with. The Chief of Staff of the Front was still General Klembovski, but General Dietrikhs had gone to Salonika in charge of a Russian brigade, and his place as General Quartermaster had been taken by his assistant, General Dukhonin, an honest man and a tremendous worker.

On April 20th all four armies of the South-West Front had been ordered by the Staff of the Front to prepare to assume the offensive. Each army commander was told to make preparations, depending solely on the forces in his army, for penetrating the enemy's front in a sector he was himself to select, the preparations to be completed by May 11th. Special emphasis was attached to secrecy, and it was ordered, in case the enemy took the initiative before the completion of the Russian preparations, that all four Russian armies should at once attack.

On May 14th the Austrian offensive in the Trentino commenced. It is generally believed that the King of Italy made a personal appeal to the Emperor for help. Brusilov was asked if he could move, and he replied that he could move as well at once as some weeks later.

The offensive was therefore launched on June 4th merely as a demonstration without the previous concentration of sufficient superiority of force to make possible a decisive success.

Some two months later Brusilov in conversation ascribed his success to the fact that for the first time the armies of the South-West Front had been ordered to advance simultaneously, so that the enemy was unable to withdraw troops from one part of the line to another. In the armies, however, opinion was very definite that the success was due entirely to the careful local preparation and that the staff of the front had little hand in it.

Three out of the four army commanders were remarkable men. Kaledin, like Brusilov, was a cavalryman, who had commanded the 12th Cavalry Division with success in the war. He was, however, not at all of the *beau sabreur* type, but short-sighted, shy and silent, more of a student than man of the world like his chief. He was married to a Frenchwoman.

Shcherbachev, of the 7th Army, a tall, thin soldierly man, was at this time fifty-nine. He had been Commandant of the Military Academy in peace time, and now had as his immediate assistants two former colleagues, Golovin, now Chief of Staff, formerly Professor of Staff Duties, and Neznamov, now General Quartermaster, formerly Professor of Strategy. The staff work and the orders in this army were said to be models.

The 9th Army had an ideal combination in Lechitski, at this time sixty years of age, a man of self-education, but of strong will, good common sense and great experience, Sanikov, a sound man (*polojitelni*), who had been Lechitski's Chief of Staff in the Far East, and the General Quartermaster, Kelchevski, who of all the ex-Academy professors most " made good " in the war.

Sakharov (sixty-three), the Commander of the 11th Army, and his Chief of Staff Shishkevich, and General Quartermaster Cheremissov, were less well spoken of.

Sakharov, like Brusilov and Kaledin, was a cavalryman, while Lechitski and Shcherbachev had commenced their service in the infantry. Kaledin, Shcherbachev and Sakharov were all graduates of the Military Academy, while Brusilov and Lechitski were not.

The 8th and 9th Armies on the right and left respectively gained the most striking immediate success. The 7th Army was successful too, but was held back by the failure of the 11th on its right.

I gathered some account of the actual operations of the successful armies some weeks later.

Friday, August 4th, 1916. ROJISHCHE.

I saw Kaledin yesterday at Lutsk for the first time. He gave me the impression of being a hard thinker, but of being, perhaps, without the necessary reserve of vital energy required to carry a difficult operation through. I asked him to what he ascribed the success in June when the attempt at the offensive on the South-West Front in

Operations on the South-West Front

December and January had proved such a failure. He said that the offensive in June succeeded because it was prepared with exceptional care.

General Delvig, who had commanded the XLth Corps till just before the battle, told me later that he ascribed the success to the secrecy of preparation and to the peculiarly favourable character of the ground, which at once favoured observation and afforded cover.

The 8th Army made its main attack on a front of twenty-five versts, of which only the centre fifteen versts, north and south of the village of Olika, were the scene of strenuous fighting. On these fifteen versts were concentrated the four divisions of the XLth and VIIIth Corps—sixty-four battalions, about three and one-third rifles per yard.

On the flanks of these two corps a division of the XXXIXth and one of the XXXIInd Corps each occupied five versts of front.

In addition to their own divisional artillery, which would normally amount to 216 3" guns, the six divisions had 60 4·8" howitzers, 32 6" howitzers, 8 4·2" guns and 12 6" (120 pud) guns on the whole twenty-five versts of front (29,150 yards).

In the fighting of June 4th and 5th the 4·8" howitzers fired 140 H.E. and 27 shrapnel per gun, and the 6" howitzers 140 H.E. and eight shrapnel.

The bombardment was carried out on June 4th, and the assault took place early on the 5th. The XLth Corps carried three enemy lines, penetrating three versts. The VIIIth Corps was less successful, but both corps held on to the ground gained, repelling all counter-attacks.

The advance continued on the 6th, and the opening in the enemy's front was widened to forty versts. The enemy's advanced fortified rayon was carried and he did not pause in his flight to defend his second rayon. On June 7th his third rayon in advance of Lutsk was carried by frontal attack and Lutsk was occupied, the breech in the Austrian front having been widened to eighty versts and the 8th Army having marched thirty-five versts and won two pitched battles in three days. Kaledin would have won a still more striking success if he had had his cavalry at hand. He had only a single division—the 12th—for the remainder of his mounted troops had been allotted a separate task by Brusilov: to penetrate along the Sarni-Kovel railway to Kovel. In this they failed.

Kashtalinski, who commanded the XLth Corps in the breakthrough, told me on August 4th that if he had had an extra infantry division when he got to Lutsk he would have occupied Kovel, though whether he would have been able to remain there was " another question." He said that his corps lost in three weeks' advance 7,500 men, but later when he sat still under heavy German gunfire his casualties amounted to 8,000 in five days.

Meanwhile the left wing of the 8th Army pressed forward and occupied Dubno on June 9th. On June 10th the Russian line ran along the seventy versts river-front from Rojishche to Dubno, the enemy holding only Torgovitsa at the confluence of the Ikva and the Stir.

On June 4th and 5th the 11th Army attacked twenty versts north-west of Tarnopol on the front Glyadki-Vorobievka, but failed.

The 7th Army selected a section on its left, opposite von Bothmer's right and directly east of the village of Jaziowec for its assault, for four very sufficient reasons. The enemy's defences there were comparatively weak, his line projected in a salient permitting of the employment of enfilade fire, the 36th Austrian Division, which held this section, was 80 per cent. Slav, and lastly, the ground offered cover for the Russian reserves and at the same time facilities for the observation of movements in the Austrian rear.

Special pains were taken to mislead the enemy. The Army Commander issued his instructions personally at repeated interviews with the corps commanders. Up to the last minute the offensive was not alluded to even in cipher telegrams. The 3rd Turkistan Rifle Division, which was detailed as reserve to the striking corps, was moved into position by night. Batteries came up on the night previous to the attack. Sapping was carried out along the whole front of the Army.

Operations on the South-West Front

On May 27th a telegram was sent to the G.O.C. IInd Corps: "In view of the transfer of the corps to another front, you will please prepare for entrainment by June 2nd at the stations of Czortkow, Vygnanka and Kopyczynce."

The uninitiated ascribed the move of the 3rd Turkistan Division to a decision to place it in front line in relief of the IInd Corps, and the intensive work on the front of that corps to the same reason. A captured Austrian Intelligence Summary stated: "Prisoners affirm that the IInd Corps will be transferred to another front on relief by the 3rd Turkistan Division."

The 7th Army contained seven infantry and three and a half cavalry divisions, or 112 battalions and 92 squadrons. The arrangements for the main effort were entrusted to Pflug, the Commander of the IInd Corps. He detailed thirty-six of his forty-eight battalions to a front of seven versts. He was given 40 per cent. of the 3" guns of the army, 56 per cent. of the 4·8" howitzers and *all* the heavy artillery, viz., in all 116 3" field guns, 20 4·8" howitzers, 7 4·2" guns and 16 6" howitzers.

The guns opened fire at 4 a.m. on June 4th. The enemy replied by firing at the Russian observation posts and batteries, but soon ceased, as it afterwards transpired, because all his telephone wires had been cut.

Fire was continued all day methodically with careful observation of each shot. After dark the volume of fire slackened and was chiefly directed upon the passages cut through the enemy's wire during the day to prevent all possibility of repair.

From 12.30 midnight to 2.30 a.m. on the 5th, fire was lifted to enable scouts to examine results. After dawn fire was once more directed on the enemy's front lines.

The results "exceeded all expectations." The first line was entirely destroyed; the second and third lines were destroyed with the exception of some of the shelters.

An aeroplane is said to have corrected the heavy gun-fire during the preparation, but practice with wireless had only commenced on May 6th, and there had been little of it on account of the foggy weather.

The Russian infantry attacked at 2 a.m. on June 6th, and two hours later had occupied all the enemy's first and second and part of his third lines. The Austrian counter-attacks were easily repulsed.

On the evening of the 6th the IInd Cavalry Corps was brought up, and on the 7th co-operated with the IInd Corps in the development of the success, the enemy retiring behind the Strypa. On the 8th the advanced guards of the two corps crossed the Strypa, and on that and the two following days the XVIth Corps and the left of the XXIInd Corps drove back the enemy on their front.

The Austrians abandoned forty-five versts of front that they had fortified for eight or nine months. The 7th Army captured from June 4th till 10th 415 officers, 15,649 rank and file, 35 guns and 37 machine guns. Its losses were 360 officers and 19,943 men.

From the 11th to the 13th the enemy counter-attacked fiercely but was repulsed with loss.

On the night of the 13th the two left corps of the 11th Army —the VIth and XVIIIth—were transferred to the 7th Army. From the 14th till the 21st Shcherbachev took 10,000 prisoners, but made little progress to the north-west. He therefore carried out a regroupment and on July 6th-8th drove the enemy across the river Barysz.

In April a captain of the general staff of the 9th Army carried out a reconnaissance of the front from the Dniester south to the town of Dobronowtz (about thirty versts north-east by north of Czernowitz), where the Austrian line lay practically on the frontier. He reported the area as particularly suitable for the main stroke, the ground being cut up by deep ravines and so complicated as to afford absolute protection from Austrian artillery fire.

It was decided to attack west from the village of Balamutovka, immediately north of Dobronowtz, in combination with an attack to the south-west by a division from the Dniester re-entrant further north. The plan was approved by the staff of the front and methodical preparation commenced.

To avoid exciting suspicion zigzag trenches were worked out

Operations on the South-West Front

from the front fire trenches all along the front of the army. The 82nd Division, on which little reliance was then placed, was moved south and its place in the XLIst Corps was taken by the 3rd Trans-Amur Division. The heavy guns were only brought up the night before the bombardment, and one gun of each battery was left to fire from the former battery position.

The Austrians were completely deceived, and expected the attack further south, though proper observation from a commanding height on their front—Hill 458—should have given them some inkling of the Russian plans.

On June 4th the 9th Army consisted of ten infantry and four cavalry divisions (160 battalions and 108 squadrons). It was opposed by eight and a half Austrian infantry and four cavalry divisions (131 battalions and 92 squadrons).

The "push" was carried through by the XLIst and XIth Corps. Of the former, the right division—the 74th—occupied in the first instance a passive section on the left bank of the Dniester. The left division of the XLIst Corps, the 3rd Trans-Amur Division and the three divisions directed by the XIth Corps, together with their supporting guns, were distributed as follows:

CORPS.	SECTION.	INFANTRY.	3″	4·8″	4·2″	6″How.	6″120 puds	6″ Canet
XLIst	Active. 2½ versts	16 batts. 3rd Trans-Amur Division	44	8	—	—	4	—
	Passive. 6 versts	4 batts. 11th Division.	18	—	—	—	—	4
XIth	Active. 3½ versts	20 batts. 11th and 32nd Divisions	105	24	3	8	19	—
	Passive. 3½ versts	4 batts. 32nd Division.	18	—	4	—	—	—
		Total Guns	185	32	7	8	23	4

The 19th Division from the XIIth Corps, attached to the XIth Corps, was placed in reserve.

More than half of Lechitski's heavy artillery was composed of 6″ 120-pud guns. These had been obtained on the initiative of the staff of the army from the Black Sea fortress of Ochakov. Though the gun dates from 1877, it did good work. It is drawn by eight to ten horses and requires half an hour to come into action. It fires a shrapnel weighing 85 Russian lbs. 7,450 yards, and a H.E. shell weighing 81 lbs. with a charge of 12½ lbs. melinite 9,100 yards.

The sections selected for the decisive assaults—two and a half versts and three and a half versts—were of course too narrow, but the guns available did not admit of the preparation of a wider stretch of front. The whole front occupied by the 9th Army was ninety versts, or sixty miles. It showed Lechitski's courage to risk the concentration of half his infantry strength on a little more than one-sixth of his front.

The right active section had sixteen battalions in front line on a front of two and a half versts (2,917 yards)—about 3·6 men per yard. The left active section had twenty battalions in front line on a front of three and a half versts (4,083 yards)—about 4·2 men per yard.

The artillery preparation commenced at 4.30 a.m. on June 4th and lasted till noon, when the infantry of the 11th and 32nd Divisions rushed the enemy's three first lines of trench, taking 8,000 prisoners. The 3rd Trans-Amur Division attacked about half an hour later, and by evening had occupied all the enemy's trenches on its immediate front.

Progress on the following two or three days was slow, owing to the enemy's violent counter-attacks, but all the ground gained was held. On the night of the 6th the enemy evacuated Sinkuv on the left bank of the Dniester, and on the following day the 3rd Trans-Amur Division fought its way forward to the outskirts of the village of Okna.

As the enemy was evidently preparing to withdraw from the left bank of the Dniester, Lechitski transferred by the 9th the 1st Trans-Amur (XXXIIIrd) and the 74th (XLIst) Divisions to the right bank, where they came into action right and left of the 3rd Trans-Amur Division. The 2nd Trans-Amur Division (XXXIIIrd) was left for the present on the left bank in observation of a front of over thirty miles.

Operations on the South-West Front 445

The capture of Hill 458 on June 10th by the 32nd Division, aided by a brilliant charge of the Tekinski Regiment (formerly called the Turkoman Horse), finally broke the enemy's resistance. He retreated in disorder to the Pruth and was only saved from complete destruction by the torrential rain which hindered the pursuit.

Opposition was met on the Czernowitz bridgehead on the 12th, but the position was carried on the 17th and the town was occupied.

In the nine days June 4th-12th, the XIth Corps alone took 564 officers, 23,816 rank and file, 9 guns and 75 machine-guns.

On June 19th the enemy was driven back to the Sereth. The further conquest of the Bukovina offered no great difficulty, but the task set the Army was to advance north-west on Przemysl, and every yard advanced lengthened the left flank, which was exposed to attack from the Carpathian passes.

The success of June 4th in contrast to the failure in January was ascribed largely to the able direction of the artillery of the XIth Corps by a lieutenant-colonel who was taken on the initiative of General Kelchevski, the General Quartermaster, from the command of a battery, and placed in charge of all the guns of the Corps over the head of the Inspector. The guns fired more shell on June 4th than during the whole fourteen days' offensive in December and January. They no doubt prepared the way, but it was the splendid dash of the infantry and Kelchevski's bold direction that completed the enemy's discomfiture.

By the middle of June, two of the four enemy armies opposing the Russian South-West Front were in full flight, and the success of Brusilov's flank armies had driven deep wedges into the Austrian defence. In the centre the inner flanks of Boehm-Ermolli and von Bothmer's armies still held their original line, though the former's left had been driven back by the left of the 8th Army and the latter's right had given way before the onslaught of the Russian 7th Army. The whole front of the 8th Army—105 miles—three-quarters of the front of the 7th Army—thirty miles—and the whole front of the 9th Army—sixty miles—had moved forward. The enemy still maintained his original line on the front of the 11th Army (fifty miles), and opposite the right of the 7th Army (ten miles). The Austrians had been driven back from lengths aggregating 195 miles of a line of 255 miles that they had fortified for upwards of nine months, and they had been driven back by an army with technical equipment far inferior to their own.

The sudden success of an enemy, whom they had thought they had decisively beaten in 1915, came as a rude and unexpected shock to the strategists of Berlin. The moment, too, was uncomfortable, for the attack on Verdun was still in full progress and was making ever-increasing inroads on German man-power. The Germans, however, came promptly to the help of their ally.

They sent troops to fill the two gaps, west of Lutsk, opposite Kaledin, and between the Dniester and Pruth, opposite Lechitski.

A new army of manœuvre was formed under von Linsingen's direction to drive back the 8th Army columns which were advancing north-west from Lutsk on Kovel. This new army contained ten divisions—one German formed from reserves north of the Pripyat, three German from the Northern Front, four German from France and two Austrian from the Trentino. In the latter half of June von Linsingen succeeded by frontal attacks in stopping Kaledin's advance towards Kovel on the Stokhod. He also attempted a great counter-offensive against Kaledin's flanks ; his right wing drove back the Russians to Boromel, south of Lutsk, but his left wing was held up on the Stir at Kolki.

Lesh's 3rd Army, which was astride the Pripyat facing von Linsingen, had now been added to Brusilov's command. Leaving his right flank—the marshy line from Vigonovskoe Lake along the Oginski Canal and east of the Pinsk salient—weakly held, Lesh concentrated four infantry and five cavalry divisions on the Stir, and on July 4th, in conjunction with Ist Turkistan and the XXXth Corps of Kaledin's right, launched an offensive against von Linsingen and drove him back towards the Stokhod, capturing from the 4th to the 7th 300 officers and 12,000 unwounded prisoners.

Operations on the South-West Front

Meanwhile in the extreme south, while three Austrian divisions had fled south across the Carpathians, the main body of the discomfited 7th Austrian Army had retreated west between the Dniester and the Pruth. Here they were reinforced by two German divisions (from the Northern Front and from the Balkans), and by three Austrian divisions from the Trentino.

Lechitski completed the conquest of Bukovina by the occupation of Kimpolung on June 24th. On the 28th his right wing advancing west defeated the enemy once more between the Dniester and the Pruth, and took 10,000 prisoners. He occupied Kolomea on the following day.

From July 6th to 10th Lechitski's left wing defeated enemy counter-attacks in advance of Kimpolung, and on July 10th his right wing occupied Delatyn.

The front of the 9th Army had now been enormously extended, and there was a pause in the operations while it awaited reinforcements from the north.

The second phase of the offensive, like the first, was remarkable for the success of the two Russian flanking armies, in the north in this case the 3rd, and in the south the ever gallant 9th. It was now fully time for the centre armies to make their contribution.

Lesh's successful advance across the Stir had removed the threat from Kaledin's right. Brusilov now launched Sakharov's 11th Army to forestall an enemy attack from the south-west against Kaledin's left.

The 11th Army, which had now taken ground to the north, attacked near Gumbin, south-west of Lutsk, on July 16th, and drove the enemy back in a south-westerly direction. Sakharov then crossed the Lipa at its junction with the Stir, and under cover of a flank guard, thrown out to the west, moved south with the bulk of his army and entered Brody on July 28th. He captured 40,000 prisoners, 49 guns and 100 machine guns in an operation which a French writer has characterised as "one of the finest victories of the whole war."[1]

---

[1] Henri Bidou, *Revue des Deux Mondes*, vol. xxxviii., p. 168.

Further south the 7th Army could make little progress against Bothmer, but the 9th Army made some advance towards Stanislau.

Brusilov threw the Guard Army on the Stokhod between the 3rd and 8th Armies in a last desperate bid for Kovel.

CHAPTER XIV

THE TRANSFER TO THE SOUTH. EVENTS ON THE NORTHERN AND WESTERN FRONTS IN JUNE AND JULY, 1916

Reference Map. No. XI.

BRUSILOV'S offensive had been launched by the Emperor as a demonstration to help his Allies. From the purely Russian point of view the local reserves on the South-West Front on June 4th were too limited to offer a reasonable probability of the attainment of results that might justify the cost of the "breakthrough." The immediate success upset all the calculations of the Russian Supreme Command.

For military reasons it became important to reinforce the South-West Front to enable Brusilov to hold what he had gained and to prevent a return to the trench warfare so little suited to the Russian temperament. It was equally important for political reasons to exploit a success which was instilling a new spirit in a population already tired of the war.

It was really a race to the South-West Front. The question was, could the Russians withdraw sufficient forces from their Northern and Western Fronts and convey them to their South-West Front in time to forestall the reinforcements which the enemy was concentrating from every theatre of war—from France, Italy and the Balkans, as well as from other parts of the Russian front? As so often happened in Russia, the Supreme Command ordered but the railways decided.

As early as June 11th the XXIIIrd and another corps from the Dvinsk bridgehead were on their way south. They were followed by a constant stream of units up to the extreme capacity of the railways.

It was soon decided to abandon the Krevo offensive. The Russian Command had found a soft place to strike and naturally disliked the idea of risking its knuckles against the German lines west of Molodechno.

On June 18th Ragoza received orders to move with the Staff of the 4th Army from Molodechno across the rear of the 10th Army, and to attack " at all costs " north of Baranovichi on July 3rd. He arrived at Nesvij on the night of June 21st and assumed control of the section of front from Dyelyatichi on the Nyeman to the Vigonovskoe Lake. This was occupied from right to left by the XXVth, IXth, Grenadier and Xth Corps. The XXXVth and IIIrd Caucasian Corps lay in rear, and two other corps were assembling.

The corps commanders were called to Headquarters on the 23rd, and it was decided to carry out the main attack on a front of 7,500 yards east of the town of Gorodishche, about fifteen miles due north of the railway junction of Baranovichi·

The section selected was in the centre of the front of the 4th Army, and it was chosen because it was the only one from the Baltic to the Pripyat then occupied by Austrian troops.

It was arranged that the IXth Corps should deliver the main stroke, its right to be covered by the 46th Division of the XXVth Corps. The Grenadier and Xth Corps were to deliver subsidiary attacks on their fronts further south.

The 247 heavy guns of the army were distributed fairly equally to corps, the idea being that the bombardment should not give the enemy an indication of the actual section to be assaulted, and that the main attack should be carried through by weight of infantry. On the 7,500 yards selected Abram Dragomirov, the Commander of the IXth Corps, deployed the 5th and 42nd Divisions with immediately in rear the 67th and 53rd Divisions of the XXXVth Corps. Further in rear lay the IIIrd Caucasian Corps as reserve of the Army Commander, while one march in rear the IVth Siberian Corps was assembling as reserve of the Commander-in-Chief.

The artillery preparation commenced at 7 a.m. on July 2nd

View in the Carpathians.

[See page 447

Bivouack of the 43rd Division in the Carpathians, N.W. of Kimpolung.

[See page 447

Bridge on the Upper Pruth

[See page 447

Prince Radzivill's House at Nesvij

[See page 450

and continued till 6 p.m. At 10 p.m. the scouts reported that sufficient passages had been prepared.

The long-range batteries were much handicapped by the enemy's complete command of the air. The Russian aeroplanes were slow, mostly without wireless and practically all without machine-guns. Air observation was only possible from the balloon in rear, and the howitzers could only destroy such machine-gun posts as were visible from the forward observation posts or from this balloon.

The assault was launched at 2 a.m. on the 4th. By 4 a.m. the 46th Division had passed all the enemy's front-line defences and had captured eleven guns. Communication broke down. Ragoza, the Army Commander, heard nothing of this division's success till 8 a.m., by which time its remains had been driven back by the German artillery to its original line.

The IXth Corps, with the XXXVth, carried the enemy's advanced trenches but failed to press the attack further. Losses were heavy among the leaders—in the 46th division the Brigade Commander and two regiment commanders, in the 42nd Division three out of the four regiment commanders.

The success had come where it was not expected, and there was no one on the spot to realise the situation and to make the necessary changes in the dispositions.

Another attempt was made with new forces on the 7th, but Germans had replaced the Austrians in the front line and had brought up several heavy batteries. Further south the Grenadiers and the Xth Corps occupied sections of the enemy's trenches but were subsequently shelled out. Fighting continued for some days later, and the Russians had lost 80,000 men, chiefly by gun-fire, by July 14th. On July 9th two whole companies of Siberians perished in a bog.

Monday, July 17th, 1916.   NESVIJ.

. . . . . .

I motored to see General Abram Dragomirov. He is small and active, and certainly "all there."

I asked him his opinion as to the cause of failure. He

said: " You may be forgiven if you make a certain number of mistakes, but if you make nothing but mistakes you cannot succeed. We hurried on the operation while our forces were only assembling; we attacked on a narrow front of seven versts; we distributed the attacking force parallel to the front instead of in depth; too large a proportion of the force was held back instead of being entrusted to the Commander on the spot; the 46th Division should have been placed under the Commander of the main attack."

This was not very convincing. Staev, the General Quartermaster of the 4th Army, told me that Dragomirov had distributed the IXth and XXXVth Corps parallel to the front on his own initiative, whereas Dragomirov said that the order came from above, *i.e.*, from Staev. Perhaps if the 46th Division had been placed under Dragomirov he would have supported it, but it is not very clear why he failed to do so on his own initiative.

All accounts agree that the men attacked with rare gallantry. No one is in the slightest degree depressed. The IXth Corps lost 55 per cent., but is now full up once more.

Sunday, July 16th, 1916.   NESVIJ.

.   .   .   .

Ragoza thinks that his offensive has been valuable as it drew all the immediately available German reserves and so made possible Lesh's advance to the Stokhod. It appears that Lesh at first attempted a direct advance on Pinsk and failed.

Ragoza is an advocate of the slow system of advance against positions as strongly fortified as those of the Germans. I objected that a slow advance demanded matériel, and he replied that matériel we *must* have.

He talked to me for an hour on the training in a moral sense of the Russian soldier. He said that the Russian soldier would do anything if properly led, but the officers are wanting in moral training and do not give an example to their men. They are hopelessly lazy. He instanced two officers who slept for weeks on the same camp-bed at the front because one of them was too lazy to get his camp kit up from the rear! He said that the Russian soldier would not stand severe discipline of the Prussian type, but he wanted officers that he could look up to and would then be ready to do all they might ask of him. Unfortunately the mass of Russian officers seemed to think that their duty began and ended with leading their men in the attack; and this, after all, was only a small part of it. They did not look after their men's comfort or give their men an example by looking after their own comfort. These are material faults.

He thought that all that could be done in war-time to raise the moral level of the officers was to choose men to command carefully, and by avoiding constant transfers to give them time to *form* their subordinates. The way in which he personally had been shifted about might be taken as a compliment, as it proved he possessed the confidence of the Commander-in-Chief; but all the same it was hard on him and it had led to no good results. Three days before the March offensive he had been transferred to take command of the 2nd Army, which had been selected to play the principal *rôle*. Then he was transferred to Molodechno because the main offensive was to take place from there. Then he was sent to Nesvij with orders to attack " at all costs " within a fortnight. He had had no time to make proper arrangements for the attack. He had had to carry it out with an army of ten corps, only two of which he had known before. One of the corps was commanded by a man who had been already four times removed from his command in the course of the present war. How could he possibly place confidence in this man's judgment? This constant shifting of corps from one army to another had disastrous results. If he were given four corps, and given them for a year, he could make his will felt down to the humblest private and could do anything with them.

There was no initiative in the Russian army, because initiative had been systematically suppressed by the higher military authorities in peace as a dangerous and uncomfortable thing.

Ragoza blamed G.H.Q. for lack of a properly-thought-out plan, and for lack of character to stick to a plan, whether good or bad. He says they are too easily impressed and constantly attracted by new ventures. Like most officers immediately concerned in the preparation of the Krevo offensive, he regrets its abandonment.

Thursday, July 13th, 1916.　　　　　　　　　　MINSK.

W—— (a Guard officer) passed through on his way to Petrograd. He thinks that the offensive succeeded on the South-West Front simply because the Germans had such perfect intelligence of our preparations at Krevo that they never expected a move in the south-west. He regrets the abandonment of the Krevo offensive.

On the other hand, Lebedev, the General Quartermaster (Director of Military Operations), of the Western Front, thinks that this offensive would have been a costly failure. He considers that the forcing of a position fortified on sound principles and held by an army of the stubbornness of the German, with the German's unlimited resources in matériel, is almost impossible. He says that the only fault he has to find with G.H.Q. is that they refused to adopt his suggestion of abandoning all idea of an offensive from the Western Front in order to develop at once the success in the south.

I asked why the attack was made north of Baranovichi, and he said that the idea was to effect a surprise, and that, though surprises have now lost half their value owing to barbed wire and machine guns, the fact that some units penetrated four versts shows that the attack might have been a success. He attributes the failure to units

The Transfer to the South 455

getting out of hand when their commanding officers were killed.

An attempt was made to take the offensive to the south-east of Riga in July. This commenced on the 16th and continued with interruptions till the 21st. The idea was to cut the Jacobstadt-Mitau railway on which the enemy depended for the supply of his troops on the Lower Dvina. This would, if successful, have forced his retirement from the river and would have enabled the 12th and 5th Armies to use once more the right bank railway without constant fear of interruption.

The attack was carried out by the VIth Siberian and the VIIth Siberian Corps, the chief part being played by the latter.

Sunday, October 1st, 1916. RIGA

I went to see Radko Dimitriev after supper. He spoke to me of the abortive offensive in July. He did not fail for lack of guns, for we had concentrated 300 light and 100 heavy guns to support the main attack by two corps on a front of four versts. The forces available were also sufficient, for Radko had a third corps in immediate reserve and the Commander-in-Chief had a fourth corps at Riga.

On the 16th there was a methodical artillery preparation of five hours, and the enemy's front line, which alone was visible, was destroyed. The troops rushed this line only to be confronted with a second line of strong entrenchments, which, being completely hidden in a wood, was intact. Kuropatkin ordered the preparation to be renewed on the following day, but the supply of heavy shell commenced to give out.

Radko considers that the offensive failed simply owing to the necessity to economise heavy shell. The preparation of the wood with its hidden defences could only be effected by heavy guns firing at sections of space. We had not enough shell for this, and in all probability never will have till the end of the war.

"What then?" exclaimed Radko. "Are we to

continue to sit still in front of an enemy half our strength ? "

He had suggested to Kuropatkin to try the effect of a surprise—to concentrate secretly, in the space of three or four days, divisions from all parts of the front, to open a hurricane fire suddenly with all the guns for half an hour, seeking moral rather than material affect, and then to rush all the enemy's three lines without pause. He allows he would lose about 10,000 men, but still believes such an attack would succeed.

An advance from the extreme right of the 12th Army was prepared for August 21st in co-operation with a landing to take place at Roen, sixty miles north-west of Riga as the crow flies.

The landing force was to consist of the 115th, 116th and 3rd Rifle Divisions. At its commander's request the XXIst Corps moved first due west from Shlok and had some success. Ships and the three divisions were collected at Riga, but at the last moment the local naval authorities refused to guarantee the safety of the transports, so the delicate part of the operation was abandoned. It was just as well, for, Riga being a hotbed of spies, the Germans had received warning and had concentrated reserves and guns on the west coast of the Gulf.

Apart from these attempts the Russians made no serious effort on the Northern and Western Fronts to prevent the enemy from withdrawing troops to the South-West Front, though in both these groups of armies they were far stronger than the enemy in rifle strength. On the Northern Front, for instance, in the middle of October the Russians had about two and a half times as many battalions as the Germans. It was considered that any attempt to advance without more heavy shell and aeroplanes would be useless butchery.

On the other hand, the Russians could not understand how the Allies, who *had* aeroplanes and shell, continually allowed the enemy to withdraw divisions from other theatres to hold up Brusilov's advance. There was evident a certain amount of

The Transfer to the South

exasperation at what was considered to be the inactivity of the Allies. Some Russians thought that Russia was being allowed to bear the whole burden of the war.

Such a Russian was Prince Dolgoruki, the Commander of the 3rd Don Cossack Cavalry Division, at whose headquarters I spent a night some versts from the Dvina.

Dolgoruki was a rich man with large estates, but had no other apparent claim to responsible command. He attacked me with the statement that England should take steps to prevent the depreciation of the rouble. He evidently considered that the labour of the war should be divided, and assigned to England all the sea-work and all the payment. I tried to explain to him that the purchasing power of the rouble had fallen even more in Russia than abroad, that England was paying for Russia's purchases of war material abroad, but that it was impossible for us to afford to arrange for him to buy foreign machinery for his estates at pre-war rates of exchange!

In the Dvinsk bridgehead a few days later General Fidotov, the Chief of Staff of the XIXth Corps, made the statement rather offensively that the Allies had "allowed eighteen divisions to leave the Western theatre since the commencement of Brusilov's offensive." I told him that it had never been expected that Great Britain would take a large share in the war on land, but that in spite of this we had called out a larger percentage of our population for the land war than Russia had. He thought that we should introduce conscription in India, and I tried to convince him that the cause would gain nothing if, for instance, we drove all the eighty millions of Bengal into the trenches in France.

On my return to Petrograd I sent General Fidotov a statement of the real situation, showing that though the German Command had withdrawn several units from the West, their places there had been taken after the commencement of the Somme offensive by new formations, so that on October 22nd the Germans had actually eleven and a half more divisions in France than they had in January (127 divisions against $115\frac{1}{2}$, or 1,299 battalions against 1,290).

The withdrawal from the West to the East had been:
- In June, when the Russian offensive was at its height, 73 battalions.
- In July, after the commencement of the Somme offensive, 37 battalions, whose place had been taken by two new divisions.
- In August, three more exhausted divisions, whose place was taken by eight new divisions.
- In September, one fresh division and one exhausted division, whose place was taken by four divisions in the west.

Such incidents were, however, only natural, and besides, they were wholly exceptional.

Tuesday, October 10th, 1916. POLOTSK.

While with the 1st Army I fed with the Commander, and we were a cosmopolitan crowd. Litvinov, the Commander, is a pure Russian, Odishelidze, the Chief of Staff, is a pure Georgian, Vartenov, the Inspector of Artillery, is a pure Armenian, Richkov, the General Quartermaster, is half Russian and half Armenian. They were all very kind to me and treated me quite as one of themselves.

Litvinov is a shrewd old fellow, and while giving one the impression that he does nothing, is thoroughly *au courant* with all that goes on in the army. His wife has sent him an English grammar to learn English, as she has determined to take him to England directly after the war. We spent much time together over the pronunciation of " th "!

Odishelidze dreams that Russia, after the war, will become a huge confederation of states on British lines. Men of brain like he is recognise at once all that England is doing.

When I went to Vartenov to talk of artillery I found two books on his table—a Life of Christ and a Russian work on the Garden Cities of England.

CHAPTER XV

OPERATIONS OF THE GUARD ARMY ON THE STOKHOD, JULY 21ST TO AUGUST 12TH, 1916. A VISIT TO THE 9TH ARMY

Reference Sketch E

GREAT things were expected from the Guard, which had been carefully nursed since the retreat from Vilna in September, 1915. In the intervening ten months it had been trained in December to Bessarabia, in January back to Volhiniya, in the spring north again to the Dvina Front, then south-west to the neighbourhood of Molodechno to take part in the projected Krevo offensive. It had travelled much, but had not been under fire. It had been retained for a great occasion, and the forcing of the Stokhod seemed to provide the opportunity.

The Guard received orders on July 9th to entrain for the south at and in the neighbourhood of Molodechno. It consisted of three corps—the Ist Guard and IInd Guard (sixty-one battalions) and the Guard Cavalry (three divisions—eighty squadrons).

The Guard Army was officially formed on July 21st, with Headquarters at first at Olika and later at Rojishche. It took up a section of front between the 3rd and 8th Armies, facing generally north-west, with its centre half-way from Lutsk to Kovel. It was commanded by General Bezobrazov, with Count Ignatiev as Chief of Staff and General Gerois as General Quartermaster, and included from right to left:

XXXth Corps: Bulatov, 80, 71.
Ist Corps: Gavrilov, 22, 24.
Ist Guard: Grand Duke Paul, 1 Guard, 2 Guard.
IInd Guard: Raukh, 3 Guard, Guard Rifle.

The three divisions of the Guard Cavalry Corps concentrated under General Khan Nakhichevanski in rear of the left flank of the army.

Monday, July 31st, 1916.   ROJISHCHE.

I called on Brusilov at 12 noon yesterday at Berdichev. He received me kindly and asked me to lunch. He is sixty-two, but lithe and active. He gives one the impression of cunning, with small, deep-set eyes and thin lips, but he is intelligent and self-reliant—not a man to lose his head in a tight place.

I gathered that he would have liked to have moved on Kovel earlier, but was held up by the state of the roads. The 3rd Army, which is only lent to the South-West Front, is to move west on Kovel. The Guard Army will move north-west on Kovel. The 8th Army on its left will move west on Vladimir Volinski. The 11th Army is to wheel on Lemberg. The 7th Army is to follow up the retreating Austrians through Brody, which fell three days ago. The 9th Army is now held up by superior enemy forces, but its turn will come when Rumania joins in.

I asked Brusilov when he expected to get to Kovel. He said it was a matter of luck, but if luck were with him he hoped to be there within a week.

He estimated the Austrian losses since June 4th at 800,000, *viz.*, 320,000 prisoners, 360,000 wounded and 120,000 killed. The Intelligence Section estimated them at 600,000, and this is probably more accurate. All agree that, though the spirit of the Austrian army is badly shaken, it is not broken. Most of the units have been refilled.

Brusilov estimated the number of German prisoners to date at " 40,000 to 50,000," but the Intelligence Section said " 5,000."

Dukhonin said that the Russian armies would have been by now in Lemberg if their technique had been up to date. The greatest needs are :

1. Aeroplanes. The Germans have about seventy planes per army to our five, few of which are fast enough. Such of ours as have machine-guns have only one, so that they can only fire when flying straight at an enemy and not when retiring.[1]

2. Automobiles, both passenger and transport cars. (I think he exaggerates this need, in view of the hopeless roads.)

3. 4·8" shell. He said he thought there was enough 3" shell for the present, though the demands of the front were never completely met.

He estimates the Russian losses since June 4th at 450,000, of which only 8 per cent, *i.e.*, 36,000, are "missing." When the operations commenced the South-West Front had 400,000 men in reserve. It has only 100,000 now, and men have been thrown into the firing-line with only six weeks' training. Dukhonin is the first Russian I have heard to express anxiety regarding the possible exhaustion of our reserves of men owing to the terrible losses—the result of our feeble technical equipment.

The Guard Army on July 25th mustered 134,000 combatants against two weak German and two Austrian divisions.

Under orders from Brusilov, the two Guard infantry corps were deployed on the eight-versts front from the Lutsk-Kovel railway to Fishko. Through the marshes on this front there were only three narrow causeways. In consequence of representations made by the Staff of the Army, permission was obtained on the 26th for the IInd Guard Corps to extend its left to the south-west. This weakened the general front, but gave some possibility of an initial success.

On July 28th and the following days the army attacked all along its front. The XXXth Corps, which had only Austrians to deal with, gained some ground on the left bank of the Stokhod.

---

[1] Russia had at the outbreak of war 244 aeroplanes; on June 1st, 1916, 320; on September 1st, 1916, 716.

The Guard took the villages of Raemyesto, Shchurin and Tristen, and drove the Austrians and Germans in their front across the Stokhod, taking forty-six guns, sixty-five machine-guns and some 11,000 prisoners.

From July 29th to the 31st the two Guard Corps made good all the ground on the right bank. The 2nd Division failed at Vitonej with heavy loss; the 3rd Division took Koloniya Ostrov, suffering severely from the enemy's machine-gun fire; the Rifle Division captured a low hill south-west of Vitonej, but the 2nd and 3rd Regiments were almost wiped out, and many of the wounded were drowned in the marshes.

Wednesday, August 2nd, 1916.   ROJISHCHE.

We were bombarded by aeroplanes from 6 a.m. till 8 a.m., casualties several horses and eleven rank and file.

I started soon after 9 a.m., and drove over dreadful roads to the Headquarters of the IInd Guard Corps. I did not see Raukh, but met the Grand Duke Dimitri Pavlovich and Cantacuzene, who sleep in a shelter together, as the Staff is bombarded daily. I then drove on through desolate country to Tristen, where I found the Staff of the Guard Rifle Division, still commanded by Delsalle, but with Suvorov, whom I had not seen for eighteen months, as Chief of Staff. He is as jolly and light-hearted as ever. As the Austrian line ran immediately in advance of Tristen, the village suffered terribly in the recent battle, and has only a single house standing—that occupied by the Staff.

The situation is pretty rotten. Alexyeev seems to have thought that the Germans would not make a serious attempt to defend Kovel, but we find we have strong defences to attack everywhere.

Units in the army seem to have been badly distributed. The Stokhod marshes are impassable, except by narrow causeways on the whole front from Linevka, east of the railway, to Maidan. This stretch is now held by a division of the Ist Corps and by the Ist Division of the Guard.

It should have been possible to relieve these two divisions by a cavalry division, and to have concentrated the whole of the two Guard infantry corps for a decisive attack further up the river. It looks now as if we will have to stop to await drafts. The XXXth Corps is reduced to 10,000 bayonets, the 71st Division on its left having suffered severely yesterday. The Ist Corps has only 10,000 bayonets. The losses of the Guard since the 25th are estimated at 30,000.

The attack on Vitonej yesterday failed completely, the village being found to be strongly fortified with many machine-guns. The fortifications were not expected, because our aeroplanes have been unable to photograph anything in the enemy's rear owing to his complete command of the air. The artillery has been hopelessly handicapped in its work by the lack of aerial observation. There is now a great want of 4·8″ shell and 3″ H.E. The unfortunate XXXth Corps asked for H.E., but was only sent shrapnel.

It does not look as if we would reach Kovel.

It is extraordinarily quiet as I write, though it is only 10 p.m. It takes a daily aeroplane bombardment at 6 a.m. to force the Russians to keep respectable hours!

Ignatiev is not as popular or as successful as Chief of Staff as he was when in command of the Preobrajenski Regiment. Bezobrazov is a difficult old man to work with, and he has never worked so well as with Domanevski. Altogether, there is an atmosphere of failure and mistrust.

Little Gershi[1] is now a man of great importance. To-day I found him holding a regular reception. Among others, Prince Aristov, the Commander of the 1st Brigade of Cavalry of the Guard, was asking Gershi to urge Bezobrazov to allow the cavalry to take over the trenches now

---

[1] Second-Lieutenant Gershalmann, A.D.C. to General Bezobrazov.

occupied by the 1st Infantry Division of the Guard in order to set free all the infantry for a decisive assault. It is a comical situation for a major-general to solicit such intervention from a boy of four years' service, but Gershi has, it is true, quite the best head on his shoulders of anyone I have met of his rank.

Friday, August 4th, 1916.   ROJISHCHE.
It was cloudy yesterday, and there is a hurricane blowing to-day, so we have been spared aeroplanes for two days.

I heard early yesterday that Bezobrazov had left with Gerois for Lutsk to meet Brusilov and Kaledin in conference at 9 a.m. In motoring to Lutsk to visit the 8th Army, I passed him returning. I hear that Brusilov spoke to him " straight," both in the presence of Kaledin and separately. The old man is " piano " to-day. He told me that he intended to advance slowly. The difficulty, he says, is that we cannot put up our balloon owing to the number of hostile aircraft, so all our gun-fire is blind.

Stogov, the new Chief of Staff of the 8th Army, a quiet and capable man, gave me Captain Bazilevich to accompany me in a visit to the XLth and VIIIth Corps. B. is chief of the Censor Department in the army, an ex-officer of the 12th Hussars, who met and married an English widow in the Far East. He is excellent company.

He told me he had twenty-five people working under him to carry out the censorship of the letters of the 8th Army and of the Government of Volhiniya, which is allotted to that army. I told him of the enthusiastic patriotism of the extracts from the officers' and soldiers' letters that Dukhonin had read me, and he laughed, and said they were either written by the Censor himself or by some ambitious N.C.O. who wanted promotion. I think so too, for the letters had not a natural tone. Why, for instance, should a man write to his sister to say that he was " still whole, but ready at any moment to die for his Emperor and country"? What a devil of a time some Russians waste in putting their heads in the sand and in trying to induce their allies to follow their example!

When we were discussing the peculiarly suspicious attitude of some of the staffs, B. told me how once in the Carpathians he had been sent with a Japanese officer and a Russian artist to visit the 69th Division. The G.O.C. the division asked him for his papers, and, as he had none with him, he asked him why he spoke Russian so badly. B. said that he had been brought up in Paris and had married an Englishwoman. The General flared up: " I don't understand your story at all. You were brought up in Paris. You marry an Englishwoman, and now you come here with a Japanese officer!" At this moment the Japanese and the Russian artist entered the room, and B. said: " I am very sorry, gentlemen, there is nothing to be done here. We must go back to the 8th Army." The General said: " There you make a mistake. You are all three under arrest till I make enquiries."

Luckily an artillery general came in who had known B. in the Russo-Japanese war. In half an hour he and B. were finishing a bottle of brandy, the General was showing all his maps to the grinning Jap, and the long-haired artist was sharpening his pencil to sketch in the General's profile.

I gather that the present strength in bayonets in the 8th Army is, from right to left, about:

XXXIXth Corps	9,000
XXIIIrd Corps	8,000
XLth Corps	17,000
VIIIth Corps	20,000

Saturday, August 5th, 1916.   ROJISHCHE.
F. and K. came in to lunch yesterday and I heard something about the attack of the Rifle Division. The section chosen—south-west of Vitonej—seems to have been

about as ill-selected as can be imagined. The men had to ford a marsh wading up to their middles. The losses, which are estimated at 70 per cent., were greater, owing to the ten months in rear having been spent too much in close-order drill.

The wounded sank slowly in the marsh, and it was impossible to send them help.

Sunday, August 6th, 1916.   ROJISHCHE.

I drove as far as possible towards the front yesterday, visiting on the way the Headquarters of the 3rd Guard Cavalry and the 3rd Guard Infantry Divisions at Tristen. The Commander of the latter gave me an officer as guide, and we walked on to the most advanced houses in the village of Babie, whence I got a glimpse of the fatal marsh. The young officer said that it was a " pity that we spared our guns so much," for if we had brought them up secretly at night to the edge of a wood, whence the enemy's defences might have been destroyed at point-blank range, we might have avoided most of the loss incurred during the attack on Koloniya Ostrov.

Similarly the officers of a battery of the Guard Rifle Division that I visited told me that they could have destroyed Vitonej, but no one told them to fire at it. The Guard Rifles were supported by the Moskovski Regiment in the attack on Vitonej, and the latter's attack seems to have been carried out without any artillery preparation, no passages being cut in the enemy's wire.

The splendid courage of the infantry was wasted, owing to the absolute lack of artillery support. I wonder if the Inspector of Artillery reconnoitred the position properly beforehand ? Of course, there was the usual lack of mutual support between units. There has been too much close-order drill and too little practice in combined manœuvre in the ten months' rest. The Russian Command spends all its time in teaching the Russian soldier to die, instead of teaching him to conquer.

I hear that at the Conference at Lutsk on the 3rd, it was decided to make another attempt to reach Kovel, and Bezobrazov received a direct order to put his cavalry in the trenches in order to release infantry to add weight to his penetration. He had been urged to do this from the first, but he had insisted on retaining his three cavalry divisions intact, in order to launch them through the breech which he hoped to make on the left. A fanatical believer in the cavalry arm, it was hard for him to resign the dream of his life.

It was decided at the Conference to make three pushes:

1. By the Ist Siberian and the XLVIth Corps in the 3rd Army.

South of these the Ist Turkistan Corps (3rd Army) is to hold a passive sector, while the XXXth Corps (Guard Army) is to attack to cover the right flank of the Ist Guard Corps.

2. By the Ist Guard Corps and the Ist Corps, who are to deliver the main stroke in a north-westerly direction from the seven-versts' front between Velitsk and Bolshoi Porsk (north of the railway and twelve versts north-west of Sokul).

The Ist and 2nd Guard Cavalry Divisions are to take over the passive sector along the Stokhod from the railway to Maidan.

3. By the Guard Rifle Division, which is to attack Vitonej again, the 3rd Guard Infantry Division and the 3rd Guard Cavalry Division acting passively on its left.

I am convinced that the direct road to Kovel should be held passively and the main operation should be undertaken west on Vladimir Volinski. The Russian Command for some unknown reason seems always to choose a bog to drown in.

I visited the anti-aircraft battery this afternoon and was present when it fired unsuccessfully at an aeroplane. This is the only battery of the kind at present in Russia.

The Colonel in command told me that his regular station was Tsarskoe Selo, where his task was to defend the Imperial Family. He had there eighteen guns and six machine-guns, and he has now brought four guns to the front " to practise " !

I hope to leave for the Ist Guard Corps at Sokul to-morrow. Podimov (C.R.E. of the army) and Gershi think this offensive will be a success. I wonder !

Monday, August 7th, 1916.   ROJISHCHE.
I heard Tilli (a General Staff officer) reporting to Gerois (the General Quartermaster) the result of a reconnaissance he had made of the line we are to attack to-morrow. His report was unfavourable, confirming in its conclusions a preliminary report he had made before the regroupment was carried out. It is curious that a line for attack should be decided upon after only a superficial reconnaissance, and that unfavourable in its conclusions.

Thursday, August 10th, 1916.   SOKUL.
I left Rojishche by car in the afternoon of the 7th, having sent the horses on in the morning.
The greater part of the village of Sokul has been burnt, the Catholic church especially having suffered from our gun-fire. I share a room in the house occupied by the Staff with Baranovski, a lieutenant-colonel of the General Staff, a nice fellow. I met Rilski, the Chief of Staff of the corps, who seems capable and a good fellow too. Called on the Grand Duke Paul—very tall and spare—talks English. He gave me the impression of being ill and nervous. His son, Dimitri Pavlovich, came out and talked to me. They are in the priest's house, 100 yards from us. Aeroplanes visit Sokul most mornings and evenings, and a groom of the Grand Duke's and his three best horses were killed by a bomb on the morning of the 7th.

July-August, 1916

Dimitri Pavlovich blamed Bezobrazov for the "wasting of the Guard." He said that the idea at G.H.Q. was that a breach should be made in the enemy's line by corps of the Line, and that the Guard should be used to extend this and to develop the success. On the other hand, Rilski told me that Brusilov laid down the exact position that the Guard Corps were to take up on the German front.

I got up at 5 am. on the 8th, and rode with Rilski to the "Woodman's Hut," south of Yanovka, the Headquarters of the 2nd Guard Infantry Division, where I remained all day, except for three hours in the afternoon when I visited Yanovka.

The strength of the troops in this area at the commencement of this phase, *i.e.*, on the morning of the 8th, was:

XXXth Corps	9,000 bayonets
Ist Guard Corps	25,000 ,,
Ist Corps	10,000 ,,

The sixty-four battalions of the Ist Guard Corps and the Ist Corps were opposed, as far as is known, by only nine German battalions (Regiments 227, 232 and 52 Reserve), in addition to the 41st Honved Division.

The enemy's front line was in a thick wood, and his movements were completely hidden. His line projected in a salient south-west of the village of Kukhari. The Ist Guard Corps was detailed to attack the north-eastern face of this salient from Velitsk to south-west of Kukhari, and the Ist Corps the south-eastern face from south-west of Kukhari to Bolshoi Porsk. Scattered trees afforded some cover to the Ist Corps, but the Ist Guard Corps had to attack across open ground. The latter corps approached its front line to a distance varying from sixty to four hundred paces from the edge of the wood on the night of August 6th-7th.

Each Guard infantry division detailed two regiments for the attack. The two remaining regiments in each division were disposed as follows : In the 1st Division, which was on the right, the Preobrajenski Regiment had orders to attack the enemy's left after the first success, and the Yegerski Regiment was detailed as corps reserve. In the 2nd Division the Pavlovski and Finlandski Regiments were concentrated on the left bank of the Stokhod, west of Padalovka.

Each of the four four-battalion regiments detailed for the immediate attack had two battalions in front line, one in second line and one in regimental reserve. The battalions in front had each two companies in firing-line and two companies in support. Each of the companies in the firing-line was extended in four successive waves of one section each, the first section being preceded by grenadiers and sappers to clear such of the wire as might have escaped the artillery.

We had no plans of the enemy's defences, and only the vaguest idea of the position of his batteries, for our airmen had been unable to venture over the enemy's lines on their inferior machines. We were ignorant of the shape and extent of the wood the enemy occupied, for our maps were last corrected nineteen years ago, the Russian General Staff having never anticipated that the army would be called upon to fight so far east.

The artillery preparation commenced at 6 a.m., and continued methodically till noon, when commanders were asked to report on the state of the enemy's wire. The general opinion was that more time was required. Potocki, the Divisional Commander, was nervous, but did his best to conceal it. We sat at a little table on a veranda built by the Austrians with pretty birchwood trellis-work. P. spoke of Kuroki fishing in similar circumstances. He himself drew on the table pictures of ladies, clothed and unclothed. When the time came to give the order, and he realised the difficulty of the task set the infantry, he said to me : " Now comes the weighty responsibility of the Divisional Commander." However, Rilski telephoned to the Grand Duke, and received the order to postpone the attack till 5 p.m.

I returned from a visit to Yanovka just before five. The excitement was intense, but we could see nothing Rilski took out his watch and said to Potocki: " It is time for prayer." Potocki went to his dug-out, followed by most of his Staff. Rilski went to the telegraph dug-out.

The first reports came from the artillery observation posts—that the Grenaderski were in the wood, then that the Izmailovski were, then that the Moskovski were. Then we heard from regiments, and they began to blame one another. The Moskovski reported that they could not establish touch with the Grenaderski; later the Grenaderski that the Moskovski were not advancing. On the right the Semenovski Regiment reported to the Staff of the Ist Division that the 71st Division on its right was hanging back—a statement that was probably accurate, as that division had only 300 casualties.

Things, however, appeared to be going well. The observation post reported that " a great crowd of prisoners " was being sent back. We sat down to supper in high spirits. Then the prisoners arrived—103 of them under a Grenaderski guard—as sorry a looking lot as one could wish to see !

Potocki was beside himself and went to meet them, cackling like one demented. He kissed the first man of the escort four times on each cheek, and then commenced repeating the performance with the next man, a particularly dirty individual who said he had taken ten men to his own bat.

The Pavlovski Regiment was ordered forward and placed at the disposal of the O.C. Grenaderski Regiment. Rilski and I rode home to Corps Headquarters satisfied, for the reserves on the spot seemed ample.

At 4.30 a.m. on the 9th, Baranovski was called to the telephone by Zankevich, the Chief of Staff of the 2nd Guard

Division, and he returned to tell me that the Moskovski Regiment had retired from the wood.

At 9 a.m. the Grenaderski Regiment retired as well.

The check came as a complete surprise to most people. There was some talk of the superiority of the German artillery, but the Russian guns fired six shell to the German guns' one during the preliminary bombardment. The Russian infantry certainly reached the wood, and, once it was there, it was thought it would be able to maintain itself against the counter-attacks of much inferior forces.

Guard officers laid the blame on their neighbours. They said that the failure of the 71st Division to attack uncovered their right, and that the 22nd Division on their left did not assault to its front, but followed the left Guards regiment, the Grenaderski, like a flock of sheep, avoiding the Germans, who were thus allowed to continue their hold on the southern edge of the wood.

I lunched with the Commander of the 71st Division, who was an old friend, on August 9th. He had watched the assault from his observation post a mile in rear of the line, and he said that the right Guards regiment, the Semenovski, like his own regiments, was prevented by the German artillery fire from entering the wood at all. He had slept in this post on the night of the 8th, and "the night had been perfectly quiet."

As far as I could ascertain, the losses in this futile attack on the Kukhari Wood were:

71st Division	300
1st Guard Infantry Division	1,500
2nd „ „ „	4,000
22nd Division	1,000
Total	6,800

It was humiliating to think that the splendid Guardsmen, physically the finest human animals in Europe and all of the best military age, were driven back by such weedy specimens as the German prisoners we had seen.

Bezobrazov told me that he had specially ordered subordinate commanders to regard the edge of the wood as the objective. He read me his instructions on the subject, which were certainly not repeated in corps, divisional or regimental orders.

G.H.Q. blamed Bezobrazov. The General Quartermaster told me that when he read Bezobrazov's instructions, he knew that the attack would not succeed, for they were rather a treatise on the attack of woods in general than definite orders for the attack of this particular wood. They were written by Gerois, who for several years taught at the Military Academy.

Only a small fraction of the overwhelming Russian force available was actually used. The attack of the 71st Division was a farce. The Ist Guard Division only used five out of its sixteen battalions, the 2nd Guard Division only eight out of its sixteen. The O.C. Grenaderski made no use of the Pavlovski Regiment which had been placed at his disposal. He explained that the regiment was unable to move forward owing to the heavy enemy barrage—an excuse which carries no weight in view of the description given me by the G.O.C. 71st Division of an " absolutely quiet night."

A large number of company commanders were killed or wounded : for instance, in the Grenaderski Regiment, ten out of sixteen, in the Moskovski Regiment, six. The Russian soldier requires leading more than any soldier in the world, and especially in wood fighting. Under the rules in force, only two officers per company went into action with the men, the remainder staying behind with the regimental reserve and going forward to replace casualties. They could not get forward in time.

The 3rd Army also failed. The Guard Rifle Division occupied Vitonej, but was driven out by the enemy's heavy artillery.

The Guard Army had failed. By the evening of August 9th it had lost 532 officers and 54,770 rank and file. It had gained a few versts of ground, but in doing so had abandoned an easily defensible position for one less easy to defend, and which at the same time offered no facilities for a further advance. The enemy had had time to fortify several defensive lines in advance of Kovel, and there was no prospect of these being forced by frontal attack from the direction of the Stokhod.

I left the Guard Army on the 14th.

Monday, August 14th, 1916.　　　　　　　　　BERDICHEV.

The German airmen gave us a bad time at Rojishche yesterday. My servant came in at 6 a.m. to say that bombs were being thrown. I was making up my mind what to do, when three fell about 100 yards off, and this helped me to decide. I spent the next one and a half hours together with eighty-two men in the cellar of the Army Printing Press, which we fondly imagined to be bomb-proof, but which was condemned later in the day as useless. Over eighty men were killed and wounded.

Some thirty more bombs were thrown at 6 p.m.

The intrigue in progress in the Guard Army is interesting. On Saturday, the Grand Duke Dimitri Pavlovich passed through Rojishche " with a big packet." At 4 p.m. on the same day Bezobrazov returned from a visit to the Ist Guard Corps, and at once despatched his A.D.C., Rodzianko, with a letter to G.H.Q. The pig did not tell me a word about his mission, but drove to Rovno, and there caught up the Grand Duke's train. The latter, like a sportsman, gave Rodzianko a seat in his wagon, but warned him that he would have to make his own way up from the station at Mogilev, as he wanted half an hour first to get his say in! Dimitri Pavlovich is going like a good son to defend his father, Rodzianko to defend his " old man." They must have had an interesting journey!

Bezobrazov told me last night, when I went to say goodbye, that he had determined to get rid of the Grand Duke Paul, who was an excellent man of peace in every way, but who was totally unfitted to command a corps. I am afraid the result will be that Bezobrazov himself will be fired out!

Sunday, September 3rd, 1916. PETROGRAD.

I arrived at G.H.Q. last Sunday and lunched the next day at the Emperor's table. After lunch, the Emperor, in speaking to me, alluded to the failure of the Guard Army, and said he had decided to transfer Gurko, " who was very active and popular," to its command from his present post in the 5th Army. I said I was very sorry about Bezobrazov, of whom I was personally very fond. He said he liked him too, especially as he had served with him in the Hussars of the Guard, but that he was not active enough.

Tuesday, September 12th, 1916. PETROGRAD.

Rodzianko gives amusing accounts of the developments in the Guard. He travelled in amity with the Grand Duke to G.H.Q. On arrival at Mogilev station they found that the Empress had arrived on a visit, and the Emperor was with her in her carriage. Dimitri Pavlovich was therefore prevented from seeing the Emperor at once, and Rodzianko took his letter straight to Alexyeev, who sent it on with other papers to the Emperor. Two days later, at lunch, the Emperor told R. to tell Bezobrazov that he was satisfied with him and with the Guard, but that he was to be sparing of life, as he was fond of his Guard.

R. returned to Rojishche in triumph, but, five days after his arrival, Bezobrazov's orderly suddenly came to tell him that he must prepare to leave with his General at once. They packed up and went to G.H.Q. There Bezobrazov told R. that the Emperor kissed him and told him to take six weeks' leave before returning to his command. Bezobrazov went to Petrograd, and R. to Rojishche to collect kit. At Rojishche, Gurko arrived to take charge of the Guard Army, which was rechristened the " Special Army." He made short work of the Staff, breaking it up completely, retaining only Gerois as G.Q.M. Then he " went into things," and telegraphed to G.H.Q. that he considered it impossible to attack on the Stokhod, and that, as Bezobrazov told me, " he signed with both hands all his (Bezobrazov's) dispositions."

Poor old Bezobrazov is convinced that he will go back, but no one else thinks so.[1]

Tuesday, August 15th, 1916. BERDICHEV.

The 3rd Army and the Guards Army were handed over to the Western Front Group at midnight on the 13th-14th. Brusilov told me he was glad to hand them over, as six armies were too many for one man to direct.

The Staff of the Front is bitter regarding the failure of the Guard on the Stokhod. Brusilov says that they are badly staffed. He considers that the operations, especially those of July 30th, failed owing to the bad artillery direction. " The Duke of Meklenburg is a very nice man, but he knows absolutely nothing. Smislovski and Gilgenschmidt " (the two corps inspectors of artillery) " are no use. War is different work from living in an hotel. The artillery was directed as it might have been after two days of war instead of after two years."

On my venturing to remark that it was unfortunate that the two fresh Guard Corps were placed on a marshy section of front, Brusilov said: " There are marshes everywhere."

Dukhonin says that Gerois is an ex-professor of the Academy, and that professors generally have not been a success in the war. He says that the Guard batteries remained too far off and did not arrange proper observation posts. The Guard delayed too long and gave the enemy time to bring up heavy artillery. The line of the middle Stokhod is now too strong to be carried, and it will be passively defended.

The 8th, 11th, 7th and 9th Armies will advance gradually. Brusilov thinks that Lemberg will be taken in five weeks, *i.e.,* by September 25th.

---

[1] This was, indeed, the end of his military career.

July-August, 1916

Dukhonin thinks that Rumanian intervention will be of no use unless she comes in at once. He thinks that Lechitski's left flank is now secure. He grudges the detachment of Zaionchkovski's Corps (two infantry and one cavalry division) to the Dobrudja, especially as it is rich in aeroplanes and motor-cars. This corps will only have an active *rôle* if Bulgaria attacks.

On August 2nd the whole Eastern Front was brought under Hindenburg. This arrangement, however, was modified a few days later, the Tarnopol-Lemberg railway being fixed as the southern limit of Hindenburg's command, and the armies south of that line being united under the nominal control of the Archduke Charles.[1]

On August 7th, Lechitski attacked the new enemy group under Koevess south of the Dniester, and drove it back thirty versts, entering Stanislau on the 10th and Nadworna on the 12th. On the latter date the 7th Army occupied Monasterzyska. Meanwhile Sakharev's movement to the south forced Bothmer on the 11th to retreat from the line he had occupied all the winter.

The 11th Army took, from August 4th to the 11th, 304 officers and 16,594 rank and file. The 9th Army, from August 1st to the 10th, took 141 officers and 10,440 men.

Bothmer halted on the Zlota Lipa and counter-attacked.

The total captures of the four original armies of the South-West Front in the sixty-nine days from June 4th till August 11th, were:

	Officers.	Men.	Guns.	Machine-Guns.
8th Army	2,384	107,225	147	459
11th Army	1,967	87,248	76	232
7th Army	1,267	55,794	55	211
9th Army	2,139	100,578	127	424
Totals	7,757	350,845	405	1,326

[1] See Map No. XII.

The front of the 9th Army had been more than doubled by its conquest of Bukovina, and every yard it advanced in Galicia increased the danger of an attack from the Carpathians on its lengthening left. The Austrian units that had wintered in front of Lechitski had been badly mauled, but the enemy had soon commenced to pour in reinforcements, the following units being identified on the dates mentioned:

June 29th.—105th German Infantry Division. From the Balkans.
July 1st.—44th Austrian Landwehr Division. From Italy.
July 3rd.—119th German Infantry Division. From Lake Naroch.
July 5th.—18th Austrian Mountain Brigade. From Italy.
July 7th.—6th Austrian Mountain Brigade. From Italy.
July 21st.—34th Austrian Infantry Division. From Italy.
August 8th.—German Carpathian Corps. From Verdun.
August 10th.—195th German Infantry Division (?)
August 12th.—1st German Infantry Division. From Verdun.

To oppose this constant stream of fresh troops, Lechitski had for many weeks only the skeleton of his original ten infantry and four cavalry divisions. I asked Brusilov on July 30th if the 9th Army was not dangerously weak. He said that its spirit was such that it did not want men.

As a matter of fact, reinforcements had already begun to arrive. The following came up about the dates mentioned:

July 23rd.—117th Division. From coast defence at Odessa.
        108th Division. From the 6th Army.
August 2nd.—37th Division. From the 7th Army.
        43rd Division. From the 7th Army.
        79th Division. From the 1st Army.
August 8th.—Staff of the XVIIIth Corps. From the 7th Army.
August 16th.—64th Division. From the 4th Army.
August 20th.—3rd Caucasian Cossack Cavalry Division. From the 3rd Army.

August 28th.—59th Division. From the 5th Army.
August 30th.—Staff of the XXIIIrd Corps. From the 8th Army.

To sum up, from June 29th till August 23rd the enemy received four or five German infantry divisions and three Austrian infantry divisions, while from July 23rd till the end of August Lechitski received seven infantry and one cavalry division.

The enemy's advance on his left still occasioned Lechitski anxiety, and on the night of August 18th he ordered two divisions back from the Western Group, south-west of Stanislau.

At midnight on August 20th-21st, the 9th Army handed over its two right corps (four infantry and one cavalry division) to the 7th Army. Similarly the 7th Army transferred its right corps to the 11th Army, and the 11th Army in turn handed over its right corps to the 8th Army.

It was arranged that the 9th Army should give its undivided attention to the forcing of the Carpathian Passes on the front Delatyn-Kimpolung.

Thursday, August 24th, 1916.   CZERNOWITZ.

The task of the 9th Army will be to force the Carpathians in order to protect the right flank of the Rumanians in case they come in. For this purpose the army has to-day on the mountain front of 110 versts from Nadworna to Dorna Watra, on the Rumanian frontier, 160 battalions and 120 squadrons, opposed to the enemy's eighty-three battalions and twenty-six squadrons.

The difficulty is that, out of these eighty-three battalions, some twenty-one are German, and the Germans use their artillery effectively. It was the threat of an enemy offensive against our left that caused the Staff of the Front to divert to the 9th Army the 64th Division, when on its way to Bender to join Zaionchkovski.

Through the main range of this section of the Carpathians there are three chief roads :

1. From Delatyn, *via* Korosmezo to Maramarossziget.

This is the only road that the Austrians have fortified.

2. From Kuty to Maramarossziget.

3. From Kimpolung *via* Kirlibaba to Maramarossziget.

The foothills of the Carpathians have more roads. In fact, this is the only Russian army in which I have found it possible to motor practically all along the front.

The Russian prisoners have been employed in road-making by the Austrians during the winter. One such road is labelled " Pflanzer-Baltin Strasse," after the General who has since been removed from his command. At one point on this road there are large wooden huts that were built for the accommodation of the Russian prisoners, and in one of these was found written up in Russian : " Work hard, my brothers, for these roads will be of use to our own people ! "

The road gradients generally are easy, and the Carpathians are not the wild, unproductive country that their height above sea level might seem to indicate. The hills are thickly wooded, mostly with fine larch. Grass is plentiful everywhere. Ordinary field artillery is little use, but howitzers, and especially our light 4·5″'s, are in great request.

Friday, August 25th, 1916.   CZERNOWITZ.

The atmosphere in the Staff mess of this army is healthier than in any other army I have visited. Everyone now evidently likes old Lechitski, though he was far from popular in the early days of the war. He is a different man from what he was in Gulevich's time. He constantly told Gulevich that, though he was his Chief of Staff, he could not trust him. Now the old man jokes and laughs with everyone. His present Chief of Staff is considered to be a useful brake on Kelchevski, who is liable to be too impetuous. Lechitski has a strong character and he understands the troops.

While junior members of the Staff think a lot of their

own commander, they have a poor opinion of their neighbours. One young officer tells me that Sakharov was a good corps commander, but is quite unable to tackle the problems of a wider nature that fall to the army commander. His Chief of Staff, Shishkevich, he characterises as "ungifted." The same youth said that Shcherbachev was always trying to carry out some complicated manœuvre that never came off. Brusilov he labelled as "uneducated," Klembovski as only "Napoleon in name," and Dukhonin as "characterless and liable to be led by others"!

However unflattering this officer's opinion may be of some of the commanders in the South-Western Group, he firmly believes that, if the troops of that group were to change places with those on the Northern and Western Fronts, they would drive the Germans before them as they have already driven the Austrians. I don't, and told him so. He argues that the experience the troops have gained means everything; they entered the war knowing nothing.

The conversation turned the other night on Pavlov, who is now in command of the VIth Cavalry Corps. I remember him well before the war, when I often sat next him at meals during the autumn manœuvres at Krasnoe Selo. He was then unemployed, being a General à la Suite, a small, neat figure and a good horseman. He served in former years in the Hussars of the Guard with the Emperor, and so runs less risk than others in at all times saying and doing as he thinks best. His subordinates like him, but he is a difficult subordinate himself.

Someone told the story of how General Tolmachev once came to inspect a regiment of Trans-Baikal Cossacks that Pavlov commanded. Pavlov met him at the station, and T.'s first question was if he had a really quiet horse for him to ride. P. said that he had one ready, and galloped off to receive the General on the parade-ground. The horse edged away as T. tried to mount, and he shouted to Pavlov: "You said you had a quiet horse for me!"

Pavlov said: "Well, the only quieter one in the regiment is that wooden dummy!"

From the Trans-Baikal Cossacks, Pavlov was promoted to command His Majesty's Lancers of the Guard.

One day, when training his regiment at Krasnoe Selo, one of his patrols trespassed on the shooting preserves of the Grand Duke Nikolai. The keeper complained, and Pavlov was asked for his reasons in writing. He commenced his reply: "With regard to the encounter between His Imperial Majesty's Lancers and His Imperial Highness's hares," etc., etc.

Such eccentricities were pardoned, but he had to give up his command because he refused on one occasion to lend his horses for a General Staff ride on the ground that the officers could not ride and spoilt any animal they touched.[1]

On August 27th Rumania declared war.

---

[1] Pavlov was sent to Rumania in command of a cavalry corps.

CHAPTER XVI

EVENTS ON THE SOUTH-WEST FRONT FROM THE MIDDLE OF AUGUST TILL THE MIDDLE OF NOVEMBER, 1916

REFERENCE MAP No. XII.

THE Special Army was very soon handed back to the Southwest Front. Its Commander, General Gurko, however, reported that very large reinforcements would be necessary to make possible a direct advance on Kovel, so that project was abandoned. Efforts were concentrated on an attempt to force a passage to Vladimir Volinski. Unfortunately the enemy had had time to bring up much heavy artillery and to construct strong lines of defence on the dry ground east of that town, and here, too, Kaledin, and later Gurko, failed.

Meanwhile, Rumania having entered the war, the Russians despatched to the Dobrudja the minimum force required by the military convention—two infantry and one cavalry division—under the command of General Zaionchkovski. Many Russians were of opinion that the Bulgarians would never fight against Russia, the liberator of their country. If Alexyeev shared this view, he made a mistake in detailing the Ist Serbian Volunteer Division, composed of former Austrian subjects, as part of the Dobrudja Detachment, for it was very certain that the Bulgarians would have no scruples about fighting Serbs. In any case, the Russian detachment was too small.

Thursday, May 3rd, 1917. PETROGRAD.

Zaionchkovski told us that when he visited G.H.Q. in July and August, 1916, he protested to Alexyeev against the detachment of Russian troops to the Dobrudja, and, secondly, if it had been decided to send Russian troops, that the force detailed was too weak.

Alexyeev replied : " I have been all along opposed to the intervention of Rumania, but have been forced to agree to it by pressure from France and England. Now that the principle has been accepted, if the Emperor ordered me to send fifteen Russian wounded men there, I would not on any account send sixteen."

When Zaionchkovski protested once more regarding the smallness of the force, Alexyeev said that he was a coward and unworthy to wear the uniform of a Russian General.

Z. says that the sending of the Serb Division was a fatal mistake. Bulgarian prisoners said that they would not have fought against the Russians, but when they found the Russian troops fighting side by side with the Rumanians, whom they despise, and with the Serbs, whom they hate, they no longer hesitated.

Bulgaria declared war on September 1st.

The Rumanians throughout September advanced successfully in Transylvania, but the Russian 9th Army, in spite of severe hand-to-hand fighting, made little progress in its attempt to force the Carpathians between Delatyn and Kimpolung. The Staff complained of the extraordinary difficulty of artillery direction in mountains, where the Russian infantry, which might be in range only a few hundred yards short of the enemy's position, would often require a couple of hours to reach it. No one, however, expected Russian troops to be experts at hill warfare. They were cumbrously equipped and notoriously slow movers. Ninety per cent. of them were dwellers in the plains. Good officers were too few to exercise proper control, and the rank and file did not excel in intelligence and initiative. The average Russian soldier was indeed very much like an Indian buffalo : he would go anywhere he was led or driven, but would not wander into uncomfortable places on his own.

Von Falkenhayn's offensive rolled the Rumanians back in October, and suddenly, on the 13th, six Rumanian battalions who occupied a position on the flank of the 9th Army, on the frontier south of Dorna Watra, retired fifteen versts in a single night. Lechitski sent Count Keller south with two cavalry divisions as a temporary expedient, but it became evident to the 9th Army that it would have to extend its left flank permanently to the south to prevent it from being turned.

Brusilov had to abandon the Galician offensive, and all the fronts had to contribute troops to defend the new ally. The migration of Russian units to the south that had commenced in June continued, but their destination was to be in future Rumania instead of the South-West Front, and their object was purely defensive. The initiative had passed to the enemy, and the high hopes of the summer were gone.

It was decided that the 9th Army should take up a front from the west of Kimpolung to a line running through Vaslui-Ocna, and the Staff of the 8th Army was transferred in the middle of October from Lutsk to Czernowitz to take over the front formerly held by the 9th Army from Delatyn to the west of Kimpolung. The 8th Army took over most of the troops that formerly belonged to the 9th, and Lechitski had to wait at Suczawa till a new army had been collected.

The units of the former 8th Army on the Vladimir Volinski Front joined the Special Army, and Gurko found himself in command of twenty-five infantry and five cavalry divisions. With a striking force of fifteen divisions on a front of twenty versts south of Kiselin, he made on October 16th-17th the last of the many attempts to penetrate to Vladimir Volinski. This was Brusilov's final effort to extend the Lutsk salient, Gurko's subsequent operations being rather in the nature of demonstrations to prevent the enemy from detaching to Rumania.

The failure of Kaledin's and Gurko's offensive to the west from Lutsk was as complete as that of Bezobrazov on the Stokhod. In almost every attack the Russian infantry reached the enemy's second and third line of trench; but was shelled out and lost heavily in retiring through his barrage. General Khanjin, who as Inspector of Artillery of the 8th Army was responsible for the first attacks, maintained that the Russian guns did all that could be expected of them. They cut the enemy's wire and made his trenches untenable. They could not fight his batteries because they had no aeroplanes to tell them where they were. He said the attacks had come to nothing because the troops were worn out and had lost most of their good officers. General Smislovski, who, as Inspector of Artillery in the Special Army, directed the guns in the later attacks, said that the first attempts failed because no batteries were detailed to combat the enemy's batteries, and the later attacks collapsed because the infantry had lost heart.

Monday, October 25th, 1916.   BERDICHEV.

Dukhonin gave me half an hour at 10.30. He is pessimistic for a Russian. Says we are undoubtedly much weakened by the intervention of Rumania, which he characterised as having been a " pure gamble." The nerves of the Rumanian soldier have not stood heavy shell. However, the 11th Rumanian Division, which is in the 9th Army, is fighting steadily.

The 9th Army will now have its right flank at Dorna Watra instead of its left. It will defend the line of the Sereth, its left at Bacau. The Carpathian Passes cannot be defended owing to the retirement in the Dobrudja. Dukhonin indicated that many mistakes had been made by Zaionchkovski, " who could command a corps, but not an army." He will be relieved by Sakharov from the 11th Army, with Shishkevich as Chief of Staff. Unfortunately, however, it is too late to retrieve the situation. The allied line in the Dobrudja is now many miles north of the Constanza railway. The Russian troops are reduced to nothing. The 61st and the Serb Division have about 3,000 bayonets each. The 115th Division was untried and has not distinguished itself. The 3rd Rifle Division was taken away at a critical moment to defend the approaches to Bucharest. There is serious danger that the enemy may cross the Danube, which is only observed, not guarded, by the 8th Russian Cavalry Division and two Rumanian cavalry divisions.

Dukhonin said that we would now be in Lemberg if Rumania had not come in. As things are, it seems likely that all Wallachia with its grain and oil will be lost to the enemy.

The winter will be the time of special danger in Rumania. If we survive till the spring, we will have had time to train and to equip the Rumanian army. We have already given it 100,000 Austrian rifles, twenty-five million Austrian S.A.A. and a large number of Austrian machine-guns.

The Rumanians seem to have learnt nothing from the experience of the war, though they had officers attached to the armies of the Central Powers. They dig trenches as shallow as in 1877. They had only three telephone apparatus for seventeen batteries. The Russians have given them 150 apparatus and 1,000 versts of wire. They do not know how to mend the telephone wire. They are without Hughes telegraph machines. The Russian telegraphists regard them with the utmost scorn!

Saturday, October 28th, 1916. LUTSK.

I left Berdichev at 6 p.m. and arrived at Rovno at 1 a.m., slept there till six and then drove in a car to Lutsk.

It was a foggy and wet day and the whole country is a scene of desolation. The local inhabitants apparently do not believe in the permanency of the Russian success, for only soldiers were to be seen, there is no cultivation, and no attempt to rebuild ruined houses.

I found the Staff of the Special Army in the Monastery, that the 8th Army had occupied in August. All swear by Gurko.

The little man talked to me for a long time in his broken English, speaking very correctly, but slowly, and often at a loss for words. He agreed that it had been a mistake on the part of the Front to send the Guard to the Stokhod, where only a small local success was possible. When our main strength was moved to the Vladimir Volinski road it was already too late, for the enemy had brought up his heavy batteries. Gurko said that he is now only attacking to prevent the enemy transferring troops to Rumania. Brusilov wanted to stop the attacks a week ago, but allowed them to continue till to-day. However, to-day's attack has been postponed on account of the fog.

The Germans have hung out a notice to the effect that the Kaiser will give Brusilov an Iron Cross if he penetrates their front. There was a proposal to reply that the Emperor would give the Kaiser a St. George if he broke through the Russian front, but a wag suggested that they had better not, as " perhaps the Germans might really try ! " However, Gurko does not fear an enemy offensive. The Germans are scraping up all they can for Rumania.

At supper Gurko spoke of his experiences in the Boer war. He saw there on one occasion a battery of four Boer guns—all of different type—in action all day behind a hill that was bombarded by sixty British guns. On his return to Russia he reported that, in his opinion, in the wars of the future, artillery would be exclusively used from concealed positions. Russian gunners laughed at him, but later on adopted his views in the course of the war against Japan.

I hear whispers that the Russian infantry has lost heart and that anti-war propaganda is rife in the ranks. It is little wonder that they are downhearted after being driven to the slaughter over the same ground seven times in about a month, and every time taking trenches where their guns could not keep them. However, I do not attach importance to this, for they will be fresh again next spring.

Sunday, October 29th, 1916. LUTSK.
Another miserable day of fog and wet. Smislovski took me with him to visit Kornilov in the XXIVth Corps. The corduroyed road was awful, and the Pierce machine

was a fair wonder to get us there and back at all. We lunched with the Staff of the XXIVth Corps, and I did not attempt to go any further, for it would have taken three hours to reach the O.P., and we would have seen nothing when we got there.

Kornilov told us of his capture and escape. His division, the 48th, was doing rearguard in the retreat of the 8th Army from the Carpathians in May, 1915, when he was wounded and captured. He was confined in a house with a high wall round it at some small town south of Vienna. He made up his mind from the first to escape as soon as possible. He therefore adopted the surliest attitude towards any Austrians who came to see him, as he did not want to make friends who might become constant visitors and so discover his absence immediately he escaped. The arrangements for the flight were made by Russian soldiers in combination with Czech friends. The General's presence was checked daily at noon when the guard on the house was relieved, but after being formally taken over by the relieving guard he could reasonably count on twenty-four hours. It was therefore important that he should escape as soon as possible after the change of guard. Just before that hour he dressed in the uniform of an Austrian soldier, covered, of course, by his Russian greatcoat and cap. At 12.5 he descended the stairs and passed the sentry, and, when his back was turned, threw off the greatcoat and cap, handing them to a Russian doctor who was attending him, and who came to meet him by previous arrangement. When the sentry turned at the end of his beat, he was merely an Austrian soldier climbing the wall.

A Czech soldier met him outside, and they went together to the station and slept there till the train arrived. Kornilov was provided with a forged railway pass and also with a certificate—to show in case of necessity—testifying that he was " Private ——, authorised to search for the escaped Russian General, Kornilov."

The fugitives arrived at Buda Pesth the same evening

and spent the night in the barracks set apart for travelling soldiers. The Austrian sisters who attended Kornilov thought he was a Transylvanian.

On the following day the companions took train to a station not far from the Rumanian frontier. There in a wood they changed their Austrian uniform for workmen's dress, which they had carried with them in a bundle. Kornilov passed fifteen more days on foot before he succeeded in crossing the Rumanian frontier. The hunger they both suffered proved too much for the Czech's prudence, and, going to a village to search for food, he was captured by gendarmes and shot. Kornilov occasionally purchased food from Rumanian houses, but the last three days before passing the frontier he lived on berries only. He lay out two nights on the rocks on the frontier studying the beat of the Austrian patrols, and crossed on the third night. He had a map and a compass. As the nights, however, were cloudy, he could get little help from the stars, and it was dangerous to strike matches to consult the map. He said his sense of direction, fostered by long travel in Mongolia, helped him. Kornilov is a Trans-Baikal Cossack with Buriat blood, small, quiet, and self-possessed. He visited India in 1903-4 and met there Generals Bindon-Blood, Smith-Dorien and Barrow.

Monday, October 30th, 1916. LUTSK.

When I went to say goodbye to Gerois he fairly burst out regarding the stupidity of the general allied direction of the war. He said that everything was going well with us and we had had the initiative all the summer. Both sides were fairly balanced, and it seemed that the intervention of Rumania would turn the scale definitely in our favour. We had so mismanaged matters that Rumanian intervention became a curse rather than an advantage.

Our failure now was worse than that of last year, for then we failed through lack of shell, now we failed through sheer stupidity. We should have incorporated the

Rumanian army in the Russian army, making a new front directly under G.H.Q. We should have taken the whole direction of the Rumanian army into our hands. If Rumania was unwilling to come in under those conditions, we were better without her—God be with her!

We should have had Russian forces ready to advance in Transylvania only sufficiently far to neutralise the Kronstadt re-entrant, then, having reached a shorter line of defence, we should have fortified it and have held it passively. Meanwhile, our main forces should have advanced from the Dobrudja and, in co-operation with Serail, have definitely conquered Bulgaria, severing Turkey from her allies.

He blamed the Russian Command for having failed to recognise in August that, with our inferior technical equipment, further progress in Galicia was impossible. He blamed the Allies for Serail's passiveness and for having failed to insist on a proper utilisation of Rumanian intervention. He would now take all the units that we could possibly spare from the South-West Front and hurl them into Rumania. That we are not doing this he could only ascribe to our miserable railway system.

Wednesday, November 1st, 1916. BERDICHEV.

I drove through Dubno on Monday to the Headquarters of the 11th Army at Kremenets. Dubno has suffered much from the Russian artillery fire during the winter, and is no longer the pleasant little town Laguiche, Leonkevich and I visited over two years ago.

Kremenets must be a pretty town in the spring, for it has many gardens and lies among steep, tree-covered hills. The Staff of the 11th Army is in an ecclesiastical college. General Sakharev and his Chief of Staff had left for the Dobrudja, and the army was temporarily commanded by General Yakovlev, a dear old man, who has been at the head of the XVIIth Corps since 1909 and has commanded it without a day's leave in the present war.

My visit was not a success, and I gathered little

information. Everyone was trembling in anticipation of the coming of the new Commander, Klembovski, who stalked in yesterday. Though we have been allies for over two years, Russians do not willingly part with information till they know one. In fact, if they applied to defeating the enemy some of the ingenuity they show in preventing proper intercommunication between allies, the war might be appreciably shortened.

I had to return to Berdichev to get to the 7th Army, as the direct road is impassable for cars.

Sukhomlin has been appointed Chief of Staff *vice* Klembovski. Brusilov has gone to Kiev to visit the Dowager Empress.

Thursday, November 2nd, 1916. BUCZACZ.

I left Berdichev at 9.30 last night and reached Tarnopol at 4.30 p.m. to-day—a miserably slow journey in a crowded train.

Tarnopol has not suffered, as the German high-water mark last autumn fell short of its reoccupation.

A car met me, and I drove with the Chief of the Red Cross of the Army the seventy-five cold and bleak versts to Buczacz.

Both Shcherbachev and his Chief of Staff, Golovin, have their wives here, so I could see neither.

Friday, November 3rd, 1916. BUCZACZ.

Shcherbachev, who was Chief of the Academy earlier in his career, makes a good impression. He is tall and thin, speaks to the point, and is evidently clever. He commanded the IXth Corps at the beginning of the war, then the 11th Army, from which he was transferred to the 7th. His silver wedding will be celebrated to-morrow, and his wife, an astonishingly young-looking woman, arrived for the celebration by the same train as I did yesterday.

Golovin was Professor of Staff Duties at the Academy, and Neznamov, the General Quartermaster, was Professor of Strategy, till both were removed by Yanushkevich, late Chief of the General Staff the year before the war, it is said because they laid stress on fire tactics, belittling the Suvorov tradition of the bayonet. The junior members of the Staff are evidently proud of this galaxy of talent.

Golovin says that the combination of the artillery with the infantry has been "ideal" in the 7th Army in the last battles. The enemy is now counter-attacking in an attempt to oust us from commanding positions, so that he may be able to hold this front with fewer troops during the winter.

The 7th Army took 82,000 prisoners in the four months June-September. Of these, 15,000 were German and 2,000 Turks. The Turks are said to have fought with even greater ferocity than the Germans. At first they killed all prisoners, being persuaded that the Russians did likewise. "The Austrians are the only gentlemen to fight with!"

The 7th Army has lost 200,000 men in the summer's fighting. "Every shell it has lacked has been paid for in blood!" All the same, it has still a superiority of force—272 battalions and 114 squadrons against 205 battalions (eighty-eight German, ninety-three Austrian and twenty-four Turkish) and thirty-seven squadrons.

This afternoon Golovin showed me an elaborate system that is being experimented with, with the idea of deceiving enemy airmen regarding the position of trenches by the use of powder of various colours. The Inspector of Artillery, who was with us, thought the system demanded too much transport, as indeed it did, and told us of a more rough-and-ready method. Two Russian gunners were told to imitate a battery in order to draw the enemy's fire. One threw down bags of dust and the other squirted kerosene from his mouth, lighting it with a match!

After supper the conversation ran on spies. Levitski

(Operations Section) told of one Jansen, an ensign of the XXXth Corps, who hung behind during the retreat from Galicia and then went over to the enemy. Targo (Intelligence Section) told of two Jews who deserted in the Russo-Japanese war. One of them settled permanently in Japan, but the other returned to Russia after the war. His wife asked him if he had received Rs.4 which she had sent to him through the regiment. The idea of losing 8s. 6d. was too much for him, so he went to the regiment to claim it. As ill-luck would have it, he was recognised by an N.C.O. and was tried and shot.

Sunday, November 5th, 1916.   CZERNOWITZ.

I left Buczacz at 10 a.m. yesterday, and motored through the mist to the Headquarters of the XLIst Corps, where we lunched with Belkovich, the Commander. We then drove, still through mist, to Stanislau, where we visited the Headquarters of the 3rd Trans-Amur Division. Stanislau is a fine town, and little damaged, though the Germans bombard it daily.

We spent the night with the XIIth Corps at the battered village of Nadworna, and I had a long talk with Kaznakov.

To-day we left the area of the 7th Army and motored through Delatyn and Sniatyn to Czernowitz, now the Headquarters of the 8th Army.

Supper was rather an uphill meal. Kaledin is not easy to talk to, and all the others are very obviously afraid for their lives of him, so they do not utter

After supper I had some talk with Stogov, the Chief of Staff, who is evidently a good man at his job, and whom I like, though people complain of his rudeness. He gives one a straight answer to a straight question, and does not try to sidetrack one from essentials to nonsense like coloured powder !

Stogov thinks that if we had had reserves available on the South-West Front at the time we broke through we might have gained a really great material success. Cavalry, if on the spot, might have done something, but extra infantry corps would have accomplished much more. He attributed the check in the offensive to a combination of several causes:

1. Lack of heavy artillery and shell. The enemy has more guns and very much more shell.
2. Lack of aeroplanes.
3. Deterioration in the general level of quality of the troops, both officers and men. This is the natural result of four months' continuous fighting, since the wounded officers and men have not had time to return.
4. Discouragement of the rank and file at having to attack repeatedly in the same area without success.

Stogov did not touch on the main reason of the check to Brusilov's offensive—the arrival of German troops on this front. The plain truth is that, without aeroplanes and far more heavy guns and shell and some knowledge of their use, it is butchery, and useless butchery, to drive Russian infantry against German lines.

Sherinski—my companion in the 7th Army—said that Shcherbachev had two faults—optimism and a tendency to waste men. Funnily enough, Bazilevich, who is in charge of me here, blames Kaledin for his total lack of regard for human life.

Tuesday, November 7th, 1916.   CZERNOWITZ.

I lunched with the Trepovs. General T. is the new Governor of Galicia. They have taken the large house of Princess Soltykov behind our Embassy at Petrograd, so they evidently do not anticipate an early move to Lemberg. Madame Trepov told me that the house is now only occupied by her old English governess, who has been forty-five years in the family, and who " elevated " both her and her mother. Russians, in speaking English, often thus translate from French. The other day someone said to me that a certain lady had had quite a "novel" with a subaltern in the Guards.

Pokrovski, the General Quartermaster, came to see me. He expressed admiration for British character and said that Russia would have made peace long ago if it had not been for England.[1] He is certain that the war will last till the end of 1918, unless peace is hastened by the internal condition of Germany, of which he knows nothing.

Thursday, November 9th, 1916.   SUCZAWA.

I drank tea the other night with some officers to meet some Russian nurses. One of the latter, who was engaged to a Kuban Cossack, said that she did not "like" infantry officers, and that she could not imagine why they were allowed to wear spurs! I walked back to the hotel with Bazilevich, who waxed eloquent on the subject of regimental snobbery. He said that the Guard Cavalry looks down on everyone, and that the Line Cavalry looks down on the infantry. In each cavalry division hussars despise lancers, lancers despise dragoons, and all three despise Cossacks! I remember that Tolstoi says something of the same sort in his book *Sevastopol*. All the same, the Russians generally are not snobs, and I think there is less of this nonsense in the Russian Army than elsewhere. I wonder when people will realise that the real hero of the war is the plain infantry private or second lieutenant?

A party of allied military representatives are here on tour from G.H.Q.—Generals Sir John Hanbury-Williams, Janin and Baron Rickel. We drove to-day to lunch with General Rerberg, the Commander of the XXVIth Corps, and he took us to visit the 78th Division, north-east of Dorna Watra. We stood for half an hour in the bright

---

[1] See end of Introduction for a similar opinion of British character by a Russian peasant.

sunlight at the edge of a wood in full view of the Austrian artillery observation posts, if there are such things. We fired a few shots, but drew no reply.

Kelchevski says that the Staff of the 9th Army pointed out repeatedly that to make the best use of Rumanian intervention it was necessary to concentrate a large new army in the south. This Brusilov, who continued to be infatuated with the mirage of Kovel, would hear nothing of. Kelchevski says that the 14th Rumanian Division fought well, but some of the officers are not up to the mark. He complains that all Rumania is a mass of spies, so many of the population actually sympathise with the enemy An officer who went to Roman to arrange billets for the Staff of the 9th Army was by no means met half-way by the local Prefect. The Russian lost patience, and exclaimed: "After all, the Russian army is coming to protect you from a German-Austrian invasion." The Prefect seemed to think that the enemy invasion would be the lesser of the two evils. The miserable capacity of the Russian and Rumanian railways makes the concentration of a sufficient force at the eleventh hour a task of incredible difficulty. The three lines *via* Czernowitz, Jasi and Reni can only carry nineteen troop trains daily, in addition to supply trains, and the Czernowitz line is behind on even this programme. A Russian army corps requires 128 trains. The transport of the IVth Corps to the Danube was completed yesterday. We have now to carry one division of the XXIVth Corps, two of the XLth, and two of the VIIIth. This may be completed by the 27th.

Friday, November 10th, 1916. SUCZAWA.

The Operations Section of the 9th Army takes a more hopeful view of the Rumanian situation. The Rumanian rank and file fight bravely. The officers' nerves have been affected by the H.E. shell, but they will get over this. The guns fire well, but the direction of the artillery is poor, and too frequent use is made of unconcealed positions. There is great hope that the short offensive of the 9th Army planned for the 28th on Csikzereda may be successful, as it may be opposed by Austrians only. This might possibly paralyse the German advance on Bucharest.

Kelchevski has asked G.H.Q. to concentrate a Russian army in rear of the left of the 9th Army, approximately in the area Adjudu-Focsani-Tecuci.

Sunday, November 12th, 1916.   SUCZAWA.

I started at 8 a.m. yesterday and drove across the Rumanian frontier to Falticeni, then across the valley of the Moldawa, and up an excellent road made in 1896-1902, over a pass 1,268 metres high, to the valley of the Bistrito. Climbing this valley to the north-west, we called at the Headquarters of the IIIrd Cavalry Corps (Count Keller), and further on, at Brosteni, at the Headquarters of the IInd Corps (Pflug). Pflug has aged much since I saw him at Tashkent in September, 1913. He has been a very successful corps commander and no one knows exactly why he was removed from his position at the head of the 10th Army after driving back the Germans in the Avgustov woods in September, 1914.

We followed the valley of a right bank tributary of the Bistrito, passing the headquarters of an infantry regiment commanded by a man I had known in the staff of the Guard Corps, and climbed a mountain to the observation post of a mountain battery which was in action right on the Austrian frontier. This battery had come from far Siberia, being quartered in Krasnoyarsk in peace time. It had fought in East Prussia and the Carpathians and had lost half its original strength.

We drove back by moonlight, arriving at Suczawa at 1.45 a.m. to-day. The scenery was everywhere glorious.

August-November, 1916

I was struck by the unlikelihood of an army as cumbrous as the Russian ever forcing a mountain range as wide and difficult as the Carpathians. The Russians have probably double the number of infantry that the enemy has, and yet are making very little progress.

Tuesday, November 12th, 1916.　　　　　BERDICHEV.

I said good-bye to my friends in the 9th Army on Sunday and motored to Czernowitz with a youth who in peace time had served in a bank in Old Bokhara, the purest oriental town in all Asia. All the way we passed long columns of infantry and transport marching south. I dined with the 8th Army on Sunday evening, and on Monday motored to Proskurov, catching a train which brought me to Berdichev to-day.

The following is the present composition of the Russian armies on the South-West Front:

Commander in Chief: General Brusilov. *Chief of Staff:* General Sukhomlin. *General Quarter-Master:* General Dukhonin. *Front:* North of the Sarni-Kovel railway to Ocna in Moldavia.

SPECIAL ARMY. Lutsk: Generals Gurko, Alexyeev and Gerois. Left flank Berestechko:
Vanovski's Column: 5th Don Cossacks, 4th Finland Rifle.
XXXIV. Shatilov, 104, 56.
XXX. Gavrilov, 71, 2nd Guard Cavalry, 102.
XXXIX. Streletski, 53, 125. Trans-Baikal Cossack Cavalry.
South of Kiselin:
XXV. Kornilov, 80, 46, 3rd Grenadier.
I. Bulatov, 24, 22, 20.

IInd Guard. Raukh, 3 Guard, Guard Rifle.
Ist Guard. Potocki, 1 Guard, 2 Guard.
Ist Turkistan. Scheidemann, 1 Turkistan Rifle, 2 Turkistan Rifle.
V. Baluev, 10, 7.
Reserve: 1 Guard Cavalry, 3 Guard Cavalry.

11TH ARMY. Kremenets: Generals Klembovski, Romanovski and Giesser. Left flank north-east of Brzezany:
XLV. Laiming, 2nd Finland Rifle, 126.
XXXII. Fidotov, 101, 105.
Vth Siberian. Voronov, 6 Siberian, 50.
XVII. Yakovlev, 3, 35.
VII. Sichevski, 13, 34.
VI. Gutor, 4, 16.
Reserve: 122, 12th Cavalry. Composite Cossack Cavalry. Trans-Amur Cavalry.

7TH ARMY. Buczacz: Generals Shcherbachev, Golovin and Nezamov. Left flank west of Delatyn:
XVI. Vladimir Dragomirov, 113, 23.
IIIrd Caucasian. Irmanov, 21, 108, 52.
VIIth Siberian. Stupin, 12 Siberian, 13 Siberian, 47.
XXII. Von der Brincken, 1 Finland Rifle. 3 Finland Rifle.
XXXIII. Krilov, 1 Trans-Amur, 2 Trans-Amur.
9th Cavalry Division.
XLI. Belkovich, 3 Trans-Amur, 74.
XII. Kaznakov, 117, 19.
IInd Cavalry. Caucasian Native Cavalry, 6th Don Cossack Cavalry.
Reserve 41st Division.

8TH ARMY. Czernowitz: Generals Kaledin, Stogov and Pokrovski. Left flank west of Kimpolung:
7th Cavalry Division.
3rd Caucasian Cavalry Division.
XI. Barantsev, 12, 11.

The Woodman's Hut south of Yanovka. Taken during the attack of the 2nd Guard Infantry Division on the 8th August, 1916. Left to right. General Rilski, Chief of Staff 1st Guard Corps, General Potocki, Commander 2nd Guards Infantry Division.

[See page 469

River Stir at Sokal.

[See page 468

Group of Military Members of the British Delegation in Riga bridgehead, February, 1917. Left to right: Major D. Davies M.P., General Sir Henry Wilson, Brig.-Generals Sydney Clive and Lord Brook.

[See page 517

Riga bridgehead. Infantry in trenches awaiting attack.

[See page 517

XXIII. Ekk, 32, 79, 82, 59.
XVIII. Zaionchkovski, 43, 37, 64, 84.
Reserve : Ussuri Cavalry Division.

9TH ARMY. Suczawa : (shortly to move to Roman). Generals Lechitski, Sanikov and Kelchevski. Left flank west of Ocna :
XXVI. Rerberg, 65, 78.
II. Pflug, 103, 3rd Turkistan Rifle, 26.
IIIrd Cavalry. Count Keller : 10 Cavalry, 1 Don Cossacks, Terek Cossack Cavalry.
XXXVI. Korotkevich, 68, 25.
Vth Cavalry. Velyarshev, 11 Cavalry, Orenburg Cossack Cavalry.
XXIV. Nekrasov, 48, 49. (Concentrating.)
XL. Bergmann, 2 Rifle, 4 Rifle. (Commencing to arrive.)
Reserve of the Commander-in-Chief (*en route* to Ocna) :
VIII. Denikin : 14, 15.

The Dobrudja Detachment has now been rechristened " The Army of the Danube." The South-West Front has sent its commander, Sakharev, no less than 60,000 drafts. His army now consists of eight infantry and two cavalry divisions distributed as follows :

On the left bank of the Danube :
IV. Aliev, 30, 40, 8th Cavalry.
In the Dobrudja :
IVth Siberian Corps. Sirelius, 9, Siberian, 61, 10 Siberian.
3rd Rifle Division.
3rd Cavalry Division.
In the rear reforming :
115th Division.
1st Serb Volunteer Division.

Summary

	Infantry Divisions.	Cavalry Divisions.
Special Army	21	5
11th "	13	3
7th "	17	3
8th "	10	3
9th "	11	5
Reserve of the Com.-in-Chief, S.W. Front	2	-
Total	74	19
Army of the Danube	8	2
Total	82	21

The immediate result of Rumanian intervention is that it has been necessary to move to territory formerly neutral in the course of two and a half months no less than twenty infantry and seven cavalry divisions, *viz.*:

To the Dobrudja in accordance with the Military Convention:

    61st Division from the 10th Army.
    1st Serb Volunteer Division from Odessa.
    3rd Cavalry Division from the 7th Army.

Later:

    8th Cavalry Division from the 5th Army to the Army of the Danube.
    XXVIth Corps from the South-West Front to Moldavia.
    XXXVIth Corps from the South-West Front to Moldavia.
    115th Division from the 6th Army to the Army of the Danube.

August-November, 1916

3rd Rifle Division from the 5th Army to the Army of the Danube.
IIIrd Cavalry Corps from Bukovina to Moldavia.
IVth Corps from the 5th Army to the Army of the Danube.
Vth Cavalry Corps from the Special Army to Moldavia.
IInd Corps from the 7th Army to Moldavia.
XXIVth Corps from the 10th Army to Moldavia.
XLth Corps from the Special Army to Moldavia.
VIIIth Corps from the Special Army to Moldavia.
IVth Siberian Corps.

Wednesday, November 15th, 1916. BERDICHEV.

Brusilov spoke about Rumania. He points out that intervention has weakened us by lengthening our front. The lengthening of the German front is of less consequence to her, as with her abundant artillery and machine-guns she can defend a passive sector with far fewer men, while her railway system enables her to concentrate rapidly a superior striking force at whichever point she desires.

Brusilov thinks that the Rumanian railways are, "if possible," even worse managed than the Russian. Russia has handed over to the Rumanians over 600 wagons and all the engines captured from the Austrians, but the Rumanians do not know how to use them. Since the Russian concentration commenced, the Rumanians should have provided 130 trains at Czernowitz to carry forward the Russian troops detrained there. They had provided only thirty and the Russian troops had to continue the journey on foot.

Rumania is a difficult ally (*tyajeli soyuznik*).

The 9th Army had offered to buy supplies for the troops now concentrating, but Rumanian officials had hastened to say that there was no need to worry, for their officers would provide everything required in four large magazines.

They had provided nothing, and the Russian concentration had to be stopped to allow supply trains to get through, for otherwise the men on the spot would have starved.

I suggested that the men fought bravely. He agreed, but said that the one idea of the officers was to go on leave to Bucharest. Some of them went there every night, and how could an army fight on such lines?

I asked if it were not possible to arrange a fourth or Rumanian Front under G.H.Q. It might be commanded by the King of Rumania, with the French General Berthelot or some Russian General as Chief of Staff. Brusilov said that the King wanted to have the 9th and Danube Armies placed under his command, but would not hear of going himself under G.H.Q.

It is evident that the present system, with the 9th Army reporting to Brusilov, the Northern, 2nd Rumanian and 1st Rumanian Armies reporting to the King, and the Army of the Danube direct to Russian G.H.Q. is rotten, though Dukhonin says that " after all, the Rumanian Armies are only semi-detached advanced posts, and the right of the Army of the Danube is almost in communication with the left of the 9th Army."

Dukhonin confesses that the losses on the South-West Front since the 4th June have well exceeded a million. Still, all armies, though weaker in artillery and machine-guns, have a substantial numerical superiority over the enemy armies in their front. The winter will give time for training, and in the spring wounded officers will have returned before the first offensive. During the winter all armies will pass officers through a two-months' "refresher" course. The two ensigns' schools on the front at present turn out 1,500 young officers every five months. Of these no less than 80 per cent. are village schoolteachers.

Dukhonin considers that improved technical equipment is necessary in order to spare life and so enable the offensive to continue long enough to attain adequate results. Brusilov's offensive really only lasted five weeks.

At present the five armies of the South-West Front have

only 412 so-called heavy guns (4.2" to 11") or less than one heavy gun per mile of front.

It was interesting to ascertain the views of various leaders regarding the work of the cavalry in the open fighting of the summer. Russia's enormous superiority in cavalry was made very little use of during the war, and the feeding of the many mounted divisions was a permanent burden on the railways. More than once it had been suggested that part of the cavalry might be with advantage dismounted and transformed into infantry.

An ex-cavalry officer then serving on the staff of the Guard Corps had embodied the idea in a scheme he drew up in 1915, but General Bezobrazov had told him, with tears in his eyes, that he was ashamed that any cavalryman should have even imagined such a thing!

October 26th, 1916.   BERDICHEV.

I had some talk with Brusilov about cavalry. He has broad views, in spite of having spent sixteen years in the Cavalry School at Petrograd.

I asked what cavalry had accomplished in the recent offensive, and he gave the astonishing reply that it had proved useful in occupying passive sections and so enabling the Command to economise infantry for the main shocks. Brusilov does not believe in far-reaching cavalry raids, and he quoted Svyentsyani as a failure. (All the same, the Svyentsyani raid forced the evacuation of Vilna, though it may have failed in Hindenburg's ambitious project of rounding up the 10th Army.)

Brusilov said that the Russian cavalry had had one great chance in the recent offensive—the IVth Cavalry Corps (Gillenschmidt) in Lesh's offensive should have crossed the Stokhod and pursued the Austrians, who were then retreating in disorder. Gillenschmidt said that he could go no further and he had been spoken to severely in consequence,

Brusilov is of opinion that there is too much cavalry in the Russian army. It costs much and complicates supply. He would assign two cavalry divisions to each army of about 160 battalions. The cavalry in armies now averages much more. He thinks that corps and divisional cavalry should be increased to one six-squadron regiment per corps of two divisions. Some corps have now as much as this, but by no means all.

He quoted from his personal experience two instances of good work done by cavalry in the war: 1. In the first big battle on the Gnila Lipa, a gap of three versts was formed between the XIIth and the VIIIth Corps. A strong enemy column was moving towards this gap and the 12th Infantry Division which was advancing to fill it was still some distance off. The 12th Cavalry Division, then under Kaledin, was sent forward and held the line by dismounted fire, pending the arrival of the infantry. 2. At the battle of Grodek, the flank of the XXIVth Corps on the left of the 8th Army was being turned, when Brusilov sent the 12th Cavalry Division to prolong the line. Kaledin used nineteen of his squadrons dismounted, and charged with success with the remaining five.

"Of course," Brusilov said, "it would be a different story if the enemy were demoralised. But when will he be demoralised? I have myself personally assisted in the 'annihilation' of the 43rd Honved Division on four different occasions. On each occasion it has been reduced to 2,000 or 3,000 men, but it has always reformed and returned after two or three weeks."

Tuesday, November 7th, 1916.   CZERNOWITZ.

I burst in suddenly on Kaledin at 12 o'clock and asked him his opinion regarding the work the Russian cavalry had accomplished in the recent offensive.

He thought for a moment, and then gave me quite a lecture on the subject.

He is strongly of opinion that the reason the Russian

cavalry accomplished so little was that lack of troops compelled the Command to use it in trenches and so prevented it from being held concentrated in rear for its legitimate work.

The flank armies on the South-West Front—the 8th and the 9th—were the strongest in cavalry. The 8th Army (Kaledin's) had the Vth Cavalry Corps, consisting of two cavalry divisions, and, in addition, two independent divisions—the 7th and the 12th. The army had a front of 180 versts (120 miles), and in order to assemble sufficient troops for the main attack it was necessary to put the Vth Cavalry Corps in the trenches to hold stretches of marshy front.

After the success of the first attack, Brusilov, in spite of Kaledin's protests, moved the 7th Cavalry Division north to join the Vth Corps in an attempted raid on Kovel along the Sarni-Kovel railway. This was a complete failure, and the Russians, who had to advance through marshes, in places above their middles, suffered large losses.

Kaledin was left with the 12th Division, which could do little by itself. He is convinced that if it had been backed by the 7th, none of the Austrian transport would have escaped. If he had had the whole of his four cavalry divisions on the spot and available at the time of the break-through he would have occupied Vladimir Volinski and have cut the railways north and west of Kovel.

He is strongly of opinion that in the state of demoralisation which then reigned in the Austrian army a cavalry corps would have been of more value than an extra infantry corps.

"The Germans," Kaledin said, "are unfortunately not yet demoralised, and naturally, for they have two years of victory to their credit. When they come to retreat they will suffer from the Russian cavalry. As it is, their infantry has more than once had a taste of it. There was the case, for instance, of the Orenburg Cossacks on the Stokhod. The XXXIXth Corps was being hard pressed, and the

German infantry was nearing the Russian guns, when three squadrons of Orenburg Cossacks charged on their little Kirgiz ponies and cut two German companies to pieces. The moral result of this sudden stroke was enormous."

Thursday, October 5th, 1916.   DVINSK.

I tried to draw Abram Dragomirov on the subject of cavalry at supper, by telling him that Sir Douglas Haig wanted details of the part the Russian cavalry had played in the recent offensive on the South-West Front. I explained that neither in the 8th Army nor in the 9th, as far as I had been able to discover, had mounted troops played any very important part.

He told me to tell General Haig from him that he firmly believed a great day for cavalry was coming. The Germans lived in dread of the Russian cavalry. If it played no great *rôle* on the South-West Front, it was because the retreat was by short laps. He believes that when the Germans come to retreat from the sparsely held Northern Front, they will do so in columns necessarily far apart, and the Russian cavalry will penetrate between and round them, and will work havoc.

This may be true if the German *morale* has by then dropped to zero, and if the Russians have at last discovered a heaven-born cavalry leader. However, the Germans and Austrians retired from the Vistula in October, 1914, without serious interruption from an overwhelming force of cavalry, and their retreat was certainly not by short laps. If they retire from their present line on the Northern Front they will do so by short laps to wired positions.

Of course, there may be something in the oft-repeated argument that the Russians would never have carried through their retreat from Poland in 1915 if the Germans had had enough cavalry.

I returned to Petrograd on November 19th, and went straight to bed, where I was laid up with scarlet fever till December 29th.

CHAPTER XVII

THE THREE MONTHS PRECEDING THE REVOLUTION

THE inadequacy of Russia's communications with the outside world led to two projects for bringing in munitions from the Arctic Ocean, both of them interesting, though one proved a failure and the other came too late to affect the general situation.

These projects were the Skibotten-Karungi sledge route and the Murman Railway.[1]

Work on the Murman railway commenced in the first winter of the war, but the slowness of its progress led the British Government in the Russian munitions crisis, in the winter of 1915-1916, to finance an undertaking proposed by an energetic Finn named Bostrom to establish a sledge route along the 500 kilometres from the port of Skibotten due south to Karungi, the terminus of the Finnish railway system north of the Gulf of Bothnia. Bostrom arranged post-houses and stabling at intervals of fifty kilometres and purchased 2,000 horses. The route was, however, only a sledge route, and the spring thaw came before 1,000 tons had been hauled to railhead. Later in the year munitions stored at some of the stages were destroyed by incendiaries, no doubt at German instigation.

The construction of a railway to an ice-free port in the Arctic Ocean had been contemplated in pre-war days, but the project had been postponed from motives of economy.

At the outbreak of war, the railway terminus was at Petrozavodsk, north-east of Petrograd. On December 12th, 1914, the Council of Ministers voted a credit, and in the same

---
[1] See Map No. XIII.

month preliminary work commenced on an extension from Petrozavodsk to Seroka bay, on the south-west corner of the White Sea.

The whole distance from Petrozavodsk to the ice-free Kola inlet was 1,061 versts (707 miles), and was divided into three sections: Petrozavodsk-Seroka, 356 versts; Seroka along the western shore of the White Sea to Kandalaksha, 440 versts; Kandalaksha due north across the Kola peninsula to the port of Romanov on the Kola bay, 265 versts.

Imperial sanction was given for the construction of the southern section in January, 1915, for the northern section in June, and for the central section in October of the same year.

The natural difficulties of constructing a line through desert country in a terrible climate were increased by the difficulty under war conditions of purchasing and delivering material for the work and for the maintenance of the constructional personnel.

Of the 1,061 versts from Petrozavodsk to Murmansk, over 250 versts, or upwards of 25 per cent. of the whole line, had to be laid through marsh. To every 1,000 yards of line there were sixteen yards of bridge. In the effort to avoid marsh, no less than 40 per cent. of the line was in the first instance laid on curves. Proper ballast was difficult to obtain. Enormous boulders had to be blasted with dynamite. During half of the year in the northern section there reigned perpetual night, yet work was carried on continuously, the only lighting being obtained from enormous torches, which had to be used, since lanterns proved useless in the strong north-east wind and continual snowstorms.

No labour or supplies of any kind were obtainable locally. Even hay had to be carried from Central Russia. The necessary material when purchased had to be conveyed to the area by a combination of several methods of transport, by rail, sledge route, by river or sea.

The provision of labour was a constant difficulty. The contract for the construction of the northern section was originally given to a British firm, but this section, like the others, was eventually completed by the Russian Administration. Some 30,000 hired labourers were brought in 1915 from the Volga

Governments, and 5,000 more from Finland. They became discontented at the wildness of their surroundings, and many of them deserted. On the conclusion of their six and a half months' contract, few of them renewed. Recourse was had to prisoners of war. In July, 1916, 53,020 men were at work on the line, *viz.*, 13,224 on the southern section, 30,342 on the central section and 9,454 on the northern section. Of these 14,503 were prisoners of war and the remainder were Russians. Arrangements were then made to secure an additional 36,000 men, *viz.*, 16,000 Russians, 10,000 prisoners of war and 10,000 Chinese.

The line was eventually opened for through traffic on November 28th, 1916, but its carrying capacity remained exceedingly small till several months later.

In late August General Byelyaev, who, as Chief of the General Staff at Petrograd, had from the beginning of the war worked in the most cordial co-operation with the allied military representatives, was, on his return from an important mission to England and France, summarily dismissed by the Minister of War, General Shuvaiev.

The Minister informed General Byelyaev by telephone that he was appointed a member of the Military Council, adding that he was " a most honourable man and a thorough gentleman " (*chestnyeishi i blagorodnyeishi chelovek*), but that work with him he could not (*Ya s vami rabotat ne mogu*) !

No one who knew the two men was surprised at this. Shuvaiev was an expansive Russian—all heart. Byelyaev, though a pure Russian, was of the meticulous German type.

Appointment to the Military Council was equivalent to retirement, for the Council met only three or four times a week at 1.30 p.m. and broke up at 3 p.m., its work being purely formal. Poor General Byelyaev, who was fifty-three, at the first meeting after his appointment sat down beside his youngest colleague and found he was a General of sixty-four.

However, Byelyaev was too useful a man to be shelved, and he was soon despatched to Rumania to act as Chief Russian Liaison Officer at the King's Headquarters. On January 17th,

1917, he was recalled from Rumania to take General Shuvaiev's place as Russian Minister of War.

Shuvaiev was not dismissed, as he might have been, for complete incompetency, but, it was said, on account of his blunt and soldierly outspokenness regarding the reactionary tendencies of the Government.

Soon after his return with the Duma Delegation from the visit to the allied capitals, Protopopov, the Vice-President of the Duma, had joined the Cabinet as Minister of the Interior, and had embarked at once on a policy of oppression, in accordance, it was rumoured, with the views of the Empress.

There was a short-lived hope of a saner policy when, on November 24th, M. Trepov, hitherto Minister of Ways, was appointed to succeed M. Sturmer as Prime Minister.

On December 30th, Rasputin was murdered at 104, Moika, the house of Prince Yusupov. The Grand Duke Dimitri Pavlovich had driven on the night of December 29th to 64, Gorokhovaya, where Rasputin lived, to fetch the impostor. He had gone to the back door, as the suisse and dvorniks were employés of the Secret Police.

Friday, October 12th, 1917.

Princess B—— at lunch recounted the story of Rasputin's murder, as told her in Moscow by a participator. Yusupov had often invited Rasputin to come to see his house. On the day in question he demurred, as he had been warned by the police that he should not go out. He was, however, persuaded. There were present the Grand Duke Dimitri Pavlovich, the Duma member Purishkevich, an officer named Sukotin, a doctor and Yusupov. They had prepared port, a poisoned bottle on a side table, and an unpoisoned bottle, poisoned pink cakes, and unpoisoned chocolate cakes. At first Rasputin refused to drink, but later took three glasses of the poisoned port and ate several of the pink cakes. The poison seemed to have no effect, so Dimitri Pavlovich and Yusupov retired upstairs to consult. It was decided to kill by shooting.

Yusupov took Dimitri Pavlovich's revolver and went down and took a seat at the table beside Rasputin, hiding the revolver in his left hand. He watched his victim for a long time, and wondered morbidly what it would feel like to shoot him: imagined the look that would come into his eyes, the scream he would utter, and how the blood would spurt. He felt he could not shoot him while sitting beside him, so drew his attention to an old crystal crucifix at the other side of the room, and, as he walked over to look at it more closely, followed him and shot him in the back. Rasputin fell with a piercing scream. The doctor said he was in his death-agony, and the whole party adjourned upstairs.

They returned some three-quarters of an hour later. The Grand Duke went out to get his car to dispose of the body and left the door open behind him. Yusupov was surprised to find that Rasputin's hands were not yet cold, and was kneeling down to feel his heart, when the monk opened his eyes and, calling him a murderer, stumbled to his feet and out of the door. They pursued him to the garden, where after a general fusillade, Purishkevich despatched him with a bullet in the neck.

The police came, but were quieted by a bribe of Rs.100 and a story that Yusupov had shot a dog. After they had gone, Yusupov's servant and the dvornik dragged the body into the house. At this point one of the party's nerves gave way, and he became temporarily deranged, throwing himself on the body and digging his nails into the flesh, so that he got up all covered with blood.

A sorry story altogether, and a fitting prelude to much that has happened since!

After the murder, the body was rolled in a sofa-cover, the arms and legs being tied together, and was conveyed by car in the early hours of the 30th to the Petrovski Bridge, where it was thrown into the river. The ties came undone, and when the body was found on Sunday morning, the 31st, the arms were stretched out to the front and frozen stiff. On January 3rd the body was thawed, placed in a coffin and taken to Tsarskoe Selo, where it was buried in the middle of the night, the Emperor, Empress and the young Grand Duchesses attending the funeral.

All classes were delighted. Perfect strangers meeting one another in the street exchanged congratulations in the exuberant Russian manner. When Prince Tumanov, the Director of Supply on the Northern Front, heard the news, he called his officers together and congratulated them officially

Wednesday, January 3rd, 1917.   PETROGRAD.

A short paragraph appeared in the evening papers of the 30th, telling of Rasputin's death, but the papers of Sunday, the 31st, contained nothing, as all mention of the tragedy had been forbidden.

It is said that Madame Virubova ran to the Palace at Tsarskoe Selo for protection when she heard of the murder.

The Council of Ministers debated whether the finding of the body should be made known. Trepov and Ignatiev, the Minister of Education, wished to conceal it, but Protopopov, acting no doubt on instructions, gave the information to the Press.

An A.D.C. from the Empress called at Dimitri Pavlovich's palace and demanded his word of honour that he would remain there till further instructions. Both he and Yusupov are now under arrest.

On the night of the 6th the Grand Duke Dimitri Pavlovich was sent off to Persia, where he was appointed to the Staff of General Baratov, the Commander of the Cavalry Corps in Northern Persia. Prince Yusupov was sent to his estate in the Government of Kursk a few hours later.

Unfortunately, the Emperor remained subject to reactionary influence. Though implored by his most devoted advisers, he refused to adopt a more liberal policy. The British Ambassador did all that was humanly possible. After a reference to England, he was authorised by the Foreign Office to make representations to the Emperor on his own responsibility.

Three Months Preceding the Revolution

In his interview on January 12th, Sir George Buchanan spoke tactfully, but certainly more strongly than any previous Ambassador had ever ventured to address the ruler of Russia's millions. He implored him to change his policy while there was yet time, pointing out the danger of a starving and exasperated capital. The Emperor listened with scarcely a word of reply, and the Russian Minister, who had an audience immediately following the Ambassador, found him trembling and distrait.

On January 9th the two more Liberal members of the Government—Trepov, the Premier, and Count Ignatiev, the Minister of Education—resigned on the ground that they were unable to continue members of a Government in which M. Protopopov held the portfolio of Minister of the Interior. Prince Golitzin, a comparatively unknown man, who had spent several years as Governor of Arkhangel, and who during the war had assisted the Empress in her charitable organisations, was appointed Premier.

General Alexyeev 'left G.H.Q. on a few weeks' leave, and is said to have warned the Emperor before his departure that the censorship of soldiers' letters showed that they wrote continually of the Empress and Rasputin. It was said that the Commanders-in-Chief of the Fronts warned His Majesty that the troops would not fight if the anarchy in the interior continued.

Officers began to speak openly of the Imperial Family in conversation even with foreigners in a way that would have been impossible a few weeks earlier. A General of Artillery, in discussing the disgraceful theft of magnetos from motor-cars and even of the leather from the seats of the British 4·5s in transit from Arkhangel, shrugged his shoulders and said: " What can we do? We have Germans everywhere. The Empress is a German!"[1]

The Duma was to have assembled on January 25th, and it was thought advisable to call up the Guard Depot Cavalry Regiment from Novgorod to help in the maintenance of order. Many of the officers petitioned to be allowed to rejoin their regiments at the front rather than risk being employed at Petrograd in defence of

---

[1] In spite of gossip to the contrary, the Empress as well as the Emperor was loyal to the Alliance. Unfortunately there is no doubt that she opposed concession to popular demands.

the Government. The only troops in the capital were the depot battalions of the Guard and some depot units of the Line. These contained each from 8,000 to 10,000 men, most of whom had never been at the front. They were officered either by men who had been wounded at the front and who regarded their duty as a sort of convalescent leave from the rigour of the trenches, or by youths fresh from the military schools. It was doubtful whether either officers or men could be relied upon in the event of civil disturbance. It was certain that, if the men went wrong, the officers were without the influence to control them. Some weeks earlier the depot battalion of the Moskovski Regiment had refused to fire on strikers, and five officers had been cashiered and fifteen men hung.[1]

On January 20th I reported: " The effect of the arbitrary action of the past few weeks has been to unite all classes in opposition to the Government, so that, if there is a revolution, little blood will be spilt."

This was a true statement of fact, but unfortunately a very false deduction!

On January 18th the opening of the Duma was postponed till February 27th.

An Allied Delegation, with British, French and Italian representatives, arrived in Petrograd on January 29th. The British Delegation was led by Lord Milner, with Sir Henry Wilson as chief military adviser. It was rumoured that there had been a proposal to send out the Duke of Connaught with a letter from the King to the Emperor. If there was such an idea, it was no doubt rejected on account of the inter-allied nature of the Delegation.

---

[1] An extract from the Diary of a later date may be interesting here:

Sunday, May 20th, 1917. PETROGRAD.

Engelhardt lunched. I asked him if he had foreseen the Revolution. He said that no one had. In December, 1916, the 1st Guard Cavalry Division had received orders to move to Petrograd, and had actually commenced entraining when the order was cancelled. Officers of the Chevalier Gardes, in talking over matters with him, had seriously discussed the advisability, if recalled to Petrograd to restore order, of carrying out a plot to arrest the Emperor and force him to grant a constitution.

On February 16th Engelhardt, Guchkov and Shulgin had drawn up a list of a possible Ministry to have ready in order to prevent anarchy in case of a revolution.

Three Months Preceding the Revolution 517

Still, it is a matter for regret that it was found to be impracticable, for it would have been easy for the Duke to advise the Emperor in a manner that was obviously impossible for Lord Milner to attempt without risk of offence.

The Delegation was entertained with the usual lavish Russian hospitality, but found time for much useful work before its departure for England at 11 p.m. on February 21st. General Gurko, who was acting as Chief of Staff during Alexyeev's temporary absence, came from G.H.Q. to attend the inter-allied strategical conferences, while the conferences on munition supply were presided over by General Byelyaev in his capacity of Minister of War.

The two Englishmen who most impressed the Russians were undoubtedly Sir Henry Wilson, who charmed them with his cordial manner, and Mr. Layton, of the Ministry of Munitions, whose astonishing grasp of detail impressed everyone.

The Delegation dined with the Emperor at Tsarskoe Selo on February 3rd, and a few days later I conducted the military members of the British Section on a short tour to the Headquarters of the Northern Front at Pskov, where they met General Ruzski; to Riga, where we were entertained by General Radko Dimitriev, lately promoted to the command of the 12th Army; and to Minsk, the Headquarters of General Ewarth, the Commander-in-Chief of the Western Front.

At Riga we learned something of the fighting that had taken place south-west of the town in the month of January. The operations were in three phases:

    (a) A Russian offensive, January 5th-10th.
    (b) A German counter-offensive, January 22nd-25th.
    (c) A further German counter-offensive, January 30th-31st.

On the night of January 4th-5th, the 2nd and 1st Lett Brigades, each eight battalions strong, broke through the enemy's lines without artillery preparation, the bomb-throwers moving in advance to cut the enemy's wire. The 3rd Siberian Division on the right of the Letts failed in its surprise attack, and further right the 4th Special Division refused to leave its trenches. The Letts were not properly supported, but the fighting up to the 10th resulted in the Germans being forced back a few kilometres.

On the 22nd the enemy, by a severe bombardment, drove the Russians back to a line slightly in advance of that occupied previous to the original Russian attack. On January 30th, after some days' rest, he launched strong infantry attacks, which were repulsed with the bayonet. On the 31st he subjected the Russian line to a severe bombardment.

Radko, who had been everywhere in the thickest of the fighting, encouraging his men, waxed enthusiastic at dinner on February 10th over the " success " of his surprise tactics. He said that if he had had three or four corps in reserve he would have gone far. He issued a triumphant order, with elaborate instructions for the carrying out of future surprise attacks by night without artillery preparation, the enemy's wire to be cut by hand.

Some members of Radko's Staff were less enthusiastic. On the active front from the Gulf to the village of Sarkanaiz the Russians had never less than ninety-two battalions, while the enemy had only twenty-two to twenty-five battalions on January 5th, and his strength never increased beyond sixty-four to seventy-one battalions. There is no doubt that the enemy was completely surprised, but the reason for undertaking the operation was not clear, for the Russians had insufficient troops of good quality on the spot to develop a real success. As it was, the attempt was only a raid, and it failed in the primary object of a raid—the improvement of the raiders' *morale*—for it cost in Russian life and *morale* before the end of the month at least six times the damage it caused the enemy.

The party returned from the front *via* Moscow, and on the afternoon of February 15th, after lunching with General Mrzovski, the Commander of the District, attended a meeting of the Moscow branch of the Military Industrial Committee. A big Moscow manufacturer took the chair and read long speeches in Russian, welcoming the Delegation, asking for every possible material from England, including steel, which Russia should have been able to produce in abundance, and incidentally abusing the Russian Government. The burden of the argument was that, as

Three Months Preceding the Revolution 519

Russia was badly governed, she was unable to make use of her enormous natural resources for the purposes of the war, therefore practically all munitions must come from abroad. Though we repeatedly explained that our resources and our shipping were limited, that our only object was to help, and to find out how we could best help within the limit of our powers, we came away without obtaining a single practical suggestion. One of the engineers followed me out and, overcome with emotion, said that he felt it was his duty to tell me that Russia was now governed by people who were deliberately preparing her defeat. He said: " Something dreadful is going to happen. We are approaching a catastrophe ! "

The artillery that the British Government had sent Russia previous to the visit of the Delegation was :

- 16 60-pounders, with 96 wagons.
- 1 9·2 howitzer with caterpillar tractor.
- 32 6" howitzers, with 8 tractors, 26 lorries, and 60 wagons with harness.
- 400 4·5 howitzers, with 637 lorries, 1,240 wagons and harness, and 500 additional 6-horse-team sets of harness as spares.

The Delegation recommended that after the opening of the port of Arkhangel there should be sent monthly :

- 4 batteries of 6" howitzers.
- 2 batteries of 8" howitzers.
- 1 battery of 9·2 howitzers.[1]

General Gurko communicated to Sir Henry Wilson his determination as soon as weather permitted to attack with about seventy divisions on all four fronts of the Eastern theatre. The offensive on the Rumanian Front was to be launched first, and to be the smallest owing to the defective railways. Brusilov's

---

[1] A minor result of the visit of Sir Henry Wilson was that, after two years and seven months of war, the important service of enemy intelligence was placed under the British Military Attaché, who was relieved of the task of liaison regarding the supply of munitions to Russia. The munition supply branch, with which the Military Attaché and his single assistant had hitherto struggled alone, was placed in the more competent hands of a special Supply Mission, under General Poole, who soon collected an independent staff of some forty to fifty officers.

offensive on the South-West Front was to be the most important. It was thought probable that an interval of about three weeks would elapse after the launching of the offensive on the Rumanian Front before climatic conditions in the north would make it advisable for General Ruzski to move.

As in 1916, Brusilov had ordered each army commander some weeks previously to submit plans by February 28th for an offensive to be undertaken by each army relying only on its own individual resources.

The appreciation of the situation submitted in reply by General Baluev, the Commander of the Naroch Group in the offensive of March, 1916, who now in Gurko's absence at G.H.Q. temporarily occupied the post of Commander of the Special Army, showed lack of confidence in success.

Baluev wrote that his army of fifteen infantry and three cavalry divisions had only 547 3" field guns and 168 so-called " heavy " guns and howitzers of calibres ranging from 4·2" to 6". He considered that at least forty light field and twenty heavy guns per verst of active front were necessary for a decisive attack and that no attack on a front narrower than fourteen versts had a chance of success. As his heavy artillery only admitted of an attack on a front of eight versts, he suggested that he should be allowed to take up a passive attitude, and that his surplus infantry might be transferred to some army where they might be of more use.

Conditions in front were, however, far more satisfactory than in rear. During the visit of the British Military Delegation to Moscow, a fine old Russian soldier—General Vogack—in discussing the situation, had invited our attention to a map of Russia. " There," he said, pointing to the frontal area, " everything is right, but here in rear everything is chaos."

The Russians asked for huge quantities of steel, and argued that they were unable to increase their own output owing to shortage of labour and defective transport. If asked why they could not make their men work more than twenty-two to twenty-four days in the month, they replied that it would be no good if they did, for the railways were unable to carry the necessary fuel and raw material. It was contended that the railways were the chief cause of the chaos.

The railways were, indeed, going through a serious crisis, owing to the exhaustion of the stocks of coal on many of the lines and the poor quality of the coal that was available. The system of inland waterways had not been used as it should have been in the summer to accumulate coal reserves at convenient centres in central and northern Russia—partly no doubt because the men had not been tied down to the mines and made to work throughout the summer. The poor quality of the coal affected the engines, and these had to work without intermission with reliefs of personnel, who had never time to clean them. Again, the long spells of very cold weather and snowstorms strained the locomotives, shortened trains, and locked up rolling-stock owing to the frequent delays of as much as twenty-four hours caused by the breaking down of engines.

Thursday, February 22nd, 1917. PETROGRAD.

I talked to Polivanov. He said the Ministry of Ways had been haggling over two years about the price of coal, and hence the miserable stuff that is ruining the engines. I asked him what he would do if dictator. He said he would call the best traffic managers together to consult. He would then place each main line under a dictator, who would have full powers on his line to hang or to do as he liked.

He says that the Russian engineers are good constructors but wretched traffic managers. The management of the railways presents no difficulties, but demands constant watching and *active* supervision. Meanwhile our statesmen sleep.

He told me that Byelyaev had not been near him since his promotion to be Minister of War. He said that he (Polivanov) was hated by the Empress, by Kshinskaya (the dancer) and Virubova (the Empress's favourite), and that, as Byelyaev wanted to keep his place, he did not care to risk a doubtful intimacy!

Thursday, March 1st, 1917.　　　　　　　　PETROGRAD.

　　The Ambassador left yesterday for Finland on a few days' well-earned holiday.

　　I had an interview with Byelyaev to give him a telegram from Sir Henry Wilson describing the disorganisation at Romanov. I put the case as strongly as I could, pointing out that it was disgraceful that our merchant seamen should risk their lives to deliver material at Romanov that the Russians made no attempt to remove. Byelyaev confessed that the Murman railway was not a real railway in the proper sense of the word, but something in the nature of a gigantic bluff. The fault lay with Trepov—late Minister of Ways—who had declared the line open on November 28th, and had so delayed necessary construction work.

　　Byelyaev told me that, since last Sunday, by the Emperor's order, the three Ministers—of Ways, Trade and Agriculture—had met daily for an hour under his chairmanship to try to co-ordinate their work. He complained that all the Ministers worked each in his own separate "corridor" (the Russian equivalent of our "watertight compartment").

　　We drifted into politics. He said that the only politician in whom he had any faith was Savich. Guchkov was clever, but he could not trust him, for, like others, he simply used the prevailing chaos as a lever to oust the Government. He acknowledged that it was Polivanov who had taught him to work, but said that for him (Byelyaev), as an honourable soldier, to work with Polivanov had been very difficult, for Polivanov constantly sought advice from the politicians.

　　He said he had remarked to the Emperor how fortunate England was in the possession of men like Layton—" a professor at Cambridge University," who worked at his job and never meddled in politics. I pointed out that this was possible in England, where we had a Government the people could trust. He sighed.

　　The narrowness of poor Byelyaev, who objects on

principle to any seeking of advice outside official ranks, neutralises all his energy and honesty. His stupidity makes it all rather hopeless. What will happen I don't know.

Monday, March 5th, 1917.   PETROGRAD.

On Saturday morning, M. Diamandi (the Rumanian Minister) telephoned that he wanted to see me. I went to him at 3 p.m. I am sorry for him, for he is a gentleman, honest and a patriot, and he feels his position acutely, for he was largely instrumental in bringing his country into the war, that has proved so disastrous for it, while its intervention has so far brought nothing but inconvenience to the Entente.

He talked for one and a half hours. First he pointed out how Rumania had been left to her fate, forty-two enemy divisions being at one time concentrated against her, how Serail's promised offensive from Salonika had been merely a demonstration, the lack of discipline among the Russian troops in Rumania, the thefts and the rape. He said that the Russians had promised 200,000 sets of uniform, and that these had been despatched from Moscow in September, but only 20,000 had so far reached Rumania, the rest having been pilfered *en route* or simply unloaded by the wayside into the snow.

I stated a little of the Russian side of the question, and he allowed that there had been mistakes on both sides.

Then he touched on the political problem, remarking on our declaration that Constantinople should be handed over to Russia, and the effect in neutral countries of the Russian retreat beyond the Danube further and further away from our acknowledged objective.

He said that in Rumania there is only enough food to last till April. The Russians have been living on the country. The harvest will not be available till August. It had been a fatal mistake to abandon the lower Danube—

a greater disaster even than the evacuation of Bucharest. The reconquest of this waterway was the only remedy.

I said it was too late, as the river would soon be in flood, and in any case the Russian troops, being without boots, were not in a condition to undertake an operation of such magnitude.

Wednesday, March 7th, 1917.   PETROGRAD.

I saw Byelyaev at 9.45 p.m. and found him much depressed. He said he would do all that was possible to hasten the conveyance of stores from Romanov, and he begged me to avoid alarming people in England into possible refusal to continue the despatch of munitions to the port. He felt everyone was against him in his fight for order, but he would continue to do his duty as long as Minister.

The disorder on the railways was chiefly caused by lack of engines, but had been accentuated by the severity of the winter. He blamed the Ministry of Ways for the low price offered for new engines and for the repair of old engines. Although Rs.150,000 were paid for unsuitable engines from America, he (Byelyaev) had had difficulty in 1916 in forcing the Ministry to raise the price for engines manufactured in Russia from Rs.57,000 to Rs.77,000. All the works were privately owned, and, owing to the poor price offered, they had naturally abandoned the construction and repair of engines for more lucrative work.

He said that in the so-called " mobilisation of industry " in 1915, many small factories had accepted Government orders with the object of getting workmen and fuel, but none of them had worked anything like their total time on these orders. In the remainder of their time they had used the labour and fuel provided by Government for national purposes to carry out profitable private orders.

I gave General Byelyaev a paper on copper production, showing that 3,995 tons of copper now lie at various stations awaiting transport, and pointed out that it was difficult for the producers to carry on with their money locked up indefinitely in copper ingots. He said he knew that the Metallurgical Committee was worthless.

Thursday, March 8th, 1917. PETROGRAD.

I saw General Vselojski, the officer in charge of military communications. He thinks that the railway situation will improve. February and March are always the worst months, and in this year the snowfalls have been heavier than usual and the frosts more severe.

I argued that the shortage of fuel of good quality was primarily owing to the slackness of labour in the mines last summer and to the slackness of the Government in allowing labour to leave the mines during the summer, when coal for the winter traffic might have been obtained and distributed by the inland waterways. He said that all the river steamship companies were privately owned, and to take them over would have required a new department, " which might have done more harm than good."

In other words, the Government shied off the task. They are in terror of any approach to socialism!

I visited Guchkov at 6 p.m., driving through Cossack and police patrols on the Liteini, for the workmen are commencing to strike for want of food.

Guchkov said that the blow the present disorganisation of transport was dealing the Russian cause was worse than any disaster in the war—worse than the defeats at Tannenberg or in Galicia. The causes are the stupidity and supineness of the present Government, and its continuance in power will make it impossible for Russia to fight through a fourth winter. He had told M. Dumergue (the Chief of the French Delegation) that, with the present Government, he need not count on Russia helping to beat Germany.

On February 7th it had been suddenly discovered that many railways had only two to five days' supply of coal.

The Ministers of Ways, Rukhlov and Trepov, had bargained with the coal owners for a year and seven months without making any contract. They depended on requisitions, which brought them, of course, the worst coal, to the detriment of the engines.

No attempt has been made to economise coal. Owing to the cost of the labour necessary to procure wood, coal, even far from the mines, is the cheapest fuel. Hence, even the Arkhangel and Polyesie lines, whose entire length runs through forest, have been allowed to work on coal.

The railways were ordered to carry nothing but coal for a week. The week was extended till March 14th. In this period of over a month it is stated that 3,100 wagons a day have been despatched to all destinations, but Guchkov doubts this, and estimates the quantity despatched in the whole period at only some half million tons.

Half of the blast furnaces in the Donetz region have stopped work altogether, and the other half are working only half time. The output of metal from the Donetz region during the month ending March 13th will fall from 260,000 tons to 100,000.

In the other great industrial region, the Urals, the output of metal will fall for another reason. The fuel used there is wood, which is carried to the furnaces by sledge. The carriers have stopped work because they have no oats for their horses. There is abundance of oats in the neighbourhood, but the peasants will not sell at the price fixed by Government.

The Putilov Works stopped yesterday. The Tula Works have stopped, and so have the Tambov and Baranovski powder factories. The Okhta and Shoshka factories are only working a third of their time.

Guchkov is thoroughly in agreement with the idea of militarisation of labour, but says such a step could only be taken by a Government that possessed the confidence of the people. He proposed the rationing of munition workers months ago, but nothing has been done.

He says that Voinski-Krieger (the Minister of Ways) is a good technical man, but without any " go." " Byelyaev is the worst of all."

The Emperor has gone to G.H.Q.

Questioned regarding the attitude of the workmen in the towns towards the war, Guchkov said that from 10 to 20 per cent. would welcome defeat as likely to strengthen their hands to overthrow the Government. The remainder are in favour of the war, and they hate the Germans, but they disclaim any idea of conquest ; their motto is national defence, but not offence. They are opposed to the idea of conquering Constantinople or Galicia.

In a pamphlet printed by this latter group it is laid down that " the whole strength of the country should be mobilised for its defence," and again, " the present political régime is not only designed for the oppression of the working classes, but seems also to be an obstacle to the mobilisation of the whole living strength of the people for defence, and is thus leading the country to military disaster."

The eleven labour members of the Military Industrial Committee, who were arrested by order of Protopopov on the night of February 5th, belonged to this group. They are still in confinement. However, Guchkov, who guaranteed that they had no revolutionary tendencies, has secured a promise that they will be eventually tried.

Saturday, March 10th, 1917.   PETROGRAD.

I dined last night with the V——s in a magnificent house on the Sergievskaya. After dinner they produced whisky, and actually Schweppes' soda—the remains of what must have been a large supply laid in before the war.

I saw Polivanov at 10.15 a.m. to-day. He says that the cessation of work at Putilov's was really owing to the defective arrangements for the distribution of food. The workmen said they could not work if they and their wives, who are also employed at the works, had to wait in queues for hours to get their small portions of bread.

The Government shows signs of yielding. Last night it agreed to hand over the responsibility for provisioning Petrograd to the Municipality. It had long refused to do this, and only does so now when the whole business is in hopeless disorder.

Polivanov says that last night at the Council of Empire the dvorniks said that as they had had no bread they could not carry up wood to heat the stoves. Accordingly the " potent, grave and reverent seniors " interviewed them, and distributed bread, after which wood was forthcoming! What a subject for an historical picture!

I saw Manikovski.[1] He said that the Tula Works had restarted, and that Putilov and most of the Petrograd works would restart on Monday. The strike at Putilov's was really a lock-out, the men turning up so unpunctually and irregularly owing to the difficulty in procuring food that the administration closed down. Manikovski confirmed generally Guchkov's statement regarding the output of metal on the Donetz and in the Urals, but estimated the drop in production respectively at: Donetz 260,000 tons to 160,000 tons, and Urals 80,000 tons to 40,000 tons.

He said: " Why can't England give us a Minister ? "

The Nevski was quiet when I crossed it at 3.30 p.m., but half an hour later the gendarmes were charging the people. Bruce (the First Secretary) arrived at the Embassy in a state of holy wrath, having conducted to her home a woman who had been knocked down in the scuffle. About 5 p.m., Head (another Secretary) telephoned from the Hotel Europe that he had just seen two civilians killed, and Lady Sybil Gray from the Anglo-Russian Hospital that a civilian had been killed on the Nevski in front of the hospital.

Tereshchenko[2] came in and told us that the labour

---

[1] The Chief of the Artillery Department. See p. 273.

[2] A rich sugar-refiner from Kiev, who had been educated at Oxford and spoke English fluently. He had been working during the war in the Military Industrial Committee on the South-West Front.

Three Months Preceding the Revolution

leaders had been to Guchkov in the morning; they were getting uneasy as the workmen were getting out of hand. Martial law was proclaimed at 11 a.m. following the murder of a police inspector. However, Tereshchenko thinks that the weather is "too cold for revolution" and that things will settle down.

I dined with the W——s, near the Marinski Theatre, and found them very pessimistic. Madame W——'s brother said he had mingled with the crowd and had found them far more determined than in the disturbances of 1905. I walked back with him at midnight, and found the streets deserted except for Cossack patrols and a few lonely policemen.

Sunday, March 11th, 1917.   PETROGRAD.

I spent the morning with Markozov,[1] whom I interrupted at breakfast at 10 a.m.

There is no lack of rye flour in Petrograd. It is true that from the 1st till the 9th only 210 wagon-loads of flour came in, but 100 wagons came in yesterday, and there are now 459,000 puds in store, in addition to quantities estimated at 20,000 puds with the bakers and perhaps 100,000 puds with private consumers.

The Food Controller issues 35,000 puds a day to such bakeries as promise to bake, and if this quantity was really baked it would be sufficient for the population.

However, there is practically no wheat flour, and there are no oats or hay. We have 60,000 horses. The market price of oats is Rs.9 per pud and of rye flour only Rs.2.80. With fuel at its present price (Rs.40 per sagene instead of Rs.5), the baker's trade has ceased to be profitable, and the baker prefers to sell the rye flour issued to him. The

---

[1] A personal friend, a retired captain of the Lancers of the Guard, who had been wounded three times in the Chinese and Japanese campaigns, and had then retired and gone into business. In the Great War he had gone to the front in charge of the Red Cross in Rennenkampf's Army and had been taken prisoner in the retreat from East Prussia. A member of the Municipal Council, a good business man and a sterling good fellow, now a refugee in England.

horseowners buy it and feed their animals on it in lieu of oats. Hence a shortage of baked bread.

Owing to the defective system of bread cards, individuals have been able to collect several rations by joining several queues in the day. Hence a still further shortage of baked bread, and workmen who have been at work all day have to go to bed hungry. Hence natural discontent.

Markozov thinks that an error was made in fixing the price of grain too low. Hence the peasants have been holding for a rise. Efforts have been made to increase the reward to the agriculturist, but the real desideratum is confidence in the Government and a patriotic sense of duty. It is impossible for the Government to requisition as the grain is scattered in small peasants' farms. It requisitioned from the merchants in 1914, and the latter have since then avoided the accumulation of large stocks.

The Government had hitherto refused to hand over the arrangements for the distribution of food to the Municipality, because the latter insisted on nominating representatives of all classes to the distribution committees, and this, the Government maintained, required the passing of a new law! The Municipality also insisted on buying grain themselves. These two points have now been conceded, and the " new law " will be passed as quickly as possible!

The question is whether the Municipality, now that everything is in a mess, will be able to restore order from chaos.

When I left Markozov's house the chauffeur pointed to a huge crowd coming down the street a few hundred yards off—the workmen from one of the outlying factories coming in to demonstrate. We were stopped by troops from returning through the Nevski, but made a wide detour and got home to lunch.

At 2 p.m., by appointment, I went to see Rodzianko in his house on the Furshtadskaya. He was much excited. He had heard that there was shooting on the Nevski and had sent his chauffeur to enquire. The chauffeur returned before I left and reported that all was quiet.

Rodzianko said that things could not go on as at present, and that he was going to telegraph to the Emperor to demand a Government representative of the people. I suggested that if the Emperor were to entrust Krivoshen[1] with the formation of a Government the people would be satisfied. He said that he could not discuss names, but thought that in some ways Krivoshen would not be the best man. I asked if he would take on the job himself. He said that he would; that he might make mistakes, but that he would do something.

He suggested, as usual, that the British and French Ambassadors should make joint representations.

Rodzianko thinks that the present crisis will pass, but that similar crises will infallibly recur, as the people are sick to death of the Government.

I am afraid Rodzianko is only big in physical bulk!

Shooting commenced at 4.30 p.m. on the Nevski opposite the Anichkov Palace. Casualties are estimated at fifty.

I saw the Ambassador at the Embassy. He looks much fitter after his change, but has come back to anarchy.

---

[1] A former very able Minister of Agriculture of Liberal sympathies.

CHAPTER XVIII

THE RUSSIAN ARMY ON THE EVE OF THE REVOLUTION

IN the autumn of 1916, eleven new twelve-battalion divisions, numbered 128-138, were formed, partly on cadres detached from regular divisions, but chiefly from depot units and Opolchenie. Of these five divisions, Nos. 128, 135-138 were formed on the Northern Front, and the remaining six—Nos. 129-134—on the Western Front. This added 132 battalions to the fighting strength.

In January, 1917, the Supreme Command issued orders for the formation of a large number of additional divisions and for the simultaneous re-organisation of the existing infantry in divisions of four three-battalion regiments, only the Guard divisions and those on the Caucasian Front retaining the normal Russian sixteen-battalion organisation.

Each four-battalion regiment in a corps with two divisions detailed one and a half battalions to form a third division, completing the parent regiment to three-battalion establishment from drafts.

Each four-battalion regiment in corps with three divisions detailed one battalion to form a new fourth division.

In the former case the new organisation gave thirty-six battalions to the corps instead of thirty-two—a net gain of four battalions. In the latter case the reorganisation brought with it no increase of strength, but involved merely a tearing asunder of existing organisations.

G.O.O. Corps were ordered to arrange for the provision of a machine-gun section of eight Maxims for each regiment in the new divisions, and parent regiments had to provide men for the new communications, sapper, mounted scout and trench gun detachments, and for the non-combatant company, for the regimental police, and for the detachment for collecting rifles.

It was calculated that the scheme would provide by the middle of March sixty-two new divisions, or a total net gain of 188 battalions to the four fronts of the Western Frontier.

No provision was made for the equipment of the new divisions with artillery, and, as a matter of fact, very few of them received any guns.

The scheme was General Gurko's, and there was a great difference of opinion regarding its soundness. It is true that a twelve-battalion division is a more convenient tactical formation than a sixteen-battalion division, and the arrangement made it easier to withdraw divisions periodically from the trenches for a rest. The allocation of guns to each division was thought to be of less importance in trench warfare, as the guns could remain in position while the infantry went back to rest. On the other hand, most officers considered that in the then condition of the Russian army the reorganisation was a grave mistake, for it demanded additional skilled personnel, such as sixty-two divisional commanders, sixty-two good staff officers and 248 regiment commanders, that was exceedingly difficult to provide, and also much additional technical equipment, such as telephones and transport.

Men like Zaionchkovski, who had returned to the command of the XVIIIth Corps, laughed at the scheme. In re-arranging his three sixteen-battalion divisions in four twelve-battalion divisions he said he felt like the Berdichev Jew, who, when one day walking into the country, saw two highwaymen approach, and taking off his hat and placing it on a stick, cried out: "Now we are two!"

In the early winter the greater part of the Rumanian army had been withdrawn to reserve to reorganise and train under the able supervision of General Berthelot and a large staff of French officers. A "Rumanian Front" was formed, under the King of Rumania, with General Sakharov, late Commander of the Army of the Danube, and his Chief of Staff, General Shishkevich, as Chief of Staff and Assistant Chief of Staff respectively. The Army of the

Danube had been rechristened "the 6th Army," and General Ragoza had taken the Staff of the 4th Army from the Western Front to form a new 4th Army between the 9th and 6th Armies on the Rumanian Front.

At the beginning of March, 1917, the distribution of the Russian army was as follows:

> G.H.Q. Mogilev. *Supreme Commander-in-Chief:* The Emperor. *Chief of Staff:* General Gurko. *General Quartermaster:* General Lukhomski.
>
> NORTHERN FRONT. Pskov. *Commander-in-Chief:* General Ruzski. *Chief of Staff:* General Danilov. *General Quartermaster:* General Boldirev.
> In Finland and on the coast of the Gulf: 5 infantry divisions and 2 cavalry brigades.
>
> 12TH ARMY. Riga. *Commander:* General Radko Dimitriev. *Chief of Staff:* General Byelyaev. *General Quartermaster:* General Sukhomnin.
> Left flank 10 versts east of Friedrichstadt.
> Total: 21 infantry and 2 cavalry divisions.
>
> 5TH ARMY. Dvinsk. *Commander:* General Abram Dragomirov. *Chief of Staff:* General Vakhrushev. *General Quartermaster:* General Cherni.
> Left flank Pitkelishki, 25 versts south of Dvinsk.
> Total: 11 infantry and 5 cavalry divisions.
>
> 1ST ARMY. Glubokoe. *Commander:* General Litvinov. *Chief of Staff:* General Dovbor-Musnitski. *General Quartermaster:* General Orlov.
> Left flank southern bank of Lake Naroch.
> Total: 8 infantry divisions.
>
> WESTERN FRONT. Minsk. *Commander-in-Chief:* General Ewarth. *Chief of Staff:* General Kvyetsinski. *General Quartermaster:* General Lebedev.

The Eve of the Revolution

10TH ARMY. Molodechno. *Commander:* General Gorbatovski. *Chief of Staff:* General Minut.
    Left flank Dyelyatichi.
    Total: 19 infantry and 1 cavalry division.

2ND ARMY. Nesvij. *Commander:* General Smirnov. *Chief of Staff:* General Gerois.
    Left flank south of Baranovichi.
    Total: 17 infantry and 4½ cavalry divisions.

3RD ARMY. Manevichi. *Commander:* General Lesh. *Chief of Staff:* General Baiov.
    Left flank Rovno-Lutsk railway.
    Total: 12 infantry and 3 cavalry divisions.
    In formation in rear by Staff of Front: 2 infantry divisions.

SOUTH-WESTERN FRONT. Kamenets-Podolsk. *Commander-in-Chief:* General Brusilov. *Chief of Staff:* General Sukhomlin. *General Quartermaster:* General Dukhonin.

SPECIAL ARMY. Lutsk. *Commander:* (temporarily): General Baluev. *Chief of Staff:* General Alexyeev. *General Quartermaster:* General Gerois.
    Left flank north-west of Dubno.
    Total: 21 infantry and 3 cavalry divisions.

11TH ARMY. Kremenets. *Commander:* General Balanin. *Chief of Staff:* General Romanovski. *General Quartermaster:* General Giesser.
    Left flank 8 versts north-east of Brzezany.
    Total: 14 infantry and 1 cavalry division.

7TH ARMY. Buczacz. *Commander:* General Shcherbachev. *Chief of Staff:* General Golovin. *General Quartermaster:* General Neznamov.
    Left flank west of Delatyn.
    Total: 21 infantry and 2 cavalry divisions.

8TH ARMY. Czernowitz. *Commander:* General Kaledin. *Chief of Staff*: General Stogov. *General Quartermaster:* General Pokrovski.
Left flank west of Kimpolung.

Total: 12 infantry and 2 cavalry divisions.
At disposal of the Commander-in-Chief of the Front: 3 infantry and 2 cavalry divisions.

RUMANIAN FRONT. Jasi. *Commander-in-Chief:* The King of Rumania. *Chief of Staff*: General Sakharov. *Assistant Chief of Staff:* General Shishkevich.

9TH ARMY. Roman. *Commander:* General Lechitski. *Chief of Staff:* General Sanikov. *General Quartermaster:* General Kelchevski.
Left flank south of Ocna.

Total: 18 infantry and 3 cavalry divisions.
With the Rumanian Army (24 kilometres of front).
Total: 3 Russian infantry and 1 Russian cavalry division.

4TH ARMY. Barlad. *Commander:* General Ragoza. *Chief of Staff*: General Yunakov. *General Quartermaster:* General Alexyeev.
Total 9 infantry and 6 cavalry divisions.

6TH ARMY. Bolgrad. *Commander:* General Tsurikov. *Chief of Staff:* General Vironovski.
Total: $20\frac{1}{2}$ infantry and 3 cavalry divisions.

CAUCASIAN FRONT. *Commander-in-Chief:* The Grand Duke Nikolas. *Chief of Staff:* General Yanushkevich.
Total on the Front: $15\frac{1}{2}$ infantry and 11 cavalry divisions.

The strength on the five fronts was therefore:

The Eve of the Revolution

	INFANTRY DIVISIONS.	CAVALRY DIVISIONS.
Northern	45	8
Western	50	8½
South-Western	71	10
Rumanian	50½	13
Caucasian	15½	11
Total on active fronts	232	50½

An analysis of the infantry formations shows the following number of divisions and battalions.

	DIVS.	BATTS.
Guard	3	48
Guard Rifle	1	16
Grenadier: 1-3, 5, 6, 1 and 2 Caucasian	7	84
Line: 1-53, 55-57, 59-62, 64-71, 73-84, 100-113, 115-118, 120-138, 151, 153-157, 159-175, 177-194	158	1,896
Rifle: European: 1-8	8	96
Finland: 1-6	6	72
Caucasian: 1-7	7	84
Turkistan: 1-5, 8-10	8	96
Siberian: 1-22	22	264
Frontier Guard	3	36
Trans-Amur: 1-5	5	60
Special: 1-4	4	48
Kuban Plastun Brigades: 1-4	2	32
Don Cossack Brigades	½	8
Composite Caucasian Divisions	2	30
Lett Brigades: 1 and 2	1	16
Serb Volunteer Divisions	2	24
Polish Volunteer Divisions	1	12
Total	240½	2,942

Certain divisions had been annihilated at the front and had not been re-formed. Such divisions were the 54th, 58th, 63rd, 72nd and 114th.

An analysis of the cavalry formations shows approximately the following divisions and squadrons :

DIVISIONS.	SQUADRONS.
Guard : 1-3	61
Line : 1-17	408
Caucasian Cavalry	24
Composite Cavalry	24
Ussuri Cavalry	24
Trans-Amur Cavalry	24
Don Cossack Cavalry : 1-4 and 6	120
Caucasian Cossack Cavalry : 1-6	144
Kuban Cossack Cavalry : 1-4	96
Composite Kuban Cossack Cavalry	24
Terek Cossack Cavalry	24
Orenburg Cossack Cavalry	24
Siberian Cossack Cavalry	24
Ural Cossack Cavalry	24
Trans-Baikal Cossack Cavalry : 1 and 2	48
Turkistan Cossack Cavalry : 1 and 2	48
2nd Composite Cossack Cavalry	24
Caucasian Native Cavalry	18

Total .... 50 divisions or 1,183 squadrons.

BRIGADES.	
Petrograd Frontier Guard	12
Polish Cavalry Brigade	6
1st Baltic and 2nd Baltic	16
Siberian Cossack	12
1st Independent Cossack Brigade	12
1st Composite Cossack Brigade	12
Don Cossack Brigades : 1-2	24

Total : the equivalent of 54 divisions or 1,277 squadrons.

The Eve of the Revolution

After two years and seven months of war the Russian infantry had expanded from a peace footing of seventy divisions and (including the Trans-Amur Frontier Guard) twenty-one independent brigades—in all, 1,282 battalions—to approximately 240 divisions containing 2,900 battalions.

The Russian cavalry had expanded from the peace footing of twenty-four divisions, seven independent brigades and a few minor units—in all, 756 squadrons—to the equivalent of fifty-four divisions—1,277 squadrons—and in addition had supplied a numerous corps and divisional cavalry to all infantry formations.

It had been found, however, that the task of feeding this number of horses was too great a burden for the Russian railways, and at the time of the Revolution all cavalry and Cossack regiments, with the exception of those of the Guard and of those in the Caucasus and in Persia, were in process of reduction from six to four squadron establishment, the dismounted men being formed into rifle divisions, which remained an integral part of the cavalry divisions.

A statement drawn up by the Russian General Staff in the autumn of 1916 estimated the strength in battalions in the *European* theatres of war as follows:

ALLIES.	BATTS.	ENEMY.	BATTS.
Russian	2,343 [1]	German	2,198
French	1,473	Austrian	937
British	793	Bulgarian	229
Italian	801	Turkish	69
Rumanian	72		
Serb	79		
Belgian	82		
Total	5,643	Total	3,433

The length of the Russian Front from Riga to the Black Sea

---

[1] This statement was drawn up when the reorganisation in twelve-battalion divisions had commenced but had not yet been completed.

was estimated at 1,720 versts, the length of the French Front at 750 versts.

On the Russian Front, 100 Russian battalions occupied 73 versts, 100 German battalions 129 versts, and 100 Austrian battalions 93 versts.

On the French Front, 100 French battalions held 40 versts, 100 British battalions held 20 versts, and 100 German battalions 57 versts.

The following comparative table gives some idea of the progress effected in the organisation of technical troops:

	1914	End of 1916
Sapper battalions	39	74
Pontoon battalions	9½	21½
Independent telegraph companies	Nil	50
Wireless units	7 companies	15 divisions (1 per army, with 1 or 2 sections in each corps)
Engineer parks	4	1 per front and 1 per corps
Railway battalions	16	35
Horse-drawn railways	Nil	3 parks
Automobile companies	1	21
Cyclist companies	Nil	39
Motor-cyclist companies	Nil	2, and in addition 41 motor-cyclists in each regular cavalry division
Armoured car sections (4 cars)	Nil	47
Chemical (gas) detachments	Nil	15
Aeroplanes	244	838

Up till the end of 1916 the Russian Government had mobilised for the army, including Cossacks, 14,500,000 men. These were called out in the following categories:

August 1st, 1914:	Regular army serving with the colours.	1,423,000
	Reservists	3,115,000
	Opolchenie	400,000
October 14th, 1914:	Class of 1914	700,000
February 7th, 1915:	,, 1915	700,000
May 28th, 1915:	,, 1916	550,000
August 20th, 1915:	,, 1917	950,000
May 28th, 1916:[1]	,, 1918	700,000
At various dates:	Remainder of Opolchenie 1st Ban. Opolchenie 2nd Ban, *except* classes of 1895 and 1894 (untrained men of 42 and 43 years of age). A certain number of "White Ticket" men (originally totally exempted)	5,962,000
	Total	14,500,000 [2]

Drafts were sent forward to the front in the years 1915 and 1916 as follows:

	1915.		1916.[3]	
	MEN.	HORSES.	MEN.	HORSES.
Infantry	3,094,250	—	2,336,000	—
Regular Cavalry	34,333	38,953	24,278	23,961
Cossacks	65,458	44,605	72,732	53,390
Artillery	70,000	—	80,000	—
Engineers	22,000	—	20,000	—
Total	3,286,041		2,533,010	

[1] On February 16th, 1917, the class of 1919 was called up. Its strength—600,000—raised the total calls on Russian man-power during the war to 15,100,000.

[2] These figures were obtained from General Saturov, the Chief of the Mobilisation Department, on October 23rd, 1917.

[3] The drafts sent forward in the eight and a half months, January to September 15th, 1917, were:

Infantry	1,692,589 men
Cavalry	52,239 men and 16,434 horses
Cossacks	27,363 men and 8,575 horses
Artillery	76,000 men
Total	1,848,191 men

It was impossible to obtain detailed and accurate information of the fate of the fourteen and a half million men who had been taken from their homes. It was said that at the end of January, 1917, there were still serving at the front and on the lines of communication seven millions, while there were two and a half millions in the interior—1,900,000 in the depot units, including training cadres 400,000 strong, and 600,000 men employed on miscellaneous duties, such as guarding railways, prisoners, etc. G.H.Q. proved on paper that there ought to be, and therefore argued that there must be, seven million men on the front. The Staff of the fronts maintained that the number was much less. The Staff of the fronts were probably right, and the balance consisted of deserters in the interior of the country, estimated by the Grand Duke Serge at one million, and possibly amounting to considerably more. These men were living quietly in their villages, unmolested by the authorities, their presence concealed by the village communes, who profited by their labour.

The wounded under treatment were estimated at 550,000, those sent on extended leave or excused all further service at 1,350,000,[1] the missing and prisoners at 2,000,000, and the dead at 1,100,000.[2]

The number of males in Russia of the ages of eighteen to forty-three was twenty-six millions. As only fourteen and a half millions had been called up, there remained in January, 1917, eleven and a half millions apparently still available. This latter figure, however, was said to include two millions left behind in occupied territory, five millions physically unfit, and three millions considered necessary for productive work in rear.[3]

---

[1] The Mobilisation Department on March 8th, 1917, estimated the number of men discharged as permanently unfit at 500,000. The remainder were on convalescent leave of several months.

[2] Information obtained from G.H.Q. and from the Mobilisation Department in October, 1917, accounted for 12,839,125 men out of the 15,100,000 called to the colours by that date. The balance—2,260,875—had presumably by that date deserted to their homes. This estimate gave the strength on all five fronts at 5,925,606, the killed, died of wounds or sickness at 1,290,000 and the prisoners at 2,900,000.

[3]
Railway construction	200,000
Railway working	1,000,000
Munitions and industry	1,200,000
Mines	400,000
Administration, Red Cross, etc.	200,000
Total	3,000,000

The Eve of the Revolution

There remained accordingly only one and a half million men of military age available. Of these only the class of 1919, which was called up in February, 1917, was of good material, and it was evident that the whole one and a half millions would not meet the demands of the front in 1917, if wastage continued at the same rate as in the previous years.

The Government proposed to call up men of forty-three years and over, but twenty-eight members of the Council of Empire and Imperial Duma, who sat as a special " Committee for the Consideration and Collation of Measures for National Defence," petitioned the Emperor, pointing out that the mobilisation of these " old men " would only provide extra mouths to feed and would at the same time " completely destroy the national fabric."

The petition suggested that any additional men required might be obtained by combing out from the lines of communication, and by taking adequate steps to reduce wastage at the front.

It pointed out that in France the strength on the lines of communication, exclusive of depot troops, was to the strength on the front as 1 to 2, while in Russia the proportion was as $2\frac{1}{4}$ to 1.

It asserted that the losses in officers and men in Russia had steadily increased, while in France they had as steadily decreased, and declared that some commanders in the Eastern Theatre " seemed to think they could make up for deficiencies in technique by lavish expenditure of blood."

General Gurko replied to this petition by the Emperor's order on February 22nd. He denied that the proportion of men on the lines of communication was as great as stated, since returns showed that on December 14th, 1916, the proportion of the army in front, including auxiliary services, was 65 per cent. Efforts were constantly made to reduce the number of men in the rear, but the miserable character of the communications rendered further reduction extremely difficult.

He pointed out the impossibility of conscripting nationalities hitherto excused military service. The inhabitants of Finland and the Caucasian tribes must, for political reasons, remain exempt. The number of members of other nationalities was small. Most of them were natural cavalrymen, and it was not proposed to increase the cavalry arm. Of the men formerly excused service in Turkistan, 263,000 had been taken as labourers and only 55,000 remained.

As regards wastage at the front, it was impossible to tie the hands of the Command, " as the result of the war depended on the campaign of 1917." However, the remainder of the 2nd Ban of the Opolchenie and the " White Ticket men " would only be called up as a last resource. General Gurko concluded : " Every effort has been made in the past and will be made in the future to economise men pending the improvement of our technical equipment, but the censure of Commanders in a matter so delicate would undoubtedly affect their spirit of the offensive. The possession of heavy artillery and of technical equipment, even if on a scale inferior to that possessed by the enemy, would, of course, lessen our losses, but of this we cannot dream for the present, at any rate, and meanwhile the enemy is determined to retain the initiative, and drags us into continuous fighting."

Fourteen and a half millions represented less than 10 per cent. of Russia's population, while France had called up no less than 16 per cent. of hers. Russians argued that 10 per cent. of the population in their country represented a greater burden than 16 per cent. involved in France, owing to the enormous distances, the scantiness of the population in contrast to the extent of territory, the lack of railways and metalled roads, the severity of the winter necessitating extra labour in the combating of snowdrifts, the poor equipment in steam power machinery—the number of H.P. in France in 1908 was fifteen times as great as in Russia— and finally the undoubtedly small productiveness, for various reasons, of the Russian labourer in comparison with the labourer of western Europe.

Other Russians confessed that the burden on the national life caused by the withdrawal of 10 per cent. of the population from productive labour was enormously magnified by the national lack of ability to organise. The bureaucracy was at once weak and inefficient, and while shirking strong government, was suspicious of popular co-operation for the national defence. It had totally failed to enlist the sympathies of the masses of the people in a struggle, success in which demanded the conscious effort of the meanest unit of the population.

Probably many of the two million men who at the end of 1916 were classed as " missing and prisoners " were really " killed." Still, the number of prisoners was far larger than it should have been, and was out of all proportion greater than in any of the allied armies. This was owing to a variety of reasons, such as lack of education, the absence of real patriotism, the failure of the officers to enforce real discipline, insufficient training and the lack of proper armament and technical equipment. Again, the number of men " sent on leave or excused further service "—1,350,000—was too large, and showed that the medical control in rear was carried out with a good-natured slackness that would have been suicidal in countries with a smaller population.

Figures regarding Russian armament were as difficult to obtain as regarding man power, and when obtained were often contradictory, the supply departments in rear having a tendency to exaggerate the quantity of equipment they despatched to the front, and the army staffs being perhaps sometimes disinclined to acknowledge the existence of guns they possessed.

The following table, which was copied from an official document in the Artillery Department, purports to give the numbers of the principal types of gun and shell, the number of rifles and of machine guns that existed on the outbreak of war, and the additional deliveries up to November 14th, 1916, *i.e.*, in twenty-seven and a half months of war :

Detail.	On Aug. 1, 1914.	Delivered till Nov. 14, 1916.
3" field guns.	6,672	7,274
,, ,, ,, shell.	5,774,780	37,411,220
3" mountain guns	440	879
,, ,, ,, shell.	657,825	2,979,855
4·8" howitzers	538	1,081
,, ,, shell	449,477	2,706,093

Detail.	On Aug. 1, 1914.	Delivered till Nov. 14, 1916.
4·2″ guns	80	185
„ „ shell	22,344	828,350
6″ howitzers	173	184
„ „ shell	99,910	1,033,751
Rifles	4,290,400	3,726,760
Machine-guns	4,157	23,788

On January 14th, 1917—the Russian New Year—there were on the four fronts, Northern, Western, South-Western and Rumanian, the following guns :

Detail.	On the Front.	Reserve of Fronts.	Total.
3″ field guns, including types of 1900 and 1902, Japanese guns and 90 4-gun anti-aircraft batteries	5,123	938	6,061
3″ mountain guns, types 1909 and 1910	284	54	338
4·8″ howitzers	720	133	853
4·5″ howitzers (British)	228	-	228
4·2″ guns, Q.F.	108	22	130
4·2″ guns, type 1877	199	11	210
6″ howitzers, field type	186	26	212
6″ howitzers, fortress type	172	13	185
6″ gun, Schneider	18	-	18
6″ gun, 120 puds	299	10	309
6″ gun, 200 puds	68	-	68
6″ guns, 190 puds	65	-	65
8″ howitzers	29	-	29
11″ howitzers	14	-	14
12″ howitzers, Obukhov	6	-	6

A comparative table, based on information slightly earlier than the above, classified the guns as " light " and " heavy," and estimated the number in the Eastern theatre at :

The Eve of the Revolution

	LIGHT.	HEAVY.		LIGHT.	HEAVY.
Russian......	5,459	1,946	German..	2,620	3,130
			Austrian	2,000	850
			Bulgarian	330	80
			Turkish ..	120	-
Total, Russian	5,459	1,946	Enemy ..	5,070	4,060

The Allies were at this time said to have on the French front 9,176 "light" and 6,369 "heavy" guns, against the German 4,349 "light" and 5,510 "heavy" guns.

The Russians had only one heavy gun to 989 yards, while in the Western theatre the British had thirteen and the French ten heavy guns per kilometre.

The quantities of the chief types of shell which the Russians possessed on January 14th and the supply which it was hoped to possess by April 14th, when it was thought that active operations would commence, were :

TYPE OF SHELL	ON JANUARY 14TH, 1917.	ESTIMATE FOR APRIL 14TH.
3" field	15,311,000	22,332,000
3" mountain	987,000	1,769,000
4·8" howitzer	1,267,000	1,958,000
4·5" howitzer	254,000	544,000
4·2" gun......................	460,000	581,000
6" howitzer	464,000	780,000
6" gun, various types	129,000	176,000

The rifles on all the five fronts on January 14th numbered 2,290,000, with 420,000 in reserve. These were of the following types :

Russian 3-line	1,800,000
Austrian	350,000
Japanese...........................	260,000
French Gras and Gras Kropatchek	300,000
Total........	2,710,000

It was hoped that the output of Russian factories would add some 400,000 more rifles by the beginning of April. There were large orders in America—Remington 1,700,000 and Westinghouse 1,800,000—but these had so far produced little. Messrs. Remington had received their first order—for 1,200,000 rifles—direct from the Russian Government in January, 1915. The firm had hoped to supply 2,000 rifles a day from September, 1915. The first consignment (15,000) arrived in September, 1916.

The armament of the depot units was varied:

Russian 3-line	223,305
,, Berdan	59,174
French Gras	203,867
Italian Vetterli	225,396
Japanese	19,989
" Mexican "	5,860
German Mauser	12,707
Austrian Mannlicher	16,093
Total	766,391

The Russian Government had given the Government of Rumania 123,000 Vetterli rifles with 62,000,000 S.A.A., and 60,000 Austrian rifles with 25,000,000 S.A.A.

The machine guns on January 14th were:

Russian Maxims	10,831
Colts	1,584
German Maxims to take Russian S.A.A.	390
,, ,, ,, ,, German ,,	81
Austrian Schwartzlose	1,145
Madsen	355
Shosha	100
Hotchkiss	450
Lewis	500
Total	15,436

The Eve of the Revolution

Efforts were being made to reach an establishment of eight machine guns per battalion by the spring, and in addition to raise 100 machine-gun companies, each with twelve guns.

The stock of small arms ammunition on January 14th was:
- Russian 3-line 730,000,000
- Japanese 279,000,000
- Mannlicher 126,000,000

Taking into account the monthly output of Russian factories, the supply of shell and of small arms ammunition promised to be sufficient for the campaign of 1917. Of shell, past experience had shewn the average monthly expenditure in winter and spring to be only 150 per 3″ gun and 4·8″ howitzer, 75 per 6″ howitzer, 100 per 4·2″ gun and 10 per heavier gun.

In periods of continuous fighting, records showed the average total monthly expenditure of the principal types of ammunition to have been:

Type.	Five Months of 1914.	Summer Months of 1915.	Summer Months of 1916.
3″ field gun	464,000	811,000	2,229,000
4·8″ howitzer	35,000	67,000	154,000
Other guns	17,000	33,000	152,000
S.A.A.	76,500,000 [1]	56,500,000	140,000,000

Historians of the war have a right to complain of the lack of patriotism or rather of education in the idea of nationality, which allowed millions of Russians to give themselves up as prisoners to replace able-bodied Germans in the fields and factories of the Central Powers. They should have nothing but admiration for the chivalrous strategy of the Russian Supreme Command.

The Grand Duke Nikolas, and later the Emperor, had a single guiding idea—to do their utmost with the means at their disposal to lighten the burden of the Allies in the West.

---

[1] In 1914 no less than fifty millions S.A.A. were returned from the front to Warsaw Arsenal to be cleaned. This quantity was, of course, collected during advances following successful engagements, and gives some idea of the amount that must have been lost in retreats.

In 1914, during the actual mobilisation, the line of strategical deployment was advanced solely in order to withdraw pressure from France. The 2nd Army was sent half mobilised to its destruction in East Prussia, but its invasion and that of the 1st Army sent trainloads of fugitives to Berlin, who shook the nerves of the German Supreme Command into detaching force from the decisive theatre as early as August 20th. Russians claim that if this force had remained in the Western theatre it might well have turned the scale at the battle of the Marne.

Meanwhile, in Galicia, Russian troops established at once a superiority over the Austrians which they maintained till the end of the war.

Throughout the autumn and winter of 1914, after the combatants in the Western theatre had settled down to trench warfare, in spite of the severer climate, the war of movement and strenuous fighting continued over a large part of the Eastern theatre. The great transfer of force to the Vistula, culminating in the victory of Warsaw, the relief of the 2nd Army by the 5th Army at Lodz, the operation of Prasnish, were deeds worthy of the best traditions of the Imperial Russian Army.

Then shell and rifles began to fail, and the Russians had to struggle alone through the bitter tragedy of the retreat of 1915, their Western Allies being unready as yet to render them effective assistance.

In the autumn of 1915 the allied prospects in the Eastern theatre looked black indeed, but in the spring of 1916 the Russian " grey great-coats " came again grandly, and the Russian Supreme Command held the initiative till the intervention of Rumania increased its liabilities without adding to its strength.

Its main operations were an unsuccessful attack in March on the Northern and Western Fronts, delivered under impossible weather conditions with the object of withdrawing pressure from the French at Verdun, and in June, on the South-West Front, a successful offensive, which was launched originally merely as a demonstration to detach Austrian battalions from the Italian front in the Trentino.

" Brusilov's offensive " was the outstanding military event of

The Eve of the Revolution

the year. In the extent of territory regained, in the number of the enemy killed and taken prisoner and in the number of enemy units absorbed, it surpassed other allied offensives. Russia, owing to this advance, and the bait of Rumania, absorbed enormous enemy forces. The following figures speak for themselves. England and France were opposed on July 1st, the date of the commencement of the Somme offensive, by 1,300 battalions. On January 1st, 1917, the number was 1,327 battalions. Russia was opposed in the Eastern theatre on June 4th, the date of the commencement of Brusilov's offensive, by 509 German and 534 Austrian battalions; on January 1st, 1917, she was occupying 854 German battalions, 708 Austrian battalions and twenty-four Turkish battalions—an enemy increase in the Eastern theatre of 345 German, 174 Austrian and twenty-four Turkish battalions, as compared with an increase of only twenty-seven German battalions in the Western theatre. This contribution to the allied cause was attained with equipment that would have been laughed at in the Western theatre, and Russia paid the price in blood. Brusilov's armies lost 375,000 men in twenty-seven days in June, and their losses up till the end of October exceeded a million.

On the eve of the Revolution the prospects for the 1917 campaign were brighter than they had been in March, 1916, for the campaign of that year.

It is true that Russia had been forced by the temporary collapse of Rumania to add 400 kilometres to a front that was already too long, but French officers maintained that the Rumanians would soon take their share once more in the struggle—a forecast that was more than justified.

The Russian infantry was tired, but less tired than it had been twelve months earlier. It was evident that the Russian Command must in future squander men less lavishly on the front, but still the depots contained 1,900,000 men, and 600,000 more of excellent material were joining from their homes.

The stocks of arms, ammunition and technical equipment were, almost under every heading, larger than they had been even on mobilisation—much larger than they were in the spring of 1915 or of 1916, and for the first time supplies from overseas were arriving in appreciable quantities. England and France were sending much-needed aeroplanes, and the French were sending some able artillery experts.

The leading was improving every day. The army was sound at heart. The men in the rest of the winter would have forgotten the trials of the past, and would have attacked again with the *élan* of 1916. There can be no doubt that if the national fabric in rear had held together, or, even granted the Revolution, if a man had been forthcoming who was man enough to protect the troops from pacifist propaganda, the Russian army would have gained fresh laurels in the campaign of 1917, and in all human probability would have exercised a pressure which would have made possible an allied victory by the end of the year.

CHAPTER XIX

THE REVOLUTION IN PETROGRAD

Reference Sketch F

I GOT up at 6 a.m. on Monday, March 12th, as the Ambassador had asked me to go with his car to the Baltic Station to meet Miss Buchanan, who was returning from a visit to the neighbourhood of Reval. I returned to the Embassy at 9.30 a.m. and about an hour later drove to the Artillery Department, a large building on the Liteini Prospekt. I was talking to friends there in the corridor on the first floor, outside the office of General Manikovski, the Chief of the Department, when General Hypatiev, the chemical expert, and M. Tereshchenko arrived with the news that the depot troops of the garrison had mutinied and were coming down the street. I heard for the first time that a company of the Pavlovski Regiment had fired on the police on the previous evening and had been disarmed and confined in the Preobrajenski barracks. The Preobrajenski and Volinski Regiments had now mutinied.

We went to the window and waited. Outside there was evident excitement, but no sound came to us through the thick double windows. Groups were standing at the corners gesticulating and pointing down the street. Officers were hurrying away, and motor-cars, my own amongst the number, were taking refuge in the courtyards of neighbouring houses.

It seemed that we waited at least ten minutes before the mutineers arrived. Craning our necks, we first saw two soldiers—a sort of advanced guard—who strode along the middle of the street, pointing their rifles at loiterers to clear the road. One of them fired two shots at an unfortunate chauffeur. Then came a great disorderly mass of soldiery, stretching right across the wide street and both pavements. They were led by a diminutive but immensely dignified student. There were no officers. All were armed, and many had red flags fastened to their bayonets. They came slowly and finally gathered in a compact mass in front of the Department. They looked up at the windows, which were now crowded with officers and clerks, but showed no sign of hostility. What struck me most was the uncanny silence of it all. We were like spectators in a gigantic cinema. Tereshchenko, who stood beside me, told me later that as he looked down on the disorderly crowd, he foresaw all the quarrels and licence and indiscipline that were to follow.

General Manikovski came out and invited Tereshchenko and me into his room. We were soon joined there by General Hypatiev, and by General Lekhovich, who a few hours before had been appointed Assistant Minister of War.

Hypatiev asked me if I reported such things to England, and I said that I certainly did. He seemed overcome by the shame of the mutiny.

Soon we heard the windows and door on the ground floor being broken in, and the sound of shots reached us.

The telephone rang and Manikovski took up the receiver. " They are shooting at the Sestroretsk Works, are they ? " he roared in his great voice. " Well, God be with them ! They are shooting at the Chief Artillery Department too ! "

An excited orderly rushed in : " Your High Excellency ! They are forcing their way into the building. Shall we barricade your door ? " But Manikovski had kept his nerve, and said : " No. Open all the doors. Why should we hinder them ? " As the orderly turned away, astonished at this new complaisance, Manikovski sighed, and said to me with the characteristic Russian click of worried anger : " Look what our Ministry has brought us to ! "

Tereshchenko went out, and most of the officers were leaving the Department by a back door. Hypatiev and I went to the staircase and looked over the banisters. Down on the ground floor, soldiers were taking the officers' swords, and a few hooligans were going through the pockets of coats left in the vestibule.

I went down and found a N.C.O. of the Preobrajenskis, who was ordering his men to take only the swords and to steal nothing. I told him who I was, and he helped me on with my coat. I returned upstairs and found Manikovski had gone.

A party of soldiers was almost timidly breaking the glass of one of the arm-stands to take out the rifles—specimens of the armament of other nations, that were without ammunition and would be of no use to them. As they went off, proud of their capture, an officer caught the arm of one of them—a young soldier with a straight, honest face—and remonstrated with him, and I heard the boy reply: " I could not help it. They forced me."

I descended the stairs and my N.C.O. gave me a couple of men to escort me through the crowd. Out in the street a ragged individual expressed his delight with much gesticulation. He yelled: " They used to beat our friends in the prison over there, to beat them with rods ! "

A hundred yards further we met the French Military Attaché, Colonel Lavergne, who was on his way to the Artillery Department in search of some prosaic details regarding the output of shell. My escort recommended him to turn back and we walked together to the French Embassy. There, as the men left us, we stood a moment on the Quay, and looked back at the stream of troops now crossing the bridge to liberate the prisoners in the Krestovski prison, and Lavergne suddenly asked me if those men were mutineers and if my escort had been mutineers. They had been so orderly and friendly that he had never dreamed that they were anything but loyal troops !

I walked on to the British Embassy. The Ambassador had gone, as usual, with the French Ambassador to the Ministry of Foreign Affairs. I telephoned to him that a large part of the garrison had mutinied and was in undisputed control of the Liteini Prospekt. I heard him repeat my message in French to the Foreign Minister M. Pokrovski, and to the French Ambassador.

I expected Colonel Engelhardt to lunch, so walked back to my flat. Engelhardt, of course, did not come, for he, with other prominent members of the Duma, was busy trying to bring the torrent of anarchy under control. He had been appointed Commandant of Petrograd.

On the 11th M. Rodzianko had telegraphed to the Emperor: "Position serious. Anarchy in the capital. Government paralysed. Arrangements for transport, supply and fuel in complete disorder. General discontent is increasing. Disorderly firing on the streets. Part of the troops are firing on one another. Essential to entrust some individual who possesses the confidence of the country with the formation of a new government. There must be no delay. Any procrastination fatal. I pray to God that in this hour responsibility fall not on the wearer of the crown!"

The same day the President of the Duma sent copies of this message to the Commanders-in-Chief of all the fronts, asking them to support his appeal to the Emperor.

Immediate replies were received from General Ruzski and from General Brusilov. Ruzski telegraphed simply: "I have received your telegram. I have carried out your request." Brusilov's reply was more cautious: "I have received your telegram. I have done my duty to my country and to the Emperor."

Early on the 12th, Rodzianko sent a second message to the Emperor: "The situation is growing worse. Immediate steps must be taken, for to-morrow will be too late. The final hour has come when the fate of the country and the dynasty must be decided."

The Emperor made no reply. It was stated afterwards that he considered the advisability of granting a representative ministry, but with the retention in his own hands of the right to appoint the Ministers of Foreign Affairs, of War and of Marine.

On Monday morning, the 12th, a decree was published by Prince Golitzin, the President of the Council of Ministers, proroguing the Council of Empire and the Imperial Duma from March 11th, "till a date not later than the middle of April, in accordance with special circumstances." This order had been signed by the Emperor at G.H.Q. on March 10th.

The Duma meeting on the morning of the 12th resolved to

disregard the Imperial order and to remain in session. Its members, however, were extremely nervous, for events were moving rapidly and they had no control.

At 1 p.m. a delegation of the mutineers visited the Tauride Palace to ascertain the attitude of the Duma. It was met by M. Rodzianko, who defined the main task of the moment as the replacement of the old régime by a new government. In the solution of this problem he said that the Duma would take the most active part, but to enable it to succeed, before everything, order and tranquillity were necessary.

An hour later strong detachments of mutineers visited the Tauride and were met and harangued by the Socialist members, MM. Kerenski, Chkheidze and Skobelev.

About 2.30 p.m. a " Temporary Committee for the Preservation of Order" was formed, representative of all parties except the Extreme Right. This was presided over by M. Rodzianko, and included two Conservatives, three Moderates, five Cadets and Progressives and two Socialists—MM. Kerenski and Chkheidze.

After lunch I went to see General Khabalov, the Commander-in-Chief of the District, and passed on the way the still loyal part of the Preobrajenski and the Keksgolmski Regiments, which were marching in good order under their officers into the Winter Palace.

I found General Khabalov at the Prefecture, a building which has since become notorious as the seat of the Bolshevik Extraordinary Commission. On the street outside a party of Cossacks stood dismounted beside their horses. I climbed the stairs to the first floor. In the centre room of the long group of apartments a few Guards officers were seated, silent and depressed. Young officers of Cossacks were coming and going with reports.

From the centre room, where I waited, through the folding doors officers and officials could be seen in the further rooms walking to and fro in earnest conversation. The Grand Duke Kiril was said to be there amongst others, but I did not see him.

General Byelyaev passed and shook hands with his usual courtly smile. I never saw him again.

General Zankevich, the General Quartermaster, talked bravely. He said: "These are only depot troops that have mutinied, and not regulars. Regular troops will very soon put the movement down."

At last General Khabalov came, and I told him that the Ambassador had sent me to ascertain the situation. He said that the position was " very serious," as a part of the Depot Battalion of the Preobrajenskis, the whole of the Volinski, Pavlovski and Litovski Battalions and the Sappers of the Guard had mutinied, and the movement might spread. He thought he could trust the Cossacks, and he said he had telegraphed to the front for troops.

I left the Prefecture with the conviction that the old régime was doomed.

From the Embassy, later, I walked with another British officer to the Liteini Prospekt. On the way we passed a very drunken soldier with rifle and fixed bayonet. The great District Court, nearly opposite the Artillery Department, was blazing. It had been set on fire early in the day, partly perhaps in imitation of the storming of the Bastille, but more, no doubt, with the practical idea of destroying all criminal records. We found a barricade across the street with three guns and some soldiers. I asked if I could go to No. 9 to see some friends, and the sentry said that I might go anywhere if I only gave up my sword. Another man immediately interrupted him with the remark: " These are Englishmen! You must not insult them!" However, the guard decided that it was better not to pass the barricade. One of the soldiers grasped my hand and said: " We have only one wish—to beat the Germans to the end, and we will begin with the Germans here and with a family that you know of called Romanov." The crowds on the Nevski on the previous day had been shouting: " Down with Alexandra!" (*Doloi Sashe!*)

Three men were coming to dine, but Ramsden (one of the secretaries at the Embassy) and Prince B—— sent apologies, the first because all hired cabs had disappeared from the streets, and the latter because, as a prominent member of the Court, he had been advised to remain at home. Only Markozov came, having walked the whole three miles from his house. He brought the news that all the regiments except the Moskovski had joined the movement. After dinner we telephoned to various people, both he, the ex-Guards officer, and I hoping for the success of the Revolution. He left me at 10 p.m. to walk back, but quickly returned to say that there was firing next door, where the headquarters of the Secret Police with its incriminating documents was being burned.

In the afternoon a " News-sheet," drawn up by a " Committee of Petrograd Journalists," was issued with the heading : " Papers are not being published. Events are moving too quickly. The Public should know what is happening." The sheet told of the occupation of the Fortress of Peter and Paul by the revolutionaries and of the liberation of all the prisoners there and in the other prisons. Unfortunately, criminal as well as political prisoners were set at large. The Arsenal had been captured and the arms found there had been distributed to the mob.

The same sheet contained the first news of the capture of Baghdad by the British.

The following paragraphs, read lightly at the time, are of sinister import, in view of later developments :

Sovyet of Working-Men

In the course of the day representatives of workmen, and soldiers and some civilians assembled in the Duma Building. A sovyet of working-men deputies was organised and it was resolved to issue a proclamation.

Proclamation of the Sovyet of Working-Men Deputies

The Sovyet of Working-men Deputies has issued the following proclamation :

Citizens !

The representatives of the workmen, soldiers and population of Petrograd assembled in the Duma announce that the first meeting of their representatives will take place at 7 p.m. to-day in the Duma Building.

All military units that have come over to the side of the

people must immediately select representatives in the proportion of one per company.

Factories must choose their deputies—one for 1,000 employés. Factories with less than 1,000 workmen must choose one deputy each.

> (*Signed*) THE TEMPORARY EXECUTIVE COMMITTEE
> OF THE SOVYET OF WORKING-MEN DEPUTIES.

The prisons were opened, the workmen were armed, the soldiers were without officers, a sovyet was being set up in opposition to the Temporary Committee chosen from the elected representatives of the people—though I did not realise it till some hours later, we were already on the high road to anarchy.

Tuesday morning, March 13th, 1917.

To-day is the critical day. It is a grand sunny day with about twelve degrees of frost (Réaumur). A biting north-east wind would have been better, as it would have kept people indoors.

Ivan, my orderly, arrives with the news that heavy firing is going on on the Viborg Island, and in the Nevski direction. The sailors have come in from Kronstadt to join the movement. Bands of excited men are motoring about in cars with rifles, cheering and being cheered by the populace. Ivan thinks that there is " perfect organisation " ! He says : " Orators have been appointed in the Mikhail Manege, and they are lecturing the people. Anyone can come and go as he likes ! " This seems to him the summit of human happiness.

The telephone does not work. One can only hope for the best. If the officers would only join the movement ! I must go out to try to find out things.

Tuesday Evening.

I made my way to the Embassy and the Ambassador sent me to the Duma. The Canadian railway expert, Bury, and his assistant, joined me and we started on our two miles' tramp through the snow. Half way, a country sledge passed us crowded with peasants in holiday dress. They waved their arms and cheered, and when we cheered in reply, they stopped the sledge and offered us a lift, an old soldier, who smelt strongly of vodka, turning other passengers off the sledge to make room for us. As we drove along, holding on to one another to avoid falling, my soldier friend breathed into my ear that the Emperor was a good man, and fond of his people, but was surrounded by traitors. Now these traitors would be removed and all would be well.

We arrived at the Duma at the moment when the Preobrajenski Regiment was being interviewed by Rodzianko. The whole wide street before the building was thronged with lorries filled with joy-riding soldiers. Our self-appointed guide walked in front of us, waving his hat and shouting: "Way for the British representative!" I felt a fool, and no doubt looked it. The Preobrajenski giants yelled: " Hurrah!"

Our man conducted us to the great Catharine Hall, in a cleared space in the middle of which I saw for a moment Rodzianko and Guchkov. Then I fell back into the crowd, while Rodzianko addressed the men, calling upon them to return to barracks and to maintain order, as otherwise they would degenerate into a useless mob. I overheard one soldier near me say to his companions: " No. We won't return to barracks, for that will mean guards and fatigues and work as before." Then I noticed an expression of sad bewilderment and disappointment come over the face of my guide, who had been listening intently to another man of the Preobrajenskis. Poor fellow! No doubt his simple, honest beliefs had been shattered and he had begun to understand that a revolution was something coarser than the gentle thing he had imagined.

Rodzianko was succeeded by the pale-faced lawyer, Kerenski, who spoke hoarsely from the shoulders of guardsmen. I could not catch much of what he said, but I am told that he is working loyally with the Duma Committee.

The other Labour members have been less patriotic, and are working on purely party lines for the Sovyet. The first news-sheet (*Izvyestiya*) of this organisation, which was published to-day, contains nothing objectionable, but a leaflet, signed " Petrograd Committee of the Russian Social Democratic Labour Party and the Party of Social Revolutionaries " is less pleasant reading for an ally, for it incites to class-war. It commences: " Proletariat of all countries, unite! Comrade workers, the hour has struck! The movement we long ago inaugurated has grown to fruition, and has cleared our way for the realisation of the eternal longing of the proletariat. The people has overthrown the capitalists and in co-operation with the army has annihilated that hireling of the Bourgoisie, the Imperial Government. The place of the latter has been taken by the Temporary Revolutionary Government, which should be composed only of representatives of the proletariat and of the army."

Harold Williams, the *Daily Chronicle* man, whom I met at the Duma, told me that things last night were very bad —worse even than they are at present—but that the Duma Committee is now gradually getting the upper hand.

The scene in the Duma to-day, however, did not show much sign of the re-establishment of order. Few people were working. Soldiers lounged everywhere. There were only about thirty officers, and they seemed ashamed of themselves. One room was being used as an extemporary cartridge factory. In another, bags of flour were piled up for the issue of rations to the troops as they arrived. In another I found poor Engelhardt trying to function as Military Commandant. He sat at a table, on which was a huge loaf of half-gnawed black bread, and tried vainly to make himself heard above the noise of a rabble of soldiers, all spitting and smoking and asking questions.

Suddenly the late Prime Minister, M. Stürmer, was brought along the corridor with an *opéra bouffe* escort, led by a solemn student with his sword at the carry. The old man, wrapped in a huge fur coat, was unceremoniously hustled along. Later came Piterim of the Holy Synod, and then the Assistant Minister of the Interior. Three parties are out looking for Protopopov, but he has not yet been found.

In my walk back from the Duma, I met Tereshchenko, who told me that efforts were being made to induce the officers to come over in order to restore order. Meanwhile, many officers are being arrested. I am probably the only one in Petrograd that now wears a sword!

I lunched at the Embassy. The Ambassador told me that the Emperor had appointed General Ivanov to be dictator. So he is going to fight! In the present state of disorder, a couple of thousand regulars with guns would make short work of the Revolution, but the city would suffer, and what of the munition factories?

All chance, however, of the re-establishment of the old régime had passed. The troops at Tsarskoe Selo, Pavlovsk and Oranienbaum joined the movement. Every trainload of troops that arrived from the front " to quell the rising " went over to the Revolution. At 4 p.m. on the 13th the Admiralty, which had been defended by three companies of the Izmailovski Regiment and some horse artillery and cavalry, was occupied by the mutineers.

At 11.15 p.m. on the same day a student standing in the open space before the Tauride Palace was accosted by an individual in an old fur coat with muffled-up face: " Tell me, you are a student?" "Yes." "I ask you to take me to the Executive Committee of the Imperial Duma. I am the former Minister of the Interior, Protopopov"; then in a lower voice with lowered head: " I also wish well to my country, and that is the reason I have come of my own free will. Take me to the people who want me."

The old régime had gone, never to return, but it remained for every citizen to prevent the new freedom from lapsing to anarchy. The harm was done on the first day, when the officers in loyalty to their oath hung back from the movement. It was impossible for such officers now to return, and the men were fast becoming demoralised, so that only stern disciplinary measures, which there was no immediate power to enforce, could have brought them to reason. On the 13th and 14th they were engaged with the crowd in hunting down and murdering unfortunate policemen, who, it was said, had been posted by the late Government on roofs with machine-guns to use in the event of disorder on the occasion of the opening of the Duma. These operations involved much disorderly firing. Other soldiers in small parties, under the pretext of searching private apartments for arms, terrorised the inmates and stole what they could. Baron Stackelberg, an inoffensive man, was dragged from his house on a false charge of having fired on the crowd, and was brutally murdered.

The mutiny of the 12th would never have developed into a revolution if the Government, by its gross stupidity, had not previously succeeded in alienating every class of the population. If the movement had been at the outset a naked class revolt, it might have been nipped in the bud by an energetic use of the armed force of the military schools in the capital. These schools probably were not used, because the cadets, like everyone else, recognised that matters had come to such a pass that some change was essential. What was wanted in the interests of Russia and of her allies was an orderly transition to constitutional government. The tragedy of the position lay in the fact that the educated patriots of the country, upon whose initiative only such a transition might have been possible, had in sheer patriotism and loyalty to their allies tried to defer revolution till the end of the war. They had hardened their hearts to bear temporarily with whatever evil the Government might impose, lest in the probable disorder of a change of government Russia's pressure on the enemy might be weakened.

Once the revolt commenced, the Duma Committee and its successor, the Provisional Government, did their best according to their lights to save the situation in the interests alike of Russia and of the Alliance.

General Polivanov was in optimistic mood on the morning of the 14th. He said that the revolution was in full swing in Moscow and Kiev, and that no troops now at the front could be trusted to quell the movement at Petrograd.

I told him of my anxiety regarding the rift between the officers and men, and while we were speaking a friend telephoned to him the text of an order issued by the Military Committee of the Duma and signed by M. Rodzianko, calling on all officers to register their names at the Army and Navy Club on the 14th and 15th " in order to organise for the defence of the capital the soldiers who had joined the representatives of the people." While at the telephone Polivanov repeated the order, sentence by sentence, and then returned to me smiling, and said : " You will see now that all will be well." I asked him if he would himself register at once, but he said that he would wait, and " perhaps go in to-morrow." He was evidently not yet sure of the success of the Revolution and was sitting on the fence.

While the Duma was working for the restoration of order, others with whom class hatred was a stronger motive than love of country were making the most of their opportunity.

On March 15th the notorious Order No. 1 was circulated as a leaflet by the " Petrograd Sovyet of Working-men and Soldier Deputies." The order was dated " March 14th," but was only circulated on the morning of the 15th. It ran :

> MARCH 14TH, 1917. TO THE GARRISON OF PETROGRAD!
>
> To all soldiers of the Guard, of the Line, of the Artillery and of the Fleet, for immediate and precise obeyance, and to the working-men of Petrograd for information.
>
> The Sovyet of Working-men and Soldier Deputies has ordered :
>
> 1. In all companies, battalions, regiments, parks, batteries, squadrons and independent military units of various type, and on the ships of the war fleet, committees

are to be immediately chosen consisting of elected representatives of the rank and file of the above units.

2. All military units which have not yet chosen representatives for the Sovyet of Working-men Deputies will select one representative per company, who will present himself with papers of authorisation at the Duma Building by 10 a.m. on the 15th inst.

3. In all their political actions, the troops must obey the Sovyet of Working-men and Soldier Deputies and its committees.

4. The orders of the Military Commission of the Duma are only to be obeyed when they are not in contradiction to the orders and ordinances of the Sovyet of Working-men and Soldier Deputies.

5. Arms of all kinds, such as rifles, machine-guns, armoured cars, etc., should be kept at the disposition and under the control of the company and battalion committees and on no account are to be handed over to the officers, even if the officers so order.

6. On parade or on duty, soldiers are to observe the strictest discipline, but off duty or parade, in their political or private life, or in their life as citizens, soldiers are not to be deprived of any of the rights enjoyed by all citizens.

"Forming front"[1] and compulsory saluting off duty are abolished.

7. Similarly in addressing officers, the use of the titles "Your Excellency," "Your Honour,"[2] etc., is abolished,

---

[1] Forming front was a special form of salute accorded to officers of generals' rank, the private soldier standing at the salute facing the general till the latter had passed.
In the crowded Nevski Prospekt this custom was a nuisance to everyone, and must have been a special worry to a modest general.

[2] In the Russian army a regular form of titles was used by subordinates in addressing officers:
A general was addressed as "Your High Excellency" (Vashe Visokoprevoskhoditelstvo), a lieutenant-general or a major-general as "Your Excellency" (Vashe Prevoskhoditelstvo), field. officers as "Your High Honour" (Vashe Visokoblagorodie) and other officers as "Your Honour" (Vashe Blagorodie).
These forms of address were taught to raw recruits on joining, together with such stock forms of reply as, for instance, " I am unable to know " (*Ni kak ne mogu znat*).
It was always much easier for the Russian soldier to use this form of reply

and these titles will be replaced by the form of address: "Mister General," "Mister Colonel," etc. All rudeness in speaking to soldiers, and especially their address in the second person, singular, is forbidden, and soldiers are obliged to bring to the notice of the company committees any breach of this rule, or any disagreement between officers and soldiers.

This Order is to be read in all companies, battalions, regiments, batteries and other combatant and non-combatant formations.

THE PETROGRAD SOVYET OF WORKING-MEN AND SOLDIER DEPUTIES.

Some of the provisions of this order were sensible and might have been welcomed if they had been issued by the Army Command; other provisions, such as the instructions for the formation of committees, and the incitement to disobey the orders of officers, were calculated to destroy all discipline, and the men who framed them at such a time acted only in the interests of Russia's enemies.

The exact origin of the Order has been the subject of discussion.

M. Stekhlov (Nakhamkes) in a speech before the Petrograd Sovyet on April 12th, stated that the Order was not written by him and M. Sokolov, as had been rumoured, but was the production of "soldier deputies fresh from the street and from the revolutionary barracks. It was to such an extent the work of the masses that the majority of the members of the Executive Committee of the Sovyet only knew of it when it had been already printed." Stekhlov attempted to justify the issue of the Order on the ground that M. Rodzianko had, on the 13th, ordered the

---

than to trouble to think, and its continual repetition became very irritating when, for instance, one lost one's way near the front.

In 1916 a story used to be told in the Russian army to the effect that a British soldier, a French soldier and a Russian soldier, all killed in battle at the same moment, appeared in heaven and were asked by St. Peter why they had fought. The Britisher said: "Because I wanted to beat those damned Germans." The Frenchman replied with gesture: "Pour la France, pour la gloire." When the turn of the Russian came he stood stiffly to attention and said: "Ni kak ne mogu znat." The story had its pathos as well as humour.

troops to return to barracks and to submit to their officers, that some of the officers attempted to disarm their men and that the soldiers demanded a formal acknowledgment of their rights.[1]

Colonel Engelhardt, who on the 14th handed over charge of the Military Commission of the Duma to M. Guchkov, told me later that that day a group of soldiers came to him and asked him to frame an order containing their demands, which were " fairly moderate, but embodied the idea of regimental committees." He went to Rodzianko and Guchkov and explained to them that these soldiers had come to him as representing the Duma Committee, and had not approached the Soldiers' Council which was sitting in the same building. Rodzianko and Guchkov would not hear of the proposal, so Engelhardt returned and informed the deputation that the Duma Committee considered the time unfavourable for the issue of new regulations. The soldiers retired. Afterwards, in the corridor outside his room, Engelhardt met a soldier who asked him what reply had been given to the deputation. When told, he turned on his heel, saying : " So much the better. We will write the order ourselves."[2]

---

[1] Izvyestiya Petrogradskago Sovyeta Rabochikh i Soldatskikh Deputatov, No. 32 (April 18th, 1917).
[2] *Diary, November 22nd,* 1917.

    A statement published by the Temporary Committee of the Duma in the Petrograd Press on or about August 12th, 1917, agrees in general with Colonel Engelhardt's version, but states that the soldiers who came to him were actually " delegates."

    Late in the evening of March 14th, when it had become apparent that all Petrograd was in the hands of the revolutionary troops, soldier delegates from about twenty units of the garrison approached Colonel Engelhardt, the President of the Military Commission, with the declaration that they were unable to trust their officers who had taken no part in the Revolution, and the demand for the publication of an order authorising the election of officers in companies, squadrons, batteries and detachments. The order proposed by the delegates touched the foundations of military discipline to a far less degree than the Order No. 1 which was published later. It provided only for the election of junior officers and for a certain measure of control by soldiers of the domestic economy of units.

    Colonel Engelhardt reported to the Temporary Committee of the Duma, all the members of which, including A. I. Guchkov, expressed themselves categorically as opposed to the issue of such an order, considering it impossible to decide such a serious matter in a hurry.

    Some time later there appeared to Colonel Engelhardt a member of the Sovyet of Working-men and Soldier Deputies, in the uniform of a soldier, but personally unknown to him, and proposed to him as President of the Military Commission of the Duma, to take part in the framing of

The Revolution in Petrograd

These two accounts from widely different sources suggest that the soldiers, after getting no satisfaction from the Duma Commission, applied to the Sovyet, the extremists of which in the absence of the Executive Committee, then in consultation with the Duma Committee, promptly met their wishes.

The Order not only prevented all possibility of the return of the Petrograd garrison to any sense of duty and discipline, but, being printed in millions, became a printed charter of licence for cowardice and anarchy throughout the armies of the front.

In my daily visit to the Duma on the 15th, I found the officers terribly depressed. They pointed out that the impossibility for men of honour to go over with the men in the first instance, followed by the delay of the Duma Committee in coming to some decision regarding officers' standing, and the issue of the infamous Order No. 1, had made their position impossible.

I saw Rodzianko for a moment and told him that I was frightened that things were taking a turn that might endanger the continuance of the war. He said: "My dear Knox, you must be easy. Everything is going on all right. Russia is a big country, and can wage a war and manage a revolution at the same time."

It was, however, precisely because Russia was a big—and unwieldy—country that the situation was dangerous. In

---

an order to regularise on the new basis the mutual position of officers and soldiers.

On Colonel Engelhardt's reply that the Temporary Committee of the Duma considered such an order to be premature, the member of the Sovyet went out with the words: "So much the better; we will write it ourselves."

M. Vladimir Lvov, Member of the Duma and Procurator of the Synod in the Governments of Prince Lvov and M. Kerenski, has stated that on March 15th he was sitting in a room in the Duma with MM. Guchkov, Milyukov and Kerenski when the Labour member, M. Sokolov, came in and showed them Order No. 1, asking that it should be circulated by the Government. Guchkov read it through and said: "I will never sign it as long as I live"; and then left the room. Milyukov expressed a similar opinion and said: "If you want to circulate it, do so yourselves." M. Lvov protested vehemently. M. Kerenski tried to stop him and followed Sokolov to another room in order to smooth over the effects of Lvov's outburst.

Petrograd there were some 219,000 factory hands and some 150,000 mutinous troops, and these constituted inflammable material that internationalists were working day and night to ignite. Meanwhile the mass of the people that lived in villages was unable to make itself felt.

Leaflets were distributed advocating the murder of officers. The outlook was black on the evening of the 15th.

Rodzianko had prepared for the Emperor's signature a manifesto granting a constitution and a Government to be chosen by the Duma, with Prince George Lvov as Premier, Professor Milyukov as Minister of Foreign Affairs and M. Kerenski as Minister of Justice. The Grand Dukes Mikhail and Kiril had countersigned this manifesto. The Executive Council of the Sovyet interfered, and at last, at 3 p.m. on the 15th, the Duma Committee was forced to agree to a decision that the Emperor should be deposed and the Grand Duke Mikhail should be appointed Regent for the Tsarevich.

A deputation consisting of the Octobrists, MM. Guchkov and Shulgin, went to Pskov to announce the decision to the Emperor. The Emperor resigned in favour of his brother, the Grand Duke Mikhail, both for himself and for the Tsarevich, from whom he could not bear to be parted, first appointing Prince Lvov to be President of the Council of Ministers and the Grand Duke Nikolai Nikolaievich to be Commander-in-Chief.

The text of the abdication, the Emperor's last official act, ran:

> "The destiny of Russia, the honour of Our heroic army, the good of the people, the entire future of Our beloved Motherland demand the prosecution of the war at all costs until a victorious end. . . . In these days that are supremely decisive for Russia, We have considered it as a duty laid upon Our conscience to facilitate for Our people the close union and rallying of all popular forces for the purpose of a speedy achievement of victory, and in concert, with the Duma, We have deemed it good to abdicate from the throne of the Russian Empire and to divest Ourselves of

The Revolution in Petrograd 571

the supreme power. Not wishing to part with our beloved son, We transmit our inheritance to Our brother, the Grand Duke Mikhail Alexandrovich, and give him Our blessing on his ascending the throne of the Russian Empire."

The Empress was meanwhile at the Palace at Tsarskoe Selo, where she was only joined by the Emperor some days later. Her children were dangerously ill. The news was brought her by the Grand Duke Paul. A chance visitor, a friend of the family, has related since how the Empress came into the room where she was with one of the Grand Duchesses, and, taking her by the hand, said: " Abdiqué," and then: " Lui, tout seul la bas ! "

As a husband and a father Nikolas II was ideal. If he failed as a ruler, the more signal failure of his successors has proved that the ruling of Russia is no easy task.[1]

Discussion continued between the Duma Committee and the Executive Committee of the Sovyet all the night of the 15th, and the republican propaganda gained ground. At noon on the 17th, leaflets were issued with the Grand Duke Mikhail's manifesto—drafted by Lvov and Kerenski—renouncing the throne unless called thereto by the vote of a constituent assembly.

Meanwhile the composition of the first Provisional Government was announced. It contained undoubtedly the most prominent public men of non-official Russia, and its loyalty to the Alliance was beyond question. The Prime Minister and Minister of the Interior was Prince George Lvov, who had been a member of the first Duma, and as President of the Chief Committee of the All-Russia

---

[1] It is strange that a German—Maximilian Harden—should have so far written the truest appreciation of the Emperor's character :

"If the second Nikolas ever had a programme, it was to be mindful of the injunction of his namesake before him, to do on the throne all that in him lay in order to win from the masses that looked up to him forgiveness for the monstrous prerogatives of the Crown. . . . Nikolas Alexandrovich, whom only light minds can already name the last of the Tsars, sought to establish peace firm as a rock, summoned the nations to disarm and banished alcohol from Russia. That he willed these three things history will some day write down to his credit in her book. His conquerors, who gave themselves out to be saviours of mankind, universal Messiahs, have worked in eight months more horror and woe than he wrought in eight years."

Zemstvo Alliance had attained some knowledge of administration. The Minister of Foreign Affairs was M. Milyukov, till banned by the late Government a professor of Moscow University, the leader of the Cadet party in the 3rd and 4th Dumas, a good speaker, a man of courage and learning and a great Russian Imperialist. The Minister of Justice was M. Kerenski, the Social Revolutionary member for the Government of Saratov, an idealist and undoubted patriot. M. Guchkov, who was appointed Minister of War and temporarily Minister of Marine, had fought with the Boers against us in South Africa. As leader of the Octobrists in the Duma, he had been a prominent advocate of army reform, and, during the present war, had been President of the Military Industrial Committee, a sort of non-official Ministry of Munitions. M. Tereshchenko was appointed Minister of Finance.

The political declaration of the Provisional Government contained the following paragraph—evidently the price it had been forced to pay for temporary agreement with the Sovyet:

> Paragraph 7.—The military units who took part in the revolutionary movement will not be disarmed or transferred from Petrograd.

It seemed necessary to ascertain the real attitude of the Labour Group towards the war, so I asked Harold Williams, who knew everyone, to introduce me to some of its leaders. As we entered the Duma on the 16th we ran into M. Sokolov, a barrister and socialist labour leader. I told him that with all our sympathy for the struggle for freedom, we were naturally anxious regarding the continuation of the war. I assured him that, from the knowledge gained by constant intercourse with the officer class during the war, I was convinced that practically all of them had been in favour of political change, but pointed out how difficult the position of the Russian officer had been made by the issue of Paragraph 7 of the political declaration of the Provisional Government, and by Order No. 1 of the Sovyet. I handed him a copy of this latter Order, and told him I considered it a deathblow to the Russian army (*gibel russkoi armii*).

Regarding the Government manifesto, Sokolov replied that it was essential to retain in Petrograd troops that the new Government could trust. Their number he estimated at from 60,000 to 80,000, and this he considered a drop in the bucket in comparison with the " eight millions at the front." This was, of course, mere prevarication. If the Government wanted troops it could trust, it and the Revolution would have been infinitely safer, protected by a single disciplined regiment, than by the armed mob into which the Petrograd garrison had degenerated. The truth was that the men of the garrison dreaded the idea of fighting at the front, preferring to remain in the capital to demonstrate, to rob defenceless women and to intimidate weak-minded Ministers, and, with the connivance of the Sovyet, they had forced their will on the Government.

Sokolov took Order No. 1 to the window and donned his pince-nez to read it, as if he had never seen it before.[1] He then said that it was " not very well written," but he justified the order regarding the retention of arms on the ground that it was not yet known which officers could be trusted.

He assured me that there would now be an unbounded enthusiasm for the war that would mean much. There would be no more bribe-takers or traitors. The Labour Party generally was in favour of continuing the war till the enemy was driven from all occupied territory, but was opposed to all conquests, not excluding even the Dardanelles. For this reason they disliked the appointment of Milyukov to the Ministry of Foreign Affairs, as it was known that he wanted the Dardanelles to be Russian.

Sokolov said that it was hoped that work in the munition factories would be resumed on Monday, the 19th. Appearances, however, were against such optimism. The " heroes of the Revolution " seemed only to want to bask in the limelight, and could not understand an ally's anxiety to " get on with the war." One soldier said to me in the Duma on the 16th : " We have suffered 300 years of slavery, you cannot grudge us a single week of holiday ! "

---

[1] This was interesting in view of the general belief that Sokolov wrote the Order himself.

Saturday, March 17th.

I walked to see the Ignatievs.[1] He was very pessimistic. He told me that the Preobrajenski Battalion had elected three commanding officers in a single day, and one of them was an ex-suisse from the Sergievskaya Street. The commander nominated by Rodzianko had been placed under arrest by the men. Ignatiev said : " I have served with the troops for thirty-two years, and they can say what they like, but they will never be able to discipline these men again." I fancy the Government understands this, but it is desperately afraid of bringing matters to a head, and besides, it has no power. Ignatiev took me to the window and pointed out the barricade in the Liteini, saying that Guchkov had ordered its removal, but the men had refused to comply. Poor Countess Ignatiev gave me her jewellery in a parcel and letters to send to her mother and children in Switzerland if the worst happened. I am very sorry for them, and tried to cheer them, but it was difficult to pretend that they are in no danger.

They told me that Count Mengden had been killed at Luga in a particularly brutal manner. His men asked him if he recognised the new Government. He said that he must first telegraph to Petrograd for instructions, and they stabbed him to death.

Poor Bezobrazov[2] was arrested and taken to the Duma, his shoulder-straps torn off. He was kept for a whole night in a chair, and was then released to walk the three miles back to his home with his gouty legs—poor old General, who never in his whole life willingly did anyone any harm !

Lavergne tells me that the commander of a brigade due to embark for France in a month came to him to-day and said that of the 3,500 men he had at Peterhof only fifty

---

[1] A retired cavalry General, son of a former Russian Ambassador at Constantinople, and brother of the Minister of Education in a late Government.

[2] See Chapters IV., VI., VIII. and XV. He escaped later to Stokholm.

remained; about 1,000 were in Petrograd doing nothing, and some 2,000 had probably gone home!

Another colonel told him that his men were being corrupted fast by socialist or anarchist speakers, and suggested that we might go into the barracks to try to talk to the troops.

Bruce's [1] quarters have been broken into twice by soldiers, who stole his wine.

I paid the last of my daily visits to the Duma on the 17th. On the following day the new Ministers commenced to function in the ministries where the Emperor's nominees had presided a week earlier. They hoped to be able there to do some work without constant interruption from the soldier mob. The Sovyet continued to sit at the Tauride Palace, and the crowd there grew somewhat less as the demonstrators grew too lazy even to demonstrate. The dirt in the rooms and passages grew greater. The sentries, who had been quick to demonstrate the new freedom by lolling against the walls, now sat on chairs or lay on the ground.

There was everywhere a passion for speech, the right to which had been so long denied, and a moment of silence seemed to every-one a moment lost. There were continual "meetings" in the streets, and these gradually multiplied in number and decreased in volume—a development popular in that it enabled more men and women simultaneously to hear the sound of their own voices. A new verb was coined, "*mitingovat*," to attend meetings. A man would ask his friend what he was going to do that evening, and the reply would be: "I will attend meetings a little" (*Ya nemnogo mitinguyu*).

Monday, March 19th, 1917.

Yesterday morning I went to see Guchkov, and told him that I was telegraphing home to recommend that no more war material should be sent to Russia till order was restored at Petrograd. He agreed, and said he hoped the

---

[1] First Secretary of the British Embassy.

Ambassador would represent this officially in order to strengthen the hands of the Provisional Government. He also asked me to represent that any attempt on the persons of the Emperor and Empress would be very badly received in England.

He said: " We have not won the game yet. The Sovyet interferes in everything. However, things are getting gradually better; they are better to-day than they were yesterday, and they were better yesterday than they were the day before."

I lunched at the Embassy, and after lunch was bombarded by officers who wanted to join the British army, first one from the Academy, then three from the Warsaw Lancers, then Madame P——, the wife of a friend in the Artillery Department. I had to tell them all that I could do nothing to help them. Madame P—— said that in the Artillery Department the clerks are trying to elect the chiefs of sections! The same thing is going on at the Okhta Powder Factory. Men place officers " under arrest " to stand for two hours with drawn swords.

Guchkov's secretary, Khlopitov, told me that an officer had shot himself at the Duma. Another officer in the Preobrajenskis first shot his wife and then shot himself.

There is only one man who can save the country, and that is Kerenski, for this little half-Jew lawyer of thirty-one years of age has still the confidence of the over-articulate Petrograd mob, who, being armed, are masters of the situation. The remaining members of the Government may represent the people of Russia outside the Petrograd mob, but the people of Russia, being unarmed and inarticulate, do not count. The Provisional Government could not exist in Petrograd if it were not for Kerenski.

I went to see him to-day at 9 a.m. He is so overwhelmed with work that he could not see me at any other hour. This is a welcome change from the old régime, when it was impossible to see anyone before 11 a.m.

The Revolution in Petrograd 577

The huge Ministry of Justice, deserted by all the old officials, seemed empty. To Harold Williams and me the new Minister's footsteps sounded hollow, as he walked to meet us through perhaps a hundred yards of reception apartments.

Kerenski seems shrewd, energetic and a man. He has a certain charm of manner.

He spoke repeatedly of his sympathy for England, and said that at the time of the Boer war he was one of the few Russians who had stood up for England.

He is in favour of the continuance of the war, but without any idea of conquest. He says Milyukov has no tact, and we are not to believe him when he says that Russia wants Constantinople. He, Kerenski, wants the internationalisation of the Straits and self-government for Poland, Finland and Armenia, the latter as a separate entity from the Caucasus.

He is instituting a search for proofs of the correspondence of the Romanov family with Germany.[1]

As long ago as September 2nd, 1914, he had prophesied that Russia would only win the war if there was a successful revolution in the middle of the war.

He said that there was a certain amount of friction with the Duma, who wanted to control the Provisional Government, but this would be avoided by giving important missions to prominent members of the Duma to visit distant parts of the Empire!

He allowed that the present position with two Governments was impossible, and assured us that the Sovyet was losing ground.

He thought that I would see the men back at their drill in less than a week. The factories were to restart work to-day. Full pay was to be given for the period of the

---

[1] Though he searched for months with all his natural vindictiveness, he found no proofs, for the simple reason that none existed. The Emperor, the Empress and their family lived and died in complete loyalty to the Alliance.

late strike. An eight-hour day was to be declared, but machinery was to be kept working the whole twenty-four hours.

There had been alarming telegrams from Alexyeev telling of disturbances on the Northern and Western Fronts on the receipt of the news from Petrograd. Kerenski hoped the Germans would try to advance, for that would bring the officers and soldiers together.

I asked what would be done with the Emperor, and he said he would go to England,[1] but that he, Kerenski, would like to know whether our Government would agree to discountenance any attempt from England at a counter-revolution. Representatives from the regiments at Tsarskoe Selo had come to Kerenski, and he had placed them on their honour that no attempt should be made on the Empress.

The Grand Duke Nikolas will not be retained as Commander-in-Chief, and probably the Grand Duke Serge also will retire, owing to the feeling against the Imperial Family. Kerenski fully understood that the Allies would like the Grand Duke Nikolas to be retained, but the soldiers were against it, and there was a general feeling amongst the Left that, with Guchkov as Minister of War, his retention would lead to the re-establishment of the Dynasty.

I pressed the necessity of making each regiment swear allegiance to the Provisional Government, pending the decision of the Constituent Assembly as to a permanent constitution. He made a note of this, and asked me to speak to Guchkov

Guchkov received me at 11 a.m., together with General Kornilov, who had just arrived to take command of the Petrograd Military District. They both welcomed the suggestion that British officers who spoke Russian might be of use in barracks to reason with the men. Kornilov

---

[1] This was prevented by the Sovyet.

said that units would have to be brought to some sort of order before the oath was administered.[1]

Kornilov commenced work yesterday by visiting the Volinski Battalion, the most turbulent of the lot.

Thornhill and I went to see him at 6 p.m., and he asked us to go to-morrow to visit the Semenovski Battalion. We arranged to go at 10.30 a.m. and to do our best. I hope the whole thing will not be too formal and that we may be able to have a sort of conversation with the men.

In the period from March 20th till April 16th, when I left the capital on a short visit to the Northern Front, Major Thornhill and I visited most of the Guard depot units in Petrograd and its vicinity. We were always received politely and we were always cheered; we were often tossed by the men in the traditional Russian way, and chaired to our car in the street. We did our best, but, of course, did no good, for any impression we may have made was wiped out in a few minutes by the next agitator.

The procedure in these visits was generally the same. We drove up in the morning, accompanied by some officer from the district staff, and were met at the entrance to the barracks by the colonel and one or two of the officers. We were shown a barrack-room, generally that occupied by the Instructional Detachment, which, consisting originally of picked men, retained some semblance of discipline longer than the ordinary companies. In one regiment we saw raw recruits who had just joined from some remote district of Siberia, their honest peasant faces bewildered by the Bedlam they had come to.

Then we generally collected the battalion committee and a few more soldiers in the officers' mess or in a barrack-room, and distributed to them photographs showing life in the British army in France and elsewhere.

I used then to attempt a short address, telling the men that I had heard in the Duma that the Russian soldier would like to hear something of the discipline and of the life in the British

---

[1] No oath was ever administered, though weeks were wasted in debating its actual form.

army. I told them of the fights in which I had seen their unit at the front, and of how they had suffered from the lack of heavy guns and shell; that England was now sending them heavy artillery, her sailors braving the German submarines to deliver the guns in Russia. Then I pointed out that the Germans were working day and night, while they (the Russians) idled. I asked what use the guns would be if they were not formed into new batteries and sent to the front. If they were not going to be used in Russia it would be better to send them to France, for there at all events they would be used to good purpose, for England would continue the war if necessary for ten years, whatever happened, and England would win in the end.

After some minutes of this sort of thing Major Thornhill used to say some words about discipline in the British army, about our system of training and the relations between officers and men. Then we invited questions, and did our best to reply.

Generally several members of the battalion committee made speeches in reply. They all spoke fluently and well, for the Russian is a natural orator, and with one or two exceptions they were loud in their enthusiasm for the continuance of the war.

In the Railway Battalion there was a pro-German of a vicious type, who asserted that Great Britain only wanted to continue the war for her own selfish ends. This man was not a Russian. A few days after our visit the Commander-in-Chief of the District offered this battalion the choice of remaining a military unit or becoming a labour battalion on the lines of communication, and about 99 per cent. of the rank and file proved themselves men of peace!

In the Semenovski Battalion we had to listen to an interminable speech from a follower of Tolstoi, who extolled the Brotherhood of Nations that he hoped would follow the conclusion of the war.

We found the Volinski Battalion commanded by an ensign, who before the war was an instructor in gymnastics at Warsaw. All the forty regular officers of the regiment had been expelled, and a sentry had been placed on the front door of the mess to prevent them from returning! We were therefore conducted in by the back door. The ensign said that the runaway officers had treated the men and officers like himself, who did not belong to the regiment, " with the greatest cruelty." " In fact," he said, " you will hardly believe me when I tell you that in the mess they had one set of pegs for their coats and another for the coats of attached officers!" It was said that only one officer of the battalion had been killed in the mutiny, the commander of the Instructional Company. He was killed by a non-commissioned officer whom he had struck on the previous night. This man was afterwards given the St. George's Cross by Kerenski "because he had first raised the banner of revolt against the old régime " —a disgraceful attempt to curry favour with the rabble.

The Izmailovski Battalion had expelled its old colonel, who was " strict," and three or four of the officers. The colonel at the time of our visit was as hoarse as any Duma orator from public speaking. He told us that he had established a " Regimental University," in which he delivered lectures himself on the " Psychology of the Masses," while his second in command discoursed on the " Military Law of Various Nations." I ventured to remark that the subject he had chosen seemed rather recondite, but he said that, on the contrary, it was of extraordinary interest. It is easy to imagine how futile such an attempt must have been to occupy and amuse men, three quarters of whom were illiterate. This poor fellow somewhat later commenced writing the regimental orders in verse, and was removed from his command by the district staff.

In this battalion a private soldier, who had been an actor in civil life, proved very talkative. I had asked the men to forbear from " experiments " at such a time, and pointed out that the experiment of electing officers had only been made once, as far as I knew—in the great French Revolution—and the result had been Napoleon. The ex-actor said: " With the ' broad Russian nature ' experiments are possible that could not be tried in Western countries. Russia will find a Dostoievski, and not a Napoleon!"

The " broad Russian nature " was always the excuse for every extravagance. What was wanted was a little narrow common sense.

In the magnificent ballroom of the officers' mess of the Finlandski Regiment we spoke from a daïs surrounded by some 50 officers to about 200 men. Some of the questions the latter put were interesting under the circumstances. One man asked what would be done to a British officer who hit a man in the face. Another asked what the punishment was in the British army for " insulting remarks." I asked for an example of the " insulting remarks," and the reply was : " If an officer came on to parade in the morning and called his men ' a lot of pig-faced cattle.' " I told them that the English language was a poor one, less rich in vocabulary than the Russian.

The officers of this battalion made a poor impression. The men chaired us into the dining-room at 4 p.m., when we had finished our talk, and as we sat down to tea no less than twelve of the officers went straight to resume the game of bridge that they had only interrupted for an hour.

What was wanted was games of another type—some such grand class leveller as football—to bring all ranks together.

Of course, all the best officers had been expelled. The 8,000 men of the Yegerski Battalion had driven away twenty-two of their officers, and were " commanded " by an ensign of six months' service, who before the war had been a lawyer. The 1st Railway Regiment only kept sixteen out of its sixty-four officers, and treated these with contempt.

At Tsarskoe Selo we visited the Garrison Committee, at the time in session in the Garrison Theatre, and found two doctors and two privates sitting at a table on the stage with about 200 officer and soldier " deputies " facing them.

The main idea seemed everywhere to do as little work as possible. One battalion committee passed a resolution that so-called trained men, with eight weeks' service, should work four hours a day, and recruits five or six hours, but any work they did must have been in the barrack-rooms, for no drilling was ever seen after the Revolution.

Meanwhile the Provisional Government was, as Prince Lvov

told an Englishman, "merely a straw rushed along by a turbulent current."

It tried to save the situation by appealing in sonorous rhetoric to the non-existent patriotism of the mob. On March 22nd it issued a proclamation to the "People, the Army, and the Fleet," appealing for unity and work in the face of the enemy. On the same day M. Guchkov and General Alexyeev in another proclamation called upon the men to trust their officers, and stated that the Provisional Government had firmly decided to continue the war to a successful conclusion, and regarded violent or insulting conduct towards officers as shameful and unpermissible.

Yet two days later the *Izvyestiya* (the official organ of the Sovyet) was allowed to publish an article advocating an appeal for peace to the proletariat of all countries, over the head of the ruling classes, in whose interest only the war was said to be continued.

The situation in Petrograd in these ten days had gone far beyond healing by proclamation. Force was required, and force could have been assembled if the Government had contained a single man of will.

The optimism, chiefly of the officials, was extraordinary. M. Kerenski said on the 24th that in eight days everything would be working normally, and he would be able to afford to sleep eight hours instead of the four he had only allowed himself nightly since the Revolution. General Kornilov said on the 27th that he would have the garrison in hand in two or three weeks. On the 30th General Polivanov said that the men were merely mad with their new liberty, and that this phase would pass. On the same day Lieutenant-Commander Romanov,[1] of the Naval General Staff, when asked for his opinion of the effect of the Revolution on Russia's conduct of the war, compared the condition of the Empire before the Revolution to that of a man mortally sick who had been deliberately poisoned by his medical attendant—the late Government. There had been a change of treatment and a dangerous operation, and now the patient lay between life and death, but there was at all events a chance of his recovery.

---

[1] See Chapter X.

On the other hand, Count Ignatiev, the former Minister of Education, frankly feared a Russian Commune. General Sanikov, the Chief of Staff of the 9th Army, thought that in a few days the Sovyet would arrest the Provisional Government, and that then there would be anarchy and massacres, to be succeeded by reaction.

The news from the front was not encouraging. Major Neilson, returning from the 4th Army at Dvinsk, said that one night at 2 a.m. two soldier deputies came to tell the Army Staff that they had done all they could, but that they could control the men no longer, so Neilson and the A.D.C. of the Chief of Staff burned their papers. A French officer described the situation on the South-West Front as " catastrophique."

The pity of it all!—for the great heart of the people was sound really, and the men were most of them merely children. A lady came on a party of soldiers crying quietly in a corner of a church, and asked the reason. They said that they cried because there were no longer prayers for the Emperor. " But," she said, " you have driven him away yourselves!" " No," they replied, " we only made a little mutiny, we did not wish to drive him away at all!"

Colonel Engelhardt suggested that the Provisional Government should invite four prominent leaders from the Sovyet to join the Cabinet, one as Minister of Labour and the others without portfolio. This was at any rate a practical suggestion, and I passed it on to the Ambassador.

Sunday, March 25th, 1917.

The Ambassador is not well yet, but got up at 6 p.m. to announce the recognition of the Provisional Government by the Allies.

Each Ambassador brought his Councillor and his Naval and Military Attachés, and we assembled at the Council of Empire—a weird-looking crew!

Grenfell was replendent with epaulettes. I was common-looking in putties. There was a general atmosphere of depression, and Galaud, the French Naval

Attaché, a jovial fellow as a rule, by way of cheering us whispered that there would soon be a general massacre of foreigners and that we would lose the war.

We filed upstairs and were met and welcomed by M. Milyukov. We wandered into a long room. M. Milyukov fetched the remainder of the Ministry, who stood in an informal group, while Sir George Buchanan, as doyen, made an inspiriting appeal for the re-establishment of discipline in the army and the energetic prosecution of the war. He then delivered a message from Mr. Lloyd George, which M. Milyukov translated into Russian.

The Italian Ambassador, M. Carlotti, associated himself with the "nobles paroles de Sir George" and somewhat bored us by reading a report of an interminable debate in the Italian Chamber on the subject of Russia. Then M. Paleologue had his say. He said that he believed in the patriotism of the Ministry and in its loyalty to the Alliance; he was also told that all the Russians were patriotic, "though appearances were against it."

While the diplomats spoke, the ministry stood looking at the ground, bowing at the conclusion of each speech. I could not think of it as a ministry of victory. I did not like to look at their faces, when they were all looking at the ground; it seemed too aggressive and unfair, so I looked at the ground too, and then I saw their boots. What an extraordinary collection of boots they were! I have never seen such boots!

M. Milyukov replied with a declaration that Russia would fight till her last drop of blood. I have no doubt that Milyukov would, but can he answer for Russia?

When this was over and the groups broke up and mingled, I attacked General Manikovski, who was acting for M. Guchkov as Minister of War. I said that these were merely diplomatic words, but what of the situation at Dvinsk, where Neilson had told me that the men were streaming back from the trenches with the officers powerless to control. I said the same thing to M. Kerenski.

He said that the great preoccupation of the Government was to restore discipline in the army, and more especially in the navy. He spoke of the proclamations issued on the 22nd. But what is the good of proclamations? It seems to me that we are moving straight to anarchy and a separate peace.

A committee consisting of thirty officers, mostly generals, was appointed under the presidency of General Polivanov, and sat for five hours on alternate nights to draw up regulations for the " new discipline." It worked through the Duma Military Commission to ascertain the minimum concessions that the Sovyet would accept. The officer members had to neglect important war duties in order to attend. In fact, the war had gone into the background everywhere. The operations staffs of the armies were more occupied with the " new discipline " than with the enemy.

The French Military Attaché and I attended by invitation one meeting of General Polivanov's Committee on March 26th to reply to questions regarding our army discipline. After four hours' talk it was decided, first, as a concession to mutinous opinion, that promotions in and to the rank of N.C.O., while nominated by the command in each company, squadron or battery, should be made subject to the veto of the men; secondly, that the officers of the Petrograd garrison should be allowed to wear mufti to protect them from continual insult.

I daily saw General Kornilov and his Chief of Staff, Colonel Balaban, an old friend from 1914 days. Kornilov gradually gave up his former optimism. On April 6th he was called to attend a meeting of the Cabinet, and said afterwards that its members showed great weakness.

He was a man, at all events, and feared no one. One day a man of the Pavlovski Battalion asked him sneeringly when he proposed to have a parade, and he replied: " Parade! How do you imagine I should show rubbish like you to the Russian people? As soon as you have established order I will have a parade."

To a man in one of the machine-gun regiments he said: " I

suppose you think that the troops at the front regard you as heroes? Well, I will tell you that they don't; they think you are merely cowards that don't want to fight."

Such remarks must have been trying hearing for men who had suddenly wakened to find themselves popular heroes. The following is an example of the incense they were treated to daily:

> "Greeting to their Soldier Comrades from the Comrades of the Petrograd Gun Factory.
> Greeting to you, Comrades and Brothers!
> Glorious Champions of the liberty of the people! Future generations will bless you ... Of you history will relate: ' That was a generation of heroes, of warriors, of Titans.' "

The 176th Depot Regiment had come in from Krasnoe Selo "to demonstrate," and finding Petrograd more interesting, wished to remain there. Kornilov ordered Lieutenant-Colonel Vilhaminov, who had been elected to the command by the men, to move his regiment back to Krasnoe Selo. Vilhaminov said that the men objected to the barracks there as unhealthy. Kornilov summoned the Commandant of Krasnoe Selo, and in the presence of Vilhaminov arranged for the allotment of new quarters. Vilhaminov then said that he did not know whether the regiment would go or not. Kornilov gave him a direct order to move the regiment to Krasnoe Selo.

The Regimental Committee passed a strongly-worded resolution, condemning "the action of the Commander-in-Chief, Kornilov, who in spite of the protests of its Colonel had ordered the regiment back to Krasnoe Selo. It wished to remind General Kornilov that it was a revolutionary wave that had elevated him to his high estate, and a similar wave might throw him down again." The document ended with the direction that it should be sent to all papers in Petrograd and to the Commander-in-Chief. A deputation brought a copy to the District Staff, but told the officer who saw it that "the matter had so far been kept secret."

Kornilov sent for the deputation and for the Colonel. He

said that he would hand over the latter to be tried by court-martial. To the men he said: "You are wrong when you say that I was raised to my present position by the Revolution. I took no part in the Revolution and I never will. I came here because I was ordered, and any advancement I have got has been solely owing to the bravery of the soldiers of the 46th Division and of the XXVth Corps. I did not want to come to Petrograd, and as soon as order is restored here I will go back to my XXVth Corps on the front, and no one will be gladder than I."

The deputation left the office somewhat depressed.

Monday, April 9th, 1917.   PETROGRAD.

. . . . . .

Thornhill and I attended by invitation a pro-war demonstration. A deputation from the 15th Siberian Division made an excellent impression. Its leader, Schreider, is a regular orator and made a dashing speech. One of the men also spoke, and asked: "Why should we die in front, while you in Petrograd wander round the streets doing no good to anyone?" A member of the Executive Committee of the Sovyet, a low type of Jew, spoke of the eight-hour day as "the banner under which all Europe was marshalling its forces," but a French officer who was present gave him the lie direct by showing how France had given up all her privileges of that kind for the duration of the war. The agitator met with a great deal of opposition and slunk out of the hall.

I arrived at the Embassy to find Kerenski with the Ambassador. Kerenski said that he considered that the Revolution in Russia had brought new capital to the Alliance, as the Russian democracy would act on the German democracy and would bring it to reason without weakening the Russian military machine. He said that all the excitement in the army would pass, and that it would be better as a fighting machine than it had ever been before. There had been propaganda in the army before the Revolution, only it had been secret and no one knew of it.

The offensive which had been prepared for the spring would not have succeeded under the old régime. Russia would never have helped the Allies to win the war under the old régime; now there was a chance that she might, and he thought that she would.

Though there was no assembly in Russia that really represented Russian opinion, Kerenski knew that what Russia wanted was a defensive war, and he hastened to explain that the word "defensive" was used in a political sense and did not exclude a military offensive. He said that the military offensive would not be delayed by any attempt to persuade the German Social Democrats. He allowed that the war must be continued till the German people submitted to the will of Europe.

To the remark that no other country at war allowed its Press to attack its Allies, he replied that the paper in question—the *Pravda*—had no influence and might be disregarded.

He thought that the Provisional Government was now master in Russia, and he found it better policy to allow the Sovyet to die a natural death than to resort to force for its suppression. The Provisional Government could depend on the regiments at Petrograd to quell disturbances, but things would not be allowed to go so far.

He said that we must allow that the Provisional Government was composed not of children, but of grown-up men with brains, who knew Russia, and that its members felt that they were pursuing the only course possible to enable them to gain their ends.

He said there was a strong feeling in Russia that England was treating the new Government with coldness, and this attitude increased its difficulties. He asked that we should facilitate the return of Russian political exiles, providing them with ship accommodation.

Kerenski seems honest, but he altogether over-estimates any possible effect of overtures from the Russian Socialists to the German Social Democrats, and he altogether underestimates the effect of the rot in the Russian army.[1]

I saw Guchkov for a few moments. I said that as an admirer of the Russian army it was difficult for me to sit still in Petrograd. He agreed, but said that the lack of discipline was worse in Petrograd than elsewhere. He was still more worried about the diminution of production in factories. In Petrograd the output of the month March 13th to April 13th showed signs of falling by from one-third to two-thirds of the output of February. If factories in some other places were doing better, it was only because the revolutionary wave had not yet reached them. He acknowledged that it would have to come to a trial of strength with the Sovyet, but the Provisional Government had not yet got sufficient physical force on which it could rely. He asked me to keep this very secret, as the Sovyet had Government cyphers and control of all the Radio stations.

The output of the factories declined chiefly because the men arrested or expelled the engineers and themselves spent most of their time in attending meetings.

Kerenski himself told me that in the first days of the revolution a man in the uniform of a captain of artillery appeared at the Petrograd Cartridge Factory and delivered an impassioned socialistic speech. He was at once elected Chief Superintendent of the factory, and actually attended technical conferences at the Artillery Department for a week, till he was exposed by his assistant as a runaway convict, who, three years earlier, had murdered an officer!

Within ten days of the Revolution the Social Democrat

---

[1] Comments on this interview in the light of after events is scarcely necessary. Russia, even under the old régime, *had* helped the Allies to victory continuously since August, 1914.

To commonsense Allied advice Kerenski, with his colossal vanity, cried "Hands off!" on the ground that he knew his countrymen, whom he imagined to be super-mortals with none of the ordinary failings of human nature. His suicidal pressure for the return of political exiles led to his own overthrow and, a matter of greater importance, the ruin of Russia.

paper *Pravda* (Truth) recommended the Russian troops to leave their trenches and to shake hands with their German comrades. Neither the *Izvyestiya* nor the *Pravda* published any account of or even allusion to the British success in the battle of Arras.

Saturday, April 14th, 1917.   PETROGRAD.

The British Labour Delegation arrives to-day.

Young Lockhart [1] has arrived from Moscow and the Ambassador is taking him with him to visit Prince Lvov.

I wrote out the following note and asked the Ambassador to lay it before Lvov :

"AGITATION IN THE RUSSIAN ARMY

Even in peace time, politics should never be allowed in an army.

The state of the Petrograd garrison is evident. Three-fourths of the officers, including all of the best, have been expelled by the men, who do exactly as they like. No work is being done. No officer dares to give a punishment.

Perhaps the state of the Petrograd garrison is unavoidable, but there seems no excuse for allowing agitators to visit troops at the front. If the visits of politicians, of every shade of opinion, to the army area were stopped, the unfortunate officers might have some chance of restoring discipline before active operations commence. If these visits continue, the Russian army will not be able to pin down the seventy-two German and forty-two Austrian divisions, now in the Eastern theatre, and a large part of these divisions will be added to the 147 divisions with which Russia's allies have now to contend in the Western theatre. In other words, it is Russia's allies that will have to pay for the demoralisation that is being allowed to set in in the Russian army in the field.

---

[1] Acting Consul-General at Moscow.

Discipline is everything in contemporary war. The discipline in the Russian army under the old régime was always less severe than in other armies. If the present agitation is allowed to continue there will be no discipline whatsoever left."

The Ambassador read this declaration to Prince Lvov, who replied that the Russian Army was a better fighting machine than it had ever been before, and that it was quite well able to deal with agitators!

CHAPTER XX

THE NORTHERN FRONT IN APRIL, AND PETROGRAD IN MAY, 1917

THOUGH the average age of the Russian commanders was, grade for grade, younger than that of the opposing German leaders, it had always been considered that the principle of selection had never been given sufficiently free play in the Russian army, and that young and able men had been unfairly kept back.

Guchkov and Alexyeev now made sweeping changes. In a conference at G.H.Q. at the beginning of April, important alterations were made in the staffs of the fronts, several army commanders were retired and no less than twenty-seven corps commanders. Other changes followed.

On the Northern Front, General Ruzski remained Commander-in-Chief, but General Litvinov handed over the command of the 1st Army to General Sukhovnin.

On the Western Front, General Ewarth as Commander-in-Chief gave place to General Gurko, and all the army commanders were changed, Kvyetsinski replacing Lesh in the 3rd Army, Kiselevski replacing Gorbatovski in the 10th Army, and Vesilovski replacing Smirnov in the 2nd Army.

On the South-West Front General Brusilov remained Commander-in-Chief and Baluev was confirmed in command of the Special Army, but Gutor from the VIth Corps replaced Klembovski in the 11th Army, and Byelkovich from the XLIst Corps replaced Shcherbachev in the 7th Army.

At the headquarters of the Rumanian Front, General Shcherbachev relieved General Sakharev as Assistant to the King of Rumania. On the Caucasian Front General Yudenich was appointed Commander-in-Chief vice the Grand Duke Nikolas, and General Prjevalski took command of the Caucasian Army.

M. Guchkov nominated Generals Novitski and Filatev to be assistant Ministers of War, and General Alexyeev summoned Generals Denikin and Klembovski to G.H.Q.

The new Minister of War released from the service all men of over forty-three years of age, and gave permission to men of from forty to forty-three years to go home till May 28th to till their fields. He promised a full amnesty to all deserters who would return by May 28th.

Owing to its proximity to "revolutionary Petrograd" and to the evil influence of the Baltic Fleet, in which anarchy reigned, discipline on the Northern Front deteriorated more rapidly than elsewhere. The events of March 12th and 13th were known the same day in Pskov, but excitement was concealed till the 14th, when copies of Order No. 1 appeared.

In April it was recognised that the Baltic Fleet could not be depended upon to defend the right flank, so the Staff of the 1st Army was transferred from Glubokoe, south of Dvinsk, to Valk on the Pskov-Riga railway to assume control by May 7th of five infantry and some cavalry for the defence of the coast line from near Narva to south-east of the Gulf of Riga.

During my visit to the Northern Front from April 17th till the 18th, I found that although only a single officer had been murdered a large number of officers, and those generally the best, had been expelled by the men. The reason given was sometimes strictness, or refusal to grant leave, and sometimes so extremely silly that it is difficult to explain the invariable acquiescence of the Command in the men's demands.

Colonel Ausen, the Commander of the 1st Lett Brigade, one of the best officers in the army, was forced to resign because, as a good soldier, he took no interest in politics, and General Radko Dimitriev, while sighing over the loss of such an officer, considered it politic to meet the wishes of the men.

The men of a regiment of the 1st Caucasian Rifle Division, when asked why they objected to their commanding officer, said: "He worries us. He wants the regiment to be always first in the division. When we are in the trenches he does not want the regiment to be relieved, and when we are in reserve he wants to get back to the trenches." This officer had to give up his command!

Against another Colonel in the 5th Army three charges were formulated:

> 1. He greeted each company separately, instead of greeting the whole regiment together. (In this he acted according to regulation, but not to the liking of the men, who wanted to get the 'greeting' over so that they might 'stand easy.')
>
> 2. He was always sending men on reconnaissance. "In fact, he was willing to sacrifice the lives of six men in order to gain a single German shoulder-strap!"
>
> 3. When embarking a reconnaissance in boats to cross the Dvina at night, he carried an electric torch, with which it was obvious that he tried to signal to the enemy.

A young officer of the Instructional Company of the 20th Siberian Division told the Divisional Commander that the men wanted to get rid of their commander, because he was "an adherent of the old régime." He quoted three facts to prove his contention:

> 1. He had ordered the speaker to attend church with his company—a manifest defiance of the declaration of the Provisional Government regarding freedom of conscience!
>
> 2. He insisted on evening roll-call.
>
> 3. He refused to allow the men to go to Riga without signed passes.

There was a general illogical mistrust of the Command, and the credulity of the men was fantastic. A N.C.O. of the 144th Regiment told me that he had himself counted 14,000 head of cattle that were driven to the front by order of the old Government in order that they might fall into the hands of the Germans when Vilna was evacuated in September, 1915. The men of the 138th Division expelled the Commander, the Chief of Staff and two out of the four regiment commanders, the objection to two of them being that they had German names—and yet these very soldiers were ready to fraternise freely with the Germans.

The men were childlike in their ignorance. General Yermolyaev, the Adjutant-General of the Northern Front, spent two hours every morning trying to reason with them. Over a month after the Revolution he asked a man just returned from leave what the news was in his village, and the reply was : " Nothing, except some agitators came from another village and said that the Tsar had been turned out, and suchlike nonsense, but we caught them and beat them."

Much could still be done by officers of adaptable temper to regain the confidence of the rank and file, but the methods employed were obviously unsuited to moments of excitement and danger, and in any case involved much waste of time.

The Colonel of the 13th Siberian Regiment was approached with a request that he should allow the men to go to the trenches daily without their packs. He explained how, when a boy, he had tried to mow hay, and on the first day found that he ached all over, but that after working a little every day he soon found out he could mow as well as anyone. He asked if they knew the reason, and they replied in chorus : " Because you got accustomed to the exercise." He explained that it was also essential that they should get accustomed to carry their packs so that they should not tire on the line of march. It was said that the men agreed, and went daily equipped to the trenches, while the men of the regiments on their right and left did not.

On another occasion the same Colonel heard that the men of a company wanted to get rid of their Commander. He went to the company and asked : " You want to get rid of your Commander ? Very good, that is your affair, but tell me, brothers, why you dislike him ? " " He hit one man in the face." " Dear me, did he, and when was that ? " " A year ago." " Now, whom did he hit ? " " He hit Bublikov." " Where is Bublikov? " " Here," said the organiser of the whole affair. " So he hit you, Bublikov ? " " Yes, he did." " That is very wrong. And why did he hit you, Bublikov ? "

April-May, 1917

Bublikov was silent, but some of the men near him smiled. The Colonel repeated the question, and asked if anyone knew why Bublikov was hit. At last the story came out : " It was in the fighting last July. The Captain told Bublikov to go to bring up cartridges, and Bublikov said, ' I don't want to go,' and then the Captain hit him." " And why did not Bublikov wish to go ? " " Because the Germans were firing heavily." " Was it necessary for the company to bring up cartridges ? " " Yes, for there were very few left." " Then Bublikov should have gone to fetch them ? " " Quite right, Mr. Colonel." " Then don't you think the Captain should be forgiven, for he was only thinking of the company being left without cartridges ? " " Quite right, for Bublikov should have fetched them, it being a military duty, but, as the firing was heavy, he did not wish to go."

It was no use appealing to higher feelings, which should have existed but did not. A regiment in reserve near Dvinsk fell in, and the men stood with their heads down, crying: " Peace ! Peace ! " Three members of the Agitation Section of the Army Committee arrived in haste. Two of them made eloquent appeals to the men's sense of patriotism, but they still kept their heads down, bellowing in reply : " Peace ! Peace ! "

The third delegate said : " You want peace, and so do I." A few heads were raised, and one or two men said, " Quite right ! " They thought they had found sympathy in an unexpected quarter. " But I wonder," the speaker continued, " what sort of peace you want, and whether it is the same peace as I want ? I don't want a peace where the Germans will come and take away my land, and one in which the police will come back and hit me about the head, where my cows and my horses will be taken, and I will be left a fugitive without home and without bread. Do you want that sort of peace ? " " No, we don't ! " " Well, I want a peace where we will get more land, and where we will be able to live as we like without anyone to order us about or to interfere with us," etc., etc. This speech settled the matter for the time being, but though the regiment ceased to cry aloud for peace, it showed little disposition to fight.

The Staff of the XIXth Corps sent me to talk to the 731st

Regiment—"an average regiment" they called it—in reserve a few thousand yards from the trenches in the Dvinsk bridgehead. After speaking to them for a few minutes, I told them that the Allies were taking the offensive in the West to give the Russian army time to settle down after the recent great change, and I asked them whether in a few weeks' time they would be ready to commence an offensive too so that the war might be quickly ended. There were cries of "No." The majority of the men very evidently did not want to fight. One man said: "The Government want us all to be killed, so that our wives and children may be starved by the landowners." Another said: "We have attacked and attacked, and nothing has come of it." Others said: "England is only beginning to fight, and we have been fighting the whole time." "Russia has not only to defend her own long frontier, but she has troops in France and in Rumania too." "We don't want to fight, we only dream of our wives and children." One man asked when the war would end. I said that it would end as soon as Russia took the offensive along with her Allies. He said: "And if we are beaten? We have had many allies, but it is all no good. The Germans are people like ourselves; we want to live in peace." An appeal to fight for the reconquest of the lost territory was futile. One man cried: "The devil take the sixteen Governments!"

To the average Russian peasant, his country was the hovel on the Volga, or perhaps in the Urals, where he happened to have been born, and to which he thought the Germans could never penetrate. Besides, an army of the size of the Russian naturally contained actively harmful elements. In a letter from a soldier of the 12th Army to his people, which was stopped by the Censor Department, the following sentences occurred: " I want you to tell me how things are with you and what you are doing. Do you know you can kill all the gentry now if you want to? Have you done this yet? Here we do what we like, and if anyone interferes with us we run a bayonet into him."

Officers at the front complained that the Government allowed the army to bear all the burden of political agitation. Endless deputations visited the front. One man with a pass signed by the

April-May, 1917

Minister of War was stopped by the Committee of the 12th Army because his programme was: "Not a step in advance under any circumstances."

At Riga there was a deputation from the Petrograd Sovyet, consisting of a working-man, a soldier and a journalist. The journalist said that in a month's time the army would fight better than it ever had, but that the war would have to end in six months, "as everyone was sick to death of it."

In the Committee of the 5th Army at Dvinsk there was a deputation from Kronstadt consisting of a pasty-faced sailor and a nervous fanatical workman, such as is produced by years of brooding over personal wrongs, imaginary or otherwise, and want of fresh air and exercise. They pretended that the defences of Kronstadt had been saved by the Revolution, as an order of the late Government for their destruction had been found in the office of the Commandant. I asked who had signed the order, and, of course, they "did not know." [1] They pretended that complete order reigned in Kronstadt. Though there were several officers of the 5th Army present, not one of them had the courage to tell these murderers that they were lying.

Many of the deputations encouraged the men to negotiate with the enemy. The *Pravda* wrote of these negotiations as of "noble, spontaneous manifestations of the will of the sovereign people." Even the *Novoe Vremya* suggested that fixed points should be selected for carrying them on!

A deputation of workmen from the Petrograd factory "Etna" visited the German trenches to consult on terms of peace. It told the Germans that they must expel their Emperor and hand back Kurland to Russia and Posen to Poland, to all of which the Germans laughed, and said "No!"

---

[1] An order was issued *after* the Revolution for the removal of the guns from Kronstadt for use in coastal defence further west. This order was signed by Captain Altvater, the Chief of the Naval Staff at G.H.Q. Enemy agents at Kronstadt cunningly misled the troops in the fortess into the belief that G.H.Q. had issued this order with the object of opening the enemy's way to "revolutionary Petrograd," and pointed to the order being actually signed by a German name!—Kerenski, *Prelude to Bolshevism*, pp. 135-137.

Altvater worked with the Bolsheviks after November, 1917. He died in 1919, it is said by his own hand.

The Command did all it possibly could to prevent fraternisation, well knowing the affect it would have on the Russian troops. The Germans detailed men specially instructed by the General Staff to interview the Russians. German visitors to the Russian lines took away with them bread and photographs of the Russian positions; the Russian peasant, in returning the visit, told all he knew of the Russian dispositions and came back happily drunk.

The proclamations passed by the enemy into the Russian trenches always pointed to England as Russia's real enemy. At first, after the Revolution, they showed their ignorance of the political situation in Russia by accusing England of having "made" the revolution. A proclamation distributed on March 23rd contained the following:

Soldiers!

In Petrograd Revolution! . . .

The English have deceived your Tsar; they forced him into the war in order, with his help, to conquer the world.

At first the English went hand-in-hand with the Tsar, and now they are against him; the English have always only sought their own selfish interests.

The English have forced your Heaven-sent Tsar to resign.

Why?

Because he was no longer willing to be deceived.

Because he understood all the deceit of the English game.

War contracts have brought the English enormous profits, have given them countless millions, and only the English can profit from the continuation of the war.

And who is waging this bloody war? The mujik, the splendid, long-suffering mujik, striving in silence, dying in silence, ignorant that he is only shedding his blood for England.

Etc., etc.

Another proclamation distributed about the same time on the Rumanian Front runs:

March, 1917. Temporary Executive Committee of the Imperial Duma. Back row. Left to right: Shulgin, Dimitryukov, Engelhardt, Kerenski, Karaulov. Sitting: Vladimir Lvov, Rjevski, Shidlovski, Rodzianko.

[See page 557

March, 1917. Soldiers posing in the Liteini Prospekt. The flag is inscribed " Down with the Monarchy ! "

[See page 587

June, 1917. Methods of travelling.

[See page 627

Trooper of the Tekinski Turkoman Volunteer Regiment.

[See page 689

Russian Warriors!

Children! Remain true to your Tsar!

At the moment when he wished to give you an honourable peace, he has been murdered, or at all events captured, by the English spies who call themselves the defenders of the Russian People. . . .

Do not betray your Emperor and your Mother Russia.

March to Petrograd to help your own people.

God save the Emperor!

However, the German Propaganda Department soon changed its line of attack.

A proclamation distributed on the Western Front stated:

Comrades!

In December last year the German Emperor offered you peace. This offer was made voluntarily, without any compulsion, solely for the love of peace and in the interests of suffering humanity. It was refused by your Tsar.

Now you have chosen your own Government. And you imagine that our Emperor could help your overturned Tsar to seize the throne once more! What madness is this!

No one of us dreams of interfering in Russian internal affairs. . . .

No matter how strong Germany may be, she will never take advantage of the internal struggle in Russia by assuming the offensive on the Eastern Front.

Germany is ready to make peace, though peace is not necessary for her. She will wait patiently to see if the new and free Russia will start peace negotiations with us in the holy holidays of Christ's resurrection.

The Russian soldier committees distributed proclamations in German in the German trenches. One of these, sent by the Petrograd Sovyet and printed in German at Riga, appealed to " all peoples who are being ruined and destroyed by this frightful war to begin a decisive contest against the aggressive tendencies of all governments." It ended:

Comrades!

    We beg of you to reply to our appeal. Do not show this manifesto to your officers. Spread it amongst your comrades of the artillery. On other parts of the front we are already in communication with your comrades.

    Long live universal peace!

It was obvious that the Russian soldier would never attack unless the death penalty was again established, but so long as he was only asked to remain quietly in his trenches, was fed by Government, and had little or no work to do, he had too little initiative to become actively mutinous unless stirred by propaganda. This propaganda was most harmful where it was conducted by some unscrupulous temporary officer.

Probably the worst division at this time in the army was the 109th, and probably the worst regiment in that division was the 436th, in which the ringleaders were Lieutenant Khaust and Ensign Sievers. Sievers was a German who had only assumed Russian nationality two years before the war.

One day early in April, when the men of this division were fraternising with the enemy between the lines, a battery of the 8th Heavy Division opened fire on the crowd. Khaust came to the battery, arrested the two officers and took them off to his regimental headquarters to be tried. They were subjected to every kind of indignity, and were only finally released owing to a threat of the gunners to open fire on the " court-martial."

On April 20th, Khaust, Sievers and nine men of their regiment appeared at the Assembly of the 12th Army and demanded the immediate conclusion of peace, the Germans and Russians to lay down their arms simultaneously. But the Assembly, though only consisting of soldiers, was not prepared to go so far, and the general attitude towards the party was so hostile that only the intervention of the Jewish soldier President, Rom, saved them from bodily hurt.

General Radko Dimitriev was fully aware of these facts, but said it was impossible to arrest the agitators, " as it would cause bloodshed," and they were allowed to continue their harmful propaganda.

Similarly, General Abram Dragomirov acknowledged that there were several agitators in the 5th Army as harmful as Khaust and Sievers, whom he could not arrest.

The cavalry and artillery were much "sounder" than the infantry, partly because a larger percentage of the men were literate, but chiefly because units still contained many cadre men. The infantry on the Northern Front after the Revolution protested vigorously whenever batteries fired on the enemy. A Battery Commander at Dvinsk told his men to try to explain something of their duty to the infantry, but they replied: "We have talked to them, but they do not understand us; their language is not ours."

The elective principle and the principle of combination had always been suppressed in Russia. Now that "freedom" had been won it was not surprising that the general ambition was to elect, or rather to be elected, and to combine, and no one who had any acquaintance with the Russian character was surprised to find that "freedom" was interpreted as freedom to talk without end and to do nothing.

The committees organised as a result of Order No. 1 developed in directions increasingly radical, owing to constant pressure by the men, and the harassed Command looked eagerly for an authoritative statement from the Government to set some limit to their powers.

On April 12th G.H.Q. issued an order on the subject, but it was simply disregarded. On April 29th the Minister of War issued as Army Order No. 213 the regulations drawn up by General Polivanov's Committee for company, regimental and army committees and for disciplinary courts. To these latter all power of punishment was handed over, officers only retaining the power to "warn" or to "reprimand." The company disciplinary court was to consist of an officer as president and two soldiers as members, elected by the company for a period of six months.

Even General Polivanov's Committee had a glimmering of the truth that in action something further was required in an army like the Russian, where in many regiments it had only been the power of the officers to inflict punishment that had enabled them to drive the men forward. Accordingly the following paragraph was added :

> In action, a superior officer has the right to undertake on his own responsibility all measures, including the employment of armed force, towards subordinates who fail to carry out his orders. Such measures are not considered to be ordinary disciplinary awards. An officer must at once inform his superior officer and the committee concerned of the steps he has taken.

This, of course, did not amount to anything. The men were being trained to disregard their officers out of action, and would continue to disregard them under fire, and the officer who might attempt to use force to compel their obedience would be simply shot.

As a matter of fact, the Order of April 29th remained as much a dead letter as that of April 12th, and the committee system developed in each army on individual lines. Working-men and soldier deputies boasted that the 12th Army was " the most democratic of all the armies." Its committees were entirely of soldiers, and would not permit officers to become members on the ground that their presence would weaken the authority of the committees with the men. In Dvinsk, on the contrary, the 5th Army Committee contained eight officers as well as thirty-seven soldiers.

As a rule the delegates chosen by the men were of a better type than one had a right to expect, though many of them were barely literate. One Sunday at Riga the men of various units stormed a brewery; many got drunk, and a few were drowned in the vats. Two members of the 12th Army Committee were sent to reason with the rioters, but unfortunately got drunk themselves. They were turned out of the organisation with every mark of contempt.

The officers and men of the Committee of the 5th Army took themselves very seriously, and their Agitation Committee constantly intervened to prevent excesses.

April-May, 1917

But if the majority of the members of the committees were sane, they had no real hold over the troops, who might be at any moment carried away by harmful agitation.

It was only natural that the committees tried to get all power into their own hands. The 12th Army Committee published in its paper an analysis of the work of its " Arbitration Committee." It stated that it enquired into ninety-six cases of quarrels between soldiers and officers (*sic*). Of these, forty-six resulted in " complete agreement between officers and soldiers to forget the past." In the remaining fifty cases the committee recommended :

    1. The dismissal from the service of three officers.

    2. The transfer to other units of thirty-seven officers, of whom twelve to be court-martialled for breach of regulations.

    3. The removal from his appointment of one doctor.

    4. The dismissal of two nurses for rough treatment of soldiers.

    5. The dismissal of six officers for criminal actions. Of these, two to be tried by court-martial.

    6. The removal from his appointment of one general.

    7. The severe reprimand of one general.

The Staff of the Army explained that this statement was issued by the committee to pretend to the men that it wielded a greater authority than was really the case. All the same, the publication of such a statement at Government expense and without a protest from the Command showed how little was being done to defend officers' prestige.

The soldier delegates were, of course, totally ignorant of military science, but they did not hesitate to worry the unfortunate Chief of Staff of the 12th Army with such questions as : " Why is the ―― Regiment on the line it now occupies and not 200 yards further back ? " This hard-worked officer had to explain for hours the necessity for avoiding interference in the detail of arrangements made by a subordinate commander.

An ensign in the 1st Army remarked : " If we are now ordered to attack, we will first send a delegate to examine the artillery position, a second to count the shell and a third to select the point of attack, and only when their reports have been received will we consent to go forward."

There was a glut of newspapers. The 12th Army had three, all of which were printed at Government expense. The *Staff News of the 12th Army* was official and daily. The *Officers' News of the 12th Army* and the *Soldier Deputies' News of the 12th Army* were published two or three times a week.

The Russian army had become enamoured of politics, and all its thoughts were directed towards the rear. It was obvious that the mistrust which had been sown by agitators between the officers and men had destroyed all fighting efficiency. Yet the Command still pretended to be optimistic. General Ruzski said that the first fight would bring the officers back to their own. General Radko Dimitriev pretended to believe that his army would be a better fighting machine in two months than it had ever been before! General Dragomirov, the Chief of Staff of the Front, said that the army would right itself if the anti-war party at Petrograd did not get the upper hand. No one dreamed of an attempt to restore discipline by force, probably because such an attempt would have been condemned by the Government as counter-revolution, yet such an attempt was possible, and it was the only chance.

Thursday, April 19th, 1917. RIGA.

The position of the officers has been so shaken that the efficiency of the army is utterly ruined. The officers have lost heart and the army therefore will do no good. The enthusiasm which carried the French through the short battles of the revolutionary period will not occur here, and, even if it did, it would not be sufficient to sustain the Russian peasant soldier through the long strain of the modern battle. He formerly fought because he was afraid of his officers and of punishment. Now he has lost all respect for his officers and he knows he cannot be punished. He has no patriotism or any possible motive force for enthusiasm.

General Abram Dragomirov, though more pessimistic than General Radko Dimitriev, seemed to look for a psychological miracle. He said that he, no more than I, could divine what was in the soul of the Russian peasant. An intelligent soldier deputy argued that the Russian peasant was swayed by the heart rather than by the head, and that the man who could seize his imagination at the exact moment could do what he liked with him. There was a good deal of truth in this, but it seemed risky to gamble on the possibility of the peasant proving a demigod. He was, through no fault of his own, without education and without lofty instincts. His selfish interests seemed all to point in one direction, and there seemed to be no doubt that, now the control to which he had been always accustomed had been removed, that was the direction he would take.

Saturday, April 28th, 1917. PETROGRAD.

I got back at 6 p.m.

The denshchiks (officers' servants) at Pskov had a meeting yesterday and decided to agitate for :

1. An eight-hour day.
2. That they should not be sent to the trenches.
3. That Jews should not be commissioned as officers, since they did not wish to serve them.

On April 30th the annual benefit performance for the Knights of St. George took place at the Mikhail Theatre and was attended by the Ambassador, at whose disposal a box had been placed. The programme, which was badly stage-managed, was devoted to the glorification of Russia and the Allies. The French section of the performance naturally led to scenes of immense enthusiasm, and Kerenski appeared in the front of a box full of soldiers who had won the Cross of St. George. He was chaired by soldiers down to the stalls and made an impassioned speech in praise of France— the France of the Great Revolution. This all seemed unreal and foolish after the betrayal of France's vital interests which had been evident at the front. After the French section, it was somewhat strange to find that the orchestra and performers proceeded next to the glorification of the United States of America, but it was evidently Kerenski's idea to place the republics of the Alliance before the monarchies.

The demonstrations of May 1st passed without disturbance. The general note of the banners was not directly anti-war, but anti-capital, advocating general robbery and confiscation.

Colonel Balaban, however, said that the position had grown worse in the last fortnight and that Lenin's Bolshevik propaganda was making progress in the garrison. The publication, therefore, on the 1st by the Provisional Government of its declaration of solidarity with the Allies aroused the keen resentment of the internationalists. On the night of the 3rd large crowds demonstrated for and against M. Milyukov before the Marinski Palace, and the Minister of Foreign Affairs, with rare courage, came out and spoke to the crowd in defence of his policy. On the 4th the whole city was bubbling with excitement, and in a collision which occurred between processions on the Nevski Prospekt two soldiers were killed by workmen. General Kornilov called out the Volinski Regiment, the Cossacks and the Equipage of the Guard, but cancelled the order owing to a visit of members of the Sovyet, who guaranteed there would be no further bloodshed. He then heard that there was firing on the Champ de Mars, and drove his car straight into the middle of a large crowd of the Pavlovski Regiment who were being harangued by civilian agitators.

He stood up in his car and, raising his hand to command silence, said that anyone who agitated in troublous times like the present was a German agent paid by the Germans. One of the civilians said: "General, you are a 'provocateur.'" The little man replied that he had looked death too often in the face to be frightened by such as he. He spoke of his wounds and of his services to the country, and in five minutes the crowd hurrahed, the agitators disappeared discomfited, and the men of the Pavlovski escorted Kornilov back in triumph to his Staff.

Such personal successes could do little to stem the tide of indiscipline and disorder fostered by the existence in the capital side by side of two Governments, each struggling for power.

During the disorders on May 4th, the 180th Depot Regiment

paraded with arms and bearing banners inscribed : " Down with the Provisional Government." Its excuse was that it had been called out by a telephone message purporting to come from the Sovyet. Ostensibly to prevent any future misuse of its authority, the Sovyet on the 5th issued a proclamation forbidding any unit to parade with arms, except for the ordinary guards, unless it received a formal order from the Sovyet on stamped paper. This proclamation placed the Provisional Government and General Kornilov in an equivocal position, and the Government on the 9th made its protest in a statement issued to the Press to the effect that orders to the troops could only be issued by the Commander-in-Chief, General Kornilov. There was, however, little doubt whose orders the troops would obey if matters came to a trial of strength between the rival powers

Friday, May 11th, 1917. PETROGRAD.

Khlopotov, M. Guchkov's private secretary, and Blair lunched. Khlopotov was very vigorous in his assertion that the French and the British were making a great mistake in regarding the Russian army as a " wash-out " (placing a cross on the Russian army). I allowed that an offensive, if successful, would bring everything right, but entirely disagreed with him when he argued that an unsuccessful offensive would not hasten the end of the Russian army. I told him that I gave the Russian army two months to exist if the offensive proved unsuccessful.

He evidently imagines we do not read the Russian papers ! Last night in the Duma the Minister of War said that the forces weakening and disintegrating the Russian army were moving more rapidly than the forces of healthy reconstruction, and Alexyeev, when asked by a Press interviewer whether he thought that the Entente would win, replied that the Allies thought so, but " the Russians unfortunately only dreamed of a quiet and peaceful life."

At the Embassy, three officers of the Litovski Regiment came to see me—a colonel and a lieutenant from the regiment and an ensign from the depot battalion. They all wanted to join the British army, and they were willing to join as private soldiers.

Later old General Torklus came with his son, also a candidate for the British army.

Next came a Pole, a native of Kalish and a German subject. I told him that he would probably be interned if he went to England and that we were not so far fallen that we had to enlist our enemies. He said he could enlist easily here, but he knew that nothing good could come of the present disorder.

The prisoners of war who were working on the landlords' estates have been liberated by the peasants, and are wandering about stealing. German and Austrian officers are walking freely about Moscow.

Balaban boasted that at least a dozen spies a day are now captured, whereas under the old régime only about one per month was arrested. I told him that, out of the million or so wandering about, a dozen a day was a very "poor bag."

There is an extraordinary wave of extravagant humanitarianism.

Surely there has never been another country at war in which the prisoners of war declared a strike for better pay and conditions of life !

The thieves of Moscow had a meeting outside the town, and the Chief of Police showed his human sympathy by attending. It is said that an unanimous resolution was passed to refrain from stealing for two days " in honour of the sun of freedom " !

Similarly the deserters met in conference at Odessa, and the Commander-in-Chief was recieved with acclamation !

In Petrograd, children have been seen parading with banners inscribed : " Down with the parental yoke ! "

The Bolshevik Press carried on an intensive propaganda in

favour of immediate peace. The *Pravda*, on May 12th, published a resolution passed by the so-called All-Russian Conference of the Social Democratic Party, demanding the formal repudiation by "the Government of landlords and capitalists" of the secret treaties "made by the ex-Tsar Nikolas II. with the capitalist Governments of England, France, etc." The resolution stated that the "Party" would by every means in its power support the proletariat groups abroad, "who even during the war were fighting against their bourgeois and capitalist Governments, and would in particular support the general fraternisation of soldiers of all the combatant armies." The Conference, however, protested against the "low calumny spread by the capitalists" that the Party was in favour of a separate peace with Germany, since it "considered the German capitalists to be bandits similar to the Russian, English and French capitalists, and the Emperor William to be a similar crowned bandit to Nikolas II. and the English, Italian and Rumanian monarchs."

On May 11th a telegram from the Foreign Office asked whether, in view of the present state of the Russian army, it was worth while to send out any more material. I strongly advised the Ambassador that we should make it clear to the Russian Government that we would stop supplies unless steps were taken to restore discipline.

Colonel Balaban told me on May 12th that it was considered that General Kornilov had proved a failure and that his removal had been decided upon. He blamed the General's "tactless attitude" towards the Executive Committee of the Sovyet. Another officer, and a true prophet, said that in any case the Executive Committee had little power, and that it would be swept away as soon as its ideas ceased to coincide with the progressively wild ideas of the majority of the garrison.

Kornilov complained of the interference of the Committee and of the weakness of the Provisional Government, who should have forced the Committee to cancel its instructions forbidding units to parade without its own written orders.

An unofficial meeting, at which apparently Balaban presided, decided that Major-General Polovtsev, lately a Colonel of the

Caucasian Native Division, was the only man to command the district.

Balaban also said that the Sovyet wanted to get rid of MM. Milyukov and Guchkov, and that Tereshchenko was thought of as Milyukov's successor, " as he would be more likely to work in with the United States, to whose policy Russia would incline more willingly than to the revengeful and grabbing policy of the other Allies."

Sunday, May 13th, 1917.   PETROGRAD.

I lunched with Thornhill to meet poor Lechitski. The old man quite touched me when he gave me greetings from his 9th Army. I can't help loving these people ; they are all heart.

He told us of how poor Miller [1] was arrested. The XXVIth Corps objected to him because he was " exacting." They said that he visited posts even in advance of those ordinarily visited by the company commanders, and that as the Germans did not fire at him he must therefore be a German. One day he took down the names of the men of a draft that had arrived from Moscow with red favours. This gave the necessary excuse. The brutes fell on him, tore off his shoulder-straps and coat, and wounded him in several places with bayonets. Guchkov, who was at Jassy, on Lechitski's advice, telegraphed to Kimpolung that Miller was to be released and to be reinstated in his command. A deputation of the soldiers of the corps arrived, and Guchkov cancelled his first order. Miller was conveyed to Petrograd under arrest and his assaulters were allowed to go unpunished.

Lechitski blames Alexyeev and Brusilov as well as Guchkov for giving way to the mad idea of democratising the army.

Professor Pares came in at 10 p.m. after dining with Guchkov, who told him that he was resigning as a protest

---
[1] General Miller, Chief of Staff of the 5th Army in 1914-1915. (See Chapter VII.) Fought at Arkhangel and Murmansk against the Bolsheviks in 1918-1919.

against the weakness of the Government and the impossibility of restoring discipline in the army. Poor Guchkov! He has been honest. His fault was that he believed too much in Russian " broad nature "!

Monday, May 14th, 1917.

I addressed a letter to-day to the Ambassador. I commenced by quoting my letter of April 14th, with Prince Lvov's reply that the army was a better fighting machine than it had ever been and that it was quite well able to deal with agitators, and continued:

" I returned to Petrograd from a visit to the Northern Front on April 28th. I gave you my opinion of the deplorable state of things at the front. Units have been turned into political debating societies; the infantry refuses to allow the guns to shoot at the enemy; parleying in betrayal of the Allies and of the best interests of Russia takes place daily with the enemy, who laughs at the credulity of the Russian peasant soldier. Many senior officers complained that the Government, to which every army has a right to look for support, had left all the burden of dealing with agitation to the army.

"In Petrograd things are growing worse daily. The tens of thousands of able-bodied men in uniform who saunter about the streets without a thought of going to the front or of working to prepare themselves for war, when every able-bodied man and most of the women in England and France are straining every nerve to beat the common enemy, will be a disgrace for all time to the Russian people and its Government.

"Even Lenin disclaims the idea of a separate peace, but his agitation tends to the same end by the utter ruin it is bringing on the Russian army.

" The movement of German troops to the Westtern theatre which you foretold to Prince Lvov on April 14th has commenced. The following are details of the accessions to enemy strength in the respective theatres from March 15th, when Germany first heard of the Russian Revolution, till May 10th :

To the Western theatre :

From the Eastern theatre, established	5 divisions.
From the Eastern theatre, surmised	13 ,,
From the interior of Germany.	10 ,,

To the Eastern theatre :

From the Western theatre, established	1 division.
From the Western theatre surmised	2 divisions.
From the interior of Germany.	3 ,,

" It is necessary for us to arrive at some conclusion as to whether the Russian army will fight. No army in the history of the world has ever fought with such anti-war agitation in rear as is now permitted in Petrograd by the Government."

I suggested certain steps as necessary : the isolation of the army from political pollution, the suppression of the most bitterly anti-ally papers, the *Pravda*, the *Soldatskaya Pravda*, and the *Novaya Jizn*, the arrest of anti-war agitators, the prohibition of parleying with the enemy.

Tuesday, May 15th, 1917.   PETROGRAD.

Tereshchenko told the Ambassador yesterday that he would probably be Minister of Foreign Affairs in the new Government, and that Kerenski would be Minister of War. The Government is angry with Guchkov, whose resignation has placed it in an awkward situation ! In my opinion, he should have resigned a month ago.

The Executive Committee of the Sovyet decided yesterday by forty-four votes to nineteen to join a Coalition Government.

April-May, 1917

The composition of the Executive Committee is said to be at present as follows:

1. Bolsheviks 21
2. Social Revolutionaries:
    (*a*) Maximalists 5
    (*b*) Others 7 12
3. Social Democrats:
    (*a*) Mensheviks 17
    (*b*) Oborontsi 13
    (*c*) Edintsvo Party 5 35
           Total 68

Yesterday's evening papers contain proclamations from the Sovyet. First to " the Socialists of all Countries ":

> "The revolutionary democracy of Russia turns to you socialists of the Austro-German Alliance; you cannot allow the troops of your Governments to become a weapon against Russian freedom. You cannot allow your Governments taking advantage of the joyful enthusiasm for freedom and brotherhood, which has taken possession of the Russian revolutionary army, to transfer their troops to the Western theatre in order, first, to destroy France, and then to attack Russia, and finally to smother you yourselves and the whole international proletariat in the world-embrace of Imperialism."

The second proclamation is addressed to the Russian army, and is an appeal to cease parleying with the enemy. This was passed, the Bolshevists abstaining from voting.

Balaban has a high opinion of Kerenski. He says that he refused to accept the portfolio of Minister of War unless a Coalition Government was first formed. His objection was that, as Minister of War, he would at once become the object of general attack, and the Government as a whole would then lose the advantage of his personal influence, which is now so valuable.

Wednesday, May 16th, 1917.   PETROGRAD.

Kerenski and Tereshchenko did not dine at the Embassy last night. The British Labour people did—three fine fellows, whose solid bulk it was a pleasure to look at after the nervous, excitable people we see here. They have grasped the situation in Russia, and will tell the War Cabinet that there is nothing to be hoped for from this side.

Friday, May 18th, 1917.

The Government has taken in five socialists. Kerenski is Minister of War.

I went to the official residence of the Minister of War—67, Moika—this morning, and was there before Kerenski arrived.

He took me into his room and introduced me to his assistants, Colonel Yakubóvich and Prince Tumánov. He will leave for the South-West Front in five or six days, "when he has restored order here." Hope that springs eternal! I told him I was glad of his appointment, for I considered him to be the only man who could save Russia.

He asked me if the Embassy was "still in panic," and when I was going away he asked me not to frighten the Ambassador by collecting "pessimistic information"!

In the afternoon I saw Yakubóvich, and asked him what it was proposed to do here. He said the programme was:

1. The proclamation of the Sovyet to the Army. This has been already issued—eight weeks too late.

2. The Peasants' Conference will pass a resolution depriving all deserters of any right to land in the approaching distribution.

3. Healthy propaganda.

I said that nothing would come of this programme unless the Government muzzled the *Pravda* and other papers of the unpatriotic Left Press, and arrested traitors like Khaust and Sievers. Yakubóvich said that these things they could not do *yet*. My impression is that they will never do them.

As Engelhardt, whom I met later, said: " The situation can only be saved by a Government that is willing to wallow in blood, and this Government will not do that."

The Ambassador told me that he had given my paper of the 14th to Tereshchenko, who said he thoroughly agreed with it. His agreement is not much use unless he forces his colleagues to act.

I am afraid the Coalition Ministry will do little to increase Russian pressure in the Eastern theatre. A milk-and-water programme such as that outlined will do no good. Our object must be to keep at all events *some* Russian troops on the line to prevent *all* German troops from going west.

Sunday, May 20th, 1917.

The Ambassador found Tereshchenko very optimistic yesterday morning, apparently because of his unbounded faith in Kerenski. He said that he hoped soon to bring 20,000 men to demonstrate before the British Embassy! He pointed to an order issued by Kerenski last night as a sign of his strength of character. In this order; Kerenski said that he would not allow any senior commander to retire, and that all deserters who did not return by May 28th would be severely punished. Such deserters, says T., will be punished by penal servitude. We will wait and see! After all, both Kerenski and Tereshchenko are only boys, and naturally full of boyish enthusiasm!

Apparently, on the 17th, the Commanders-in-Chief of the Fronts asked for the abolition of committees in the army, and Kerenski refused. The Commanders-in-Chief then expressed a wish to resign, and Kerenski told them that if they did they would have to serve as soldiers. Balaban is enthusiastic over this evidence of " Kerenski's strong will," but it is much easier to take up a strong attitude towards these unfortunate men than towards the mutinous soldiery.

Balaban told me that Kornilov was offered the 5th Army vice Abram Dragomirov, who has been promoted to command the Northern Front, but he asked for "something further from Petrograd," so poor Kaledin is to be removed from the 8th Army to the 5th to make room for Kornilov at Czernowitz.

Polovtsev was summoned from the army on the night of the 17th to be Commander-in-Chief of the Petrograd Military District.

Kerenski is to start going round units—the same old game as poor Kornilov played. His speeches will be more frothy and the effect will last an hour or two longer.

Engelhardt and Pares lunched. Engelhardt says that Kerenski has no fixed plan. He is going to work by propaganda. E. had seen him yesterday and the day before on the subject.

Tuesday, May 22nd, 1917.

Kerenski came to see the Ambassador at 6 p.m. yesterday. Young Lockhart interpreted during the first part of the interview, I being only called up later, because, I fancy, the Ambassador thought I might " go for Kerenski."

Kerenski said that he would go often to the front. We insisted on the necessity of his speaking to the troops detailed for the attack on the eve of the offensive. He is working by propaganda. "The best orators and literature are being sent to the army. The Sovyet is exhorting the army to carry out all the orders of the Provisional Government and not opposing the latter, as it formerly did."

Kerenski calmly says that the great difficulty he has to contend with is the "fright" of the officers, who "do not realise the position and are not rising to the occasion." This comes well from him. It is his duty to restore the officers' prestige. Has he taken any steps to do this? He will fail as Guchkov failed.

At Helsingfors, according to Kerenski, all is well. The fleet is working well. The U-boats have gone out to the German zone, the torpedo-boats are preparing to go out, and in a few days the battleships will leave for their firing practice! According to him all is for the best in this best of all possible worlds. We will wait and see whether his eloquence and the adventurer and convict whom he is placing in charge of the District here will be able to induce the troops to work and the dvorniks to sweep the streets.

Regarding the formation of Polish units, Kerenski said he was opposed to the idea of separate Polish regiments, first because the mass of the Polish people were not Socialists, and secondly because such a formation would cause disorganisation in the Russian army. The second objection is a natural one, but it was characteristic of the speaker that he placed it only second. I pointed out that in many regiments at the front the Russians had run away and had left the Poles to fight alone. He said: "Let them fight!"

Balaban visited eight units with Kerenski on the 20th and eight more on the 21st. Kerenski formed each unit in a square and spoke to the men for ten minutes. He spoke out straight and told them that he insisted on discipline, that the army should be one whole with the people, etc., etc. In the Moskovski Battalion he called out the warrant officers who had been "elected" by the men to command companies, and asked them who had appointed them. They replied that they had been chosen by the men. "And what have you done in the last two months?" One frothy-mouthed individual replied: "We have maintained and defended the liberty we have gained." Kerenski said: "I will make you ensigns now, but mind, you will have to work and to see that others work."

Balaban's impression is that Kerenski's influence is such that if he ordered a regiment to go to the front it would go at once. "He could be dictator if he wished and if he were not a man of principle."

Then Balaban told me of Kuzmin, the new assistant to the Commander-in-Chief of the Petrograd Military District. He served nine months as a soldier, and passed later through the Politecnique at Paris. In 1905, when a civilian, he was chosen as President of the "Krasnoyarsk Republic." When order was restored in Siberia, he was sentenced to be hanged, but the sentence was commuted to one of penal servitude for life. He was released after the Revolution. On May 17th he was promoted to be Second Lieutenant, and on the 18th to be Lieutenant.

Balaban says that he gives the impression of a very serious and very innocent child; he knows nothing.

Yesterday he announced his intention of addressing the commanders of forty units at the District Staff at 8 p.m. on the subject of the domestic life of the troops in barracks, the restoration of discipline and the instruction of the men.

While I was at the Staff, Balaban told his assistants to place a long table in the room and to have tea ready for the séance. One of them said that there were only ten glasses and that there would be at least forty officers present, and Balaban said: "We won't give them tea, they will leave all the sooner."

The idea of assembling forty officers, of the rank presumably of colonel, to hear the ex-convict's views on such subjects, is very Russian.

Thursday, May 24th, 1917.

Balaban tells me that the "General Lieutenant," as he calls him, did not attempt to teach the eighty commanders of units who met last night and the night before, but sat and listened while they discussed discipline, etc., in the usual manner, without plan and without arriving at any conclusion.

Balaban was at his dinner when I went to see him at

3 p.m. He was constantly interrupted by officers while he ate the usual Russian meal of thick soup, cutlets and tea.

While we talked, a draft company passed with red banners and without any sembance of order. I asked: "Do you think that men that leave for the front in order like that will fight when they get there? Do you imagine that the officers at the front will be glad to see them arrive?"

An article in the *Pravda* of the 23rd ends: "Comrades . . . Russian soldiers! Are you willing to fight for this, that the English capitalists should rob Mesopotamia and Palestine? Are you willing to support the Russian Government of Lvov, Chernov, Tereshchenko, Tseretelli, tied to the interests of the capitalists and afraid to speak the truth?"

At the Embassy this morning I saw a telegram to the effect that the War Cabinet was sending out Mr. Henderson at the head of a special mission, as it considered it essential to get into touch with the Russian Socialists. It was suggested that the Ambassador should take some weeks' leave, returning to England to report on the situation. This will do no good. It is evidently thought that it is possible to appease and to win over the Extreme Party—Lenin and his followers. The Extreme Party is either German-paid or so fanatical that no one, who is in favour of the continuance of the war, has a shadow of a chance of its confidence. The Ambassador's visit to England will be looked on as a great victory for the German party.[1]

---

[1] Some days previously I had telegraphed pointing out the increase of socialistic and peace influence, and the danger that the anti-Allied agitation might so increase as to make a separate peace a question of weeks. I asked, as the only chance, and even that a poor one, if it were not possible to reconsider our agreements with the Allies in order to show that our vital aims in the war were something that even Russian Socialists could fight for.

* Proof that the Entente ideals were something finer than the proposed partition of Asia Minor would have deprived the Internationalists of a useful plank in their platform, but in the light of after events I am now certain that the rot in the

Friday, May 25th, 1917.

The new Commander-in-Chief, Polovtsev, is due to arrive on the 28th. I heard something of him to-day. He has loved much. He is "beau garçon," very rich and intelligent, but said to be an adventurer and a thorough egoist. It will be interesting to see how he works with the "General-Lieutenant," for it is impossible to imagine two men more diametrically different.

Balaban attends the meetings of the Executive Committee of the Sovyet every evening. He says that the Committee funks the application of force to deal with the "anarchists"; its policy is to remain on good terms with the Extreme Left, as it fears the reproach that it is "conspiring against the people's liberties."

Balaban thinks that not more than 5 per cent. of the garrison is Bolshevik in sympathy.

Saturday, May 26th, 1917.

Colonel D—— came to see me yesterday at the Embassy. I had known him when he was in charge of the Armoured Car Section of the 1st Army in the retreat from Poland in 1915. After the Revolution his Section was placed in the trenches between the 120th Division of the XXXVIIth Corps and the XVth Corps. The 120th Division had always been bad and had corrupted the neighbouring units of the XVth Corps.

When D——'s men fired at the Germans, they were fired on by the men of the 120th Division and one man was killed and two wounded. The 120th Division fired volleys

---

Russian army had already gone too far and no appeal to any idealism would have induced the men to fight.

Writers like Mr. Wells, who have attacked the attitude of the Allied diplomatic representatives in Petrograd, have only shewn their complete ignorance of the situation. The few poor overworked British diplomats in Petrograd had no power to dictate the war policy of Great Britain. They only did their best in Petrograd, as their duty was, in the interests of that policy, while England was fighting for her life and Mr. Wells' friend, Maxim Gorki, was daily attacking England in his paper, the *New Life*, as effectually as if he were in German pay.

We can claim that we "saw it through," and our task was a less pleasant one than Mr. Britling's.

at its own battery, but as the battery was 2,000 yards distant, caused no casualties. The men of the Division went over to the German trenches and pointed out the position of the battery, so that the German gunners fired at it all day.

The Armoured Car Section was sent to Pernau to quell a mutiny in one of the regiments of the 135th Division. The men of the regiment had come to their Colonel and had demanded that he should take off his shoulder-straps "as a mark of sympathy to their brothers of the Baltic Fleet." He said : " Be sensible, brothers, how can I do such a thing ? " They urged : " Shoulder-straps are a sign of the old régime We ask you to remove them." He said he could not do so. " We order you to remove them ! " " I won't." " Well, take that ! " and they murdered him.

A long article in to-day's *Pravda*, by Kamenev, whose real name is Rosenfeldt, points out that the adoption by the Provisional Government of the formula " Peace without annexations " is a pretence unless accompanied by action leading to the withdrawal of all troops from occupied territory by all the powers at war. England must withdraw her forces from India, Egypt and Ireland !

Sunday, May 27th, 1917.

A Declaration of the Rights of Soldiers, dated May 24th and signed by Kerenski, is published. This contains no new concession to licence, but confirms those already granted, such as permission to wear mufti when off duty, the abolition of compulsory saluting and of summary punishment, and shows that Kerenski is not going to take any practical steps to restore discipline.

There is also published an " Order for the Offensive of the Army and Fleet," dated the 25th, in which Kerenski writes that " without discipline there can be no safety " and appeals to the " freest army and navy in the world " to prove that " in freedom there is strength and not weakness."

Colonel Yakubóvich spoke for three hours at the Conference of Peasant Deputies on the night of the 25th, and was gloomy. He said that the army has enough shell for six months' maximum expenditure, but there is a shortage of food, and horses in places only get one pound of oats a day. There are mass epidemics of scurvy. The open deserters number several millions, secret deserters a million officers and men, who are skulking in rear under various pretences. Anarchy on the railways. Companies at the front reduced to forty to seventy bayonets. Of drafts 1,000 strong despatched from depots in rear, only 150 to 250 men reach the front. Men despatched to the Western Front decide *en route* that they prefer to go to the South-Western Front, and go there they do!

I telegraphed that I feared the situation was desperate. The Ambassador told Tereshchenko that he could not blame me for pessimism when the Assistant Minister of War made such statements.

The output of coal fell 20·2 per cent. in the month of April, as compared with the corresponding month last year. The production of pig-iron fell 17·6 per cent. in the first quarter of 1917 as compared with that of the first quarter of 1916. The factories generally produce 40 per cent. less, owing to the introduction of the eight-hours' day, combined with the refusal of the men to work overtime and the lack of sufficient skilled labour to arrange additional shifts. On an average, 40 per cent. of the engineers have been expelled by the men, in one case 80 per cent.

The demands of the men are without limit. In eighteen metal works in the Don region, which allotted 18,000,000 roubles to dividend in 1916, the men demand increases in pay amounting to 240,000,000. The masters offered to give up all profit, but the men refused. In the Urals the men demand increases of 300,000,000 roubles in works where the turnover is only 200,000,000!

A young officer of the Preobrajenski says that it is

quite impossible to do anything with the men. Thirty thousand deserters pass through Kiev daily.

A battalion commander of the XVIIIth Corps told me that his companies were still 150 strong. None of his men had deserted, but everything in rear had gone, transport drivers, depot units, etc. His men are absolutely without boots and are wasting away from sickness. He said he looked upon the Russian army as finished, and Russia's existence as an independent power ended.

I dined with R——, who threw out dark hints of a counter-revolution. He asked if we could supply arms for a brigade at Arkhangel, but I reminded him of the fact that we were in alliance with the Provisional Government.

Then he said that he foresaw that Great Britain and France would make peace and would establish joint control over Russia!

Monday, May 28th, 1917.

On my way to the Embassy in the morning I met Lechitski. He does not believe in an offensive by "the most democratic army in the world," for the Russian is by nature and early home conditions most undisciplined, and he has no idea of patriotism or sense of duty. Poor old Lechitski, I wonder if I will ever see him again! I have the very greatest regard and respect for him.

I was told a story of a Colonel Kotlarevski, a technical artillery officer of the Caucasian Front, who arrived at Moscow in the very middle of the Revolution and had to find the military staff on urgent business. He found a door over which "Military Council" was written. He told the sentry he had business with the military council, and he was ushered into a room where he found six ensigns, some doctors and a few soldiers sitting at a table with lighted candles. They asked him what he wanted, and he said he had come to get the component parts of mountain guns. They consulted together for a few moments and then the President stepped forward and said: "By the will of the people, you are appointed the Commander-in-Chief of the Moscow Military District." The bewildered Colonel did his best to avoid the honour. Colonel Gruzinov came in and he pointed him out as a man in every way more suitable. Gruzinov said that he would serve as his assistant, but Kotlarevski said: "This is not the time to worry about such trifles as rank. Though you are a Lieutenant-Colonel and I am a Colonel, I will serve as your assistant." He served in this capacity for a month, and was then exceedingly glad to get away with a whole skin.

CHAPTER XXI

THE SOUTH-WEST FRONT IN JUNE
KERENSKI'S OFFENSIVE IN JULY

Reference Map No. XII

I LEFT Petrograd on May 29th and travelled *via* G.H.Q. and Kiev to the headquarters of the South-West Front at Kamenets-Podolsk.

At G.H.Q. I met for the first time General Denikin, who was now acting as Chief of the Staff. He had commanded the 4th Rifle Division (the " Iron Division ") most of the war, and he gave the impression of being a man of nerve.

From G.H.Q. I travelled in luxury with General Dzyevenovski, who was in charge of Military Communications on the South-West Front. There was a strike of waiters at Kiev, but the General took me to some charming Poles, who entertained us royally.

Appearances at Kiev and on the railway did not promise well for the coming offensive. The station at Kiev was constantly full of men who should have been at the front. Permission had been given for 5 per cent. of the rank and file up to forty years of age and for 15 per cent. of men of forty to forty-three to go on leave every three weeks. Very many more than the percentage allowed left the front, and few returned. The roofs of carriages as far as Kiev were crowded with soldiers, but when we turned west from Kiev the train was comparatively empty.

I arrived at Kamenets-Podolsk on Sunday, June 3rd, and spent a month in the 11th, 7th and 8th Armies.

General Brusilov was promoted to succeed General Alexyeev as Supreme Commander-in-Chief, and left the South-West Front for his new post on June 6th, with three princes, his personal Staff. French officers considered it a fatal mistake to remove the only man who might have induced the troops to attack just as the hour for the final effort arrived. General Brusilov himself said that he had told Kerenski that if he had decided to transfer him, the transfer should have been made before. " However," he added, " as my name is synonymous with the offensive, my new appointment will have automatically an encouraging effect on the leading on all the fronts."

Most officers were very outspoken regarding what they termed " Brusilov's political gymnastics." One said that he had been necessary to the South-West Front before the Revolution, but that since the Revolution he was necessary nowhere. Another said that, though Brusilov had character and common sense, he suffered from the lack of higher military education, and that at Mogilev he would be " a positive danger, as he would give way in everything to the politicians."

General Brusilov's method was to persuade by talk. On June 4th I waited with many Russian generals in his ante-room while he reasoned for four hours with an ensign who had arrested his divisional commander, and had refused to attend the summons of either his corps or army commander. The General told me next day that this particular division recognised no one, neither the Provisional Government nor the Sovyet, and its only " programme " was to leave the front and to avoid fighting. In a military sense these four hours were entirely wasted. There was only one way to deal with this division and with the boy that had misled it, and Brusilov, as an officer with over forty years' service, must have known it.

Officers said that Brusilov tried to curry favour with the revolutionaries by telling them that he had been the first Russian general to demand the abdication of the Emperor, and they recalled the fact that he kissed the Emperor's hand twice on the occasion of His Majesty's last visit to the South-West Front.

He took leave of the men on the evening of the 5th in a speech in which he said : " I carry luck everywhere with me. The 8th Army was always victorious, and so has been the South-West Front under my leadership. Now I will lead all the armies of Russia to victory."

"Kerenski's Offensive"

In command of the 8th Army, officers said that he had been luckier than he deserved; that he had been on the point of ordering a retreat at the Gnila Lipa on August 27th, and again in the fight of September 11th, when the Austrians gave way. They argued that if the 3rd and 8th Armies had advanced with more energy they would have cut off the Austrian main armies, and the Russian Guard might have been sent north to help Samsonov as had been originally intended.

I was present at the ceremony of the General's departure, which was attended by the " delegates " in force, and where he made three more speeches, the last from his carriage window. At lunch afterwards one officer characterised him as merely an opportunist, sincere in nothing and searching only for popularity. Another maintained that he saw all the folly of his antics, but believed that he was taking the only course possible to restore some sort of discipline in the army.

The new Commander-in-Chief of the South-West Front was General Gutor, who had commenced the war as Chief of Staff of the 4th Army. In 1915 he had been transferred to the command of the 34th Division, and he had since commanded the VIth Corps and the 11th Army. He had been wounded more than once. He appointed General Dukhonin, late General Quartermaster, to be his Chief of Staff.

In an interview on June 5th, General Dukhonin said that the Italian representatives at G.H.Q. had asked for a Russian offensive, and he explained that such an offensive " could not go far " ! When the 1916 offensive was launched all units in front were up to strength and there were 200,000 drafts in rear, but now units in front were 200,000 short of establishment and there were only 60,000 men behind. The horses were half starved. Still, he thought that the offensive would remind the Germans that they had still to reckon with the Russian army, and might make them ask for peace ! He would be satisfied with 200,000 prisoners !

I spent the next week with the left army of the group, the 8th, in Bukovina. General Kaledin had proved too honest to give way to all the demands of the army committee and had been in consequence removed by General Brusilov. His successor,

General Kornilov, had only arrived on May 25th. The general opinion was that the spirit of the army was improving. A patriotic captain of the General Staff, Nyejintsev, was busy trying to organise a storm battalion of volunteers who promised to try to live without politics and " meetings," and who " agreed to attack when ordered," and the idea was to raise eventually one of such battalions in each division, " to show the way to the other units."

The idea was good, but what was wanted was rather something behind to drive bad units forward. The time for influence by example had passed.

General Kornilov's plan was to strike north-west through Nadworna. He did not believe in piercing the Carpathians. Neither did the troops. One of the men of a unit in the Carpathians said to him: " Mr. General, we will attack, only this place is not convenient for attacking. If we take a mountain, there is always another in front of us, and there is no end and no profit in it."

Here in the far south there were fewer complaints of the visits of agitators which so plagued the Northern Front, but officers spoke of the evil influence of the Left papers. The Colonel of the Engineer Regiment of the XIth Corps said that his men subscribed for ten copies of the *Pravda*, and received forty additional copies free, and the men who could read to a certain extent —perhaps 20 per cent. of the rank and file—had been so long accustomed under the strict censorship of the old régime to regard the printed word as of guaranteed truth, that they believed all they read.

Thursday, June 7th, 1917. CZERNOWITZ.

At lunch in the Army Staff we had a visit from a revolutionary doctor, who, on account of his political opinions, had been promoted from the post of junior doctor in a hospital to be P.M.O. of the whole front. He spoke of Lenin as of a " clean-minded idealist." We all attacked him on the question of discipline and the folly of abolishing the death penalty. He was a simple idealist with no practical acquaintance with the every-day routine of the control of troops, many of whom are naturally cowards, in action. He quoted with pride, as an example of his method of appealing to the better feelings of the men, one of his orders, which ended: " I demand, I beg, I hope that this order will be carried out." Damned ass!

The C.R.E. of the front, General Velichko, came to supper. He told an anecdote to illustrate the difficulty of getting money out of the Government. A lieutenant-colonel spent Rs.7.50 of his own money and claimed refund from Government. The correspondence continued for eight years. The officer retired, but being a man of strong principle, still continued to agitate. At last he took to his death-bed, and when he was already unconscious a letter came to say that he was " the creditor of Government for Rs.7.50."

The decision came too late to afford the dying man any pleasure, but the widow, imagining the formula to which she was unaccustomed to be some tardy recognition by Government of her husband's life-work, wrote on his tombstone: " Here rest the ashes of Lieutenant-Colonel ——, Creditor of the Russian Government."

On June 8th, Kerenski degraded General Gurko from his position as Commander-in-Chief of the Western Front, and appointed him to command a division in the Kazan Military District. The General had resigned on May 28th, refusing to be responsible for his command after the publication of Kerenski's " Declaration of the Rights of Soldiers."

After supper on the 11th, General Kornilov asked me to come into his study for a talk. The room, which also served as a bedroom for the General, was in the Palace of the Austrian Viceroys of the Bukovina, and looked out on a garden with a beautiful statue of the murdered Austrian Empress. I had talked in the same room during the preceding year with Generals Lechitski and Kaledin, two of Russia's finest soldiers who had been already sacrificed to the hatred of the mob.

Poor Kornilov was very pessimistic. He said that the way Gurko had been treated showed clearly that the present Government was determined to remove everyone who had decision of character and possessed some influence with the troops, and to keep only such men as Brusilov, who agreed to any madness they proposed. He agreed with me that, if the coming offensive failed, the Allies would have nothing more to hope for from Russia, and he said: " If Russia stops fighting, I hope you will take me as a private soldier in the British Army, for I will never make peace with the Germans."

I left the 8th Army the next day and spent the succeeding three weeks in the 11th and 7th Armies, which had been detailed to deliver the main attack.

Thursday, June 14th, 1917.   KREMENETS.

On the road from Tarnopol there were everywhere signs of disorganisation. The artillery of the Guard was seen halted in one village. The guns and horses were distributed without system, just where they happened to be unbuckled. There was no sentry over the guns. I can imagine how the unfortunate officers' sense of order must suffer. In several places we passed transport wagons, the horses unhitched and tied up without food, while the men slept under a tree.

After supper I asked the officer in charge of the Intelligence Section who would do the leading in the coming offensive, the officers or the committees. He said that of course the officers would, and added that the position of the regimental officer is now so desperate that he does not care whether he is killed or not.

The other day, when fraternisation was in progress at the front, some German officers came over, and there was an informal discussion regarding the causes of the war. The Russian and German officers naturally disagreed, and a Russian soldier said he preferred the word of a German officer to that of a Russian. In taking leave, the German officers told the Russians that they were "really sorry" for them, for their "position was dreadful."

I blame the whole of the Higher Command for the martyrdom the officers are now suffering—Guchkov, Alexyeev and all the others. They should have insisted at once on a firm line being drawn to protect the army. There are whole units on this front which only read the *Pravda*, printed and distributed with German money, and what can one expect from ignorant men poisoned by such stuff? Other units receive hundreds of copies daily of the Russian paper published by the German General Staff, which makes a speciality of attacks on England.

What can the Russian soldier know of "Peace without annexations and without contributions"—the formula produced in Berlin for his special misleading? Many of them think that "Anneksiya" and "Contributsiya" are two towns, and one of them, when asked if he understood the motto, said that he did not know where "Anneksiya" was, but that "Contributsiya" was "somewhere in Turkey!" He thought of Constantinople!

I spent the night of June 16th in the XLIXth Corps, and found the Commander, General Selivachev, quite a character. He had undoubtedly Jewish blood and an extraordinary pineapple-shaped head, a ludicrous feature which officers asserted had prevented his appointment to the General Staff, though he passed the Military Academy.

In the afternoon I visited the Czechs, 4,000 of whom were being concentrated to take part in the coming offensive—grand men, with chests like Aldershot gymnastic instructors. Their orchestra sang "God Save the King" at supper. I slept in the General's room, and left for the front with him at 6.30 a.m. the next day. We returned at 3.30 p.m., after trekking some twelve miles through trenches in a hot sun. Certainly General Selivachev was physically the most energetic Russian general I had met. He had everywhere a cheery word for the men; he was doing all that was humanly possible.

The following day I spent with General Notbek,[1] the Commander of the VIth Corps. In visiting the trenches, he shook hands with every soldier he met, a sudden departure from the former Russian custom of only giving the hand to officers. The simpler plan would have been to have abolished the custom of hand-shaking all round, as a habit as useless as the wearing of the sword, and there seemed to be a tendency in this direction in the Staff of the 11th Army, where every room had a notice on the door: " Hand-shaking is abolished in hot weather."

In the three months since the Revolution the VIth Corps had changed its commander twice, also all its three division commanders, eight out of its twelve regiment commanders, and had expelled from five to six officers, mostly regulars, from each regiment. It was no wonder that there were 3,000 officers " at the disposal of the Commander Kiev Military District " awaiting appointment to units where the men might be pleased to accept the offer of their services!

The men in some units had said: " We will attack, but if we fail, we will kill the Corps Staff." A soldier at a meeting had proposed that in the attack the corps commander should lead, followed by the three divisional commanders, followed by the twelve regiment commanders and all the officers, the men coming last of all.

The worst regiment in the XLIXth Corps was the 13th Finland Regiment, which had been corrupted by Ensign Kirilenko, a half-crazy individual who was later to attain an unenviable notoriety. This man, in a speech in the committee of the 11th Army on May 12th, had expressed his belief in the existence of secret treaties between Great Britain and Germany.

---

[1] General Selivachev was promoted in July, 1917, to command the 7th Army. General Denikin told me in London in 1920 that he is now dead. He was forced by the Bolsheviks to command an army against the Volunteer Army, and later, when on his death-bed, confessed to the priest that he had done all that in him lay to facilitate the success of the Volunteers.

General Notbek was later promoted to command an army—I think the 1st. He, too, was forced to serve under the Bolsheviks, and was in command at the town of Samara when that town was captured from the Bolsheviks by a revolt of Russian officers under Captain Kapel in 1918. As he had failed to take an active part in this revolt he was mistrusted by the corps of officers in Siberia, and accordingly did not receive a command in Kolchak's army.

On the same occasion he reported the result of a " plebiscite " he had organised in the 13th Finland Regiment to decide the course of action to be followed by Russia in each of the following eventualities :

    1. If the Allies abandoned all claim to annexations but Germany did not.
    2. If both the Allies and Germany refused to abandon the idea of annexations.
    3. If the Allies refused to abandon their claim to annexations, but Germany agreed to do so.

The reply, he stated, was in each case "War," but in the third case " War against the Allies." He calmly contemplated war against the world, and said that the worst that could befall Russia would be the loss of the Caucasus, Finland, Siberia and Poland.

Kerenski had appointed "commissaries " to each army to assist in the maintenance of discipline. These men were all hall-marked revolutionaries, and most of them had spent several years in penal servitude. The commissary of the 11th Army had been six years an exile in Siberia; the commissary of the 7th Army, Boris Savinkov, had been the chief organiser of the murder of the Grand Duke Sergei Alexandrovich. Since then he had lived in exile as a journalist. Under the pseudonym of " Ropshin " he had written a weird tale, " The Pale Horse." In principle, the appointment of commissaries was, of course, wrong, as it diminished the prestige of the officers, but both of these men were working with courage and in complete harmony with the Command to re-establish order.

The Commander of the 7th Army at Buczacz, General Byelkovich and his Chief of Staff, General Neznamov, were more optimistic than officers nearer the front. General Obruchev, of the XXIInd Corps, said that the further forward the men were, the less inclined they were to attack. His corps was 12,000 men under establishment, and one of his divisional commanders said that he had only received 400 men in drafts since the Revolution. These had arrived in ten draft companies, the survivors of 2,500 men who had been despatched with banners as heroes from Tver.

There were patent signs of indiscipline everywhere. The bivouack of every mounted unit had numbers of horses galloping about loose. Guns were never parked. Men were everywhere bathing, lying drying in the sun or tea-drinking. The only people who seemed to be doing a day's work were the cooks, the men, no doubt, seeing to it that they, at all events, worked. The roads which, when taken over from the Austrians the year before, had been good, were now in a disgraceful condition, and no attempt was made to repair them.

Everywhere Government transport was used for work for which it was never intended; one of its chief duties seemed to be to carry delegates to and from their meetings.

The one idea was politics. I was sitting with the General Quartermaster of the 7th Army *the day before* we moved to the front for the offensive, when two members of the Petrograd Sovyet were announced. They had come to lecture on two themes, " Peace and War " and " The Constituent Assembly." Were they not ridiculous enough, these demagogues, to dream of such abstract subjects on the very eve of an offensive that might decide the fate of Russia !

The only chance seemed to be that the men might be impressed by the number of guns concentrated for the support of the attack. One gunner I talked to said he had fought for three years and had " never seen anything like so many guns " !

The one object of the Command seemed to be to avoid bloodshed, and it was only by bloodshed that discipline could have been restored. What streams of Russian blood shed since might have been saved if only loyal units had been used to restore order with energy at the outset of the rot in the army.

The history of the VIIth Siberian Corps may serve as a typical instance of the vacillation of the Command. This corps was formed near Riga in the autumn of 1915 from the 12th and 13th Siberian Divisions. It was badly commanded, and seems to have been already corrupted by German propaganda before its transfer to the 7th Army in the autumn of 1916.

Towards the end of May, 1917, the corps was resting with its newly-formed division—the 19th Siberian—at Kolomea, when it received the order to return to the trenches. Ten thousand men obeyed and the remainder refused. The Commissary reported to the Minister of War, and orders were issued for the disbandment of four of the regiments. The men were, however, fully armed, and as they refused to give up their rifles the Commissary, in order to avoid bloodshed, decided to " give them another chance."

Five thousand more men now agreed to obey orders. Meanwhile, the first ten thousand men had been formed into a Composite Siberian Division, and steadily refused to receive back their former comrades. The five thousand men remained in the second line transport.

There remained some 3,000 men, who complained that they were ill. When, however, a medical board was appointed, only 800 men appeared before it. These were all granted from two to four months' leave to depot regiments to recuperate.

On the night of June 28th, the IInd Cavalry Corps was despatched south to bring the remainder to reason. The mutineers were surrounded and given till 6 p.m. on the 29th to surrender. They actually began to entrench, but a few rounds of shrapnel fired high up in the air made them change their minds, and they gave up their rifles. When Savinkov reported to General Gutor on the evening of the 29th, and asked what should be done with the 1,500 men disarmed, the General said, " They will attack." Apparently he had decided that they should not be punished.

Some days after the 800 men had obtained sick leave, General Byelkovich, the Commander of the 7th Army, drove to the Composite Siberian Division to talk about the coming offensive. The men were holding a meeting and he was invited to attend. He was asked why he had given leave to 800 mutineers and had compelled them, the loyal 10,000, to go to the trenches. The question was a difficult one, and Byelkovich said that he really did not know about it as he had not seen the telegram. A one-year volunteer then asked him how he called himself the Commander of the Army if he did not even know what telegrams were sent. This so affected the General that he fell back in a dead faint.

The offensive was postponed to allow of the arrival of Kerenski with a joint proclamation of the Conference of the Sovyets of Working-Men and Soldier Deputies and the Executive Committee of the Alliance of Peasant Deputies. On the face of it, the document he brought with him was scarcely worth waiting for. It is true it called on the men to attack, but to attack in order by " proving their organisation and strength to add weight to the voice of revolutionary Russia in its appeal to enemy, neutral and allied countries, and so to hasten the end of the war." This was not very enthusing. Kerenski's Order of June 29th was better, but the phrase, " I call on the army, fortified by the strength and spirit of the Revolution, to take the offensive " must have seemed a hollow mockery to officers at the front.

Kerenski on arrival went with his usual energy to try the effect of his eloquence on one of the worst divisions in the army—the 2nd Guard Infantry.

Saturday, June 30th, 1917.   COMMANDER-IN-CHIEF'S TRAIN, KOZOWA.

When Kerenski visited the 2nd Division of the Guard yesterday the men formed into two groups, 6,000 surrounding him, cheering, while 4,000 held another " meeting " some hundreds of yards distant. Kerenski said he wanted to speak to all of the men, and asked the hostile group to come over. They refused, called him a " bourgeois," and said they only wanted to fight the bourgeoisie. They refused a hearing to an officer who tried to persuade them. They yelled: " Down with the war ! " " Down with everything ! " Kerenski was with the division two hours and very few of the opposition crowd strolled over. The Grenaderski Regiment is the worst regiment in the division, partly because it has lost more officers killed than any other Guards regiment and partly owing to the activities of a Polish ensign, who was educated near Lemberg. Of the 1st and 2nd Divisions of the Guard, the Preobrajenski, Semenovski and Izmailovski Regiments are said to be all right, but the other five regiments are all bad.

It is well that Kerenski has had a rebuff, for it will show him the present state of things, of which, judging from his conversations with the Ambassador, he seemed to be ignorant.

To-morrow is Sunday, July 1st. What will it bring?

Sunday Evening, July 1st.
There will be no success.

It had long been decided that the main offensive of the year should be launched on the South-West Front, and that this stroke should be accompanied or succeeded by minor offensives on the other fronts. The section selected for the main attack was twenty-eight miles in length, of which thirteen miles north of the village of Kuropatniki lay in the area of the 11th Army and fifteen miles south of that village lay in the area of the 7th Army.

The plan was, briefly, to gain the western bank of the Zlota Lipa and then to wheel north-west and advance on Lemberg.

Two subsidiary offensives were also arranged by the South-West Front:

(*a*). By the Vth Siberian Corps on a narrow front, nineteen miles south of Brody. This movement was to be supported by the 6th Grenadier Division from the Special Army and was postponed owing to the refusal of that division to fight.

(*b*). By the XIIth Corps of the 8th Army, west of Mariampol.

The object of the two subsidiary offensives was to hold the enemy in their immediate front. The XIIth Corps section was selected because certain Austrian units on the line there had more than once urged the Russians to attack quickly so that they might have time to surrender before German troops arrived who might force them to fight.

With the idea of encouraging the men, General Gutor moved the Staff of the Front forward from Kamenets-Podolski to the village of Kozowa, seven miles from the German trenches, and ordered the Staff of the 11th Army to move from Kremenets to Jezierna, and of the 7th Army from Buczacz to the village of

Teliache. General Gutor's Staff consisted of General Dukhonin as Chief of Staff, with General Rattel as General Quartermaster; General Erdeli commanded the 11th Army, with General Boris Gerois as Chief of Staff and General Markovski as General Quartermaster; and General Byelkovich was in charge of the 7th Army, with Generals Neznamov and Zapolski.

Most of the Staffs had been changed a short time before the action. General Gutor had only succeeded General Brusilov on June 6th. The Commander of the 11th Army had been changed twice in the previous two months, and General Erdeli only arrived five days before the offensive. General Gerois had occupied his post for two months, but his General Quartermaster had arrived only ten days before the attack. Both the Commander and the Chief of Staff of the 7th Army had been appointed in April. All the corps commanders and most of the division commanders had been changed in the three months preceding the attack.

However, all the regular officers that had survived the war and the revolution worked heroically to stem the tide of cowardice and indiscipline.

The main striking force consisted of the following units :

11TH ARMY :
    XVII. 35th Division.
    XLIX. Selivachev, 4th Finland, Czecho-Slovak Brigade. 6th Finland, 82.
    VI. Notbek, 2nd Finland, 4, 16, 155, 151.
    Reserve of Army Commander :
        Trans-Baikal Cossack Cavalry Division.
        V. Miliant, 7, 10. (To complete concentration north of Tarnopol by July 7th.)
    Reserve of Commander-in-Chief :
        I Guard, Ilkevich, 1 Guard, 2 Guard. (West and north of Tarnopol).

7th Army :
    XLI. Melgonov, 113, 5th Trans-Amur, 3rd Trans-Amur, 74.
    VII. Siberian. Ladovski, Composite Siberian, 108.

XXXIV. Skoropadski, 19th Siberian, 23, 104, 153.
XXII. Obruchev, 5th Finland, 1st Finland, 3rd Finland,159.
    Reserve of Army Commander :
      Guard Rifle Division.
      Polish Division.
      2 cyclist battalions.
      II. Cavalry, Tumanov, 9th Cavalry, Composite Cavalry Division.
    Reserve of Commander-in-Chief :
      3rd Guard Infantry Division.
      V. Cavalry, Veliarshev, 11th Cavalry, Orenburg Cossack Cavalry.
      XLV. 122, 126, 194. (To complete concentration from the 9th Army by July 13th.)

The Russian superiority in bayonets was, as usual, considerable, and the Command had succeeded for the first time in the war in concentrating a superiority in guns and aeroplanes.

Apart from specialist detachments numbering over 50,00 men, the twenty-three and a half divisions of the corps in front line had 174,701 bayonets in the companies against, as far as was known at the commencement of the operation, eighteen German battalions, forty-eight Austrian and twelve Turkish, a superiority of three or four to one.

Classified according to the Russian system, the Russians had 693 light field guns opposed to 284 enemy guns, 84 light howitzers opposed to 178 enemy, and 337 so-called heavy guns and howitzers opposed to 66 enemy.

The 11th Army had about fifty aeroplanes and the 7th Army about seventy, including six of large type.

The enemy had known all along of our selection of this area, but he did not imagine till June 23rd that we had serious intentions of attacking. Information given him by deserters enabled him to follow every move. For instance, it had been necessary to relieve the Guard Corps from the right of the 11th Army in order to concentrate it in rear of the striking force. The day after the relieving corps, the 1st Turkistan, took its place in the line, a N.C.O. and a private went over to the German trenches and returned two hours later drunk and with supplies of cognac and propaganda literature. An officer ordered his men to fire on them as they staggered back, but the men refused. Enemy spies passed freely backwards and forwards through the lines of the XXXIVth Corps. It was wished to concentrate by night, but many units refused to march except in the day.

Few of the infantry units were actively mutinous, but almost every division had one bad regiment. The cavalry and artillery were sound.

The corps inspectors of artillery proposed to destroy the enemy's first line trenches by five hours' fire and then to attack, but this proposal was over-ruled by the Commander-in-Chief on the advice of Captain Vagneux, of the French Artillery. It was finally arranged that the 11th Army, together with the XLIst Corps of the 7th Army, should commence their artillery preparation at daylight on June 29th, and the other corps of the 7th Army— VIIth Siberian, XXXIVth and XXIInd—at daylight on the 30th. The attack was to be launched at 10 a.m. on July 1st, but the 4th Finland Rifle Division and the Czecho-Slovak Brigade postponed their attack till the morning of the 2nd.

The artillery preparation, to which the hostile guns made little reply, destroyed the enemy's wire and all the defences in his first fortified zone.

The VIth Corps took the enemy's first three lines of trench in twenty minutes, practically without loss. The village of Koniuchy was occupied by the 2nd Finland Division, but as liquor was found there,[1] the other divisions of the corps were

---

[1] This danger was foreseen. In VIth Corps Order No. 28 of June 23rd the preparatory order for the attack, Para. 15, runs:

> Measures are to be thought out in the divisions for dealing with deserters and malingerers who shirk fighting. For this purpose the widest use is to be made of divisional, regimental and company deputies. It is particularly important that deputies should be present at dressing-stations and advanced hospitals with cooking-carts and at river crossings.
>
> Divisions must also take steps with the co-operation of the deputies to contend with drunkenness by appointing special individuals and detachments to destroy spirits and wine in trenches captured from the enemy. The troops are to be warned that prisoners state that the Austrians are going to leave for our men in their trenches poisoned spirits which will cause death or serious illness.

held back. General Maimaievski, the Commander of the 4th Division, marched to the attack at its head.

Progress was, however, much interfered with by the indiscipline and stupidity of the men. The left regiment of the 16th Division had been allotted a passive task. While the artillery preparation was in progress, the Divisional Commander was informed by the regimental committee that the men refused to move because only two passages had been prepared for them through the wire, while eight passages had been prepared for the neighbouring regiment. To destroy the wire that worried these men much shell had to be wasted that would have been otherwise used against the enemy's trenches. The extra passages were not required, and the enemy's trenches being insufficiently destroyed the regiment that had raised the objection suffered more heavily than it need have done in the attack.

Further to the right in the XLIXth Corps, the 24th Regiment of the 6th Finland Division refused to attack, and so exposed the 6th and 8th Regiments of the 2nd Finland Division to heavy counter-attacks in which they lost twenty-five and thirty officers respectively.

In the 7th Army all the divisions that had been allotted an active task occupied the enemy's trenches as far as these had been destroyed by gunfire, but, with the exception of the divisions of the VIIth Siberian Corps, showed little inclination to press further.

On the edge of an oak forest, on high ground south-east of Brzezany, there were many artillery observation posts. In one of these General Gutor took up his position with the Minister of War. From another more to the left I got a fine view of the advance of the Composite Siberian Division along the summit of the hill on our immediate front.

All the observation posts were crowded not only by artillery officers but by correspondents and soldier "delegates." On the other hand, there was no proper liaison with the firing line. The watch of the artillery Colonel in my O.P. was eight minutes slow, and he continued firing at the enemy's trenches after ten o'clock, till notified by one of the batteries that the trenches were already occupied by the Russian infantry.

About 2 p.m. I went back to the headquarters of the 7th Army, where I sat in the General Quartermaster's room and obtained a general idea of the progress of the operation. At first the Staff were in good spirits, but from 3 p.m. the picture began to change.

The 74th Division was making no progress and complained of heavy gunfire from its left. The Commander-in-Chief telephoned that many men of this division were streaming to the rear, and ordered that all available delegates were to be sent to hearten the waverers. No doubt Kerenski had suggested the delegates, his universal panacea. He was to see how ineffective they were to stop a panic as compared with the officers whose prestige he had allowed to be undermined.

The Composite Siberian Division continued to make progress and was reinforced by the 108th Division.

General Skoropadski, the Commander of the XXXIVth Corps, soon began to call for help. "Two regiments of the 19th Siberian Division had reached the second line of German trench, but the other two regiments could not be brought up owing to the enemy's barrage. The 23rd Division had three regiments already in line and was suffering much from the German fire. He feared a counter-attack. The 153rd Division had so many men down with the scurvy that only forty rifles per company were left." At 4 p.m. he telephoned that he had two German divisions against him, as he had taken prisoners from both the 15th German Reserve and from the 24th German Reserve Divisions. As a matter of fact, these two German divisions were not only holding up Skoropadski's four divisions, but also the two divisions of the VIIth Siberian Corps and one division of the XLIst Corps!

General Skoropadski proposed that his corps should be relieved that night by the IInd Guard Corps, and the Army Staff recommended this course on the ground that it was necessary to restore confidence at the outset of the operation.

By 5.30 p.m. the XXXIVth Corps had retired to its original trenches.

The XXIInd Corps on the left shared the same fate. At first all three divisions made good progress, and especially the 1st Finland in the centre. The 5th Finland Division on the right captured two lines of Turkish trench, but retired, owing to a counter-attack, and the other two divisions followed its example.

By 6 p.m. on July 1st, all the Russian units, with the exception of the VIth Corps and the VIIth Siberian Corps, had retired to their original trenches. The VIIth Siberian Corps held on to the ground it had gained for about forty-eight hours longer and was withdrawn. A few gas shells had caused a panic in the 3rd Trans-Amur and 74th Divisions. The enemy's fire was never heavy and the Russian artillery worked under practice camp conditions.

Most of the infantry behaved badly. The men were some of them impressed by a supporting artillery fire to which they had been little accustomed, and they went as far as the enemy's trenches had been destroyed. They had lost many of their officers and had no incentive to further effort; in fact, they knew that further progress would be attended by risk and they knew they could retire without fear of being punished. To dig themselves in where they were was too much trouble, so they went back to their old ready-made defences. As a Russian artillery General expressed it, "They felt lonely in front and went back to their dug-outs to sleep."

Many of the officers behaved heroically. One officer, after fruitless efforts to induce his men to advance, tore off his shoulder-straps and swore he would "never again try to lead such swine," then he took a rifle and went over the top like a man. Another—a machine-gunner—was seen three times to go forward and each time to return to appeal to his men to follow, but without result.

The Propaganda Mission from the Black Sea Fleet, consisting of twelve sailors, attacked with the troops in the 11th Army.

The army staffs reported the capture on July 1st of the following prisoners: By the 11th Army, 164 officers and 250 German and 8,010 Austrian rank and file. By the 7th Army, 23 officers, 1,214 German, 577 Austrian and 191 Turk rank and file. The 11th Army captured five guns.

The 81st Czech Regiment surrendered *en bloc* to the VIth Corps, and next day marched through Tarnopol headed by its band and with a small Cossack escort.

The first return of losses sent in was incredibly large, and

General Dukhonin talked all lunch on the 2nd of the enormous losses in the 23rd Division, of which "only 2,000 bayonets remained." Next day it transpired that the losses of the whole 7th Army were less than those ascribed in the first report to this one division. It is probable that a large number of men hid in the woods and only returned when they got hungry and were sure that the fighting was over. The return finally given out was 17,339 killed, wounded, and missing.

The Chief of Military Communications of the South-West Front superintended the evacuation of the wounded from Kozowa on July 1st, and told me that the sights he saw effectually cured his former optimism. In a train with 850 cases he saw only some fifteen men really wounded; the remainder "had wounds nearly all in the left hand, many in one finger and all very suspicious looking. Formerly men were liable to the death penalty for self-wounding, but now such doctors as were not working in committees were afraid to arrest the men."

Though Kerenski worked hard as Minister of War, he was still, before everything, the revolutionary. When three German prisoners—the first taken—were led past his observation-post, he sent to ask them, not the number of German troops on their left and right and rear, but to what political party they belonged, and whether there would soon be a revolution in Germany. The honest men replied that they did not belong to any political party. They did not know anything about the interior of Germany, but at the front, where they had been the whole war, there was no sign of a revolution.

The Minister of War either really thought or pretended he thought that a great victory had been gained. He sent off a rhetorical telegram to the Premier: "To-day has furnished the reply once and for all to the malicious and slanderous attacks on the organisation of the Russian army, based on democratic principles. I earnestly beg of you to sanction urgently, in the name of the free people, my presentation of red revolutionary standards to the regiments which took part in the battle of July 1st." Prince Lvov replied, sanctioning the proposal and stating with unconscious truth that "July 1st has shown to the whole world the might of a revolutionary army, organised on democratic lines and inspired by a fervent belief in the ideals of the revolution."

On the night of July 1st the IInd Guard Corps occupied the area formerly held by the XXXIVth Corps. General Skoropadski went into reserve with the 23rd Division. The 19th Siberian Division was handed back to the VIIth Siberian Corps, and the 153rd Division was transferred to the XXIInd Corps. The units of the XLIst Corps gave it to be understood that they would not attack again. The offensive in the 7th Army had come to an end.

On July 2nd the 11th Army continued its advance, and the XLIXth Corps, in conjunction with the 35th Division on its right, made good progress. The Commander of the Corps, General Selivachev, was fortunate in being opposed only by Austrians. Airmen had seen the Germans travelling south on the day before by all available roads, in order to resist the advance of the VIth Corps. General Selivachev confessed the next day with emotion that he owed his success to the Czecho-Slovak Brigade, and the list of captures confirms this view:

TAKEN BY:	AUSTRIAN OFFICERS	AUSTRIAN R. AND F.	GUNS.
4th Finland Division	50	1,600	3
Czecho-Slovak Brigade	70	3,200	20
6th Finland Division	40	1,000	3

Monday, July 2nd, 1917. KOZOWA.

The Czech officer has just been in to tell me that his people captured twenty guns to-day. The 35th Division and the 4th Finland Division took two more guns.

The Czechs complain of unsympathetic treatment. No less than 20,000 of the Czech prisoners, who, of course, surrendered voluntarily, are said to have perished on the Murman railway. Even now only 10 per cent. of the prisoners are allowed to volunteer for the front, the remainder being detained to work on farms in the rear.

Kerenski said that they should make a revolution in Austria instead of coming to fight on the Russian front.

The VIth Corps failed to make further progress.

The disaffection in the 1st Guard Corps, the only reserve concentrated in rear of the 11th Army, had prevented full advantage being taken of the success of the VIth Corps on July 1st, for General Erdeli had considered it necessary at the last moment to hold back the 151st Division of that Corps as army reserve, and the Commander of the Corps was therefore left without the necessary weight to push his initial success.

Again General Selivachev's success with the XLIXth Corps on July 2nd was of no avail, for the 1st Guard Corps was still too far distant to drive the attack home. Simply on account of the disaffection in this Corps the whole advance of the 11th Army had to stop on the 3rd, 4th and 5th.

On the morning of the 3rd I met the Pavlovski Regiment marching, it is true, towards the front, but without any semblance of order. I mentioned the fact half an hour later to the Commander of the Division, General Rilski, whom I met at the staff of the 11th Army, and he was greatly surprised, for, though the move had been ordered, he did not in the least expect the order to be obeyed.

The Grenaderski Regiment refused to move till the 4th, when it suddenly changed its mind. On the morning of the 5th only two battalions of the 1st Guard Corps had come up into line to relieve tired units of the XLIXth Corps, and especially the Czech Brigade, which had suffered severely on the 2nd. It is not surprising that when the attack was renewed on the 6th the enemy was found to be dug in and in greater strength.

It seemed evident on July 4th that no further progress could be hoped for from the main offensive, and everything seen confirmed the previous impression that the Russian army had been irretrievably ruined as a fighting organisation. I therefore decided to return to Petrograd to telegraph my conclusions to England.

Wednesday, July 4th, 1917.   Kozowa.

I heard that Ignatiev wanted to see me, so I drove in the little Ford at 10 a.m. to the headquarters of the 1st Guard Infantry Division.

He took me into his small tent to have a quiet talk. He was very pessimistic, and as he is a man of good digestion, with plenty of robust common sense, his opinion is valuable. He thinks there is no hope.

I put three questions to him, whether Russia would:
1. Fight as she fought before the Revolution;
2. Fight as she has fought since the Revolution till the general peace; or
3. Make a separate peace.

To the first question he said emphatically, "No." He was inclined to say "Yes" to the second, but with hesitation, and he was unable to deny the possibility of a separate peace.

He pointed out that peace is essential for Russia, and that if there is not peace soon there will be a general massacre. The prolongation of the war is drawing Russia to the brink of economic ruin. Even at the beginning only an inconsiderable number of the peasants wanted war. The educated classes did, but the one dream of the peasant soldiers at the front has long been peace.

He said: "If you were now to go out on the village square and to proclaim that the war will end at once, but only on one condition—that Nikolai Romanov returns to power, every single man would agree and there would be no more talk of a democratic republic."

I asked if he thought that the reconsideration of the objects of the war would have any effect on Russian public opinion. He said that it would on the conscientious people, but that the mass of the soldiery only wanted an excuse for saving their skins—they were not Bolsheviki or Mensheviki, but simply 'Shkurniki' (fearers for their own skins).

He allowed that Russia was doing a dirty action, and foresaw that no foreigner would speak to a Russian for twenty years. In England's place he would get out of the war as quickly as possible while there was yet time! He had always hoped that the war would end militarism, but he now saw that militarism would be increased immeasurably by Germany's victory.

He said that no one could possibly picture the present position of officers—they were martyrs and not officers. Some nights ago a company commander in the Yegerski Regiment was riding along with his company when the men called to him to get off, as they did not see why a bourgeois should ride when they had to walk. He got off! Then they began to consider whether, after all, he had not better ride so that he might be able the quicker to find them billets when they arrived. He mounted, but he had no sooner mounted than they required him again to dismount. This officer asked permission to leave the regiment, but he was persuaded by his brother martyrs to remain. Of course he cannot have been much of an officer, but his superiors have certainly not given him an example in firmness.

Ignatiev told me that his mother had died of a broken heart. She had spent all the latter years of her life in charitable work in the village where she had started and maintained a school for forty-five children. The village "Committee" decided to boycott this school "lest the feeling of gratitude should be inculcated in the children." The President of the Committee announced that anyone who kissed the old lady's hand would be fined Rs.25, but one woman had the courage to say: "I will kiss her hand, for the old Countess was the only person who came near me to sit with me when I was ill, and I will not pay your fine!"

Thursday, July 5th, 1917.   TRAIN, KAMENETS TO KIEV.

I said good-bye to the staff of the front last night. I think Gutor and Dukhonin are really far less optimistic than they pretend.

Dukhonin protested when I said that the whole operation would be over in four more days. He said: "My God! What a pessimist you are!" He argued that he could continue for fourteen more days with the strength he now possessed. Selivachev has been given command of the 7th Army, vice Byelkovich, and after he has studied the position for a few days a decision will be come to as to whether the offensive should be continued in both armies or only by the 11th!

Both Gutor and Dukhonin absolutely deny the possibility of a separate peace. They think that the Russian army can and will fight a fourth winter. Gutor, however, said that on economic grounds it would be better if we could make peace sooner.

I asked Dukhonin what steps he considered necessary in order to restore the army to something of its old *morale*. He said that Kerenski should be pressed to restore their power to officers in order to raise their prestige, to do away with committees and to give courts-martial in the area of armies engaged in offensive operations the power of inflicting the death penalty.

Gutor asked for a military law as opposed to civil law—that military courts in time of war, whether at the front or in rear, should have power to inflict the death penalty. He suggested that I should see Tseretelli or perhaps Chkheidze, point out the actual condition of things and ask them to help. Kerenski has no longer the power; the change must come from the Sovyet.

Gutor thinks that the socialisation of the terms of peace would make little difference. The people who do not want to fight use the formula "Without annexations and without contributions" as an excuse without the faintest idea of its meaning.

The thing that strikes one most in these operations is the extraordinary passivity of the Boche. He could take the offensive and knock the Russians into a cocked hat!

General Denikin was appointed to command the Western Front, vice General Gurko, and General Klembovski to command the Northern Front, vice General Abram Dragomirov resigned.

At Supreme Headquarters General Brusilov appointed General Lukhomski to be his Chief of Staff, and General Romanovski from Chief of Staff of the 8th Army to be General Quartermaster.

General Kaledin was elected Ataman of the Don Cossacks.

The war in Russia was coming more and more to be regarded as a secondary matter.

In a speech at Kiev in June, Kerenski, then Minister of War, told his audience that the Constituent Assembly could not be summoned before October, because the people would be at work in the fields. It did not occur to him to mention the war, which had been sufficient to prevent all elections even in a small country like England.

General Prjevalski, the new Commander-in-Chief in the Caucasus, in taking leave of his corps committee, thanked them for their co-operation and told them that they had two tasks before them in the future: *first* the preparation of the army for the Constituent Assembly, and *secondly* the restoration of discipline!

General Klembovski, the Commander-in-Chief of the Northern Front, said in a speech at Riga that the present offensive was all-important, because a winter campaign was impossible and all the combatants would soon begin negotiations for peace.

CHAPTER XXII

PETROGRAD IN JULY AND AUGUST. KERENSKI'S CHANCE

Reference Sketch F

I RETURNED to Petrograd on the evening of July 8th, to find the state of the garrison very much as it was at the end of May. There was no work and no discipline. The political situation had changed to this extent, that the Sovyet was now working in nominal co-operation with the Provisional Government, and the Extremist element among the troops had begun to look more and more to the Bolshevik faction, whose demand of an immediate peace was more popular than the tardy appeal of the Sovyet in the interests of national defence. Lenin, from the balcony of the house of the dancer Kshinskaya, on the right bank of the Neva, opposite the British Embassy, harangued crowds nightly without interference from the authorities.

Tuesday, July 17th, 1917.

I saw Yakubóvich, the Assistant Minister of War, yesterday afternoon, and he told me that he thought, " one way or another," the death penalty would be reintroduced in the army in a month's time. The ministers are becoming less idealistic and they only speak now of the re-establishment of order. Lvov is the great obstacle, for he is a confirmed idealist, and it would be a blessing if he would retire. Kerenski returned on the 15th and left again last night, this time for the Western Front.

I asked what would happen if the death penalty were not re-established. Yakubóvich said: " There will be an end of the Russian army by October." I said, " That means a separate peace ? " He replied, " No. It means that the army will sit in the trenches."

Tumánov, the other Assistant, came in, and I read them both the " Instructions to German Agents before leaving for Russia," of which I had received a copy from England. When I reached a paragraph recommending that every effort should be made to cause dissension between the Provisional Government and the Sovyet, Tumánov remarked : " They have missed the point there ; they should work for dissension between the men and their representative committees ; that is the real danger."

On the night of Monday, July 16th, the first Bolshevik revolt was launched in Petrograd.

The prime mover was the 1st Depot Machine-Gun Regiment, one of four depot machine-gun regiments formed in the autumn of 1916 to supply trained machine-gunners to regiments of the line. At the outbreak of the Revolution, on March 12th, the regiment numbered 19,000 men. By July 16th it had dwindled to 6,000-7,000, simply owing to desertion, for in the intervening four months it had not supplied a single man to the front. Immediately after the Revolution it had established its headquarters in the People's Palace, and for weeks had refused to move back to barracks, in spite of the efforts of the workman Godev, who had been specially detailed by M. Guchkov, when Minister of War, to reason with the men.

As in the case of all bad units, the disaffection was led by an ensign—in this case Semashko. This man was arrested early in July as a deserter by order of Kerenski, but he was liberated soon afterwards by the Guard on the demand of the men. Next day he led the regiment through the main streets of the capital in procession, trailing its machine-guns. The Government did nothing and the citizens trembled.

On Sunday, July 15th, the regiment held a meeting, in which " the proceedings," according to the *Pravda*, " were remarkable for the exceptional enthusiasm of the ripening revolutionary movement." The men were addressed by the two Bolsheviks, Trotski (Bronstein), and Lunacharski, and were finally roused to grim indignation by the description of a soldier just returned from the front of the brutal disbandment of the Grenaderski Regiment of the Guard for having merely refused to obey an order to go to the trenches!

The Depot Battalion of the Grenaderski Regiment, which had corrupted by its drafts one of the finest fighting units of the Russian army, agreed to demonstrate with the machine-gunners.

The Bolsheviks held an all-night sitting at Kshinskaya's house. Lenin himself was absent and only returned from Finland on the 17th.

On Monday delegates were sent to all the units of the Petrograd garrison, inviting them to join the armed demonstration, but the invitation met in most cases with a flat refusal.

About 9 p.m. the 1st Machine-Gun Regiment, with Semashko at its head, the Grenaderski Depot Battalion, and about 1,000 men of the Moskovski Depot Battalion, marched south across the Troitski bridge and past the British Embassy, accompanied by large crowds of armed workmen. They seized all the automobiles on the streets and armed them with machine-guns, men with fixed bayonets as usual lying along the splashboards to impress onlookers. The demonstration was joined by part of the Pavlovski Battalion, by the 1st, 3rd, 176th and 180th Depot Regiments, the 6th Depot Engineer Battalion and the 89th and 90th Drujini of Opolchenie.

The more respectable members of the "Militia," who had been masquerading as police since March, drawing as much pay per diem as the police who had protected life and property under the old régime drew in a whole month, went home; the others joined the rioters.

The crowd separated into two groups, one going west to the Marinski Palace where the Ministry usually met, the other east to the Duma. Banners proclaimed: "Down with the Ten Capitalist Ministers," and "All power to the Sovyet," mottoes that showed little power of imagination, for several of the "capitalist ministers" had resigned a few hours before, and the Executive

Committee of the Sovyet had repeatedly stated that it was working in complete harmony with the Provisional Government and had no wish to usurp its powers.

The Ministry was not sitting at the Marinski Palace, so the western column of rioters proceeded to the Nevski Prospekt, and practical men commenced looting shops.

At the Duma a meeting of the working-men's section of the Executive Committee of the Sovyet had been hastily summoned. It consisted largely of Bolsheviks. Zinoviev (Apfelbaum) appealed for stronger measures against the anti-revolutionary tendencies of the bourgeois Ministers, of the officers at G.H.Q. and of the permanent officials at the ministries. "The counter-revolutionary agitation," he proclaimed, "is being carried on with the participation of prominent allied diplomatists. . . . In the environs of Petrograd there are stationed Cossack regiments of anti-revolutionary tendencies, about which even Kerenski is ignorant." Kamenev (Rosenfeldt) proposed a resolution demanding that the working-men section of the Sovyet should assume the supreme power—he did not mention the soldier section. The representatives of all non-Bolshevik parties withdrew, and the resolution was passed.

The Commander-in-Chief of the District, General Polovtsev, had taken such measures as were possible. Some weeks before, he had wheadled 380 of its 800 machine-guns from the 1st Machine-Gun Regiment and had sent them to the front. He had removed the shell from the Mikhail School of Artillery, so that the guns which the insurgents captured were of no use to them. On Monday evening he called out eight squadrons of Don Cossacks—the only immediately available troops on which he could depend for active work—to form a mobile reserve in the courtyards of the Anichkov and Winter Palaces. He sent the Volinski Battalion to guard the Duma, "as in the days of the Great Revolution," a happy thought that showed that one general, at all events, was learning the new political method of command! He called a guard of the Preobrajenski Battalion to protect the District Offices.

The Staff remained cool and unperturbed throughout, though

none of its members slept for three nights. They had not sufficient force at first to attempt to interfere with the demonstration, and had to wait till the bulk of the garrison declared itself.

There was a certain amount of shooting on the Monday night, but none by supporters of the Government. An insurgent car drove up the Nevski Prospekt with a machine-gun, and when a few of the onlookers hooted, opened fire, killing and wounding a large number of spectators and about forty demonstrators from the Pavlovski Battalion. Possibly this incident cooled the ardour of the Pavlovski, for I met them straggling back to barracks as I made my way from the Embassy to the District Staff Office along the Milionnaya about 11 p.m.

To all outward appearances the town was completely in the power of the insurgents all Tuesday, the 17th. General Polovtsev told me in the morning that 6,000 men were coming in from Kronstadt with barbed wire, and as Ramsden and I walked back across the Troitski Bridge to lunch we met the rabble marching south—an evil-looking crew, with such inscriptions on their banners as: "A separate peace with William!" and "Down with the French and English capitalists!"

At 3 p.m. the situation was critical. The socialist minister, Chernov, tried to address the Kronstadt mutineers at the Duma, but was very roughly handled, and was only saved by the intervention of two anti-war socialists a shade more unpatriotic than himself.

The Executive Committee of the Sovyet issued a proclamation strongly condemning the armed demonstration. On the other hand, some extreme gentlemen seized the *Novoe Vremya* offices and issued leaflets, signed "Petrograd Federation of Anarchists," ridiculing Kerenski as a "little Napoleon" who had sacrificed 500,000 men in his recent offensive, and calling on the troops to elect delegates to a "revolutionary committee to control the Executive Committee of the Sovyet."

At this time the Staff had in hand for active operations eight squadrons of Cossacks, a few squadrons of depot cavalry, a battery of horse artillery and some 240 yunkers of the Paul and Vladimir Military Schools. It was known that the bulk of the garrison—all the depot units of the 1st and 3rd Guard Infantry Divisions—had so far refused to join the insurgents, but it was thought doubtful whether any reliance could be placed on these units for repressive measures.

It was about this time, when the fate of the Government seemed in the balance, that a group of officials at the Ministry of Justice took the step that saved the situation. The Ministry was in possession of material proving that the Bolsheviks, through the intermediaries Parvus, Ganetski, Sumenson and Kozlovski, had received money from the German General Staff. The officials thought that the Provisional Government was doomed, and they knew that the triumph of the Bolsheviks meant the destruction of such inconvenient material. They took their information to the District Staff and, with the consent of the Minister of Justice, made a communication to an evening paper, the *Jivoe Slovo* (" The Living Word "). As time was pressing, they considered even this step insufficient, and they accordingly communicated the broad outline of the contents of their dossier to the men of the Preobrajenski Battalion. The Minister of Ways, Nekrasov, in order to obtain favour with the Committee of the Sovyet, certain members of which had good reason to fear disclosures, did all he could to prevent the patriotic move of the officials, but failed. The news spread rapidly and had an excellent effect on the wavering troops.

Thursday, July 19th, 1917.

On Tuesday afternoon Balaban told me that he was sending out mixed detachments of each one squadron Cossacks, half a squadron cavalry and fifty rifles of the Preobrajenski to clear the streets. I suggested that fifty rifles was too little, and he said he would consult the O.C. Regiment. As a matter of fact, the Cossacks went out alone.

Thornhill had slept in the Embassy on Monday night. I moved there on Tuesday, and we both remained there till to-day.

Princess Soltykov came across to dinner, and we were just finishing when William, the Chasseur, ran in to say that the Cossacks were charging the sailors. Some ninety

Cossacks had charged across the Champ de Mars on 200 Kronstadt sailors, who fled precipitately into the Marble Palace. We arrived late for the fun, but saw the Cossacks ride past, many of them with three or four rifles slung across their backs. They rode past the front of the Embassy up the Quay.

In a few minutes two Cossacks returned on foot, escorting a prisoner, who appealed to a crowd of idle Pavlovski men to rescue him. One Cossack dropped him, but the other, a big fellow, held on to him like a man. He was one against twenty, and the cowards surged round him and overpowered him. The prisoner got free and at once bolted. A hero of the Pavlovski drew the Cossack's sword, and, while the others held back, gave him a swinging blow with it on the head. It seemed like cold-blooded murder of a man who had remained true to his salt, and we in the window above, being diplomats, could do nothing, not even shout, much less run down to tackle one or two of the brutes.

The Cossack, however, was only stunned for a moment, and then collected himself and ran off after his squadron. The other man ran in the opposite direction, and the insurgents fired several shots at both, but without hitting either.

A few minutes later there was a stampede of riderless horses down the Quay, and some five of them fell on the pavement at the corner in front of the Embassy. We learned later that the squadron had been ambushed and had suffered several casualties from machine-gun fire.

I read in the paper next day that a motor conveying dead and wounded Cossacks across the bridge was stopped by the crowd, all the bodies were thrown out, and the wounded were beaten. Can anything be imagined more detestable than some of the creatures that masquerade in the uniform of our " noble allies " !

There was heavy rain on Tuesday night and on Wednesday morning, and this helped to cool down excitement.

I awoke at 4 a.m. on Wednesday, and from my room in the Embassy saw several lorries pass with armed guards of sailors convoying shell. Then an armoured car with an enormous red flag came across the Troitski Bridge, evidently to scout, and soon ran back again. At 7 a.m. a guard arrived to open the bridge, and it was a relief to find that it had been sent by the Government.

Polovtsev sent out the yunkers of the military schools and detachments of the Preobrajenskis to disarm all troops found wandering in the streets, and some thousands of rifles were collected.

In the afternoon I was at the District Staff when about fifty automobiles were brought in by these detachments. While I was there, the Bolshevik, Kamenev (Rosenfeldt), came in with Lieber and a friend of the same race to ask for a pass for their automobile. When the Preobrajenski guard heard who they were they asked that they should be detained.

Polovtsev explained that he had not given orders for their arrest, but that it was the wish of the soldiers. Lieber, with a fine show of indignation, asked if the soldiers commanded in the Petrograd Military District and not the Commander-in-Chief! How very much easier it is to sow than it is to reap! Polovtsev retained the trio till later, and then allowed them to go free.[1]

In the same way on Wednesday morning the offices of the *Pravda*, which had been occupied by the troops, were evacuated by order of the Government and all the captured documents were returned!

By Wednesday evening all the troops who had taken part in the revolt, with the exception of the 1st Machine-Gun Regiment and the 180th Regiment, expressed their regret, and promised to be good in future.

---

[1] Lieber was not a Bolshevik. He was one of the three members of the Sovyet—Lieber, Dan and Gotz—who, whenever Kerenski showed signs of sanity, appeared to warn him of the dangers of the counter-revolution and that the "revolutionary democracy" would not tolerate strong measures. Unfortunately for Russia and for Kerenski, such intervention was always successful.

The troops ordered from the front—the 14th Cavalry Division, a cyclist battalion and a brigade of the 45th Division—commenced to arrive on Wednesday night.

This morning (19th) at 6.30 Thornhill came to my room to tell me that the fortress of Peter and Paul was going to be attacked and that we were required to evacuate the rooms on the south and east side of the Embassy in case the rebels should fire. Tereshchenko sent to invite the Ambassador and his family to take temporary refuge in the Ministry of Foreign Affairs, but the invitation was refused with thanks.

We had a weary time watching the preparations. Wave after wave of men crossed the bridge. Kshinskaya's house was occupied at 7.30, the Leninites having fled to the fortress. At 3 p.m. the fortress surrendered, and the 700 blackguards there, chiefly from Kronstadt and of the 1st Machine-Gun Regiment, were disarmed and—released! When I heard of this release at the Staff to-day I went for Polovtsev and Balaban and said that either the Russians were the cleverest people in the world or else the biggest fools. I pointed out that they had everything in their hands if they would only take strong measures, but that there would be an end of their co-operation as allies if they allowed the present opportunity to pass. Polovtsev said that he had not got a free hand, and had only orders to arrest Roshal, the Kronstadt leader, and he only sighed at my bloodthirstiness and said that I was " a hot-headed Irishman."

He gave me a specimen of a rough engraving depicting the sacrifice of a young girl by Jews, said to have taken place in Hungary in 1882, and told me that a large quantity of such anti-Semitic stuff had been found in Lenin's quarters in Kshinskaya's house.

Yesterday I wrote out the following paper. The Ambassador gave it to Tereshchenko, who said he agreed with it with the exception of the first point:

"If the Government gains the upper hand in the

present crisis, and wishes to continue the war *effectively* in concert with the Allies, it is suggested that it should :

"1. Re-establish the death penalty throughout Russia for all individuals subject to military and naval law.

"2. Require the units who took part in the unlawful demonstration of the 16th and 17th to give up agitators for punishment.

"3. Disarm all workmen in Petrograd.

"4. Establish a military censorship of the Press, with authority to confiscate the machinery of papers inciting the troops or the population to conduct to the prejudice of good order and military discipline.

"5. Establish a " militia " in Petrograd and other large towns under wounded officers from soldiers who have been wounded at the front, choosing preferably men of forty years and over.

"6. Disarm all units in Petrograd and district who do not agree to the above conditions and transform them into labour battalions."

If the Government does nothing now, I consider it is their very last chance.

It is rotten to sit here and to think that we can do nothing.

Friday, July 20th, 1917

Thornhill and I left the Embassy this morning.

Events have moved with dramatic quickness. Kerenski returned from the front last night and, in a stormy meeting of the Ministry, demanded dictatorial powers in order to bring the army back to discipline. The socialists disagreed. Lvov and Tereshchenko did their utmost to reconcile the diverging views. Kerenski left to meet the Mitava Hussars (14th Cavalry Division). While addressing the men he was handed a telegram telling him of the disaster on the South-West Front, where the Germans have broken through. He took back the telegram to the

Petrograd in July and August

Ministerial Council and the attitude changed. Lvov has resigned and Kerenski will be P.M. and Minister of War.

The Minister of Justice has resigned. He was strongly attacked by Tereshchenko and Nekrasov on account of having given the substance of the charges against the Bolsheviks to the Press before they could be arrested— as if Nekrasov would ever arrest anyone!

There is little sign of strong measures. Apparently only individuals suspected as German spies are to be arrested and the organisers of the military rising of the 16th and 17th are to go unpunished.

In order " to reassure the workmen," the Executive Committee of the Sovyet has published a notification that mass searches for arms will not be carried out.

Saturday, July 21st, 1917.

After 2 p.m. to-day the whole Palace Square was crowded by troops surrounding the men of the 1st Machine-Gun Regiment who had been disarmed. This regiment agreed last evening to bring its arms to the Palace Square by 9 p.m., but coolly put off the surrender while it sounded other units of the garrison once more in search of support. Semashko, the ringleader, has been arrested, but it remains to be seen whether he will be punished.

I had a talk with Polovtsev. Tereshchenko met Kerenski at the station on his return and complained that Polovtsev had shown weakness in constantly consulting the Sovyet. The chauffeur, who overheard the conversation, came direct to Polovtsev and offered to organise a hostile demonstration in front of Tereshchenko's flat on the Quay! Polovtsev explains that he had to work with the Committee of the Sovyet as most of the units of the garrison refused to move without their orders.

He told me that Kerenski on arrival wrote out a list of twenty Bolsheviks whom he was to arrest at once. Kerenski then came back and said that Trotski (Bronstein) and Steklov (Nakhamkes) were not to be arrested, as they were members of the Executive Committee of the Sovyet. Polovtsev explained that orders had already been issued, and Kerenski jumped into a car to go to cancel the orders. He finally gave authority for the arrest of six Bolsheviks and as many others as might be incriminated by the Anti-Espionage Section.

M. Kerenski, it is true, prohibited the publication of the *Pravda*, and of its Riga offshoot, the *Okopnaya Pravda* ("Trench Truth"), but he refused to permit the use of force to disarm the workmen of the capital who were in possession of rifles.

In a single afternoon Polovtsev had collected over 1,000 rifles from the workmen of the Sestroryetsk factory without bloodshed, but the Government preferred persuasive methods, and placarded the town with proclamations ordering individuals to bring their arms in themselves within three days, forgetful that General Kornilov had recourse to the same system in April and did not get a single rifle.

General Polovtsev was replaced by a Cossack General of thirty-seven years of age, Vasilkovski. General Balaban and his assistant Engineer Parshin left the Staff, and the former was replaced by General Bagratuni, with whom I had travelled in Central Asia in 1913. In Balaban the Government lost what the Russians call a "golden man," one who was always patient, full of human sympathy, with a wonderful capacity for work, a clear head and a strong sense of humour. He and Parshin had worked ever since the Revolution to restore order without bloodshed, single-eyed, without hope of reward.

The Cossacks who had been killed in the abortive Bolshevik rising were given an official funeral, and about twenty allied officers attended. M. Kerenski drove up amidst the cheers of the populace in the Emperor's automobile. He made an emotional speech from the steps of St. Isaac's Cathedral.

A lady overheard a soldier in the crowd of onlookers point out the British and French officers to his companions. He said: "The ones in protective colour (khaki) are Germans, and the ones with the blue trousers are Austrians. It is nice of them to come to the funeral."

While M. Kerenski was losing his chance of saving his country by restoring order in the capital, events at the front were following their natural course.

Kornilov's 8th Army had broken the Austrian front west of Stanislau on July 8th, and on the following days captured Halicz and Kalusz and crossed the river Lomnica.

The success was shortlived. The enemy counter-attacked, and Russian resistance, in spite of the heroic self-sacrifice of the officers, very soon broke.

Kalusz was evacuated on July 16th. Three days later the enemy broke through the front of the 11th Army east of Zloczow, owing to the mutinous retirement of a regiment of the 6th Grenadier Division.

The rout in the 11th Army became general. The official communiqué of the 22nd stated:

" West of Tarnopol, the enemy continued his offensive in the general direction of Tarnopol and to the south along the course of the Strypa.

" Our troops in a state of total insubordination continued their retreat beyond the Sereth. Some of them surrendered.

" Only the 155th Division and the armoured cars offered any resistance to the enemy.

" In spite of our great superiority in strength and, in this area, in technical equipment, the retreat was almost continuous. This was owing to the complete unreliability of our troops, to their debates as to whether or not they should obey the orders of the Command and to the criminal propaganda of the Bolsheviks."

It was the same everywhere. The communiqué of the following day states:

" In the Vilna direction, our troops attacked the enemy and occupied a part of his trenches, penetrating in places to a distance of three versts and capturing over 1,000 German prisoners.

" An attempt to develop the success showed the unreliability and weak *morale* of certain units. The officers acted nobly, falling in masses in the execution of their duty."

The rout in the 11th Army was followed by the rout of the 7th Army. By July 23rd Halicz had fallen, and the Russian 11th,

7th and 8th Armies were retreating in disorder on a front of 150 miles. On the following day Tarnopol and Stanislau were lost.

In Stanislau and Tarnopol the runaway troops pillaged and violated, but it was in Kalusz that the " freest army in the world " committed outrages that surpassed in sheer brutality every horror of the Great War.

The late Minister of War, M. Guchkov, had joined the Caucasian Native Division in the 8th Army. On his return on leave to Petrograd he was interviewed by the Press. He said: " The things that were done in Kalusz baffle description. I arrived there on the eve of the evacuation. It was enough to see the terrified faces of the inhabitants as they peeped from cellars. . . . Eyewitnesses related that forty to fifty men in turn outraged old women of seventy and young girls. The drunken soldiery robbed without pity, and murdered if the inhabitants refused to give them money. They snatched her child from the breast of a Polish mother and threatened to hurl it from the window if she did not hand over her valuables."

A correspondent in the 8th Army afterwards sent a more detailed account to a Petrograd paper. The town had been captured by storm battalions with a firing-line composed of officers. As these passed on, two regiments were brought up to consolidate the position. The men found wine and gave way to an orgy of drunkenness. The officers did their best to restore order and many were killed by their own men. " The retiring Germans bombarded the town, but the noise of the bombardment was literally drowned by the cries of women, as soldiers outraged them or cut off their arms or their breasts. No mercy was shown either to old women or to eight-year-old girls."

Some of the unfortunate inhabitants placed their last savings in little bags and hid them on the persons of their children. " But this did not help. Soldiers stripped little girls naked, ripped open the bags, and one after another, there on the street, violated the children and then cut them to pieces."

The Caucasian Native Division sent two squadrons to restore order, but these could only dismount eighty men—too few to deal with over 4,000 maddened savages. Some of the Russian infantry, less drunk than their fellows, actually dragged machine-guns into position and drove the Caucasians with threats back to the firing-line to hold back the German advance while the orgy continued. The Caucasians asked permission to charge. They said that they would cut down many of the rabble before they were overwhelmed themselves, but the officers decided that such a death would be too ignoble. They must have made a wonderful picture, these brave, proud mountaineers, whose religion forbade them to drink, as they looked scornfully at the degradation of the sons of the men who had conquered them.

On July 21st General Gutor was replaced in command of the South-West Front by General Kornilov, and General Cherimisev, who had commanded the XIIth Corps in the recent offensive, was promoted to command the 8th Army.

General Kornilov, with the support of Savinkov, now the Commissary of the South-West Front, had the courage, on his own responsibility, to order officers to take " exceptional measures, including shooting," to restore order. At the same time, he telegraphed to the Supreme Commander-in-Chief, General Brusilov, recommending the re-introduction of the death penalty in the theatre of operations, " otherwise all responsibility would fall on those who think of controlling only by words on fields where reign death and disgrace, treachery, cowardice and selfishness." The Government decided on July 25th to re-establish the death penalty in the theatre of war only. Kornilov prohibited all meetings at the front.

On July 29th Kerenski presided at a conference at G.H.Q., which was also attended by Tereshchenko and General Alexyeev; by General Brusilov and his Chief of Staff, General Lukhomski; by Generals Ruzski and Klembovski, former and present Commanders-in-Chief of the Northern Front; by General Denikin, then Commander-in-Chief of the Western Front; and by Savinkov, Commissary of the South-West Front. General Denikin spoke out as a brave and experienced soldier, demanding the abolition of all elected committees in the army and the restoration of all authority and disciplinary power to officers. He seems to have been only half-heartedly supported by his comrades, and no definite decision was reached.

On August 1st General Kornilov issued an order, pointing out that the Russian army from the very beginning of its existence had never known such disgrace as had been earned by the treachery of " certain units " of the 11th and 7th Armies. " In the gloomy nightmare of those days it was only the valour of those infantry units that remained true to their duty, of all the storm and cyclist battalions, of all the artillery, Cossack and cavalry units, that opposed the advance of the enemy." The order ended with a recognition of the heroism of the officers : " Officers and you few soldiers of infantry who have remained faithful and have not disgraced yourselves by shameful flight and treachery, I turn to you. Your feats are immortal, your heroism is worthy of history, of the veneration of future generations. . . . Abandoned by treacherous soldier comrades misled by mad propaganda, you alone remained at the front, and opposing the enemy masses with your personal bravery, you fell in an unequal fight, one against hundreds."

But the coward rabble was without shame. Two days earlier, on July 30th, a meeting at Kronstadt, addressed by delegates from the 5th and 11th Armies, had passed a resolution, demanding amongst other " reforms " the abolition of the death penalty and of the military censorship, the disbandment of all storm units, the confiscation of the printing-press of the bourgeois papers and the admission of delegates to Tsarskoe Selo to satisfy themselves that the ex-Emperor was guarded sufficiently strictly.

On July 31st General Brusilov was removed from his position as Supreme Commander-in-Chief and was replaced by General Kornilov, who, however, did not assume control till August 5th. General Radko Dimitriev resigned command of the 12th Army, nominally on grounds of ill-health, but really because he had at last found that even his concessions were unable to keep pace with the growing demands of the men. He was succeeded by General Parski. General Cheremisev was promoted to command the South-West Front.

While the army was going to pieces in front, in rear there was an economic and food crisis. The demands of the workmen exceeded all bounds, the technical officials were expelled or murdered and the Government proved powerless to restore order. The peasants held back their grain, the paper currency having lost value and there being no manufactures which might induce them to part with their produce. The production on the great estates had diminished, as the owners had been expelled, and the peasant expropriators awaited a "legal title" before commencing to till. The railways were rapidly deteriorating. In August, 1917, 26 per cent. of the engines and 8 per cent. of the wagons were under repair as compared with 18 per cent. and 3 per cent. in August, 1916. The autocracy in the war had brought Russia very near to disaster, but the flabbiness of the Government which succeeded it did more harm to the country in four months than the autocracy accomplished in two and a half years.

Sunday, August 5th, 1917.

I had a long talk with Prince Tumánov, the Assistant Minister of War. He thinks that the Sovyet has lost power and that it is only kept alive by the personal ambition of some of its members. It has had great influence in the country as representative of the democratic will, and it is not clear how it will be replaced; possibly by a disguised dictatorship or by a "concilium" of committees and social organisations in Moscow.

To wake him up, I gave him some figures indicative of the economic and transport crises. He said: "You base your pessimism on naked figures, but you do not take into account the wonderful Russian spirit!"

I said that I had heard a lot about the "wonderful Russian spirit" since the Revolution, but that I thought less of it since I had seen crowds of able-bodied men lounging, chewing sunflower seeds every day, and watching women train to fight while they shirked their duty. I had never seen or heard of any tribe in India or elsewhere which allowed its women to do its fighting. He said that the deadness of shame in the men was the direct result of the vodka policy of the late Government. Yes! but what of the wonderful Russian spirit as a practical factor of regeneration now?

Later we spoke of the outrages at Kalusz, and Tumánov said that the Russian was good-natured at ordinary times, but a wild beast when drunk or in panic.

The worst of it is that he is now generally in drink or in panic.

Another characteristic was touched on by Balaban, who said: "I do not understand the Russian. He will always talk ten times more than he will act, and he will always talk to people freely to whom he has no right to talk."

On August 4th the Executive Committee of the Sovyet passed a resolution of confidence in "Comrade Kerenski," authorising him to form a cabinet of members of all parties. The voting was 146 to 47, with 42 abstentions.

The "Save the Revolution" Government which was formed on August 6th included M. Savinkov in the subordinate position of acting Minister of War, the portfolio being retained by Kerenski. No one believed very much in the Government, but some of its members believed in Kerenski.

Two days later an all-Russian Conference of Bolsheviks and Internationalists opened at Petrograd. Yet Russia was still nominally at war! Elections at certain factories at Petrograd showed a great increase in Bolshevism.

The capital was outwardly quiet, but there were no signs whatsoever of the garrison being taken in hand. A garrison order complained—without effect—"Sentries have lost all military appearance; they sit, smoke and quit their posts of their own free will."

The Socialists feared a counter-revolution. A few people who wished to restore order looked to Kolchak, later Commander of the Black Sea Fleet, as a possible leader, but Kerenski appointed him Chief of a Russian naval mission to the United States and showed indecent anxiety to hasten his departure. Others thought of General Gurko, who had been called by General Brusilov from leave in the Caucasus to attend the conference at G.H.Q. on July 30th. On arrival there he was told that certain members of the Government objected to his presence, so he proceeded to Petrograd, and he was there arrested on account of a letter of sympathy he had written to the ex-Emperor.

Savinkov understood the necessity for discipline in the army, but he hoped to restore it by strengthening the hands of the commissaries, and he explained in a Press interview that there was a danger, since the reintroduction of the death penalty, that the officers, having regained their influence over the men, might use their power for political purposes. He disclaimed all idea of abolishing the committees. If he had had more experience he would have realised that no army with committees ever has fought or ever could fight.

Neither Kerenski nor Savinkov had any strong assistants in the Ministry of War. General Manikovski, who was in charge of the supply departments, said on August 9th that he had not been able to see his Minister for two months. He said : " Sometimes I want to put a bullet into my own head, and sometimes into somebody else's." His subordinate, the Chief of the Military Technical Department, said that there was no real work being done in his office. Officers in the Artillery Department, when asked how they came to have so much time to spare, explained that productive work had fallen generally 50 per cent. in Russia since the Revolution, and they were doing their best to follow the times!

General Manikovski spoke of the other two Assistant Ministers of War, General Yakubovich and Prince Tumánov, as his " nursery." Other officers labelled them " carrierists." Both agreed with officers who urged strong measures to save the situation, but both probably also agreed with Kerenski when he preached caution.

Kerenski was still the only individual who had any hold on the mob, and the nation was evidently doomed if it failed soon to produce a bigger man. He had the theatrical qualities of a Napoleon, but none of his moral courage or useful ruthlessness.

He sat in Alexander III's study at the Winter Palace and slept in his bed, and, his name being Alexander, he was nicknamed "Alexander IV." He drove in Nikolas II's Rolls-Royce. He still dreamed childishly of a peace with Germany by consent. The editor of the official military paper proposed to publish some reports received from two returned Russian doctors to illustrate the ill-treatment of prisoners in Germany, but Kerenski said he was "not to worry the Germans too much"!

After the rising of July 16th and 17th, General Polovtsev, the Commander-in-Chief of the district, received a cipher telegram from Kerenski, who was at the front, telling him that he would return on a certain day and that he wanted the streets lined with loyal troops from the station to the Winter Palace. The little Socialist Minister wished, no doubt, to thank the men as he drove past in triumph. The order was issued, and, of course, instantly became known in the Sovyet, where it occasioned no small commotion. The Minister of Labour, Skobelev, hurried to the District Staff to implore Polovtsev to cancel instructions which he thought had been issued solely to curry favour with the Minister of War. When he saw the telegram, he drove at once to the Council of Ministers and whispered the news to Tseretelli, who was beside himself, as he had for long foreseen a Napoleon arising from every bush to destroy the "beautiful fabric of the Revolution." At length Prince Lvov was appealed to, and proved, as ever, accommodating. He wrote across the order: "These instructions are not to be carried out," and the situation was saved.

The power of the Executive Committee of the Sovyet had been weakened by the revelations of the Intelligence Department, for though the majority of the members was opposed in theory to the Bolsheviks, the Sovyet drew its influence from the effect of the propaganda of the Extremists on the nerves of the Government. In the eyes of educated and patriotic people, it had made a bad blunder in trying to cover the exposure of the connection of the Bolsheviks with German propaganda, by appointing a committee of five full-blooded Jews to enquire into the charges—Messrs. Lieber, Dan, Gotz, Krokmal and Goldman.

On the other hand, the people were all sick of the war. They did not want to fight, and in their ignorance and moral deadness were ready to welcome any shibboleth, however shameful or hollow, that would provide an excuse for peace.

It was difficult to hope that it was not already too late to save the army, but there was the one chance that Kerenski might lend his own popularity to support Kornilov, leaving the latter a free hand as to methods, and that Kornilov might prove the giant that the situation demanded.

Sunday, August 12th, 1917.

On July 25th and 30th, when the Ambassador hoped to have an interview with Kerenski, I wrote out certain notes on the military situation. As yesterday he hoped at last to see him I gave him a short summary of these notes.[1]

Possibly as a result, the Ambassador brought back a message yesterday that Tereshchenko wished to see me. He, no doubt, knows that I am going on leave and wishes me to give an optimistic view of the situation when I reach England!

I went to see him at 11.30 to-day. Our conversation covered most of the ground, but I left the room little impressed by his easy optimism. He said that Kornilov would have a free hand. The Sovyet had attacked him as a counter-revolutionary, but when, two days later, he had been appointed Commander-in-Chief, it had stopped its opposition and had not restarted.

He agreed about the officers and discipline. I said that some excellent officers had been expelled, and he said that this had been done by Guchkov! Kaledin will return at once as Inspector-General of Cossack Troops or to command one of the fronts. The matter of the police is still " under consideration."

I asked if he really thought Russia would fight through

---

[1] The notes of July 30th and August 11th are in Appendix B.

the winter. He said : "We have *got* to think it." Savinkov, whom I saw later, said that discipline would be restored by the autumn, and the troops would then be retained in the trenches by fear of punishment.

I suggested to Tereshchenko three reasons that, apart from the demoralisation of the army, might interfere with the war in Russia in the winter: an economic crisis, a breakdown of the railways, and the holding back of grain by the peasants.

He thought that the economic situation would right itself, and that the workmen, after starving for a little and perhaps burning a factory or two, would consent to accept wages that their employers could afford to pay. In this opinion he is much more optimistic than the majority, who think there will be much burning and murder before the workmen learn sense.

He said that the Government would militarise the railways as soon as they got a decent excuse. The holding back of their grain by the peasants was the most difficult matter of all, and he did not indicate how the Government, with no goods to barter, is going to induce the peasants to part.

Tereshchenko said that another rising in Petrograd in unavoidable, but that the troops will put it down. The workmen still have 100 machine guns and 40,000 rifles, and no one knows how much small arms ammunition.

Savinkov makes a good impression as a fearless and honest man. He said that he was in complete agreement with Kornilov, and that as long as he remained in the Government I could be assured that Kornilov would have a free hand.

He acknowledged that Russia was now in the middle of financial, economic, food, railway and military crises, and that the future entirely depended on whether the Government could take a strong line. He referred twice to Chernov, the Minister of Agriculture, by name, and said that it was impossible to undertake any contentious measure such as the militarisation of labour as long as a Minister who would not risk his popularity remained in the Government.

He said that a separate peace, or a peace in which Russia had no voice, would be the ruin of Russia, and for that reason he, though against war on principle, was determined that Russia should fight to the end. Another point that people forgot was that demobilisation in the present state of the Russian army was impossible, for the troops would destroy everything on their way home.

Savinkov was surprised at the large majority of the British Labour Party that had voted in favour of attending the Stokholm Conference. I said that they probably thought it desirable to go because the Russian delegates were going in any case, and I asked him if the Russian Government favoured the idea of the Conference. He said that he personally, and he thought that most of the Government agreed with him, only favoured it for one reason—that it would get rid of the delegates for a certain time.

I spoke freely of the sufferings of the officers, and said that if discipline was to be restored the best soldier must be taught to look up to the worst officer as to a little god. He said that he would have to go gradually. There will be a commissary at G.H.Q. (Filonenko), one at each front, and one, with three assistants, at the headquarters of each army.

Unfortunately, Savinkov is handicapped by want of experience. He said, when speaking of the shortcomings of Russian officers: "Officers often lack tact in their treatment of the men. I have known a regiment that refused to go to the trenches but that went immediately its Commanding Officer was changed." Of course such a regiment was spoilt irretrievably by the Higher Command having given way to the mutinous demands of the men, and it was of no importance whether it was in the trenches or not, for in any case it would not fight.

Of course poor Russian officers often show a deplorable

lack of character. P—— yesterday was *very* guarded in his reference to the slackness of the troops as long as a certain one-year volunteer was in the room. When the latter left he changed his tone so rapidly that I asked who the man had been and learned that he was a member of the Sovyet!

Friday, August 17th, 1917.

I hope to start on my way home to-morrow.

I dined last night with Tereshchenko to meet Kerenski, Savinkov, Kornilov and my French colleague, Lavergne.

Kerenski looked tired and nervous. I said something to him about overwork and he sighed and spoke of the "continual disputes" (*postoyannie conflikti*). As he left the house to get into his car and drive off to try to settle some new "dispute," I noticed that half a dozen lazy soldiers lounging on the parapet opposite did not trouble to stand up or salute.

I drove at midnight to have a talk with Kornilov, but did not learn much. He talks of wide schemes for militarising the railways and industry, but does not seem to see that meanwhile nothing is being done.[1]

I saw poor little Diamandi. He wants, in order to save the last bit of Rumanian soil, that the Russians should be induced to send their best troops to Rumania, and that the Allies in the west should press their offensive energetically. He says that the Rumanians hate the Russians, who, in Milyukov's words, have betrayed them twice, first by dragging them into the war and then, after getting them in, by refusing to fight.

In saying good-bye I said I hoped to see him on my return. He said: "I only hope I will not then be the representative of a country that has ceased to exist."

---

[1] On the occasion of his next visit to Petrograd General Kornilov presented a demand for the militarisation of railways and factories, a demand which met with a flat refusal from the Provisional Government.—*Prelude to Bolshevism*, by Kerenski, p. 73.

CHAPTER XXIII

KERENSKI LOSES HIS LAST CHANCE

Reference Sketch F

I ARRIVED in London on the morning of August 30th, and reported ont he following day to the Directors of Military Intelligence and of Military Operations, but only appeared before the War Cabinet a week later—on Friday, September 7th.

Asked to make a statement on the situation in Russia, I said that there was grave danger of a separate peace and urged that a joint note should be sent by the Allies to the Russian Government, expressing sympathy with Russia's difficulties, but pointing out that events in Russia since the Revolution had not only prolonged the war by a twelvemonth, but threatened, by bringing a German victory within the bounds of possibility, to put back the progress of democracy throughout the world for a whole generation. I asked that the name of General Kornilov should be mentioned, and that Kerenski should be asked tactfully to give him a free hand to re-establish discipline in the army.

The Prime Minister and Lord Curzon were absent. While the proposal was being discussed, the Prime Minister's Private Secretary came in to say that Mr. Lloyd George had made a speech on Russia at Birkenhead, and the consideration of the note was postponed till the receipt of the text of the speech.

On Saturday the 8th—a fateful day in Russia—the War Cabinet did not meet. On Monday, the 10th, on arrival at noon at 10, Downing Street, I found a press telegram reporting the outbreak of the open quarrel between Kerenski and Kornilov. It was too late. After all, the sending of a note was only a gamble, but in war it is always better to do something than to let things take their course, and it was very certain that if Russia had been

Germany's ally Germany would never have allowed matters to lapse to their present chaos.

On the 12th I asked that a telegram should be sent to Kerenski asking him in the interests of the Alliance to come to terms with Kornilov. In Dublin, on the 14th, I read of Kornilov's failure, and wrote urging our diplomatic intervention in favour of Kornilov, who had fought the battle of the Alliance.

It was all too late.

The War Cabinet had hitherto given Russia everything she asked, even at a sacrifice to ourselves, and had supported Kerenski as the only man who stood between us and disaster to allied interests in the Eastern theatre. Opinion was now hardening, and our Government was not prepared to make further concrete sacrifices. I suggested that we might demand from Kerenski a considered statement of the part the Russian army would be able to play in the spring campaign. The statesman I put the suggestion to replied: "It would not be of the slightest use, for when the spring comes Kerenski will not be Prime Minister." He further said that there would not be an inter-allied conference to reconsider the terms of peace, for any Minister the Russians might send to attend such a conference would be certain to be "kicked out" before he got back to Russia. He waxed bitter when he spoke of the parrot cry of "Without annexations and without indemnities." "When the Russians are running away like blazes, running away like blazes *on their own territory*—that is my point, *running away like blazes on their own territory*—they have the damned cheek to ask us to relinquish territory that we have spent hundreds of thousands of lives in conquering!"

I believe this statesman voiced the opinion of England. Russian officers told me that carters in the East End of London called out to them: "When are you Russians going to fight?" Even our gardener in Ulster had asked: "Why do those Russians not fight?"

The conflict between Kornilov and Kerenski was inevitable from the first, for the two men were of very different character and stood for diametrically opposed principles. Kornilov was a hard-headed soldier of strong will and great courage, a tried patriot, but no politician. He was simple and honest, without a spark of personal ambition. With him Russia and Russia's national honour stood first. Kerenski, the petty lawyer from Saratov, had spent his life in political agitation. He was subtle, vain and ambitious. Prior to the Revolution he had been a pacifist. With him the Revolution came first and Russia only second.

Both men were of humble origin. Kornilov was the son of a non-commissioned officer of Trans-Baikal Cossacks, and his mother was a Buriat woman. Kerenski's father was a schoolmaster and his mother is said to have been a Jewess.

Kornilov was a man of wide education, and spoke several of the languages of Europe and Asia. He had fought his way to high command even under the old régime, without interest, by sheer hard work and ability. He was the first leading general the Russian army had found since the Revolution with the courage to risk everything in defending its vital interests from political interference. Kerenski had never been in a position of responsibility till suddenly called to power in the re-shuffle of the Revolution. His assets were his unbounded energy, his eloquence and his juggling political adroitness.[1]

The State Conference at Moscow was called by Kerenski with the object of bringing all parties together, but it only revealed and widened the gulf between the Nationalists, who stood for the restoration of order, and the Internationalists, who wanted peace at any price in order to continue their social and political experiments. Under the influence of his political associates, Kerenski became convinced of the danger of a counter-revolution from the Right.

Among the experienced military leaders there was only one opinion. On August 28th General Alexyeev delivered a long speech to the Conference. He drew a contrast between the army of the old régime, poor in technical equipment, but strong in its

---

[1] A note-book of General Alexyeev's discovered after his death in 1918 contained a remark jotted down during the sitting of the Moscow Conference in August, 1917: " Kerenski is a political juggler " (Kerenski *figlyar vlasti*).

warlike spirit, and the present army, well supplied with arms, but completely poisoned and enfeebled by the ill-interpreted and ill-applied doctrines which had split it into two opposite camps, so that now irreconcilable differences existed between officers and men. He declared that the committees, though useful economically, were fatal to discipline, and that the commissaries created an extremely dangerous duality of power. He said that after the publication by the Government of the Declaration of the Rights of Soldiers the men had lost all respect for their leaders, and the officers had become veritable martyrs, who had had to pay dearly for the offensive and the subsequent retreat. For instance, the force launched in one attack consisted of twenty-eight officers, twenty non-commissioned officers, and two soldiers, and the others looked coldly on while these heroes perished.

In conclusion, Russia's foremost military authority asserted publicly that it was impossible to carry the war to a successful issue unless the strongest possible efforts were made by the troops themselves, and by the Provisional Government, to re-animate and regenerate the army.

Kornilov had waited all August for the strong measures that the situation demanded. He had waited while Kerenski, who, if he had been a man of action instead of a mere talker, might in July have finally crushed the Bolshevik movement, did nothing. As Commander-in-Chief he remained powerless when on September 3rd the Germans captured Riga, the Russians refusing to fight. His visit to Moscow had shown him that he had at all events the support of the great majority of the Intelligentsiya. He had the practically unanimous support of the corps of officers. It seemed to him to be his duty to act before it was too late.

The Deputy Minister of War, Savinkov, as a man of action who had fought the old régime by terrorist acts while Kerenski attacked it in floods of speech, stood also for strong measures. It was primarily on his nomination that Kornilov had been appointed Commander-in-Chief of the South-West Front on July 19th, and had been offered the post of Supreme Commander-in-Chief on July 30th. Savinkov, however, understood, which many of the officer corps ignored, that in the then political conditions the active co-operation of Kerenski was necessary to enforce the desired reforms.

Kerenski mistrusted Kornilov, and temporised. Savinkov has related how almost from the first day of his appointment as Deputy Minister of War he had marked differences of opinion with his chief, who almost daily spoke of removing Kornilov from his command, with the idea apparently of taking the post himself.[1]

Kornilov and Savinkov had constantly urged the reintroduction of the death penalty in rear as a necessary preliminary to the restoration of order. Kerenski at length agreed on August 30th. He further agreed on September 2nd to the declaration of martial law at Petrograd and to the transfer of a cavalry corps from the front to enforce it.

Savinkov, sent by Kerenski, arrived at G.H.Q. on September 3rd and assured Kornilov that the Prime Minister was at last going to take a strong line.

On his return to Petrograd on the 6th, he found a telegram from the Commander-in-Chief asking if the death penalty had been introduced in rear. Though asked twice by Savinkov on the 7th, and again on the 8th to submit the decree which had been prepared by his instructions to the Provisional Government, Kerenski temporised.

At G.H.Q. Kornilov was urged to action by his orderly, Zavoiko, a former Marshal of Nobility of the Government of Podolya, and by many of his officer advisers. Kerenski's procrastination played directly into the hands of these hotheads, who altogether exaggerated the strength of their effective support in the country, and who had an easy task in pointing out that further delay was useless, even disastrous.

Kerenski was influenced by Nekrasov, originally a professor at the University of Tomsk, who had been a Cadet at the time of the Revolution, but had since worked much in co-operation with the Sovyet, by Galpern, a pacifist Jewish lawyer, and by a relation, Baranovski, an ambitious but inexperienced soldier. These

---

[1] Savinkov, *K Dyelu Kornilova*, p. 14.

men preached political caution, either failing to understand or preferring to disregard the danger to the army. They were of the common political type, preferring to gain temporary peace by compromise rather than risk anything by decision.

The whole Russian fabric rested on the shoulders of Kornilov and Kerenski, " the pillars of Hercules," as Filonenko, the Commissary at G.H.Q. named them in the private code he invented for use in communication with his chief, Savinkov. With their divergency in character and aims, only an irresponsible well-wisher to both was required to complete the quarrel. This *rôle* was filled by Vladimir Lvov, a Cadet and late Procurator of the Synod in the Provisional Government. Lvov's object seems to have been to act the friend to everyone and to prevent bloodshed. After a conversation with Kerenski on the 4th, he went to G.H.Q., and on September 7th suggested, as understood by Kornilov on Kerenski's initiative, the choice of three possible solutions of the Government crisis. Kornilov agreed with the last alternative, which proposed his proclamation as dictator by the Provisional Government. Lvov lunched with Zavoiko, who accompanied him to Mogilev station, and said to him at the last moment : " You have to remember three things—Petrograd under martial law, Kornilov military dictator, and the Cabinet to resign."

On the afternoon of September 8th Lvov came to Kerenski in the Winter Palace and brought him a formal ultimatum purporting to come from Kornilov, demanding that martial law should be proclaimed in Petrograd, that all military and civil authority should be placed in the hands of the Generalissimo, that all Ministers should resign pending the formation of a Cabinet by Kornilov, and that Kerenski and Savinkov should come at once to G.H.Q.

Lvov had far exceeded the commission he received from Kornilov, who, though naturally mistrusting Kerenski, had no idea of sending him an ultimatum.

At 8 p.m. Kerenski spoke with the Commander-in-Chief by direct wire, telling him, which was untrue, that Lvov was present. Kerenski, pretending that he was Lvov, asked Kornilov whether he confirmed his message. Kornilov only

Kerenski Loses His Last Chance

confirmed his request that Kerenski and Savinkov should come to G.H.Q.[1]

A man of real patriotism and of bigger type than Kerenski would have done all he could to smoothe over the conflict. Savinkov has recorded that from his conversation by direct wire with Kornilov on the night of the 8th he was convinced that the incident might be liquidated, but on going to the Winter Palace on the 9th he met Nekrasov, who told him that he had already ordered the publication of Kornilov's " treachery." Nekrasov was delighted that Lvov's visit on the 8th had made it possible " to explode the already prepared mine two days before the time fixed for it." [2]

On the 10th, Savinkov, Milyukov and Alexyeev all interceded, but Kerenski declared that " any negotiations of the Provisional Government with a man acting criminally were out of the question." Savinkov asked him if he realised that this conflict would finally ruin the army, but Kerenski, in his blind vanity, replied : " On the contrary. The army, inspired by the victory over the counter-revolution, will swarm against the Germans and will conquer ! "[3]

On Saturday morning, the 9th, Kornilov received a telegram from the Prime Minister, calling on him to resign. The Commissary, Filonenko, found him sitting in the garden of his house at Mogilev with the telegram in his hand, and was asked to explain its contents, of which the General could make nothing.

The Chief of Staff, General Lukhomski, to whom Kornilov had been ordered to hand over the command, telegraphed his refusal. General Klembovski, the Commander-in-Chief of the Northern Front, also refused. The commanders of all the groups on the Western Frontier unanimously telegraphed their protest against the change of the Supreme Command at a time so dangerous.

Kornilov was confronted with the choice of acquiescing in the

---

[1] Kerenski, *Prelude to Bolshevism*, pp. 169-170.
[2] *Ibid.*, p. 163.
[3] Savinkov, *K Dyelu Kornilova*, p. 27.

demand of the Government by resigning, and so abandoning the army and the country to its fate, or of risking everything by open revolt. He chose the latter alternative, and on September 10th appealed to the army and to the people. In his last Order—No. 900—from Mogilev, on September 11th, he explained his action. This Order ends : " I pledge you my word of honour as an officer and a soldier, and assure you once more that I, General Kornilov, the son of a simple Cossack peasant, have by my whole life, and not by words only, shown my unfailing devotion to my country and to freedom, that I am opposed to all counter-revolutionary schemes, and stand on guard over the liberties we have won, desiring only that the great Russian nation should continue independent."

This Order did not appear in the Press. On the day of its issue there was published an Appeal to the Army from the Executive Committees of the All-Russia Sovyet of Working-Men and Soldier Deputies, and of the All-Russia Sovyet of Peasant Deputies. This Appeal commenced : " Comrade officers and soldiers! General Kornilov has rebelled against the Revolution and the Provisional Government. He wants to re-establish the old régime and to deprive the people of land and liberty. To forward his criminal object, he is ready to open the front to the Germans and to betray his country."

No impartial judge can doubt for a moment which spoke the truth, the Order or the Appeal.

General Alexyeev declared in a letter he wrote from G.H.Q. to the editor of the *Novoe Vremya* on September 25th :

" Of what exactly did the Kornilov affair consist ? It was not the attempt of a handful of adventurers. It was based on the sympathy and help of wide circles of the Intelligentsiya, the sorrowful witnesses of the sufferings of their country, led to the brink of disaster by the unsuccessful choice of rulers.

" The movement was not directed against the system of government which existed on September 9th-13th. There is nothing to prove that it was. It was directed exclusively against the Ministers, who were constantly changing and were unable to give Russia lasting and firm government, but were, on the contrary, leading the state to final disaster. The object of the movement was not to change the existing form of government, but to change only the individuals governing and to find out men able to save Russia."

It is now very evident that Kornilov could not have succeeded, but on September 8th and 9th, many of the politicians at Petrograd were exceedingly nervous, and some of the Bolsheviks actually fled. Nekrasov said to Kerenski: " It is all up. We will have to resign and let the Sovyets defend Petrograd." [1]

There was a good deal of comic opera.

Tuesday, October 16th, 1917.

Ragosin, Polovtsev's A.D.C., came to lunch. He told me that Polovtsev, having tired of idleness, went to G.H.Q. to ask for employment. Kornilov told him to go to Petrograd, as he would come there soon and would want him. He went to Petrograd. At 1 a.m. on Sunday, September 9th, he was called for by Palchinski, Tugan-Baranovski and Tumánov [2] and taken to Kerenski, who shook him by the hand for five minutes and then asked him to take command of the troops at Petrograd. Polovtsev declined, but they sat talking over tea till 6 a.m. Then Kerenski, said: " I am more sorry than I can say that I cannot overpersuade you, but tell me—here is a map—where would you place your guns if you were ordered to defend Petrograd ? " Polovtsev said that he did not know the ground. He noticed, however, that the future Supreme Commander-in-Chief was placing all his guns on the tops of hills.

Monday, October 29th, 1917.

I dined with Madame R——, and met Prince

---

[1] Conversation with Savinkov, Diary, October 24th.
[2] Palchinski, an able engineer and a revolutionary.
Colonel Tugan-Baranovski, an officer of the General Staff who was serving in the Mobilisation Department at the time of the Revolution and was called by Colonel Engelhardt to assist him in his work in the Duma Military Committee.
Colonel Prince Tumánov, Assistant Minister of War.

Chefchavadze, who had commanded a brigade in the Caucasian Native Division and gave an amusing account of the march on Petrograd.

The division, which marched at the head of Kornilov's forces, was isolated, all communication with G.H.Q. having been severed by order of the Sovyet.

Its advanced guard detrained near Pavlovsk, seventeen miles south of Petrograd, and sent a party of forty men forward to select billets in the village. The forty came upon a battalion of the Pavlovski Regiment drawn up with machine-guns "to defend the Revolution," and the battalion fled.

The Caucasians wondered, and finally decided that they had stumbled on manœuvres. They said: "These men seem to be learning how to fight, but they do not know how to commence!"

When the main body of the Pavlovski Regiment was reached, one of its men called out to ask the cavalry where they were going. The Caucasians replied that they were on the way to Petrograd to quell a Bolshevik rising. Then the Pavlovski men said: "We will go with you in that case; we thought you were coming to make a counter-revolution."

Delighted that there was no fighting to be done, they all walked together to the headquarters of the Army of Defence, where they found the Assistant Commander of the Petrograd Military District, the simple and gentle Lieutenant Kuzmin, in a conservatory, surrounded by telephones. Before the newcomers had time to explain the situation, a wild man with long hair rushed out and promised each man an extra two and a half acres of land in the coming general distribution if he would fight for the revolution. This was Chernov, the Minister of Agriculture. As there did not seem to be any immediate danger in fighting for the Revolution, everyone agreed.

Savinkov had asked Kornilov on the 3rd September to send

a cavalry corps to Petrograd, but had stipulated that this corps should not be commanded by General Krimov and that it should not contain the Caucasian Native Division.

The IIIrd Cavalry Corps, however, was detailed under the command of General Krimov, and the Caucasian Native Division, which formed part of the corps, was not replaced by regular cavalry. Further, General Krimov had received orders from the Supreme Commander-in-Chief: "On hearing from me (Kornilov) or from local sources of the commencement of a Bolshevik rising, advance on Petrograd immediately, occupy the city, disarm those divisions of the Petrograd garrison which joined the rising, disarm the population and disperse the Sovyet." [1]

An officer who had formerly served with Krimov [2] was sent to Luga to meet him, and returned with him to Petrograd by car. This officer has since stated that in his interview with Kerenski in the Winter Palace, Krimov told the Prime Minister: "Frankly, I will not deceive you. I had wished to hang the lot of you." Kerenski demanded that he should write down this statement. Krimov came into the officer's study, and was left there with paper and ink. He there shot himself through the head.

The open quarrel between Kerenski and Kornilov destroyed all hope of renewal of effective co-operation of the Russian army with the Allies.

Kerenski's active denunciation of the "conspiracy" immediately placed all officers at the mercy of the soldiery. Their position had been difficult before; it became at once impossible. The cavalry regiments of the Guard expelled all their officers. The officers of the battleship *Petropavlovsk* at Helsingfors were called upon to sign a declaration condemning Kornilov as a traitor. Four of the younger ones had the courage to refuse, and were arrested. They were sent ashore under a guard of fourteen men, who, after using all their ammunition without killing them, finally kicked them brutally to death.

---

[1] Kerenski, *Prelude to Bolshevism*, p. 149.
[2] Captain Juravlev of the General Staff.

Sunday, October 21st, 1917.

Poor Neverdovski [1] came to see me at the Embassy yesterday. He and his wife escaped from Viborg disguised and by the skin of their teeth. The massacre of officers lasted two days, and was organised by sailors who came from Helsingfors, and called the local garrison " Black Hundred Reactionaries," because they had not shed any officer blood.

At 2 p.m. on the first day a few of his men came to Neverdovski and asked him to explain Kornilov's movement. When N. complied, one man said: " All the officers say that they are for the Government, but they are all secretly for Kornilov. They should all be wiped out." Another man said: " Come along and don't talk," and they all went out.

Two hours later he saw some forty soldiers running with rifles, and soon afterwards he heard that General Oranovski, the Commander of the Troops in Finland, General Vasiliev, the General Quartermaster, and General Stepanov, the Commandant of the Fortress, had been arrested. Later a lady came in to say that they had all been murdered. They were thrown over the bridge and shot in the water.

Neverdovski spent the night in a house with friends. He was about to go to his office in the morning but was implored by his officers to wait while a junior officer spied out the land. This boy soon returned with the news that it had been decided to murder all officers of field rank. N. managed to find a hired carriage, which took him for an exorbitant fare to the house of a colonel he knew some twenty miles off. There he hid six days before venturing to escape to Petrograd. The Finnish peasants helped him and gave him a rifle, saying: " The Russian soldiers are bad men. We will defend you."

---

[1] A colonel of the Litovski Regiment of the Guard, and an old friend. He was on special duty at Viborg.

General Marushevski, the Chief of the General Staff, told me later that he had warned the Government as early as July that this massacre was coming at Viborg. Twenty-six officers were murdered.

Kerenski's Government was, of course, powerless to punish the murderers. The Helsingfors Sovyet refused even to enquire into the murder of the officers of the *Petropavlovsk*. It is true that the Viborg garrison was transferred to the Northern Front. On arrival at Pskov, it sent a delegation to the Commander-in-Chief, General Cherimisov, to report that the strategical situation demanded the return of the garrison to Finland. It then marched to the station, seized wagons and commenced to entrain. Luckily, a member of the Front Committee obtained the services of some cavalry, and stopped the entrainment by threatening to open fire. After all this, Cherimisov, who was a true "revolutionary general," promised the mutineers that they should remain in reserve!

General Kornilov and his Chief of Staff, General Lukhomski, were arrested at Mogilev. General Denikin and his Staff and General Erdeli were arrested on the South-West Front. They were conveyed to Bikhov, not far from Mogilev, and were there guarded by the faithful Turkoman Regiment, which was devoted to Kornilov, and undoubtedly saved the party from lynching. Kerenski proclaimed himself Supreme Commander-in-Chief, and General Alexyeev patriotically went to Mogilev for a time as Chief of Staff to try to preserve the unity of the front. He was relieved later by General Dukhonin from the South-West Front.

A large number of changes were made in the command at the front. General Cherimisov was promoted from the 8th Army to command the Northern Front, General Baluev from the Special Army to command the Western Front; and General Volodchenko to command the South-West Front.

Savinkov resigned his position as Deputy Minister of War on September 13th, and was succeeded by Verkhovski, a general of thirty-four. Verkhovski had been a cadet in the Corps des Pages in 1903, when, during some civil disturbances, a Lancer regiment was billeted in the corps riding school. He had gone to the men and had harangued them, advising them to refuse to fire on their fellow-citizens. He was expelled from the corps. He went to the Far East as a volunteer, and was promoted to be 2nd Lieutenant for service in the field during the Japanese war. He passed through the Military Academy and in the Great War fought in the 3rd Finland Rifle Division at Lyck and Koziowa. He was wounded, and gained the Cross of St. George and the Golden Sword. After the Revolution he naturally came to the front as "one who had suffered under the old régime." He was fairly successful as Commander of the Moscow Military District. As Minister of War he showed lack of administrative experience, and even of mental balance, but his task was an impossible one.

Friday, October 19th, 1917.

I lunched with Claude Anet (the correspondent of the *Petit Parisien*), to meet Savinkov and Filonenko. Savinkov said that Kornilov was led into his movement by Kerenski, who failed him at the last moment owing to his vanity and "regard for the Sovyet." I suggested that he failed too because of his lack of moral courage, and Filonenko strongly agreed. He instanced Kerenski's defence when attacked at the Moscow Conference for having permitted the reintroduction of the death penalty, "Wait till you see me sign a death sentence," as being particularly cowardly. Savinkov related that one day, when he was seeing Kerenski off at a station at Petrograd, a telegram was delivered to Kerenski which he read and passed to him, telling him that it was his business to deal with it. This was a petition from a woman to Kerenski personally, asking him to remit a death sentence passed on her son at the front. As Savinkov comments, Kerenski did not give any indication of the reply to be sent, and it was easy for him in this way to avoid for years the signing of death sentences !

Savinkov suspects German work in the Kornilov

Kerenski Loses His Last Chance

business. His point is that there were three possible outcomes of the " adventure " :
1. Agreement between Kerenski and Kornilov.
2. Victory of Kornilov.
3. Victory of Kerenski.

The first and the second solutions would have been in Russia's interests. Only the third was in Germany's interests, and the third was the actual outcome.

Wednesday, October 24th, 1917.

Savinkov, Filonenko and Gravier [1] dined. Savinkov thinks that Kerenski is honest, but says that Trotski (Bronstein) and Kamenev (Rosenfeldt) could be bought. Lenin and Kolontai are fanatics. Filonenko said that up till last night he would have said that Kerenski was honest, but his confession yesterday that he had set a trap for Kornilov on September 8th by pretending that Lvov was at the telegraph apparatus made him ready to believe anything of him.

Savinkov thinks that a conspiracy of Russian officers never could succeed. Lukhomski sent 100-150 officers to Petrograd before the Kornilov attempt, and Savinkov's ante-room was soon crowded by a number of them who came to denounce the conspiracy.

The Russians, like ourselves, during the war were inclined to attribute the result of their own shortcomings to the machinations of the enemy. There is no evidence that German intrigue had anything to do with the Kornilov affair. It seems clear from the evidence available that Kornilov was led by his conversations with Lvov, whom he imagined to be a friend of Kerenski, and with Savinkov, whom he knew to be Kerenski's deputy in the Ministry of War, into the belief that Kerenski would support him in carrying out the plan which he and every officer of experience knew to be the only chance of restoring discipline in the army. Kerenski's

---

[1] A very able French officer and personal friend.

telegram ordering his resignation came as a bolt from the blue on September 9th, and he believed that in the interests of the country and the army he had no choice but to refuse.

Officer elements who surrounded Kornilov, and who naturally hated Kerenski, failed to understand that the co-operation of the Prime Minister was essential. They exaggerated to a criminal degree the strength of the forces at their disposal.

Still, the worst *rôle* was played by Kerenski, who, whether or not he had " led Kornilov into the movement," though urged by Savinkov, Alexyeev and Milyukov, refused to liquidate the incident quietly and peacefully. Kerenski writes that Kornilov's adventure was fatal to Russia, " for it shook profoundly and painfully the consciousness of the masses," and again, " it was only September 9th that made November 7th possible."

On the contrary, Kornilov's adventure might have proved the salvation of Russia if Kerenski had come out boldly on the side of the patriot General. This was perhaps too much to expect from a man of Kerenski's past, but ordinary patriotism should have suggested a quiet compromise. The Prime Minister, however, feared any negotiations, because the adoption of such a course might have provided the Extremists in the Sovyet with a weapon with which to attack his own political position.

Unfortunately, Kerenski was far from the great man that the times required.

Friday, October 12th, 1917.

Ragosin told me a story of Kerenski. One day, some weeks ago, the little Tsarevitch was playing at Tsarskoe Selo with a toy gun that the Cossacks had presented him with in the old days and of which he was passionately proud, when an officious soldier took the toy from him " lest he should shoot the sentries."

The boy cried bitterly, and a few days later when Kerenski and Polovtsev, then Commander-in-Chief of the Petrograd Military District, were visiting Tsarskoe and were being entertained to lunch by the Commandant, the latter asked what he should do in the matter. Kerenski allowed Polovtsev to reply first. Polovtsev said: " Give it back. After all, the child has no cartridges ! " The great man Kerenski then spoke. He said : " No. That would be dangerous, for the feelings of the soldiers are aroused. It is better not to give the rifle back. The soldiers might not like it."

CHAPTER XXIV

THE BOLSHEVIK COUP D'ÉTAT. OCTOBER-DECEMBER, 1917

Reference Map No. XIII. and Sketch F

WHEN I left England on October 2nd little further effective help from the Russian army was expected in the war. I went back to see the end. The autumn and early winter months in Petrograd were heart-breaking for one who had known the Russian army at its best. We were powerless to help our friends and remained impotent spectators of the general decline.

Friday, October 12th, 1917.

Colonel G—— (a General Staff Officer from the Northern Front), has just been in to see me. He, of course, wants to go to our army, and if there is a separate peace he will go as a private soldier.

He says that the men in the trenches are short of boots and warm clothing, and many of them are without great-coats. They gamble away their boots. Commanding officers cannot carry out inspections of clothing; as this duty is supposed to be performed by the committees!

He says that if Bolshevism wins all along the line in rear, it is very doubtful if the men will remain in the trenches. It is certain they will all leave a few hours after they hear of the commencement of peace negotiations.

He suggests that we should call in the Japanese and the Americans, that we should bribe widely, and employ murderers to get rid of Lenin, etc.—gas-bombs in the Circus when the Bolsheviks meet!

Tuesday, October 16th, 1917.

I dined last night with General Judson, the American Military Attaché, who has taken a palace of a house, and has A.D.C.'s, etc. He had Stevens, the American railroad expert, with De Candolle, our railway man, to talk to him, Verkhovski, the new Minister of War, and Colonel Polkovnikov, the new Commander of the District. I sat on Judson's left; opposite Verkhovski.

Verkhovski is intelligent, but very young. He looks twenty-eight, but is really thirty-four. He is young in his ideas and is an enthusiast with an enthusiast's lack of common sense. I am not sure that he does not talk for effect.

Some of his conversation shows the man. At dinner we talked English at our end of the table. Judson asked Verkhovski if it was not true that he was expelled from the Corps des Pages on account of his radical ideas. Looking straight in front of him, his eyes blinking through his glasses, he replied : " Not exactly. I sought the truth, and they did not want me to find the truth." Later on; in the theatre; Count Prjetski told me that the reason of the expulsion was that when a Lancer regiment was billeted in the Corps des Pages during some civil disturbances Verkhovski went to the men and told them not to fire on the people.

I asked Verkhovski what sort of propaganda he thought might do good in the Russian army—if he had a million pounds set apart for that purpose how he would spend it. He said : " In providing the men with books and literature, in cinemas and in tea-huts, to widen their outlook on life and to make them comfortable." It is quite true that this sort of thing has been too much neglected in Russia throughout the war.

Later in the smoking-room I sat beside him on a long divan. I asked if he thought the men would remain in the trenches during the winter. He said : " Of course they will remain. They remained after the Revolution."

I asked how many deserters there had been, and he said: "Four millions, but out of twelve millions." I denied that there were 12,000,000 men in the army at the time of the Revolution, and he tried to prove that there were, but was not convincing.

He slapped his knee and said: "We will restore the Russian army and make it in a fit condition to fight by the spring!"

He said that the movement against the officers in the army was elemental and that our task was to regain the confidence of the masses. I said that the destruction of the army was the work of agitators; who worked on the natural desire of the masses to save their skins, and that if a few of these agitators were shot all would be well. He said that a great number had been shot on the South-West Front. I said: "Nothing in comparison with the number of men shot in the Western theatre."

Verkhovski has an idea that the Allies should make an offer of peace to the Germans, but on such conditions that they would refuse. The refusal would show the Russian soldier that there was nothing left for him but to fight. I pointed out that I could not imagine what reservation the German Government might make sufficiently big to induce the Russian soldiers in their present mood to fight. I asked if he thought they would fight for Kurland. He agreed that they would not, but said they understood one thing; and that was their pocket, and they would fight for a good commercial treaty. While I stared at him in amazement he went on to say that he had talked to hundreds of soldiers and they understood that owing to the tariff agreement arranged after the Japanese war they had been paying annually huge subsidies to Germany. This is pure moonshine!

Polkovnikov is also far too young for his job. He told me that everything was splendid in his district, but I remarked that no training was being done.

I hear that a certain General G—— read the two proclamations of Kornilov and of Kerenski to his Corps and asked the men to choose which they would obey. The men said they preferred Kerenski, and the officers Kornilov. Could idiocy go further?

I saw Markozov this morning. Production is still at a minimum; for instance, in the railway works at Tver, 500 wagons per month were produced before the Revolution. March and April gave nothing, May and June forty and fifty. Later output was raised to 170, but now it has fallen again.

Kuzmin, the Assistant Commander of the district, though a friend of Kerenski, thinks that the latter's career is finished. He thinks that all the garrison is Bolshevik.

Thursday, October 18th, 1917.
Allied military representatives met at the Minister of War's house at 9.30 a.m. to hear a summary of the steps proposed to raise the *morale* of the army.

It is proposed to reduce its strength by the elimination of the older classes from the 10,000,000 it is now supposed to contain to 7,500,000, of which 4,000,000 will be combatants, 500,000 depot troops and 3,000,000 auxiliary services. Storm battalions are to be encouraged. Mounted and dismounted "militia" units are to be raised from wounded officers and soldiers to maintain order in the interior. After the elections for the Constituent Assembly which are to take place on November 15th, all political agitation is to be stopped in the army. Committees and Commissaries are to be retained.

Many of the proposals are excellent and others are fantastic. The suggestion to abolish the death penalty drew strong protests from General Niessel, who is quite an orator, and from me. We told the Minister that we considered it quite impossible for commanders deprived of the power of inflicting this penalty to stop a panic.

Verkhovski, finally, very pale and nervous, agreed that no army would fight without it, but he added that if it was found impossible to retain it, we were to understand that it was not his fault.

I saw Tereshchenko at 5.30 for half an hour. There are now 43,000 officers unemployed out of a total of 210,000. One corps in four will be withdrawn from the front line to train. The first corps to be withdrawn under this scheme is the IInd Guard. Result—it got hold of vodka in Podolya and is completely out of hand.

Tereshchenko fears that the German operations in the Gulf of Riga are preliminary to an attempt against Petrograd. He bases his idea on the size of the German fleet employed —sixteen dreadnoughts out of twenty-seven. He foresees a landing at Hapsal, the destruction of the Russian Baltic fleet, the sweeping up of the mine-fields with a simultaneous advance along the coast to the capital—an affair by land and sea of one and a half months, or if by sea only of three weeks. He is convinced that Germany has decided to have peace by Christmas, and is now determined to attain a strong strategical position, at whatever risk, before opening up negotiations. Germany had said all along that she would only risk her fleet at the end.

On the other hand, Germany has transferred seven divisions to the Western theatre in the last fortnight, *viz.*, one from Galicia, one from Lake Naroch and no less than five from the Riga front. This proves to me that though she may contemplate a raid, she can hardly intend a considered land-and-sea operation against Petrograd, even taking into consideration the present state of the Russian army.

Tereshchenko acknowledged that a " big offensive " was not to be expected from the Russian army next spring.

All he hoped for was that it would retain the "130" divisions now opposite it and "perhaps draw off more." (The number of divisions now opposite the Russian army is 121, *viz.*, 85 German and 36 Austrian.)

Friday, October 19th, 1917.

General G—— came to see me this morning with a proposal to send Russian officers to China to raise an army there secretly to restore order! He said the Germans might be in Petrograd in a month, and that only ruin awaits Russia as long as Kerenski is in power.

I saw Bagrutuni, the Chief of Staff of the District, in the afternoon. He told me he had had five commanders-in-chief in the two months since I last saw him. He is very keen on the formation of Armenian troops, and proposes two corps of Armenians and one of Georgians.

Savinkov thinks that Kerenski is finished, as he has lost all support from the right. At present the Cossacks control the situation in the capital. They will not take the initiative against Kerenski, but might move against the Sovyets, and would move with pleasure against Chernov. If Chernov succeeds Kerenski, Savinkov only gives him a week.

Chernov ran a paper in Switzerland which was circulated by the German Government among Russian prisoners of war! He is said to be a hypocrite, too, for when poor Kornilov was making his report to the Provisional Government and relating the excesses at the front, he shook his head more and more and was finally reduced to a state bordering on tears.

Sunday, October 21st, 1917.

The following is reported to be the detail of the members of elected organisations on the South-West Front, *i.e.*, of fighting men engaged in talk :

	MEN.	OFFICERS.	OFFICIALS.
Armies at the front	63,690	7,055	1,162
Depot units	1,769	228	19
Rear units	9,568	911	546
Totals	75,027	8,194	1,727

Grand Total, 84,948.

Monday, October 22nd, 1917.

I took Generals Danilov (Black) and Manikovski to the Ambassador to receive their K.C.B.'s. Danilov is pessimistic. He says it is possible to restore the fighting efficiency of the army, but work must be started at once. Manikovski roared out that Konavalov had told him that the Moscow party in the Government had made up its mind to force Kerenski to strong action, or, failing that, to reduce him to the portfolio of justice. He says that the Bolsheviks may try soon to arrest the Provisional Government, but that the latter should be able to " down them."

Tuesday, October 23rd, 1917.

The Foreign Office sent a very sound wire refusing to have anything to do with the wild Baltic adventure, and expressing its disgust that a nation that had forgotten the first duty of nationality—to defend its own territory—should, while retiring before inferior numbers, ask its ally to undertake an impossible naval operation in order to save it.

Friday, October 26th, 1917.

On Wednesday, on my way to and from the Ministry of Ways, where I went to collect information about the state of the railways, I passed through a seething crowd of 2,000 to 3,000 soldiers busily engaged in selling boots and clothing to civilians. This is called the " Equipment Market " ! What is the good of sending stuff to such people?[1] I drove to see the Minister of War, to protest, and to ask why our sailors should risk their lives to carry these things to Russia. Verkhovski said he thought that steps *might* be taken to prevent such sales. He had prevented them when commander of the Moscow District, etc., etc.

Saturday, October 27th, 1917.

I collected information to reply to telegram from home regarding the situation on the Northern Front. My opinion, in brief, is that the enemy will not attempt to get to Petrograd this year, but if he should attempt there is nothing to stop him except climate and space.

Verkhovski has published a good order arranging the formation of local and railway " militia " from wounded officers and soldiers. If this formation had only been carried out seven months ago when I first urged its necessity!

Tuesday, October 30th, 1917.

I lunched with Verkhovski—also Niessel, Golovin, Marushevski and Levitski.[2]

After lunch Verkhovski said that the five classes which it is now proposed to dismiss meant a million men. Dukhonin says that more than this cannot be spared from the front. On the other hand, the Ministers of Finance, Food and Commerce ask for from one to two millions more to be demobilised.

Verkhovski returned to his old plan that the Allies should offer terms of peace to Germany.

I was struck by the frank pessimism of the four Russian

---

[1] In the course of the year 1917 Great Britain despatched to Russia from the United Kingdom nearly fifty million pounds' worth of material, including 1,804,650 pairs of ankle boots and 1,259,600 pairs of long boots!

[2] General Golovin had been detailed to go as Liaison Officer to France. He is now in Paris.

General Marushevski was Chief of the General Staff. General Levitski had been promoted from the Staff of the 11th Army to be Chief of Kerenski's Military Cabinet.

officers present. There is evidently not the slightest hope that the Russian army will ever fight again.

S.——(a Russian) came in to see me with a wonderful story of a new Government forming in Moscow and of Kaledin marching on Petrograd!

General S—— came to talk of his Chinese army. When he came in I was reading the White Paper on the Cruelties of the Germans in East Africa. He said that no one could be as cruel as Russians, and instanced the murder of a divisional commander in the Special Army, who was tortured when wounded in a manner which for sheer bestial brutality it would be impossible to beat.

Thursday, November 1st, 1917.

Tereshchenko talks of pushing Kerenski out and of knocking the Sovyets. *If* they were only strong enough!

The Bolshevik trial of strength is expected for Wednesday, November 7th.

Information from G.H.Q. states that there are now 5,925,606 of all ranks on all the six fronts, including depot troops, yet of these only 2,143,500 are combatants. On the other hand, the Chief of the General Staff here says that these numbers cannot be relied upon, that a census is being taken at the front, and that he will tell me the result!

G.H.Q. states that there are now 5,929 3" guns on the western frontier and 524 in the Caucasus. It estimates the total of large calibre at 2,030 in addition to 1,277 "fortress guns" on the western frontier and 181 in the Caucasus. The estimate of the Artillery Department is considerably larger.

An enormous quantity of artillery ammunition of every calibre has been accumulated. For instance, each 3" gun has 2,200 rounds actually at the front and there are 10,000,000 rounds in rear ready charged. Then there are large accumulations at Arkhangel and Vladivostok. It is all too late. If we could only get back to life again the men who died in 1915 through lack of shell!

Sunday, November 4th, 1917.

Night before last I dined with Savinkov at M——'s house. There were also present M——, Tumánov, Filonenko, Gravier and another Frenchman.

Savinkov gave us an amusing account of how he was examined regarding his political opinions by three Jews before he went to the 7th Army as commissary. They commenced by asking him his ideas regarding peace. He replied that we had to win before we talked of peace, and that his job as he conceived it was to go to organise victory. "Yes," they said, "to organise victory, but at the same time you have to organise peace."

Savinkov, in relating this, said : "You know at times I am very stupid, and just then I could not for the life of me grasp what they meant, so I said : 'I am sorry, gentlemen, but I am afraid I do not understand what you mean.'" There was silence for some moments, broken at length by one Goldmann, who was more sensible than the others and who remarked that such conversations were of little use.

On Friday night Verkhovski stated at the Committee of the Pre-Parliament on Military and Foreign Affairs that he was unable to raise the fighting spirit of the army unless the men knew why they fought, and to teach them this we must offer Germany peace on terms. He was opposed by everyone and has tendered his resignation.

An armed demonstration of the garrison in favour of the Bolsheviks had been openly talked of for November 7th. The Provisional Government called up two cyclist battalions from the front and expressed its confidence in its ability to quell any rising. In fact, Kerenski and Tereshchenko pretended only to fear that the rising might not be attempted and that they might therefore be deprived of the opportunity of annihilating the movement once and for all.

Since the fall of Riga the Provisional Government had discussed the advisability of removing the seat of Government to Moscow, ostensibly because of the possibility of a further German advance, but also probably because of a hankering after the calmer political atmosphere of the older capital.

The Petrograd Sovyet, of which Trotski had now become president, proclaimed that it had no trust in the Government, and that it would accordingly take upon itself the defence of the capital. It formed on November 2nd a " Military Revolutionary Committee " under the Bolshevik, Antonov, to control the district staff. This Committee appointed its commissaries to all units of the garrison and to arms factories. It interfered in all orders issued by the district staff and rendered the position of the latter impossible.

Tuesday, November 6th, 1917.

I was to have gone to Pskov last night, had packed my kit and made all arrangements. At 7 p.m. Smith [1] heard from the Guard of junkers in the Embassy that they and the other guards defending embassies had been ordered to hold out to the end in case of attack, but that the guards on Tereshchenko and Konovalov's houses had been told if attacked to give up their arms without resistance. The boys said that these orders had been given them that day at the Military School. Bruce went to warn Tereshchenko, who thanked him and said he would not sleep at home. I went to the District Staff, where Podryelov, the General Quartermaster, told me that it was quite impossible that such an order had been issued. He was, however, very pessimistic and told me that he did not know whom he could trust. He advised me to postpone my departure for the front, as there would certainly be

---

[1] Captain Rowland Smith, Translator to the British Embassy. An excellent fellow and a hard-working and able public servant. Died on his way to Siberia in 1918.

interesting developments in Petrograd in the next few days.

I telephoned to the Ambassador, who asked me to sleep in the Embassy. I dined at home and got over at 9.15. Bruce also slept there. The night was quiet.

To-day Bagratuni told me that Kerenski had decided to arrest Trotski and the members of the Military Revolutionary Committee. This Committee, among other things, in the last few days prevented the despatch of 10,000 rifles from the Arsenal to Novocherkask. I asked if we were strong enough to carry out this programme, and Bagratuni said we were. Podryelov said : " We can take the risk."

About 1,000 women marched past the Embassy this morning on their way to be inspected by Kerenski on the Palace Square. They made the best show of any soldiers I have seen since the Revolution, but it gave me a lump in the throat to see them, and the utter swine of " men " soldiers jeering at them.

All automobiles were stopped in the streets and were collected in the Palace Square. About 6 p.m. on the 6th the district staff opened the bridges, posting guards of cyclists and volunteer battalions. Later in the evening a meeting of the Cossack regiments at Petrograd, the 1st, 4th and 14th Don Cossack Cavalry, was held to decide on a course of action. The men expressed their unwillingness to support Kerenski, who had called them " counter-revolutionaries " and their chosen leader, Kornilov, a " traitor." Further, they pointed out that an attempt to put down a Bolshevik rising, unsupported as they were by infantry, would result in bloodshed and would probably fail Later a deputation visited Kerenski, and his refusal to declare the Bolshevik organisation illegal confirmed the Cossacks in their resolution to remain neutral.

On the morning of November 7th, Savinkov was visited by

two officers. One, a colonel, told him that no officers would move a finger to support Kerenski ; another, a lieutenant of the district staff, told him that a group of officers had actually decided to arrest him.

Thursday morning, November 8th, 1917.
We are fairly in the middle of it again !

The papers yesterday morning made it pretty clear that the Bolsheviks had it all their own way. My walk to the Embassy in the morning made it still more plain. The Government troops of the night before had disappeared ; everywhere were patrols of the local garrison. Trams were running and there was perfect order. Ivan managed to buy me papers, but the greater part of the *Bourse Gazette* had been suppressed by the Bolsheviks.

I had sandwiches at the Embassy and then walked down the Milionnaya to see Bagratuni. At the Winter Palace bridge a crowd of men of the Preobrajenski Regiment waited on one side, ready at a moment's notice to sweep away the few poor junkers on guard near the Hermitage.

Polkovnikov, the Commander of the District, pretended to be hopeful. He said that he was certain he would be able to turn the whole situation round in favour of the Provisional Government. I asked him what he had to go on, and he said that there were " already certain indications of a reaction." He was a very brave but rather pathetic optimist !

Poor Bagratuni made less concealment. He had not slept for three nights, neither had he shaved, and when an Armenian does not shave it is noticeable. He told me that he had never been in such a position, for he could not depend on any single order being carried out. The troops called in from the front had gone over in the night. The whole town, with the exception of the Palace Square, was in the hands of the Sovyets. Some officers had gone to the Winter Palace to offer their services to the Provisional

Government. The latter was still sitting and had decided to hold out to the last. Troops were on their way from the front, but had been delayed. He thanked me quite touchingly for having come to see him.[1] I got the same impression at the District Staff as I had gathered at the Prefecture on the first day of the big Revolution—forced optimism with nothing to go on.

I met Ragosin just returned from the Cossack Conference at Vladikavkaz. He was in high spirits, and told me, as we walked across the Palace Square, that the Cossacks had come to a complete agreement with the Caucasian mountaineers regarding the formation of a federated state. They will hold back grain and coal and oil from the north. I said: " What of the war ? " He replied : " So far they have said nothing of the war, but they stand to go on with it." Everyone has forgotten the war !

The junker garrison of the Palace was working halfheartedly at the construction of a breastwork of firewood a few yards in advance of the main entrance.

I said good-bye to Ragosin; and entering the Palace by the garden gate climbed the stairs to look for Levitski, the Chief of Kerenski's Military Cabinet. He had gone. On the stairs many workmen were busy cutting down and removing the tapestries.

As I walked back across the Square to the General Staff building a fusillade broke out and the crowd ran. No bullets came my way.

Nearly all the officers had left the Staff Building; as the Pavlovski Regiment had announced that it was about to occupy the building.

I saw Golyevski, the General Quartermaster, and Durnovo, who had come to Petrograd to work in the Intelligence, and found them quite unperturbed. Golyevski

---

[1] General Bagratuni was arrested four hours later and was for long confined in the fortress of Peter and Paul. He is alive and was last heard of in Paris.

explained that the quarrel between the Government and the Sovyet did not concern the General Staff, much less foreign representatives! My officers sealed up the door of our room and took our ciphers to the Embassy.

At the Embassy I heard that Kerenski had borrowed a car from the Americans at about 5 a.m. and had escaped to Pskov. He was forced to borrow a car; as all the magnetos from the cars collected in the Palace Square had been stolen by the Bolsheviks in the night. He sent back a message to the American Ambassador, asking him not to recognise the new Government for five days, as before that time he would return and restore order. In my opinion he will not return.

I walked back to dine and took with me Wardrop, who had arrived from Bergen to be Consul-General at Moscow.

At 8.30 O—— came in. He was on his way to Moscow. He complained bitterly of the District Staff, which he said had blocked his efforts to fight the rising by its red tape. His idea was to organise at Moscow and to join the relieving troops.

Heavy firing broke out at the Winter Palace about 8.45. The cruiser *Aurora*, which had steamed up the Neva; and the fortress guns took part. The fusillade continued till midnight, though all resistance at the Palace must have been over long before.

It is a dull grey day to-day. Trams are running, but firing is still audible, though not in great volume.

On the 7th the Minister, Kishkin, was appointed Dictator by the Provisional Government, and the engineer Palchinski succeeded Colonel Polkovnikov in command of the Military District. When I parted with Ragosin at 4 p.m. on the 7th he went to see Palchinski, who insisted on his working with him; much against his will, on the ground that he was the A.D.C. of General Polovtsev and Polovtsev was Palchinski's friend! Ragosin objected that he had only come to Petrograd for a few days on purely private affairs, but finally reluctantly gave way. He was sent round the town in a car " to collect reliable officers,"and after finding three who promised to come, returned to the District Staff and was sent to report on the Palace defences.

The garrison of the Palace originally consisted of about 2,000 all told, including detachments from junker and ensign schools, three squadrons of Cossacks, a company of volunteers and a company from the Women's Battalion. It had six guns and one armoured car, the crew of which, however, declared that it had only come " to guard the art treasures of the Palace and was otherwise neutral " !

The garrison had dwindled owing to desertions, for there were no provisions and it had been practically starved for two days. There was no strong man to take command and to enforce discipline. No one had any stomach for fighting; and some of the ensigns even borrowed great coats of soldier pattern from the women to enable them to escape unobserved.

The greater part of the junkers of the Mikhail Artillery School returned to their school, taking with them four out of their six guns. Then the Cossacks left, declaring themselves opposed to bloodshed ! At 10 p.m. a large part of the ensigns left, leaving few defenders except the ensigns of the Engineering School and the company of women.

The Government was the whole time in communication with the front, and at midnight was elated by a message that troops were on the march for their relief. Then a report came that the Fleet Committee was coming to the Palace with provisions.

During the bombardment the Ministers moved about from room to room. Ragosin afterwards related that when he had to report on some subject he found " the Minister of Marine sitting in a window smoking a pipe and spitting. Other Ministers were seated at a table. Tereshchenko walked up and down like a caged tiger. Konovalov sat on a sofa nervously pulling up his trousers till they were finally above his knees." Ragosin, however, considered himself merely an unconcerned and irresponsible onlooker. In reality the plight of this handful of men must have been terrible. Deserted by their leader and surrounded from

6 p.m. on the 7th, refusing to leave their post, though powerless to effect anything, they waited their fate at the hands of the rabble.

The defence was unorganised and only three of the many entrances were guarded. Parties of the attackers penetrated by side entrances in search of loot. At first these parties were small and were disarmed by the garrison, but they were succeeded by larger bands of sailors and of the Pavlovski Regiment, in addition to armed workmen, and these turned the tables by disarming the garrison. This was, however, carried out, as an officer of the garrison afterwards stated, " in a domestic manner," with little bloodshed. The garrison fired little and is said to have only lost three junkers wounded.

Ragosin related later that, finding he could do nothing, he handed his sword to one of the Palace servants and escaped across the wood pile in the Square, only to run into some sailors, who arrested him and took him to the Central Telephone Station, where they handed him over to a guard of the Keksgolmski Regiment. As he sat there one of the soldiers, after gazing fixedly at him for a long time, said : " If I could only run my bayonet into you, run it in right up to the hilt ! " Ragosin pretended not to understand, and asked the officer in charge of the guard what was the matter with the man. The officer was a " diplomat," and diverted the soldiers' attention by talking to them about their tobacco, about the poorness of the electric light, etc. Finally he told Ragosin he might go. Ragosin asked for an escort, and to his horror was sent out with the same soldier. He walked along expecting every moment to have a bayonet in his side. When they reached the hotel he bid the man good-night and told him he had left his pipe in the telephone station. The soldier said he would go and get it, and ten minutes later knocked at the bedroom door and appeared with the pipe. Ragosin gave him Rs.10. So rapidly do Russian soldiers change !

At 2.30 a.m. on the 8th the Palace was " taken." The Ministers were arrested and marched through execrating crowds across the Troitski Bridge to the Fortress of Peter and Paul. The garrison was disarmed and taken to the barracks of the Pavlovski Regiment on the Champ de Mars. In an account published later a junker named Rosinn stated that he and his comrades were lined up against a wall and were about to be shot when they fled in all directions and were many of them shot down by soldiers. A few escaped, himself among the number, after hiding all night in the wood piles on the Champ de Mars.

According to Bolshevik accounts the company of women offered the most serious resistance, and a report stated that three of them were stripped and thrown into the Neva. The remainder, 137 in all, were marched to the Pavlovski barracks, where they were "searched for bombs in an unnecessary manner." They were then passed on to the barracks of the Grenaderski Regiment. These women were volunteers recruited from all classes, but mostly from the *Intelligentsiya*. Their real patriotism formed the brightest spot in the general apathy since the Revolution.

Thursday evening, November 8th, 1917.
I have had a busy day.
I walked with Wardrop in the morning to the General Staff. Nothing had been touched. I saw Marushevski and Golyevski. The latter said that very few men had been killed in the fighting last night. He had spent the night with Marushevski in the official quarters of the Chief of the General Staff, and they had several times sent out to ascertain how things were going. Golyevski himself had "even gone out once," but not a single wounded man had been seen. The attitude of unconcerned aloofness astounded me.

I crossed the Square to the District Staff Building and found it occupied by a large guard of mutineers. A N.C.O. with whom I talked asserted that 500 men had been killed and wounded.[1] He was of a truculent type, very different from the N.C.O. of the Preobrajenski who had helped me on March 12th.

I lunched at the Embassy and then went to the Town

---

[1] This was a gross exaggeration. The total casualties are believed to have been about ten.

Hall to get a new Embassy guard and passes for members of the Chancery. I saw Aksentiev, Nabokov, Galpern and others. They said that all the non-Bolshevik Socialists had seceded from the Sovyet and were forming a Committee of Public Safety. This Committee has no power behind it at present but hopes for support from the troops coming in from the front. Kerenski is said to have had a good reception from the relieving troops at Dno. It is expected that they will be here to-morrow or next day. Aksentiev said he gave the Bolsheviks "about two days."

When I returned to the Embassy I found Lady Georgina in great excitement. Two officer instructors of the Women's Battalion had come with a terrible story to the effect that the 137 women taken in the Palace had been beaten and tortured, and were now being outraged in the Grenaderski barracks.

I borrowed the Ambassador's car and drove to the Bolshevik headquarters at the Smolni Institute. This big building, formerly a school for the daughters of the nobility, is now thick with the dirt of revolution. Sentries and others tried to put me off, but I at length penetrated to the third floor, where I saw the Secretary of the Military Revolutionary Committee and demanded that the women should be set free at once. He tried to procrastinate, but I told him that if they were not liberated at once I would set the opinion of the civilised world against the Bolsheviks and all their works. He tried to soothe me and begged me to talk French instead of Russian, as the waiting-room was crowded and we were attracting attention. He himself talked excellent French and was evidently a man of education and culture. Finally, after two visits to the adjoining room, where he said the Council was sitting, he came back to say that the order for the release would be signed at once.

I drove with the officers to the Grenaderski barracks and went to see the Regimental Committee. The commissary, a repulsive individual of Semitic type, refused to release the women without a written order, on the ground that " they had resisted to the last at the Palace, fighting desperately with bombs and revolvers." He said that they were now under a guard apart from the soldiers, unmolested and quite safe. He refused to let me see them, though I asked twice. It was an extraordinary scene, the officers speaking French, which the commissary probably understood, and urging me not to believe a word he said; the half-dozen soldiers of the Regimental Committee, not of a bad type, but stolidly indifferent and taking no part in the discussion; the commissary of a race which has been oppressed for centuries but now holding all the cards, not arrogant but determined. We tried to telephone to the Smolni to ascertain if the order had been despatched, but could get no reply. I returned to the Embassy and, telephoning through to the Sovyet, was told that the order for the release had been sent by special messenger.

The Bolsheviks in this instance were as good as their word. The order arrived at the Regiment soon after my departure, and the women were escorted by a large guard to the Finland station, where they entrained at 9 p.m. for Levashova, their battalion headquarters. As far as could be ascertained, though they had been beaten and insulted in every way in the Pavlovski barracks and on their way to the Grenaderski Regiment, they were not actually hurt in the barracks of the latter. They were, however, only separated from the men's quarters by a barrier extemporised from beds, and blackguards among the soldiery had shouted threats that had made them tremble for the fate that the night might bring.

On the night of the 11th a deputation of four of the women came to the Embassy to thank me for my help. They asked if it were possible for them to be transferred to the British Army, as they could do nothing more to help Russia. I told them that Englishwomen were not allowed to fight, and that they would be jealous if their Russian sisters were permitted to go to the front. After they went out I vented my feelings on the officers who accompanied them, by telling them that no nation except the Russian had ever allowed its women to fight, and certainly the British nation never would.

The heroic effort of these women had had no effect on the men, who were past all shame. They were insulted by the soldiers whenever they came to Petrograd, so kind women friends provided them with civilian clothing and they dispersed to their homes.

I received many letters of thanks for my visit to Smolni from the Knights of St. George, from the Censor Department, from the All Russia Women's Alliance. The President of the latter wrote, on November 10th:

> MONSIEUR LE GÉNÉRAL,
>
> L'Union des Femmes de toute la Russie a l'honneur et la joie de vous remercier pour votre noble démarche d'hier. Vous avez fait ce que chaque mère, chaque père aspiraient à ces funestes heures. Vous avez tiré hors d'un grave danger les pauvres petites femmes heroiques et abandonnées. Monsieur, nous sommes habituées à considerer les Anglais en nobles protecteurs de femmes et des faibles, mais cette fois ci vous dépassez la limite où l'on admire et remercie.
>
> Nous nous inclinons devant votre grande Patrie.

On the night of November 7th poor Prince Tumánov, the Assistant Minister of War, and the most honest of the soldiers who had come to the front since the Revolution, was wantonly murdered by sailors. He had been arrested and escorted to the barracks of the Keksgolmski Regiment, but was claimed by a party of sailors ostensibly to convey him to the Main Guard. He had no sooner reached the street when one of them felled him by a blow from a rifle-butt from behind and the others stabbed him to death when on the ground and threw his body into the river Moika. It was truly said that the Russian sailors killed many more Russian officers during the eight months after the Revolution than they had killed German officers in the preceding three and a half years of war.

The Military Revolutionary Committee proceeded with its policy of disorganising the army, and despatched the following telegram to all fronts on November 8th:

> The garrison and people of Petrograd have overthrown the Provisional Government of Kerenski. The Petrograd Sovyet of Working-men and Soldier Deputies has welcomed the change with acclamation, and pending the formation of a Government of Sovyets has assigned authority to the Military Revolutionary Committee. In informing the army in front and in rear of this fact, the Military Revolutionary Committee enjoins the revolutionary soldiery to observe attentively the conduct of the senior officers of the army. All of the latter who do not openly and without reservation acknowledge the Revolution which has taken place should be at once arrested as enemies of the new Government's programme—the immediate offer of a democratic peace, the immediate transfer of all landowners' land to the peasants, the transfer of all power to the Sovyets and the faithful calling of the Constituent Assembly.
>
> The revolutionary army must not permit the despatch to Petrograd from the front of untrustworthy units; it must dissuade such units by speech and by argument, and where necessary by force.
>
> This Order will be at once read to units of all arms. Disobedience to it by army organisations or by the soldier masses will be regarded as the greatest of crimes against the Revolution and will be punished with all the strictness of the revolutionary law.
>
> Soldiers for peace, for bread, for land and for power for the people!
>
> MILITARY REVOLUTIONARY COMMITTEE.

On November 9th a Government of People's Commissaries was formed, with Lenin as President, Trotski Commissary for Foreign Affairs, and Military and Naval affairs in the hands of a committee consisting of Antonov, Kirilenko and the sailor

Dibenko. Four million copies of the Decree of Peace were sent to the front.

Most of the officers of the General Staff remained in hiding, and, as it was necessary to re-establish communication with the front, we had ourselves to apply to the rebels on the 10th. In the District Staff I asked the suisse, who was a stout supporter of law and order, how long he thought this phase would last. He said he did not know, " but long it could not be." Upstairs were two unknown ensigns drinking tea and munching black bread. I explained that by the stoppage of all communication with the front the Military Revolutionary Committee was merely playing into the hands of the Germans. I guaranteed that we would send no messages concerning internal politics, and suggested that a censor might be detailed by Smolni to read our telegrams. One of the youths telephoned to Smolni. At 4 p.m. I went to see General Manikovski, who had been appointed Minister of War in succession to Verkhovski just in time to be arrested together with the other members of the Provisional Government. He had been released from the fortress on the 9th to take charge especially of the service of supply, which was falling into a state of chaos owing to the boycott of the new Government by the officers and officials. Manikovski had agreed to assume the direction of the Ministry on condition that he was given a free hand and was not required to meddle in politics. I found the General in his private apartment, in a room with his pet dog and cat, the one of whom he called " Bolshevik " and the other " Menshevik." He was none the worse for his uncomfortable experience, and laughingly said that he had been Minister two days, and for that fault he had sat exactly two days in prison.

Savinkov, who escaped from Petrograd on the 9th and joined the relieving force at Gatchina on the 10th, found that its commander, General Krasnov, had not a cavalry corps, as was reported at Petrograd, but only some squadrons of the 9th and 10th Don Cossack Cavalry Regiments, three squadrons of Ussuri Cossacks and a composite squadron of Cossacks of the Guard—in all about 600 sabres with twelve guns. The 15th Ussuri Cossack Regiment had refused to join the column.

October-December, 1917

Krasnov had taken Gatchina on the 9th, and on the 10th approached Tsarskoe Selo, which was garrisoned by 20,000 men. The garrison sent delegates to ask for terms, and Krasnov demanded they should lay down their arms. Unfortunately, however, Kerenski appeared in his motor and gave vent to his usual speech about saving the Revolution, etc. This resulted in the usual "meeting." Some of the Bolshevik soldiery gave up their arms and others did not. Krasnov fired four rounds of shrapnel and all opposition disappeared. He occupied Tsarskoe Selo by nightfall.

The 20,000 Bolsheviks endeavoured with some success to convince the 600 Cossacks that they had really nothing to fight about. Both parties found a common ground in their dislike and mistrust of Kerenski.

The relieving force was expected to arrive in Petrograd on Sunday the 11th, and to assist its entry the Committee of Public Safety organised the so-called rising of the junkers. On Saturday night these boys had seized the Garage, and early on Sunday they occupied without much opposition the Central Telephone Station and the Engineer Castle. At about 8 a.m. the junkers of the Vladimir Military School overpowered their Bolshevik guard. The school was retaken at 3 p.m. after bombardment by artillery, and many of the junkers were murdered. The rising was badly organised, and only a handful of the thousands of officers in the town took any part. A few of them joined in the defence of the Telephone Station, but very few. While the firing was in progress there I met an officer I knew walking in the next street arm-in-arm with a lady friend. I expressed my astonishment that he took no interest in the fighting, and he said that it had nothing to do with him! By nightfall on Sunday the town was once more in the hands of the Bolsheviks.

That day Krasnov's force had rested. Savinkov had an interview with Kerenski and implored him to refrain from further speeches.

On the morning of the 12th Krasnov advanced once more on Pulkova, but his handful of men, though they fought bravely all day, were quite unable to drive back the Bolsheviks, who outnumbered them by ten to one and were in an entrenched position. The soldiers of the Petrograd garrison had no stomach for fighting, but the armed workmen and the sailors were evidently directed by men who knew their business. Captured sailors stated that there were seven German officers in the rebel staff, and from another source it is affirmed that during the operations all conversation on the Bolshevik telephones was in the German language.

No infantry came up in support, and towards evening the Cossacks, who were running short of ammunition and were in danger of being surrounded, retired on Gatchina.

That night the Cossack officers elected Savinkov as their Commissary, commissioning him to use his influence to prevent Kerenski from interfering in the work of the Staff. The appointment had to be confirmed by Kerenski, and was opposed by Stankevich, the Commissary from G.H.Q., on the ground that Savinkov was a " counter-revolutionary " ! Savinkov, on his part, considered it to be his duty to inform Kerenski that he did not, and never had, agreed with his policy. He wrote afterwards: " I told him that I had long ago made up my mind that his continuance in power meant ruin for Russia, that I had fought him with every lawful means, and I was ready to fight him with every unlawful means, as I considered him to be one of the causes of the complete destruction of Russia and the precise cause of the Bolshevik rising, to meet which he had totally failed to take timely measures. I did not like to say any more," Savinkov characteristically adds, " as he was so depressed that I pitied him " ! Kerenski listened to him till the end, and then confirmed his appointment as Commissary.

At midday on the 13th a council of war was held and the opinion of Stankevich that negotiations should be opened with the Bolsheviks prevailed. Savinkov denounced this decision as a crime against the country, and left Gatchina that evening to try to obtain help from the XVIIth Corps, then at Nevel. He soon found that the failure of the infantry to come up was to be ascribed to the contradictory orders and probable treachery of General Cherimisov, the Commander-in-Chief of the Northern Front.

Finally, on the 17th, orders were received from General Dukhonin that no troops were to be sent to Petrograd. Krasnov's handful of Cossacks had before this come to terms with the Bolsheviks. Krasnov himself was arrested, but soon released. Kerenski escaped dressed as a sailor and wearing chauffeur's spectacles.

There were few casualties in the open fighting in Petrograd, but many murders of unarmed men. On the 8th the manager of the National City Bank, looking out of his window at 11 a.m., saw an unarmed jukner pass a group of sailors. After he had passed, one of the latter raised his rifle and shot the junker dead. This was within a hundred yards of the British Embassy. Next morning a soldier was murdered under the Embassy windows as he tried to escape from a band of Red Guards. On the 10th, when the Red Guard was trying to prevent the distribution of anti-Bolshevik papers on the Nevski Prospekt, a student caught hold of one man's rifle. His companion fired four shots, killing a girl. This caused great excitement, a civilian dipping his handkerchief in the girl's blood and running into the middle of the street to deliver a theatrical speech. Resistance, however, was only in speech or in the refusal of service by all the officials of the various ministries except those of the Ministry of War, who, in the interests of the army and the national defence, continued work.

Wednesday, November 14th, 1917.

Verkhovski came to see the Ambassador, and I interpreted. Incidentally he said that Kerenski had not wanted to let the Cossacks suppress the rising " on their own," as he knew that would be " the end of the Revolution." I suggested that " perhaps it would have saved Russia." Verkhovski disagreed, and said it was a mistake to imagine that the Cossacks could conquer Russia. All the same, I believe they could if they were not handicapped by men of the type of Kerenski, for they represent the only force that has any approach to discipline, and if they acted quickly and resolutely all the elements that stand for law and order might rally to their side.

Verkhovski professed to believe that the moderate socialists still have a chance. I doubt it. I agree with Trotski that the only opposition the Bolsheviks had to fear was from Kornilov's and Kaledin's party, and that is now past.[1]

Kapnist, the Chief of the Naval General Staff, sent for me to go to his flat to have a long talk, because, he said, I liked Russia and knew her present situation. He argued that it was in England's as well as in Russia's interest to make peace. The Russian forces could do no more in this war. He did not believe in a separate peace, on the ground that it would not be in Germany's interest to conclude such a peace, since the Russian army in demobilising would lay waste all Western Russia and would make it impossible for Germany to obtain any supplies for many months, and also because Germany did not want Russian socialists to upset the temper of her people, and this propaganda would become far more dangerous if peace enabled the fanatics to enter Germany.

He baited his arguments with the usual appeal to England's well-known greed! He said if war were continued Germany would take Petrograd and a large slice of the Ukraine next spring. This would extend Germany's market at England's expense, and might make it impossible for Russia to pay her debts.

Like many decent Russians, he sees that the Bolsheviks are determined to make peace, and in the interest of Russia's honour he wants the peace to be a general and not a separate one.

---

[1] Verkhovski was a man of undoubted courage. In a letter which he wrote on November 14th, but which appeared later in the Press, he indignantly contradicted the rumour that he was about to join the Bolshevik Ministry. He wrote prophetically of the Bolsheviks: "These people, while promising everything, will give nothing—instead of peace, civil war; instead of bread, famine; instead of freedom, robbery, anarchy and murder."

October-December, 1917

Sunday, November 18th, 1917.

Kirilenko's new Declaration of the Rights of Soldiers was read at the general meeting of the Sovyet last night, but was not published as the majority of the Sovyet thought it should be first elaborated in detail. It provides for the election of commanders, the abolition of rank and of badges of rank, the abolition of military schools for the preparation of officers, the extension of the rights of committees, the responsibility of the command to committees for the success of operations, the levelling up of the rates of pay of officers and men.

Neilson returned from the Western Front, which he left on the 13th, spending the time since at G.H.Q. He was not allowed to visit the armies. Fraternisation is rapidly increasing. There now serve in committees on the front 54,000 men with allowances of Rs.250,000 a month, yet the committees, like the officers, have lost all power. Desertion is not increasing, and officers say the men will remain in the trenches in the winter if clothed and fed and not asked to fight. The truth of it is that they lack the initiative to leave. The ordinary soldier gets up at 10 a.m., lounges about and perhaps plays cards till 1 p.m., when he dines. He then sleeps a little, and perhaps takes a short walk, so passing the time till 5 p.m., when he starts playing cards—the real business of the day—and this he continues till 3 a.m.

Wednesday, November 21st, 1917.

I dined with the Z——s, a Polish family. W—— told a yarn of the 3rd Guard Infantry Division which is now engaged in looting in Podoliya. A Russian soldier went into a church to loot. He was seen to balance an eikon on his arm. Then he solemnly crossed himself three times and finally dashed the eikon to the ground!

Meanwhile every town in Russia was going through its small

revolution. In Moscow on the night of the 8th the Military Revolutionary Committee issued orders to all units to obey only instructions issued or countersigned by its representatives. On the following day, Friday, the 8th, the men of the 56th Reserve Regiment in the Kremlin seized the Post and Telegraph Office and the Governor's House. On Saturday the junkers struck back, rushing the Kremlin. The 56th Regiment retired across the river, and it was imagined that the fighting was over. The Bolsheviks, however, finally succeeded in surrounding the junkers in the Kremlin, and the boys were forced to surrender at 5 p.m. on Thursday, the 15th, because they realised that their position was hopeless and there was no one in all Russia with the courage to come to rescue them. The junkers were helped by a few volunteers and a few—a very few—officers. Out of a garrison of over 100,000 men only some 15,000 took part in the Bolshevik rising, and these were driven by some 400 fanatics. Many of the remainder of the garrison deserted by every train to their villages. The civilian population of over 2,000,000 looked on apathetically, hoping, many of them, that the junkers would win, but fearing to help them.

CHAPTER XXV

THE PREPARATION OF THE SEPARATE PEACE

Reference Sketch F

THE Bolshevik *coup d'etat* in Petrograd was the work of a handful of fanatics. It succeeded partly because these fanatics, being men of action, had seduced by money, wine and promises the armed workmen, the sailors, and a small part of the garrison, but chiefly because Kerenski, in his desire to please the moderate socialists, who were only talkers, had failed entirely to govern, and had so alienated the only men of action who might have defended him, the officers and the Cossacks.

Once in power, the Bolsheviks lost no time in consolidating their position. The support of the army was necessary, and they knew that nothing could buy that support so certainly as an unblushing policy of peace at any price, regardless of the national interests of Russia or of her Allies. They realised the impatience of the army, with winter approaching and bread in the trenches growing scarce, and they published their decree of peace twenty-four hours after the fall of the Winter Palace.

Eleven days later, when their authority had been acknowledged in all the principal towns in Russia—on the night of November 20th—they despatched a wireless message to General Dukhonin, the Supreme Commander-in-Chief, notifying him that all the Allied representatives in Petrograd had been already warned, and ordering him to propose an immediate cessation of hostilities to the enemy Command with a view to the commencement of negotiations for peace. It was quite untrue that the Allied Embassies had been previously notified. General Dukhonin received the message at G.H.Q. at 5.5 a.m. on November

21st. The French Embassy was notified at 5.30 p.m. on the same day, the British Embassy at midnight and the Japanese Embassy some days later.

On the evening of the 21st Trotski said at a meeting of the Sovyet: " We confront the Allied as well as the enemy Governments with the fact that the Russian people and the Russian army wish to bring the war to an end, that we have no Imperialistic ideas of conquest, that we throw into the waste-paper basket of history all the old treaties which assigned us alien territory, that we are advocates of a real peace, and for this reason we make a formal offer to commence peace negotiations and to conclude an armistice.

" All governments feel the pressure of their peoples, and our policy will be a force to increase this pressure. This is the sole guarantee that we will attain peace, and that the peace will be an honourable one, not a peace that will ruin Russia, but one in harmony with the peoples of Western Europe."

As no reply was received from the Commander-in-Chief, Ensign Kirilenko, who had assumed charge of the Ministry of War, and his chief, Lenin, called him up on the telephone at 2 a.m. on the 22nd. Dukhonin asked whether the Government had had any reply to its peace proposals from other Governments; secondly, what was to be done with the Rumanian army which formed part of the Russian front; and thirdly, whether Kirilenko wanted negotiations opened with the Germans only or with the Turks as well. When pressed for a definite reply, Dukhonin finally, at 4.30 a.m., said that only a Government recognised by all Russia could advantageously negotiate for the peace which he too agreed was necessary in Russia's interests.

The conversation was broken off, and Lenin published an Order dismissing General Dukhonin from his post as Commander-in-Chief and appointing Ensign Kirilenko as his successor.

At the same time, Lenin and Kirilenko issued a proclamation to all regimental, divisional, corps and army committees, informing them that General Dukhonin had been dismissed and calling on them to elect their own representatives and to commence at once negotiations for an armistice.

The Preparation of the Separate Peace

Lenin was attacked on account of this proclamation at the next meeting of the Sovyet. It was pointed out that such instructions would lead to separate agreements on every verst of front. Lenin explained that it was necessary to work for peace " from below," and said that he had issued the proclamation relying " on the military experience " of his colleague. If humour had not been completely absent at Smolni, this remark would have occasioned comment, for Kirilenko was before the war what is called in Russia an " everlasting student " ; in other words, an individual who occasionally attended lectures at a university but never took a degree. During the war he deserted, but after the Revolution came to the front in the 11th Army as a specialist in disorganisation.

On the afternoon of the 22nd, Colonel Muraviev, who had been appointed Commander-in-Chief of the Petrograd Military District, received an application for a train to convey a unit to the front, and wrote on it : " The war is ended. An armistice is being declared on all fronts."

The same day Kirilenko left Petrograd for the Northern Front, which, being the nearest to Petrograd, had been since the Revolution in every sense the worst. He announced his appointment to be Commander-in-Chief and his departure for the front in " Order No. 1," which ended with the following exhortation, surely the most original ever penned by a new Commander-in-Chief :

> Soldiers and Comrades of the Russian Army ! The fight for peace is now in your hands. Misery, sickness, famine, deprivation and death confront you.
>
> Comrades in the fight for peace, we must conquer. Long live immediate peace !
>
> *Supreme Commander-in-Chief and People's Commissary for Military Affairs*, N. KIRILENKO.

General Dukhonin was supported by the Army Committee at Mogilev and appealed to the fronts to await a peace in complete concert with the Allies. The responses of the Front Committees from Rumania and the South-West were favourable, but these were only the responses of the committees, and no one who knew the state of the army could imagine that they for a moment represented the ideas of the soldiery. Dukhonin's half-hearted battle was from the first hopeless, for the Russian soldier had been taught that he was master in his own house, and had for months wanted nothing but peace.

In his Order No. 2 of November 26th the new Commander-in-Chief, Ensign Kirilenko, announced his first victories. General Cherimisov, the Commander-in-Chief of the Northern Front, had refused to present himself at the station at Pskov, so was removed from his command. For a similar reason Boldirev, the honest and capable Commander of the 5th Army, was arrested at Dvinsk, and was replaced by Antipov—the same Antipov who had stood out for his remarkable incompetence as Chief of Staff of the Guard Corps in the retreat of 1915.

Kirilenko had chosen the 5th Army, that under General Plehve's command had added many a glorious page to Russia's military history, and the XIXth Corps, one of the best corps originally in the Russian army, for the disgrace of despatching delegates to the enemy's lines. The party reached the German trenches at 4.10 p.m. on November 26th. It consisted of Lieutenant Sheur, of the 9th Kiev Hussars, an adventurer of doubtful reputation, and two members of the committee of the 5th Army, the military doctor, Sagalovich, and the volunteer, Meren. It returned next morning with the consent in principle of the German Command, and the next meeting was arranged for December 1st.

At 3 p.m. on the 27th a note from Trotski was handed to the military representatives of the Allies at Petrograd to the effect that his Government wanted a general and not a separate peace, but was determined to have peace. It ended: " In so far as the Allied Governments reply with a bald refusal to recognise us or our initiative, we will continue to follow our path by appealing to the people against their Governments.

" Should this policy result in the separate peace which we do not desire, the responsibility will rest with the Allied Governments."

On the 28th Lenin and Trotski issued a proclamation " To the

Peoples of all Countries at War," asking if they were content to allow their reactionary diplomats to let slip so great an opportunity for attaining peace, and giving due warning that " the reply to this question must be given at once, and not in words but by action. The Russian army and the Russian people cannot, and will not, wait any longer."

The foreign representatives were powerless. My French colleague, who understood something of Trotski's ideas through the French socialist Sadoul, thought that we should remain in Russia in touch with patriotic Russian elements " pour embêter les Bolsheviks." General Judson was impressed by his voluble compatriot, Colonel Robins, who had arrived in Russia a few weeks earlier as second in command of the American Red Cross Mission. He believed that the Bolsheviks might be open to sane influences, and imagined that when they found it impossible to make peace with Germany they would turn to the Allies for help to enable them to continue the war. He visited Trotski himself on December 1st, and was flattered by his favourable reception.

I did not believe in the power of the Ukraine Rada or of any other organisation in Russia to force its soldiers to continue the war against the Central Powers, and failed to see any use in supporting any organisation without that power. It seemed, too, to be at least irregular for us to enter into relations with groups openly opposed to the Government, such as it was, from which, as diplomats, we claimed protection. On the other hand, I did not believe in the wish or power of the Bolshevik Government to continue the war. Nothing more was to be hoped from the corps of officers, who were powerless, and it was useless as well as cruel to reproach them with Russia's treachery and to try to exact our pound of flesh. There was danger, too, that our relations with Russia after the war might be embittered by remembrance of our present unsympathetic attitude. There seemed, therefore, to be arguments in favour of making a virtue of necessity, and of leaving Russia; after issuing a magnanimous note to the Russian people relieving them from the promise made on their behalf by the Emperor's Government on September 5th, 1914.

Trotski, who was the most energetic member of the Bolshevik Government, had no reason to love the British. He had been arrested during the war as an enemy agent, and had spent some time in a Canadian internment camp at Halifax. He had only been released and allowed to return to Russia at Kerenski's request. He blustered and threatened.

Wednesday, November 28th, 1917.

Trotski told a French officer that he did not complain of the Ambassador on account of the attitude taken up by our Government, but because he knew he was in constant touch with Kaledin.[1] He said he might even have to arrest him! If the Allies break off relations, he will retain some of us as hostages. He told Woodhouse (British Consul-General at Petrograd) that he would not allow any British subjects to leave Russia till the pacifists Chicherin and Petrov, now interned in England, were released. Woodhouse remarked that there were 20,000 Russian subjects in England as compared with only 2,000 British subjects in Russia.

The Ambassador was quite unperturbed.

Saturday, December 1st, 1917.

Little Proctor has arrived from Arkhangel in a deuce of a panic. He says that the Ambassador and his family and all British subjects should at once go home *via* Bergen, and that the Embassy should move to Arkhangel to escape the massacre that will take place when the northern armies descend in hunger on Petrograd to loot and murder. I told the Ambassador of his ideas, but the old man said he did not want to see him, that it bored him to be told constantly that his throat was going to be cut: if it was, it was, and that was an end of it!

Monday, December 3rd, 1917.

I dined with the W——s. They say that Smolni talks

---

[1] This was, of course, quite untrue.

The Preparation of the Separate Peace 729

of arresting the Ambassador, Thornhill and me. Thornhill " because he pushes his nose in everywhere," and me as the " âme damnée " of the Embassy.

Durnovo also sent me a warning that I should not sleep at home for two or three nights.

The Bolsheviks, however, did not go so far yet as to arrest their allies.

Saturday, December 1st, 1917.

I was with Marushevski at half-past one to-day when his secretary came in to tell him that a telegraphist wanted to give him some very secret information. Marushevski went out, and returned presently with a long face to tell me that Dukhonin had been surrounded last night and taken prisoner with all his Staff. He had intended to move south, but had delayed too long.

This information was premature by a few hours. Dukhonin made no resistance, and surrendered to a detachment of sailors, who accompanied Kirilenko to G.H.Q. When about to leave Mogilev by train, he was dragged from his carriage and murdered, The savages then stripped the body and mutilated it. Before the war Dukhonin, then a colonel, was in charge of the Intelligence Section of the Kiev Military District, and in that capacity travelled frequently in Austria. In one of these journeys, in which he was accompanied by his wife, he was arrested by the Austrians and kept in custody for forty-eight hours. On this occasion he made the acquaintance of a German officer then employed by the Austrian Counter-Espionage. It is said that this officer, disguised as a Russian sailor, accompanied Kirilenko to G.H.Q., and seeing that Dukhonin had recognised him, determined to get rid of him, and to that end excited the rabble.

Kirilenko witnessed the murder, and, it is said, tried to prevent it. In his triumphant Order, celebrating the " fall of G.H.Q., which brings new strength to the fight for peace," he condemned " the sad fact of the lynching of the former Supreme Commander-in-Chief," but at the same time excuses it by the remark : " The people's hatred boiled over. . . . General Kornilov's escape on the previous day was the cause of the excess."

If the hatred of these cowards and criminals had boiled over, who was more to blame than Kirilenko and men of his type, who had spent months in rousing savage passions that they could not hope to control ?

Sunday, December 2nd, 1917.

I saw Marushevski to-day. He told me that he had gone to the Smolni at 3 p.m. on Saturday. Trotski threatened him with the " Trubelskoe Bastion " (that is, with imprisonment in the Fortress of Peter and Paul) if he did not at once detail General Staff officers to take part in the negotiations for a separate armistice. Feeling ran high, and the little man had said finally : " I will talk to Podvoiski. I do not want to have anything more to do with you ! " He said that Trotski made " the very worst impression " on him.

Podvoiski over-persuaded him, and he sent, as I had recommended, officers to take part in the negotiations as technical experts, and, as such, to safeguard as far as might be possible the interests of Russia and of her Allies. Colonels Shishkin and Stanislavski have gone.

Tuesday, December 4th, 1917.

Both Manikovski and Marushevski were arrested at 5 a.m. yesterday (Monday).

Manikovski's offence is that when released by the Bolsheviks to take charge of the office of the Minister of War he sent a circular telegram telling his subordinates that they could only be removed from their posts with his consent. This had, of course, been done merely to calm their nerves and to induce them to work in the interests of the army and the country. Marushevski's crime was, first, that he had continued to address General Dukhonin as " Supreme Commander-in-Chief," and had so encouraged

The Preparation of the Separate Peace 731

him to persist in the contumacious course which ended in his murder; secondly, that he had sent in his resignation rather than take any part in the negotiations for a separate armistice.

Their cross-examination was carried on at the Smolni till 3 a.m. to-day.

The General Staff published a declaration to the effect that they were out of sympathy with the project of a separate armistice, and that their representatives only joined the Delegation as technical experts to protect the interests of the Russian army and of its Allies.

The Delegation finally consisted of the Jew, Yoffe, as President, with eight members, of whom the only individuals known were the Jew, Kamenev (Rosenfeldt) and the librarian of the Military Academy, a Pole called Mstislavski. Four of the remaining members were respectively a workman, a peasant, a soldier and a sailor, who were chosen haphazard to give a democratic complexion to the Delegation. The sailor happened on the afternoon of the day the Delegation left Petrograd to have taken his clothes to the wash in the neighbourhood of the Bolshevik headquarters at Smolni. While waiting for his laundry he went to Smolni to see a friend. In the passage he ran into Kamenev, whom he had never seen before, and was told that he was to accompany the party, which was to leave for Dvinsk in three hours.

The professional advisers consisted of two naval officers and seven colonels and lieutenant-colonels of the General Staff. The senior was Admiral Altfater—an admiral of thirty-five. The Delegation had an enthusiastic send-off from the Army Committee at Dvinsk, where Kamenev enlarged on the democratic character of its composition, while the workman, the peasant, the soldier and the sailor blushed apathetically.

Some account of the Delegation's journey was given later in a Press interview by Lieutenant-Colonel Fokke, one of the military experts. The party, numbering in all twenty-eight, was met by the Germans in the Russian trenches south-west of Dvinsk, and, after the examination of papers, was conducted to the German lines. Here the Russian General Staff officer was astonished by the dryness of the German trenches, their cleanliness, their excellent construction, and by the fact that they were actually fitted with duckboards!

The Delegation was conveyed from the trenches to the nearest station on the broad-gauge line by a narrow-gauge railway, which the Germans stated had been specially laid for its benefit.

At noon on December 3rd the party arrived at Brest Litovsk, and was met by the Commandant of the German Staff. After mutual greetings—one can imagine the heel-clicking!—the delegates were escorted in automobiles by their hosts to the Citadel, where accommodation had been prepared. " As characteristic of the precision of German methods, Fokke remarked that on each delegate's table were five sheets of ruled paper and five envelopes, one pen and one pencil, one inkstand, two packets of cigarettes and one box of matches."

Sunday, December 9th, 1917.

Yesterday I got hold of Stanislavski, who had accompanied the Delegation to Brest. He told me that the delegates were asked on arrival to dine in the officers' mess, but they said they would like, if possible, to dine apart. The Germans, however, explained with many apologies that this was impossible, as they had only one large dining-room. They therefore all dined together, Germans and Russians sitting alternately.

The first meeting took place at 4 p.m., when Prince Leopold spoke a few words of welcome. Yoffe then made the usual speech on the advantages of a democratic peace, but General Hofmann replied that such matters only concerned politicians. He said, for his part, he could only pass on the request that an armistice should be offered to the whole Entente, but he had little hope that anything would come of it, as his Government had already three times offered peace and had not even received a reply.

On the night of the 3rd the Russian technical officers drew up the Russian proposal for a six-months' armistice, with the proviso that the enemy should in that period transfer no military unit or technical equipment to other fronts and that he should evacuate the islands in the Gulf of Riga. Yoffe accepted the proposals of his military advisers except as regards Para. 1, where the soldiers had suggested that the armistice should date from the day that all the Entente Powers should sign the agreement. This he of course changed.

The delegates met for the second time at 9.30 a.m. on the 4th, and the Russians presented their terms, which fairly staggered the gentle Hun!

The Germans categorically refused to accept terms which they said could only be applied to a beaten country. They then put up their own terms.

On the evening of the 4th Yoffe spoke to Trotski by direct wire, and was told that he must on no account give way in his two demands for the evacuation of the islands and for the engagement to stop transfers to other fronts.

The evacuation of the islands was demanded with a view to safeguarding Petrograd during the armistice. The transfer of units in the event of German agreement it was proposed to control by means of special missions to be left at selected points in rear of the German lines.

At the meeting at noon on the 5th Yoffe read a declaration that the Russians had decided to break off negotiations in order to return to consult their Government. The enemy delegates were visibly annoyed, but brightened considerably when a temporary truce was arranged, to expire at noon on December 17th, and they agreed during this period to move only such units of the strength of a division and over, instructions regarding the transfer of which had been already given previous to December 5th.

Yoffe's idea is to carry on propaganda among the German troops. He argued for half an hour to try to induce the Germans to allow fraternisation during the truce, but without result. He asked that Russian peace literature should be admitted to Germany. Hofmann suggested that it would be better to send it to England and France, as Germany had enough of her own. Yoffe replied that he would do that in any case.

Stanislavski was astonished by the " decent attitude of the politicians." The general opinion of the Russian service delegates is that the Bolsheviks really want a general peace, and that the Germans want peace too. In my opinion the Germans simply and naturally want a separate peace in order to enable them to transfer force to the West, and this they can easily do, even under the terms of the truce, by systematically " milking " their divisions on the Russian front.

Most of the delegates behaved themselves, but the peasant got drunk and very argumentative. The soldier tried propaganda on his own, and got a rebuff. He tried to reason with a German soldier : " We have kicked out our Nikolai. Why don't you do the same with your Wilhelm ? " The German said : " Why should I pull a sound tooth out of my head because you had toothache a year ago ? "

I am so sorry for Stanislavski, who is an honest man and feels his position acutely.

Thursday, December 13th, 1917.

The Russian Delegation left Petrograd to return to Brest suddenly on the night of the 10th. Stanislavski, who had been sitting with me a few hours before, knew nothing of it, and Potapov, who is supposed to be Chief of the General Staff, says he did not know of the departure till noon on the 11th. Altfater has gone, and so has Skalon.[1] The Delegation did not wait for the arrival of

---

[1] I had known Skalon for six years. Before the war he was Chief of the German Section of the Intelligence in the General Staff Directorate at Petrograd. He had acted in a similar capacity at G.H.Q. throughout the war. He married in 1915. Though in character somewhat taciturn, he was a hard-working, conscientious and able officer. His more light-hearted friend Samoilo, who was Chief of the Austrian Section, now holds high command in the Bolshevik Army.

The Preparation of the Separate Peace

officers from the Rumanian and South-West Fronts. We may hear any day that an armistice has been arranged.

Why this indecent haste? It seems likely that the Bolsheviks have determined to play Cromwell with the Constituent, and they naturally want as a political asset to be able to point to the conclusion of the armistice as a much-desired step on the road to peace. This is also evident from their proclamation of the 11th, ordering the arrest of the Cadet leaders. They know that the Cadets, together with the Right Social Revolutionaries, will have a majority in the Constituent. The proclamation ends:

> "Down with the bourgeoisie! There must be no place in the Constituent Assembly for the enemies of the people, the landowners and the capitalists. The country can only be saved by a Constituent Assembly formed of representatives of the working and the exploited classes. Long live the Revolution! Long live the Sovyets! Long live peace!"

And this is democracy!

A few hours after the Delegation reached Brest, General Skalon shot himself. According to the published report of the secretary of the Delegation, the Russian representatives had not yet met the Germans and were discussing matters privately, when Skalon left the room to consult a map. This was at 3.5 p.m., and nearly an hour later—at 4.2 p.m.—the German officer attached to the Delegation burst into the room with the news that he had shot himself.

Saturday, December 22nd, 1917.

I saw Madame Enkel yesterday. She had been to her cousin Skalon's funeral on the 20th. She said that his relations were annoyed because there were two huge crosses from General Hofmann and from the " German Delegates to the Armistice Negotiations," and because the Russian Delegation had sent a wreath with the inscription: " To

General Skalon, a Participant in the Peace Negotiations." As she said, this latter was a wanton insult, for he died rather than take part in the betrayal.

On Saturday the 15th an armistice was signed to commence at noon on the 17th and to continue till noon on January 14th, 1918. The *Izvyestiya* wrote of the meeting as "historic."

"Exactly at 6 p.m. the delegates of the Central Powers and the Russian Peace Delegation approached the table, on which the secretaries of the Delegations had drawn up the terms of the agreement in the Russian and German languages.

"Hofmann and Yoffe in turn read aloud the agreement in German and in Russian, and asked their assistants to sign.

"At 6.45 p.m. the agreement had been signed by all the delegates.

"After this the President of the German Delegation said: 'Now we are no longer enemies. We are friends.'

"To this Yoffe replied: 'The Russian democracy has always been the friend of the other democracies of the world.'

"After the signing of the agreement, a state banquet was given at the headquarters of the German Staff in honour of the Russian Peace Delegation."

It is easy to imagine this scene. A stiff German trying to unbend and to make things pleasant for his strange guests, the revolutionary mouthing the inevitable platitude!

During the period of the armistice the signatories agreed not to transfer from the front between the Baltic and the Black Sea any military unit for the purpose of an offensive with the exception of those the transfer of which had already commenced. It was arranged that on the front of each Russian division three points should be marked with white flags at which the soldiers might exchange newspapers and engage in trade.

The principle of the election of officers had now been intro-

The Preparation of the Separate Peace

duced, and those not elected were reduced to the rank of private. The following account of the ceremony of the dismissal of officers of the Petrogradski Regiment of the Guard was published in the Press:

> "On December 19th the officers assembled and were informed of the result of the elections, and those not elected were notified that they would in future receive pay and rations as private soldiers.
>
> "After hearing this they adjourned for the last time to the officers' mess. Almost all of them wore decorations won in the field, and the senior colonel wore the Sword of St. George.
>
> "After a short conversation, the colonel, with tears in his eyes, took his sword, with its knot of St. George's ribbon, and cut off his own and his comrades' shoulder-straps.
>
> "Many burst into tears. . . .
>
> "When their emotion had somewhat subsided, the officers took counsel together and decided to seek some form of physical labour in order to save their families from starvation.
>
> "Negotiations with the Railway Administration resulted in an offer of work as porters at the Nikolas station.
>
> "On December 22nd thirty-five officers of the Petrogradski Regiment of the Guard commenced work."

At Kiev General Dietrikhs, late Chief of Staff to General Dukhonin, who had escaped from Mogilev when the latter was murdered, supported himself for several weeks by unloading barges.

It was only the lucky ones who were young and strong enough to earn their living by manual labour. Poor old General Van der Fliet, late Commander of the Petrograd Military District, who had completed fifty-four years in the service of his country, had his pension cancelled. His wife searched for a room to live in as they could no longer afford to remain in their flat. Yet they both suffered far more from the disgrace to their country than from the material difficulty of their own position.

AAA

Five days before we left Petrograd a large deputation of officers' wives came to my room at the Embassy to ask for advice, as their separation allowances had been reduced—as they said pathetically, "just on the eve of the holidays"—from Rs.70 and Rs.35 to Rs.15. This was, of course, because their husbands had been degraded from their rank as officers. Many of them cried bitterly.

Naturally, individuals were elected to the position of officer who combined the gift of rhetoric with a wide complaisance. The soldiers did what they liked. Some units gave nightly dances in barracks. Others found highway robbery more profitable, so that after nightfall cab-drivers refused to convey fares past certain barracks. Many specialised in the robbery of wine-cellars. One day the guard on the Winter Palace broke into the Imperial cellars and got drunk. The orgy here lasted several days, successive guards, after much shooting, arresting their predecessors, only to get drunk in turn themselves. Finally peace was restored in this part of the town by the happy expedient of flooding the cellars, and incidentally drowning a few of the weary warriors.[1] This was, however, only a local remedy. "The freest army in the world" turned its attention to private cellars, and for weeks there was drunken shooting every day in one district or another. The Left Press wrote that this cellar-looting was the result of bourgeois propaganda, which of course was nonsense. It was simply the natural result of removing all control from armed men, of continuing to feed them, and of giving them nothing to do.

And what of the army at the front? The Communiqué of December 28th ran as follows:

> G.H.Q. *December* 28*th*. NORTHERN FRONT.—Quiet. No breach of the armistice. Re-election of officers. Near Ratnek fraternisation. In N—— Division the Germans have invited our people to a Christmas-tree. In the sector

---

[1] Lunching with some friends one day, I was given some excellent Madeira, and noticed that the bottle came from the Imperial cellar. My hostess's little boy of five, while playing in the Alexandrovski garden with his nurse, had found two bottles in the snow.

The Preparation of the Separate Peace

occupied by N—— Regiment the Commissary and members of the committee have gone to hand over literature to the Germans. Western Front.—Quiet. Fraternisation and trade by barter. . .

Assistant Commissary at G.H.Q., TUROV.

Trotski published practically daily attacks on the Allied Governments and appeals to our population to revolt. He vilified as only such a master of venom could the high ideals of our race in India and throughout the world, and the cause for which the best of our men were dying daily in France. We were helpless, and had to sit still under insults that the Republic of Hayti would hardly have suffered.

On December 27th General Boldirev was tried by a "revolutionary tribunal" consisting of three uneducated workmen, and was sentenced to three years' imprisonment for having failed to report himself as Commander of the 5th Army to Ensign Kirilenko when the latter went to Dvinsk to start the peace negotiations. Soldiers who had served under the General, who was himself the son of a peasant, gave unsolicited evidence on his behalf, and he received an ovation from the general public.

Thursday, January 3rd, 1918.

There has been a hitch in the peace negotiations. The *Pravda* ("Truth") publishes articles such as "The Mask Torn Off," and as the *Novaya Jizn* ("The New Life") says, makes big eyes of innocence! The hitch has come over the interpretation of the principle, "No annexations." The Germans refuse to withdraw their troops from Poland and Kurland and from parts of Latvia and Esthonia on the ground that these provinces have declared that they are in favour of absolute separation from Russia and of independence within the German sphere of influence.

Trotski is now making warlike speeches and talking of a volunteer army !

The question is, how can an able man like Trotski have

expected anything else, and, if he expected this, why did he allow the Russian army to be destroyed?

1st solution: He is an idealistic fool. Unlikely!

2nd solution (Judson's): He was unable to prevent the dissolution of the army and had to swim with the current.

3rd solution (Russian officers'): He foresaw everything and, is acting throughout as a simple German agent.

4th solution: He is an Internationalist and does not care a damn for Russia. I believe this is the true solution, but it would, all the same, appear to have been bad policy to make Russia helpless before the Imperialists of the Central Powers. Probably he and his merry men have allowed themselves to be fooled into believing in the imminence of a revolution in Germany and—in the Allied countries.

We left Petrograd on the morning of January 7th. The party consisted of the Ambassador, Lady Georgina and Miss Meriel Buchanan, Admiral Stanley, Commander Spenser-Cooper and Paymaster Collis, Majors Scale, Neilson and myself. The "People's Commissariat of Foreign Affairs" had refused to reserve us accommodation, but a bribe of two bottles of brandy had proved more successful with the officials on the spot, and we had a comfortable carriage. Most of the Allied representatives and of the British colony came to the station to bid farewell to the Ambassador, who, like the big English gentleman he is, had fought their battle to the end with rare courage, devotion and ability. Only one Russian came, Madame B——, but no doubt many more would have come if they had dared, for no Ambassador that England had sent to Petrograd ever loved Russia more or worked harder in her interests.

APPENDIX A
Some Data Regarding Russian Field Guns in Use in 1916.

GUNS.	Calibre. Inches.	Length in calibres.	Weight of gun. Lbs.	Weight of gun with carriage. Lbs.	Weight of H.E. shell. Lbs.	Bursting charge. Lbs.	Approx number of bullets in shrapnel.	Range o fH.E. Yds.	Range of shrapnel. Yds.	Number of guns in battery.	Time to bring into action.	Traction.	Number of shots per minute.
3" Field Q.F., 1900-1902	3	30	760	4428	13.4	1.57 T.	260	9330	9330	6	—	Horse	10
3" Mountain, 1909.	3	16.5	459	2700	13.4	1.57 T.	260	7700	7700	8	—	Horse	10
3" Mountain, 1904	3	13.5	216	996	13.4	1.57 T.	260	4650	4550	8	—	Horse	6
3" Anti-aircraft, Tarnovski, 1915	3	30	936	21888	13.4	—	260	—	9330	4	10 min.	Auto	30
4.2-line, Schneider	4.2	28	1872	5544	36	4.5 T.	600	11650	11650	4	—	Horse	5
4.2-line, 1877	4.2	35	2880	6798	36	4.05 M.	625	10500	8050	4	30 min.	Horse	1
6" Siege—120 poods, 1877	6	21	4320	8208	72	11.25 M.	630	9100	7260	4	30 min.	Horse	1
6" Siege—200 poods	6	30	7200	13032	90	19.35 T.	680	13250	12360	4	30-40m.	Horse	1
6" Q. F., Schneider	6	28	5436	9600	90	12.42 T.	680	13530	12360	2	20 min.	Horse	3
6" Canet	6	45	12636	12600	90.9	6 T.	680	14460	9800	2	2 days	Rail or Horse	5
Howitzers:													
48-line-field, 1909-1910	4.8	14	1044	5220	51.3	10.57 T.	500	8400	8400	4	—	Horse	2
6" Fortress, Schneider	6	14	2416	6732	90	19.35 T.	690	9560	9560	4	10 min.	Horse	2
6" Field, Schneider	6	12	1833	5544	90	19.35 T.	685	8400	8400	4	10 min.	Horse	2

Note: T.=Trotil. M.=Melinite.

APPENDIX B

LETTER ADDRESSED TO THE AMBASSADOR BY THE MILITARY ATTACHÉ ON JULY 30TH, 1917

THE MILITARY SITUATION IN RUSSIA

July 30th, 1917.

THE AMBASSADOR,

Three days after the commencement of the Russian revolution I spoke to you of the danger to the Russian army. I have written or spoken to you on the same subject every day that I have been in Petrograd since. I know that you have missed no opportunity of impressing the danger on the Provisional Government. You have had repeated interviews with Prince Lvov, M. Milyukov, M. Kerenski and M. Tereshchenko. We were told that we were pessimists and that we did not understand the Russian character.

In the opinion of the best informed Russian and Allied officers we had every reason to hope before the revolution that the campaign of 1917 would prove decisive. The French army was not exhausted, the British army had reached its maximum strength in numbers and equipment, the Russian army for the first time was receiving adequate technical equipment. The entrance of the United States of America into the war could not fail to discourage the Central Powers.

All these hopes have been falsified by events in Russia.

In apparent fear that the army might be used for a counter-revolution, the Russian Government has stood aside in the past four months and has allowed an organised attempt to reduce the Russian army to an undisciplined mob. The Government thought that it would be possible to rebuild the army on a democratic basis. Every officer of experience knew the difficulty of such a task in the middle of a great war, but the

Government dismissed everyone who had the courage to protest.

Propaganda was allowed to continue. As a result we had the armed demonstration in the streets of Petrograd on July 16th and 17th, and we now see for the first time in history three Russian armies in full retreat before a foe a third of their strength and poorer than they in technical equipment.

The experiment in army administration practised by the Government will in all probability prolong the war by a year, and will cost the Entente many hundreds of thousands of lives, Allied as well as Russian.

We have been patient. We have waited while the gutter-press in German pay has been allowed to attack an ally in a manner that would not be permitted in any other country at war. Our King has been called a " crowned highway robber "; the cause for which the best of our people are dying daily has been described as the " cause of capitalist freebooters."

The Government has at last taken certain measures. The death penalty in military law has been re-established and the most harmful of the pro-German publications have been suppressed.

We have a direct interest in the establishment of order in Russia and of discipline in the Russian army, and it is our duty to point out that the measures taken are altogether insufficient. We hear that other steps are in consideration, but why does the Government delay when every day costs hundreds of lives and millions of money?

A few instances:

1. The Commander-in-Chief of the Petrograd Military District has been removed and no successor has been appointed. It is thought that it would have been advisable to select the new man before summarily dismissing the old. The Chief of Staff, Colonel Balabán, one of the best officers in the Russian army, who has worked day and night since the revolution with single-hearted patriotism, has been dismissed.

The disarmament of the workmen was commenced by General Polovtsev and 1,000 rifles were recovered from the men at Sestroryets Works, without, it is believed, any blood shed. The Government, however, climbed down at once on the cry of " counter-revolution " being raised, and issued the usual proclamation beseeching the workmen to return the stolen arms. General Kornilov issued a similar proclamation three months ago and did not get a single rifle. How many have been recovered now?

It is evident that there can be no security for life or property in Petrograd with 20,000 workmen in possession of rifles.

2. There is no training being done by the men of the Petrograd garrison. The Press thought it worth while mentioning the fact that a certain depot battalion started work yesterday and drilled from nine to eleven. British recruits drill from eight to ten hours a day, and they start with a higher level of education.

3. The excuse for not training is that the garrison has to provide 20,000 men a day for police. But why do not the balance train instead of fishing in the Neva or lounging about the streets? Why is not a proper police formed from wounded soldiers under wounded officers to replace the militia scarecrows at present sitting smoking at street corners? It is said that a project is under consideration. How much more consideration is necessary?

4. If Russia is to be prevented from going to absolute ruin discipline must be restored in the army as a first step to the restoration of order in the country.

The Government has now unlimited powers if it would only use them. The two steps taken—the restoration of the death penalty and the suppression of the " Pravda "—have come too late to gain the end without additional measures.

(*a*). The prestige of officers must be restored by every possible means. With this object they must be given back their disciplinary powers of summary punishment. The practice of saluting at all times and places must be restored. Sentries must be no longer allowed to lounge on benches, smoke, and talk to women as they do in no army in the world except those of the republics of Central America. All committees should be done away with except the company committee,

Appendix B

which should only concern itself with the soldier's stomach. These demands are not made in order to gratify the officers' vanity. They are the minimum which the experience of generations has proved to be necessary to instil in the mass of the soldiery the habit of respect for their officers so that they may obey them implicitly under the stress of battle.

No class of the population has suffered so much as the Russian officers during the past four months, and no class has come so well out of the ordeal. They have proved themselves to be the best patriots of Russia. Many of them have been murdered without a word of public protest from M. Kerenski, who, however, was driven to an outburst of indignation when M. Sokolov, reputed to be one of the authors of the notorious Prikaz 1, was beaten by some soldiers at the front.

There are believed to be now some 60,000 officers unemployed—men who have been driven from their regiments because they tried to do their duty.

(b). The re-establishment of discipline in the army by restoring their prestige to officers must be followed by the re-establishment of order in the interior. The civil population in the rear can only be made to work when the army has recovered its discipline.

If more time is lost it will become impossible for Russia to continue the war till the spring.

Industry is handicapped by lack of coal and the railways very nearly broke down for the same reason last February. The situation is now infinitely worse than it was at this time last year. The individual miner in May, 1915, produced 772 puds of coal; in May, 1916, 636 puds; in May, 1917, 462 puds. The result is not to be wondered at, for the number of days' work he put in in the latter month was $13\cdot7$.

The percentage of sick engines and of sick wagons rose in June, 1917, to $24\cdot2$ and 8, as compared with 18 and $4\cdot5$ in the corresponding month last year. If the men in the repair shops are not compelled to work, the railways will not be able to feed the army and the population of Petrograd and Moscow throughout the winter.

INDEX

Aegusa, H.M.S., 355
Aga Khan Shiklinski, General, 433
Agar, Colonel, 420
Aksentiev, M., 712
Alexander I., Emperor's oath, 39
Alexander III., 672
Alexander IV., 672
Alexandra, The Empress, 558
Alexyeev, General, 47, 94, 96, 137, 186, 244, 281, 285, 296, 301, 330, 331, 332, 350, 351, 387, 395, 409, 427, 431, 462, 475, 483, 484, 499, 515, 517, 536, 578, 583, 593, 594, 609, 612, 627, 633, 667, 679, 683, 684, 689, 692
   previous career of, 49
   Viceroy, 45
Alftan, General, 236
Aliev, General, 234, 319
Allenstein, 56, 58, 60, 70, 81, 84, 85, 87, 401
Altfater, Captain, 367, 731, 734
America, 222, 411, 416 422, 424, 425, 548
Amiens, 364, 365
Amur Bay, 425
Anders, Captain, 57, 62, 67, 68, 70, 71
Andreev, 115, 116, 117, 118, 119, 120, 122, 127, 195, 197
Andrjespol, 209, 210
Anet, Claude, 690
Angerburg, 69, 89, 90, 238
Anichkov Palace, 531, 656
Annopol, 127, 142, 175, 177, 184
Antipov, General, 302, 304, 341, 726
Antonov, 704, 716
Antwerp, 151
Arctic Ocean, 509
Aristov, Prince, 463
Arkhangel, 352, 354, 355, 356, 417, 424, 426, 515, 519, 526, 625, 702, 728
Arlanza, H.M.S., 356, 357, 358, 360, 361
Artamonov, General, 69, 71, 80, 93
Arys, 55, 89
Assanovich, Colonel, 49, 54
Auffenberg, 96
Ausen, Colonel, 594

Austin Cars, 257
Austria, plan of campaign against, 47
Avgustov, 89, 90, 239, 240, 259, 337, 498

Babie, 466
Babikov, General, 57
Bacau, 486
Baghdad, 364, 430, 559
Bagratuni, General, 664, 699, 705, 706
Baiov, General, 298, 347, 535
Bakhan, S. S., 356
Balaban, Colonel, 608, 610, 611, 612, 615, 617, 618, 619, 620, 622, 658, 661, 664, 670
Balamutovka, 442
Balanin, General, 316, 535
Balkans, 478
Baltic, 280, 292, 296, 333, 344, 434, 450, 700, 736
   station, 553
Baluev, General, 405, 406, 409, 410, 411, 500, 520, 535, 593, 689
Baranovichi, 44, 45, 46, 49, 54, 223, 235, 275, 277, 327, 450, 454, 535
Baranovski, Colonel, 468, 471
   General, 681
Baranow, 104
Barantsev, General, 500
Baratov, General, 514
Bariatinski, Prince, 50
Barlad, 536
Barrow, General, 490
Barysz, 442
Bazaine, 394
Bazarov, Colonel, 146, 147
Bazilevich, Captain, 495, 496
Belkhatov-Kamensk Line, 204
Below, General Von, 325
Bender, 479
Benderev, General, 241, 246, 250
Bendin, 41, 109, 113
Bendkov, 206
Benedek, 394
Benkendorf, Lieutenant, 147
   Count, 419
Berdichev, 50, 347, 385, 401, 402, 404, 434, 460, 474, 476, 486, 487, 491, 492, 499, 503, 505, 533

748　Index

Berestechko, 53, 499
Bergen, 708, 728
Bergmann, General, 501
Berlin, 38, 84, 91, 167, 367, 413, 446, 633
Berthelot, General, 504, 533
Bessarabia, 384, 459
Bethlehem Steel Co., 275
Bethmann-Holweg, 427
Bezobrazov, General, 76, 153, 164, 182, 189, 193, 196, 241, 244, 246, 248, 249, 250, 254, 256, 257, 259, 260, 261, 262, 263, 264, 301, 302, 303, 315, 332, 383, 432, 459, 463, 464, 467, 469, 473, 474, 475, 476, 485, 505, 574
Bibikov, Lieutenant, 100
Bindon-Blood, General, 490
Black Sea, 48, 286, 539, 736
　Fleet, 645, 670
Blagovyeshchenski, General, 93
Blair, Captain James, 40, 267
　Mrs., 355, 357, 358, 359
Bobr, River, 240, 249, 255, 256, 316, 320, 321, 322
Bobr-Narev front, 265
Bobrinski, Count, 290
Boehm-Ermolli, General, 434, 445
Boer war, 488
Boldirev, Colonel, 196, 254, 537, 726, 739
Bolgrad, 536
Bologoe-Syedlets Railway, 45, 143, 264
Bolshevik revolt, 1917, 136
Bonch-Bruevich, General, 344, 394, 395
Boris, Grand Duke, 224, 429, 430, 431
Borisov, General, 296,
　　railway engineer, 339
　　bridge at, 338, 429
Bosphorus, 285, 286
Bostrom, 509
Bothmer, General Von, 448, 477
Bothnia, Gulf of, 509
Boulogne, 362, 366
Brandenburger Thor, 399
Bratiano, 399
Bratolyubov, Engineer, 413, 414
Bredov, Colonel, 52, 53, 402
Breslau, 168, 185, 200, 214, 219
Brest Litovsk, 42, 93, 231, 294, 732, 735
Brezini, 191 206, 208, 209, 210, 211, 212,
Brjozovski, General, 321, 322
Brody, 299, 434, 447, 460
　-Lemberg Railway, 96
Brotherhood of Nations, 580
Bruce, First Secretary British Embassy, 528, 571, 704, 705
Brusilov, General, 47, 48, 54, 55, 96, 104, 149, 151, 168, 171, 197, 200, 287, 289, 299, 347, 403, 427, 428, 434, 436, 437, 438, 440, 445, 446, 449,

Brusilov, General (cont.)
　456, 457, 460, 461, 464, 469, 476, 478, 481, 485, 488, 492, 495, 497, 499, 503, 504, 505, 506, 507, 519, 520, 535, 550, 551, 556, 593, 612, 627, 628, 629, 632, 640, 652, 667, 668, 671
Brzesany, 434, 500, 535, 643
Buchanan, Sir George, 515, 585, 740
　Lady Georgina, 712, 740
　Miss, 553, 740
Bucharest, 486, 504
Buckley, Colonel, 363
Buczacz, 492, 494, 500, 535, 635
Buda-Pesth, 333, 489
Budberg, Baron, 238, 241, 316
Bug, River, 95, 292, 312, 313, 315, 317
Bukovina, 243, 394, 445, 447, 478, 503, 629
Bulatov, General, 459, 499
Bulgaria, 398, 399, 477
　declared war, 484, 491
Butovich, Madame, 221
Byelkovich, General, 593, 635, 637, 640, 651
Byelostok, 47, 57, 58, 59, 83, 84, 85, 199, 241, 246, 248, 249, 294, 315, 316
　-Brest Railway, 324
Byelsk, 315, 318, 320, 322
Byelyaev, General, Chief of General Staff, 267, 268, 270, 415, 418, 419, 420, 511, 517, 521, 522, 524, 534, 557
　General 12th Army, 298, 345
Bzura River, 200, 224, 226, 276, 292, 294, 396, 401
　-Ravka-Nida-Dunajec river line, 212, 218

Cantacuzene, Prince, 105, 107, 129, 147, 462
　General, 118
Carlotti, M., 585,
Carpathians, 97, 137, 149, 182, 236, 265, 280, 281, 327, 331, 394, 447, 465, 478, 479, 480, 484, 489, 498, 499, 630
Caucasian Front, 532
Caucasus, 377, 398, 422, 635, 671
Chantilly, 364, 365
Charles, Archduke, 477
Charpentier, General, 114, 210
Chefchavadze, Prince, 686
Chelnikov, M:, 387
Chenstokhov, 44, 113, 128, 160, 173, 177, 179, 185, 199
　-Bendin Front, 116
　-Olkush-Myekhov, 152, 159
Cherboni Bor, 312, 315
Cheremisev, General, 438, 667, 668, 689, 718, 726

Index

Cherni, General, 534
Chernov, Socialist Minister, 621, 657, 674, 686, 699
 Colonel, 52
Chertkov, Staff-Captain, 196, 197
Chicherin, 728
Chkheidze, 557, 651
Churin, General, 234, 292, 297, 320
Cobban, Captain, 355
Collis, Paymaster, 740
Connaught, Duke of, 516
Constantinople, 259, 523, 527, 577, 633
Constanza Railway, 486
Cromwell, 263, 735
Czechs, 489
Czernowitz, 285, 348, 384, 442, 445, 479, 480, 485, 494, 495, 497, 499, 500, 503, 506, 536, 618, 630
Czortkow, 434, 441

DAN, SOCIALIST, 672
Danilov, General "Black," 42, 43, 45, 55, 234, 249, 301, 330, 331, 332, 534, 700
Dankl, General, 96, 284
Danube, 486, 497, 502, 506, 523, 534
Dardanelles, 259, 285, 430, 573
De Candolle, General, 695
Delatyn, 447, 484, 485, 494, 500, 535
 -Kimpolung, 479
Delcassé, M., 270, 352
Delsalle, General, 141, 462
Delvig, General, 439
Demidovka, 52
Deniken, General, 137, 501, 594, 627, 651, 667, 689
Diamandi, M., 523, 67
Dibenko, Bolshevik sailor, 716
Dietrikhs, General, 347, 401, 402, 403, 437, 737
Dimitri Pavlovich, Grand Duke, 462, 468, 469, 474, 475, 512, 513, 514
Dniester, 285, 290, 292, 442, 443, 444, 446, 447, 477
Dobrudja, 477, 483, 486, 491, 501, 502
Dolgorouki, Prince, 49, 182, 184, 457
Dolgov, General, 393
Domanevski, Colonel, 155, 163, 164, 249, 252, 383, 463
Dombrova, 240, 426
Don River, 126, 624
Donetz, 426, 526, 528
 Basin, 272, 273
Dorna Watra, 479, 485, 486, 496
Dostoievski, 581
Downing Street (No. 10), 677
Dragomirov, General Abram, 287, 450, 451, 452, 508, 534, 603, 607, 618
 General Vladimir, 48, 51, 196
Dreyer, Colonel, 106, 138

Dubno, 47, 51, 52, 434, 440, 491
Dukhonin, General, 435, 437, 499, 460, 461, 476, 477, 481, 486, 487, 504, 629, 640, 645, 650, 651, 701, 719, 723, 724, 726, 730, 737
Dukla Pass, 236
Dumergne, M., 525
Dunajec, 179, 215, 224, 244, 281, 282, 283, 395, 397
D'Urban, General, 365
Durnovo, Colonel, 105, 707, 729
Dvina River, 94, 136, 320, 328, 329, 330, 344, 392, 395, 404, 455, 457, 459, 595
Dvinsk, 93, 136, 296, 325, 337, 338, 344, 345, 350, 393, 396, 404, 407, 433, 449, 457, 508, 534, 584, 585, 594, 597, 598, 599, 604, 726, 731, 739
Dzyevenovski, General, 627

ECKE, GENERAL, 236
Ednorojets, 243, 261, 310
Eichhorn, General, 239, 325, 336
Einem, von, General, 252
Eitel, Friedrich, Prince, 169
Ekk, General, 501
Ellershaw, Colonel, 273, 274, 275, 362, General, 383, 411, 419, 420, 421
Engalichev, Prince, 295
Engelhardt, Captain, 155, 156, 159, 163, 170, 176, 183, 247, 249, 263, 264, 303, 555, 562, 568, 584, 617, 618
England, 422, 580, 648, 678
Enkel, Madame, 735
Entente, 523
Erdeli, General, 105, 106, 119, 121, 123, 124, 127, 131, 133, 135, 136, 225, 226, 242, 244, 245, 640, 648, 689,
Etter, General, 189
Ewarth, General, 55, 104, 147, 159, 168, 236, 294, 298, 309, 345, 349, 351, 352, 409, 517, 534, 593
Eydkuhnen, 41

FALKENHAYN, GENERAL VON, 484
Federov, Colonel, 216, 354, 355, 364, 365, 421
Ferdinand of Coburg, 398
Fidotov, General, 457, 500
Filonenko, M., 682, 683, 690, 691, 703
Finland, 49, 426, 511, 522, 543, 577, 635, 655, 688, 713
Findlandski Regiment, 154, 184, 187, 188
Fitzgerald, Colonel, 363, 420
Fliet, Van der, General, 199
Foch, General, 365
Fokke, Lieutenant-Colonel, 731, 732
France, 344, 422

Index

Frankenau, 60, 63, 64, 65, 68, 80, 87
Franz Ferdinand, Grand Duke, murder of, 38
French, Sir John, 366
Friedrichs, Count, 387, 414
Friedrichstadt, 329, 333, 534

GALAUD, CAPTAIN, 584
Galicia, 96, 137, 140, 171, 199, 200, 264, 267, 285, 287, 290, 292, 314, 394, 478, 491, 494, 495, 525, 527, 698
Galieni, 363
Galkin, Colonel, 158
Gallipoli, 364
Gallwitz, General, 336
Galpern, M., 681, 712
Ganetski, 658
Gatchina, 716, 717, 718
Gavrilov, General, 459, 499
Gerard, Sir Montague, 43
Germany, war on Russia declared, 39
 feeling against, 43
 plan of campaign against, 47
Gerois, General, 459, 464, 468, 473, 475, 490, 499, 535, 640
Gershelman, 2nd Lieutenant, 179, 181, 184, 463, 468
Giesser, General, 500, 535
Gillenschmidt, General, 287, 476, 505
Gnila Lipa, 292, 506, 629
Gnilaya-Pripyat, 385
Goeben, 167
Goldmann, the Socialist, 672, 703
Golitzin, Prince, 44, 515, 556
Golovin, General, 187, 193, 195, 348, 383, 435, 438, 492, 493, 500, 535, 701
Golyevski, Colonel, 707, 711
Gondurin, General, 407
Gorbatovski, General, 231, 293, 298, 320, 329, 330, 345, 535, 593
Gorimikin, Premier, 334
Gorlice, 236, 282, 283
Gorodishche, 450
Gotz, Socialist, 672
Gough, Colonel John, 38
Grabbe, Colonel, 153, 160, 172
Gravier, Captain, 691, 703
Gray, Lady Sybil, 528
Grenfell, Captain, Naval Attaché, 40, 584
Grey, Sir Edward, 362, 363
Gribkov, Ivan, 41, 227, 560, 706
Grigoriev, General, 326, 327, 328
Grodek Lakes, 289, 506
Grodna, 57, 89, 93, 238, 240, 245, 260, 297, 323, 328
Grove, British Consul, 76
 arrested with Knox, 77
Gruzinov, Colonel, 626

Guchkov, Monsieur, 77, 87, 271, 278, 294, 412, 522, 525, 526, 527, 529, 561, 568, 570, 572, 574, 575, 576, 578, 583, 585, 590, 593, 594, 612, 613, 614, 619, 633, 654, 666, 673
Gulévich, General, 43, 76, 104, 146, 147, 148, 149, 191, 235, 295, 296, 313, 330, 480
Gullenbegel, Captain, 397
Gumbinnen, important action at, 55
 Germans defeated, 56, 57, 88, 90, 238, 239
Gura Kalvarya, 142, 150, 313
Gurko, General, 57, 400, 407, 475, 483, 485, 487, 488, 499, 517, 519, 520, 533, 543, 544, 593, 632, 671
Gurski, M., 118
Gutor, General, 500, 593, 629, 637, 639, 640, 643, 650, 651, 667

HAIG, SIR DOUGLAS, 508
Hamilton, Sir Ian, 43
Hampshire, loss of, 420
Helsingfors, 38, 619, 687, 688, 689
Henderson, Mr., 621
Hindenburg, General Von, 56, 86, 90, 91, 92, 140, 199, 202, 213, 236, 342, 477, 505
Hofmann, General, 732, 734, 735, 736
Hypatiev, General, 553, 554

IGNATIEV, COUNT, 162, 188, 192, 308, 364, 365, 383, 459, 463, 514, 515, 574, 584, 650
 Countess, 574
Ilovo, 66, 71, 80, 81
 Cossacks cause panic, 72
India, 424, 490, 623, 669, 739
Insterburg, 69, 88
Irmanov, General, 166, 263, 319, 500
Isaacs, St., Cathedral, 664
Islam, 233
Italy, 400, 422, 478
Ivangorod, 76, 97, 99, 100, 101, 102, 106, 117, 118, 127, 134, 135, 142, 144, 145, 146, 147, 149, 150, 151, 152, 153, 154, 155, 156, 157, 164, 165, 175, 227, 251, 294, 298, 309, 313, 315
 -Radom Railway, 159, 162
Ivanov, General, 47, 49, 50, 58, 96, 140, 147, 149, 150, 151, 193, 195, 215, 220, 236, 244, 281, 285, 296, 298, 332, 347, 401, 402, 403, 436, 563

JACOBSTADT, 94, 136, 329, 330, 404, 406, 407
Janin, General, 496, 497
Japan, 44, 85, 168, 216, 422, 488, 494
Jaroslau, 104, 112, 282, 283, 285, 289

Index

Jaslo, 283
Jaworow, 289
Jaziowiec, 440
Jedwabno, 73
Jezierna, 639
Jilinski, General, 42, 49, 56, 58, 62, 79, 83, 89, 93, 251, 365
    control of 1st and 2nd Army, 47
    his previous career, 45
Joffre, General, 193, 219, 363, 364, 365
Johannisburg, 58, 89, 238, 239
Joseph, Ferdinand, Archduke, 282, 294, 434, 436
Judson, General, 695, 727
Junkovski, 334, 388, 389

KALEDIN, GENERAL, 435, 436, 437, 438, 439, 446, 447, 464, 483, 485, 494, 495, 500, 506, 507, 536, 618, 629, 631, 652, 673, 702, 720, 728
Kalish, 41, 44, 179, 226, 610
    -Chenstokhov-Bendin, 162
    -Velyun Line, 177
Kalusz, 665, 666, 670
Kalvariya, 298
Kamenets-Podolsk, 384, 433, 436, 535, 650
Kamenev, the Bolshevik, 623, 656, 660, 691, 731
Kapnist, Count, 720
Karakin, Prince, 49
Kashtalinski, General, 329, 440
Kaznakov, General, 210, 246, 494, 500
Kelchevski, General, 354, 355, 362, 364, 366, 438, 445, 480, 497, 498, 501, 536
Keller, Count, 485, 501
Kerenski, 557, 561, 570, 571, 572, 576, 577, 578, 581, 583, 585, 588, 589, 590, 607, 608, 614, 615, 616, 617, 618, 619, 623, 628, 631, 635, 638, 639, 644, 646, 647, 651, 652, 653, 654, 656, 657, 662, 663, 664, 665, 667, 670, 671, 672, 673, 676, 677, 678, 679, 680, 681, 682, 683, 685, 687, 689, 690, 691, 692, 693, 697, 699, 700, 703, 705, 706, 707, 708, 712, 715, 717, 718, 719, 723, 728
    origin of, 679
Khabalov, General, 557, 558
Khan, Nakhichevanski, General, 57, 460
Khanjin, General, 485
Khaust, Lieutenant, 602, 603, 617
Khimets, General, 243, 244, 245
Khlopitov, M., 576, 609
Kholm, 97, 173, 231, 288, 294, 296, 298, 301, 307, 401
    -Lyublin-Novo Alexandriya Railway, 47, 304

Khorjele, 57, 75, 79, 243
Kiev, 47, 50, 221, 332, 492, 625, 627, 634, 650, 652, 729, 737
Kimpolung, 447, 480, 484, 485, 500, 536
Kiril, Grand Duke, 45, 557, 570
Kirilenko, the agitator, 634, 716, 721, 724, 725, 726, 729, 730, 739
Kirlebaba, 236, 480
Kiselevski, General, 593
Kishkin, Minister, 708
Kitchener, Lord, 273, 274, 275, 276, 361, 362, 363, 367, 411, 412, 419, 420
Kiyanovski, General, 345
Klembovski, General, 401, 403, 435, 437, 481, 492, 500, 593, 594, 651, 652, 667, 683
Klyuev, General, 69, 93
    surrender of, 86
Koevess, General, 95, 477
Kola, 510
    -Kandalaksha, 356
Kolchak, Admiral, 368, 670
Koloniya Ostrov, 462, 466
Kolontai, Madame, 691
Kolyushki, 206, 208, 209, 211
Komarov, General, 93, 96
Kondratovich, General, 93
Königsberg, 168, 244, 280
Konovalov, Minister, 413, 700, 704, 709
Konstantin, Konstantinovich, Grand Duke, 247
Kornilov, General, 137, 488, 489, 490, 499, 578, 579, 583, 586, 587, 608, 609 611, 618, 630, 631, 632, 664, 665, 667, 668, 673, 674, 676, 677, 678, 679, 680, 681, 682, 683, 684, 686, 687, 688, 689, 690, 691, 692, 697, 699, 705, 730
    origin of, 679
Korotkevich, General, 501
Kotlarevski, Colonel, 625
Kotsubé, Prince, 43, 45, 54, 193, 194
Kovel, 231, 298, 440, 446, 448, 459, 460, 462, 463, 467, 473, 483, 497, 507
Kovna, 39, 239, 280, 291, 297, 320, 325, 326, 327, 328, 329, 336
Koziowa, position of, 285, 690
Kozlovski, the spy, 658
Kozowa, village of, 638, 639, 646, 647, 648
Krakau, 97, 104, 106, 109, 111, 112 164, 168, 171, 172, 174, 177, 179 182, 185, 193, 197, 199, 211
    -Bendin-Chenstokhov Line, 97, 140
Krasnik, 96, 99, 100, 101, 134, 142, 143, 145, 146, 147, 226, 294
Krasnoe Selo, 481, 482, 587
Krasnoselts, 258, 260
Krasnostav, 301, 304, 308

Index

Krasnov, General, 716, 717, 719
Kremenets, 52, 434, 435, 491, 500, 632, 639
Kreuzburg, 325, 329, 330, 433
Krevo, 432, 433, 450, 454, 459
Krilov, General, 500
   -Dashov-Komarov-Grabovets, 96
Krimov, General, 687
Krivoshen, M., 531
Krokmal, the Socialist, 672,
Kronstadt, 273, 491, 560, 599, 657, 659, 661, 668
Krulevshchizna, 343, 346
Kruzenstern, General, 162, 165, 171, 172
Kshinskaya, the dancer, 521, 653, 655, 661
Kukhari Wood, 469, 472
Kurland, 290, 291, 325, 395, 396, 599, 696, 739
Kuropatkin, General, 332, 393, 394, 400, 455
Kuzmin, Lieutenant, 620, 686, 697
Kuzmin-Karavaev, General, 216, 220, 275
Kvyetsinski, General, 225, 331, 345, 409, 534, 593
Kyeltsi, 116, 117, 119, 120, 121, 122, 123, 126, 165, 169, 171, 172, 173, 174, 177, 186, 190, 309

LAGUICHE, GENERAL, MARQUIS DE, 41, 43, 46, 49, 50, 54, 55, 57, 67, 71, 80, 167, 170, 218, 491
   expressed sympathy, 90
Lallin, Colonel, 305
Lambton, General, the Hon. W., 366
Latvia, 739
Lavergne, Colonel, 555, 574, 676
Layton, Mr., 517, 522
Lazienki Gardens, 295
Lebedev, General P. P., 331, 345, 352, 353, 402, 534
Lechitski, General, 47, 76, 104, 138, 140, 141, 147, 148, 152, 168, 182, 187, 299, 302, 348, 436, 438, 443, 444, 446, 447, 477, 478, 479, 480, 485, 501, 536, 612, 625, 631
Lekhovich, General, 554
Lemberg, 95, 96, 97, 171, 175, 287, 289, 290, 292, 460, 476, 487, 495, 638, 639
   Krakau Railway, 168
Lenin, 608, 613, 621, 630, 653, 655, 661, 694, 715, 724, 725, 726
Leonkevich, Colonel, 41, 49, 57, 71, 80
Leopold, Prince, 732
Lesh, General, 287, 288, 289, 295, 296, 301, 302, 303, 306, 347, 446, 447, 452, 505, 535

Letts, 517
Levitski, Colonel, 493, 701, 707
Libau, 291
Lieber, the Socialist, 660, 672
Liebknecht, 367
Linsingen, General von, 446
Lipton, Sir Thomas, 355
Lithuania, 111
Litvinov, General, 199, 225, 297, 309, 310, 343, 346, 458, 534, 593
Lloyd George, Mr., 354, 362, 367, 417, 585, 677
Lockhart, Acting Consul-General, 591, 618
Lodz, 92, 165, 185, 191, 199, 203, 204, 206, 207, 209, 212, 258, 282, 342, 393, 396, 550
Lomja, 57, 237, 238, 241, 242, 243, 246, 249, 250, 254, 255, 260, 261, 266, 292, 294, 308, 314, 315, 316
Lomnica, R., 665
Lötzen, 58, 89, 238, 239
Lovchin, Colonel, 153, 160, 172
Lovich, 185, 197, 199, 207, 208, 209, 210, 211, 212, 214
Ludendorff, General, 56, 91, 92, 200, 202, 237, 242, 321
Lukhomski, General, 534, 667, 683, 689, 691
Lunacharski, the Bolshevik, 655
Lutsk, 434, 438, 439, 440, 446, 447, 459, 464, 485, 487, 488, 490, 53 5
   -Kovel Railway, 461
Luxembourg, Rosa, 367
Lvov, Prince, 570, 571, 582, 591, 592, 613, 621, 646, 653, 663, 672
   Vladimir, 682, 691
Lyck, 55, 57, 89, 237, 690
Lyon, General Frank, 366
Lyublin, 80, 96, 97, 98, 99, 100, 101, 102, 135, 139, 141, 142, 143, 144, 145, 146, 147, 148, 149, 150, 151, 152, 161, 168, 169, 175, 176, 177, 285, 294, 295, 298, 301, 304, 307
   battle raging to south, 76
Lyubomirov, Lieutenant, 354, 357, 358, 359, 362, 364, 367
Lyubomirski, Prince, 234

MACKENZEN, GENERAL, 84, 202, 203, 206, 213, 214, 281, 282, 283, 286, 290, 292, 294, 299, 300, 301, 308, 315
Magyars, 159
Maimaievski, General, 643
Maklakov, M., 277
Mala Vyes, 292
Manikovski, General, 273, 274, 275, 528, 553, 554, 555, 585, 671, 700, 716, 730

Index

Mannerheim, General, 100, 141, 158, 164
Maramarossziget, 479, 480
Mariampol, 89, 639
Marienburg, bridge guarded, 38
Markovski, General, 640
Markozov, Captain, 529, 530, 558, 697
Marne battle, 92, 550
Martos, General, 57, 60, 62, 64, 65, 69, 71, 87
   wounded, 79
   surrender of, 86
Marushevski, General, 689, 701, 711, 729, 730
Masuria, 56, 61
Masurian Lakes, 47, 237, 394
Maxim, civilian servant, 41, 44, 77, 102, 110, 116, 198, 227, 234, 358
McKenna, Mr., 419
Mecklenburg, Duke of, 172, 476
Mengden Court, 574
Menshukov, Colonel, 208
Mezo-Laborez Pass, 236, 282
Michael, Grand Duke, 413, 570, 571
Miliant, General, 48, 205, 414
Miller, General, 48, 205, 225, 227, 228, 230, 234, 296, 345, 612
Milner, Lord, 516, 517
Milyukov, M., 570, 572, 573, 577, 585, 608, 612, 676, 692
Minsk, 98, 335, 337, 343, 345, 346, 349, 350, 351, 352, 403, 404, 406, 409, 454, 517, 534
Minut, General, 535
Mishinets, 57, 78, 80, 258
   -Prasnish Road, 258
Mitau, 292, 308, 325
Mlava, 60, 61, 62, 70, 71, 72, 78, 82, 98, 168, 169, 198, 213, 234, 241
Mogilev, 330, 427, 428, 474, 475, 534, 628, 682, 683, 684, 689, 725, 729, 737
Mogilnitsa, 227, 228, 230
Mohammedans, 232
Mohun Sound, 393
Moldavia, 498, 499, 502, 503
Molodechno, 338, 339, 343, 349, 432, 450, 453, 459, 535
Moltke, 205
Monasterzyska, 477
Moscow, 205, 228, 231, 267, 269, 276, 291, 387, 393, 418, 512, 518, 520, 523, 591, 610, 612, 625, 669, 679, 680, 690, 702, 704, 708, 722
Moseiska, 98
Motkovitse, 116, 117, 118, 120
Mrzovski, General, 518
Mstislavski, Peace Emissary, 731
Mühlen, 70, 94
   -Jankowitz danger point, 71
   -Nadrau-Lansk Line, 67

Munkacs Pass, 236
Muraviev, M., 355, 357
   Colonel, 725
Murman railway, 509 674
Murmansk, 356, 510
Myasoyedov, Colonel, 277, 278
Myekhov, 108, 114, 115, 116, 117, 173, 174, 175, 176, 178, 181, 184, 186, 187, 190, 193, 194, 195, 197

NABOKOV, MINISTER, 712
Nadrau, 79, 81
Nadworna, 477, 479, 494, 630
Nadzimov, Colonel 266
Naglovitse, 108, 109, 117
Napoleon, 182, 481, 581, 671, 672
Narev River, 47, 84, 137, 241, 242, 243, 245, 253, 295, 311, 312, 313, 316, 319, 320, 321
Naroch, Lake, 93, 338, 403, 404, 478, 534, 698
Narva, 594
Naselsk, 77, 242
Neidenburg, 41, 56, 57, 58, 60, 62, 63, 68, 69, 70, 71, 72, 73, 75, 78, 79, 81, 82, 83, 86, 87, 311
   careless staff work, 65, 67
Neilson, Captain, 167, 198, 207, 209, 210, 216, 218, 223, 224, 267, 284, 286, 287, 288, 296, 304
   Major, 584, 585, 721, 740
Nekrasov, Minister, 501, 658, 663, 681, 683, 685
Nemierow, 96
Nesvij, 347, 450, 451, 452, 453, 535
Neudon, General, 365
Neva River, 653, 708, 711
Nevel, 384, 385, 718
Neverdovski, Colonel, 688
Nevski Prospekt, 528, 530, 531, 558, 560, 657
Neznamov, General, 438, 492, 500, 535, 640
Nida River, 116, 117, 120, 121, 171, 283
Niessel, General, 697, 701
Nikolas II., 571, 611, 649, 672
Nikolas, Grand Duke, 40, 43, 228, 273, 277, 482, 536, 549, 570, 578, 594
Norres, Captain, 357, 359, 360
Nostitz, Count, 153, 154, 163, 182, 186, 225, 244, 245, 246, 247, 259, 263, 301
Notbek, General, 634
Nova Alexandriya, 127, 133, 135, 142, 144, 149, 151, 152, 155, 157, 158, 159, 187, 313
Novemyasto, 284
Novikov, General, 104, 106, 135, 137, 138, 210, 225, 226
Novitski, General, 351, 394, 594

BBB

754 Index

Novocherkask, 705
Novo-Georgievsk, 181, 242, 245, 314, 315, 320
Novogrod, 250, 254, 311, 515
Novoradomsk, 113
Novorossisk, 167
Novo Svyentsyani, 338
Nyejintsev, Captain, 630
Nyeman, 90, 240, 245, 253, 256, 291, 292, 327, 395, 450
  Bobr-Narev Line, 263
  -Front, 265

O'Beirne, Mr., 362, 363, 420
Obolenski, Prince, 385
Obruchev, General, 635
Ochakov, 444
Ocna, 499, 501, 536
Odessa, 236, 285, 286, 383, 413, 424, 426, 478, 502, 610
  H.Q. of 7th Army, 48
Odishelidze, General, 225, 297, 310, 321, 346, 350, 387, 458
Ojarov, 102
Okhta, 526
Okna, 444
Oldenburg, Duke of, 276
Olika, 439, 459
Olita, 239, 240, 336
Olukhov, General, 161, 292, 303, 336, 337, 341
Omsk, 323, 368
Opatov, 122, 125, 127, 130, 138, 141
Opolchenie, 45, 54, 154, 199, 241, 268, 269
Opole, 151, 752
Orani, 336
Oranienbaum, 563
Oranovski, General, 47, 83, 93, 235, 242, 244, 245, 260, 314, 342, 688
Orel, 75
Orjits River, 241, 258, 260, 261, 295, 297, 310
Orlau, 60, 63, 66, 79
Orlov, Prince, 334, 388
Ormulev, 258, 261
Orotava, SS., 361
Ortelsburg, 56, 57, 58, 60, 62, 66, 84
Osovets, 76, 238, 239, 241, 242, 248, 256, 265, 321, 322
Ostend, 105, 328
Ostrolenka, 57, 59, 60, 62, 68, 72, 74, 75, 77, 78, 79, 80, 222, 241, 242, 243, 260, 261, 312, 314
Ostrov, 52, 57, 78, 80, 242, 246, 255, 258, 312, 315, 319
Ostrovets, 99, 101, 102, 122, 126, 131, 132, 141, 173, 174, 175, 184, 297
Otsyesenki, 121, 122

Padalovka, 470
Paget, General Sir Arthur, 275
Palchinski, Engineer, 685, 708
Paleologue, M., 428, 585
Palitsin, General, 296
Palovski, Count, 111
Panchulidzev, Captain, 159
Pares, Professor, 612, 618
Paris, 362, 365, 465
Parshin, 664
Parski, General, 668
Parvus, the spy, 658
Paul, Grand Duke, 367, 459, 468, 571
Pavlov, General, 481, 482
Pavlovitse, 151
Pavlovski Regiment, 154, 553
Pawlings, Messrs., 356
Pernau, 623
Persia, 266, 514
Peter and Paul Fortress, 559, 661, 710, 730
Peter, Grand Duke, 43, 49
Peter the Great, 426
Peterhof, 42, 574
Petrograd, 83, 92, 93, 94, 97, 127, 136, 148, 166, 167, 191, 194, 195, 196, 198, 199, 212, 216, 217, 219, 220, 221, 222, 235, 263, 266, 267, 272, 273, 275, 276, 278, 279, 282, 286, 291, 302, 320, 323, 328, 329, 333, 334, 339, 344, 345, 354, 355, 361, 362, 367, 368, 383, 387, 388, 397, 399, 400, 411, 413, 415, 418, 421, 424, 426, 427, 429, 430, 431, 433, 454, 457, 475, 483, 495, 505, 508, 509, 511, 514, 515, 516, 521, 522, 523, 524, 525, 527, 528, 529, 556, 559, 562, 563, 565, 567, 569, 572, 573, 574, 575, 578, 579, 583, 586, 587, 588, 589, 590, 591, 601, 607, 614, 616, 627, 648, 654, 656, 662, 666, 670, 674, 681, 686, 687, 688, 690, 691, 694, 698, 699, 701, 702, 704, 705, 707, 714, 715, 716, 717, 718, 719, 720, 723, 725, 728, 731, 733, 734, 738, 746
  defence of, 47
  -Kiev-Odessa Line, 426, 427
Petrokov, 186, 191, 195, 197, 204, 206
Petrokovitse, 121
Petrov, 728
Petrovski Bridge, 513
Petrozavodsk, 509, 510
  -Serotka, 356
Pflanzer-Baltin Strasse, 480
Pflug, General, 90, 337, 441, 498, 501
Philomonov, General, 80, 93
Pierce machine, 488
Pilitsa, 147, 224, 236, 237, 245, 280, 292, 293, 295

Index 755

Pillkallen, 238
Pinchov, 113, 115, 121, 122, 137, 170, 171, 172
Pinsk, 137, 328, 446, 452
    marshes, 404
Pissa, River, 249, 254
Piterim, 563
Pitkelishki, 534
Plehve, General, 47, 48, 53, 96, 104, 112, 168, 204, 205, 225, 227, 228, 229, 230, 234, 242, 246, 248, 249, 255, 256, 257, 260, 263, 292, 296, 302, 325, 329, 345, 392, 393, 394
Plevna, 399
Plonsk, 311
Plotnikov, Captain, 116, 137
Plotsk, 203, 242, 243, 310, 323
Plyeshkov, General, 405, 406, 409
Podimov, General, 308, 468
Podolya, 681, 693, 721
Podryelov, Captain, 704, 705
Podvoiski, the Bolshevik, 730
Poiret, French airman, 70, 72, 144
Pokrovski, General, 496, 500, 536, 555
Poland, 46, 90, 123, 165, 199, 269, 279, 280, 283, 293, 315, 318, 324, 353, 363, 383, 425, 426, 508, 577, 635, 739
    Advance into South, 47
    South-West, 168, 185
Polichna, 134, 156, 158, 166
Polish bastion, 139
Polivanov, General, 222, 277, 351, 394, 412, 413, 414, 416, 521, 522, 527, 528, 565, 583, 586, 603
Polkovnikov, Colonel, 695, 696, 708
Polotsk, 338, 343, 458
    -Molodechno Railway, 343
Polovtsev, General, 611, 622, 656, 657, 660, 661, 663, 664, 672, 685, 692, 693
Polyesie, 434, 526
Ponevyej, 404
Popov, General, 241, 297, 346
Poremba-Djerjna, 196
Poremba Gorna, 183, 184, 185, 188, 191
Port Arthur, 53, 231
Portales, Countess, 44
Posen, 168, 213, 599
Postovski, General, 48, 60, 61, 68, 69, 79, 80, 82, 87, 92
Potapov, General, 734
Potocki, General, 172, 174, 262, 471, 500
Potok, 436
Prasnish, 60, 62, 75, 214, 241, 243, 258, 259, 260, 265, 310, 311, 315, 342, 550
    Makov, 258
    -Mlava-Neidenburg Line, 70
    -Tsyekhanov Line, 311

Preobrajenski Regiment, 100, 161, 162, 184, 188, 189, 191, 192, 246, 250, 252, 383, 463, 470, 553, 624
Pri-Amur, 48
Pripyat River, 293, 434, 446, 450
Prittwitz, General von, 56
Prjetski, Count, 226, 695
Prjevalski, General, 594, 652
Proctor, Captain, 356, 728
Proskurov, 47, 96, 348, 499
    -Kamenets Rail, 384
Protopopov, 413, 512, 514, 515, 527, 556, 563
Pruth River, 285, 445, 446, 447
Przemysl, 98, 112, 140, 149, 168, 225, 237, 244, 280, 285, 287, 321, 445
    siege raised, 143
Pskov, 329, 344, 345, 351, 392, 395, 399, 517, 534, 570, 607, 689, 704, 708, 726
Pulkova, 717
Pultusk, 242, 258, 312
Purishkevich, M., 399, 512, 513
Pustovoitenko, General, 330, 431
Putilov Works, 257, 413, 526, 528
Pyesechno, 150

Radin, 307, 313, 314
Radkevich, General, 241, 259, 336, 337, 339, 341, 342, 346, 432
Radko Dimitriev, General, 142, 143, 149, 165, 168, 169, 171, 173, 174, 179, 181, 182, 189, 193, 197, 200, 215, 224, 244, 282, 283, 284, 286, 288, 301, 304, 333, 395, 397, 398, 399, 401, 455, 517, 518, 534, 594, 602, 606, 607, 668
Radom, 106, 119, 130, 132, 134, 149, 151, 153, 162, 164, 165, 166, 169, 170, 173, 174, 197
    -Kyeltsi Railway, 165, 168, 175, 178
    -Novo-Alexandriya Road, 132
    -Opatov Line, 140
    -Petrokov, 160
    -Skarishev, 162
Radonka, 159
Radymno, 285
Raemyesto, 462
Rafalovka-Gorodnaya, 347, 434
Ragosin, Captain, 685, 692, 707, 708, 709, 710
Ragoza, General, 158, 330, 347, 410, 432, 450, 451, 452, 454, 534, 536
Raigrod, 239
Rakov, 122, 123
Ramsden, Secretary British Embassy, 558, 657
Rasputin, 333, 334, 388, 389, 411, 412, 414
    murdered, 512, 513, 514

756 Index

Rastenburg, 89
Ratnek, 739
Rattel, General, 640
Raukh, General, 459, 462, 500
Ravka, 200, 227, 233, 276, 292
Rawa-Ruska, 51, 96, 292
Redl, 278
Reiovets, 301, 303
Remington, 548
Reni, 497
Rennenkampf, General, 48, 55, 57, 58,
   59, 60, 61, 69, 84, 88, 90, 92, 167,
   168, 170, 199, 203, 204, 205, 207,
   209, 212, 215, 263, 310, 326, 401
  considerable losses, 54
  exposed position, 80
  in command of 1st Army, 47
  ordered to retire, 79
Rerberg, General, 496, 501
Revel, 348, 393, 553
Richkov, General, 310, 458
Rickel, Baron, 496
Riga, 137, 291, 292, 296, 325, 329, 330,
   344, 345, 389, 390, 391, 393, 397,
   399, 407, 426, 455, 456, 516, 539,
   599, 601, 604, 636, 652, 680, 698,
   704, 733
  Gulf, 594, 595
Rilski, General, 648, 468, 469, 470, 471
Roberts, Lord, 401
Robertson, General Sir William, 363
Robins, Colonel, 727
Rodzianko, Colonel, A.D.C. 76, 153, 157,
   159, 160, 161, 165, 166, 167, 178,
   181, 184, 186, 187, 189, 190, 193,
   194, 196, 199, 238, 248, 250, 253,
   261, 304, 349, 474, 475
  M., President of the Duma, 277,
   388, 530, 531, 556, 557, 561, 565,
   568, 569, 570, 574
Roen, 456
Rojan, 60, 75, 242, 245, 312, 313, 314, 319
Rojishche, 438, 440, 459, 460, 462, 464,
   465, 466, 468, 474, 475
Rom, 602
Romanov, Lieutenant-Commander,
   354, 357, 360, 361, 362,
  Port 510, 522, 524
  Family of, 558, 577
Romanovski, General, 535, 652
Ronjin, 427
Rosenfeldt, the Bolshevik, 623
Roshal, the Bolshevik, 661
Rosinn, junker, 711
Rosog, 80
Rovno, 49, 50, 51, 54, 298, 401, 433,
   435, 487
  H.Q. of S.W. Front, 46
Rozanov, Colonel, 183, 184, 263
Rozwadow, 105

Rudniki, 126
Rukhlov, Minister, 526
Rumania, 364, 383, 394, 399, 400, 483,
   484, 485, 486, 487, 488, 490, 491,
   497, 503, 523, 550, 551, 676, 725
  declared war, 482
Russian horse-rations, 127
Russin, Admiral, 354, 362, 366
Ruzski, General, 48, 52, 55, 93, 96, 98,
   104, 204, 215, 245, 281, 296, 329,
   344, 351, 352, 392, 394, 517, 520,
   534, 556, 593, 606, 667
  control of 3rd Army, 47
Ryabikov, Colonel, 395, 396
Ryejitsa, 345
Rzeszow, 282, 287

SADOUL, French Socialist, 727
Sagalovich, Doctor, 726
St. Omer, 365, 366
St. Petersburg, 77, 98
Sakharov, General, 383, 435, 447, 477,
   481, 486, 491, 501, 533, 536, 593
Salonika, 417, 437, 523
Salza, Baron, 47, 48, 55
Samarkand, 60, 310, 424
Sambor, 97, 285
Samoilo, Colonel, 42, 45, 352
Samsonov, General, 47, 48, 55, 57, 58,
   61, 62, 69, 70, 71, 72, 76, 80, 81,
   82, 83, 86, 87, 88, 89, 90, 94, 98,
   103, 176, 263, 310, 394, 629
  and Staff join XVth Corps, 74
  death, 77, 78
  declares position critical, 73
  description of, 59, 60
  dramatic incident, 68
San, River, 97, 98, 139, 142, 143, 148,
   151, 152, 162, 165, 174, 200, 203,
   283, 285, 286, 312, 394
Sandomir, 101, 102, 103, 105, 127, 128,
   130, 131, 140, 141, 143, 162, 165,
   168, 169, 222
Sanikov, General, 299, 348, 436, 438,
   501, 536, 584
Saratov, 386
Sarkanaiz, 518
Sarni-Kovel Rail, 499, 507
Savich, General, 285, 298, 347, 401, 522
Savinkov, M., 637, 667, 670, 671, 674,
   675, 676, 680, 681, 682, 686, 689,
   690, 691, 692, 699, 703, 705, 716,
   717, 718
Savrimovich, General, 354, 360, 361
Sazonov, M., 275, 293, 389, 419
Scale, Major, 740
Scarborough, 266
Schäffer, General, 206, 208, 211
Scheidemann, General, 92, 168, 203,
   204, 205, 206, 212, 500

Index   757

Scholtz, General, 336
Schreider, Captain, 588
Schweppes' soda, 527
Selivachev, General, 647, 648, 651, 633
Semashko, Ensign, 654, 655, 663
Semenovski Regiment, 161, 180, 246
    Battalion, 579, 580
Semlin, 180
Sencha, General, 133, 136, 137
Serail, General, 491, 523
Serbia, 180, 344, 394
    -Austrian Ultimatum, 38
Sereth, 445, 486, 665
Serge, Grand Duke, 271, 273, 274, 275, 415, 419, 428, 542, 578
Sergei, Alexandrovich, Grand Duke, 635
Seroka Bay, 510
Serotsk, 312
Sestroryetsk, 554, 664
Setsekhov, 156
Shapojnikov, Captain, 107, 109, 112, 116, 127, 128, 132, 134, 137
Shatilov, General, 499
Shavli, 291, 325
Shcheglovitov, Minister, 277
Shcherbachev, General, 285, 348, 383, 435, 438, 442, 492, 500, 535, 593
Shcherbatov, Prince, 277
Shchuchin, 241, 243, 248, 250
    Byelostok Line, 245
Shchurin, 462
Sheur, Lieutenant, 726
Shishkevich, General, 435, 438, 481, 486, 533, 536
Shishkin, Colonel, 730
Shlok, 390, 456
Shoshka, 526
Shulgin, M., the politician, 570
Shumsk, 243
Shuvaiev, General, 415, 429, 511, 512
Shuvalov, General Count, 207, 208
Siberia, 49, 77, 221, 263, 368, 579, 635
Sichevski, General, 500
Sieniawa, 283, 285, 286
    Jaroslau Line, 139
Sievers, General, Commander 10th Army, 90, 169, 200, 238, 241, 263
    General 5th, 12th and 6th Armies, 227, 228, 297, 345
    Ensign, 602, 603, 617
Silesia, 193, 200, 202, 203, 215, 219, 244
    South, 167
Sipnevo, 249
Sirelius, General, 83, 93, 405
Sitsina, 129, 130, 132
Skala, 178
Skalbmyerj, 117
Skalon, Colonel, 41, 45, 46, 734, 735, 736

Skarishev, 130, 163, 166
Skernevitsi, 143, 169, 206, 207, 211
    -Lodz Railway, 208
Skibotten-Karungi, 509
Skinski, General, 314
Skobelev, 234, 557, 672
Skorjisk, 174, 181, 184
Skoropadski, General, 644, 647
Slutsk, 347
Slyusarenko, General, 207, 407
Smatyn, 494
Smirnov, General, 225, 298, 405, 535, 593
Smislovski, General, 476, 486, 488
Smith, Captain Rowland, 704
Smith-Dorien, General, 490
Smolni Institute, 712, 714, 716, 725, 728, 731
Smorgoni, 338, 339, 342, 343
Snow, General, 366
Sofia, 362, 398
Sokal, 51, 298, 299, 468
Sokhachev, 143
Sokolov, 285, 309, 313, 316, 567, 572, 573
    -Lancut-Jawornik Line, 142
Soldau, 41, 60, 62, 69, 70, 78, 80, 311
    heavy losses, 72
Soleika Volya, 129, 130
Solets, 108, 160
Soli, 342
Soltykov, Princess, 495, 658
Somme, 457, 458, 551
Sosna, 322
Sosnitse, 109
Spencer-Cooper, Commander, 740
Stackleburg, Baron, 72, 564
Staev, 452
Stallupönen-Insterburg, 55, 57
Stanislau, 95, 281, 494, 477, 665, 666
Stanislavski, Colonel, 730, 732, 734
Stankevich, the Socialist, 718
Stanley, Admiral, the Hon. Victor, 740
Stashov, 122, 123
Staviski 243, 246
Stavrov, General, 346
Stegelman, General, 134
Stein, Von, Quartermaster-General, 91
Steklov, 567, 663
Stepanov, General, 688
Stevens, Engineer, 419, 695
Stir River, 440, 446, 447
Stogov General, 464, 494, 495, 500, 536
Stokhod, River, 446, 448, 452, 459, 461, 462, 467, 470, 474, 475, 476, 485, 487, 505, 507
Stokholm Conference, 675
Stolypin, 277
Stopnitsa, 106, 108, 122, 181, 184
Streletski, General, 499

758 Index

Strikov, 203, 208, 209, 211
Strumets, 385
Stryj, 95, 285
Strypa, 442, 665
Stsiborjitse, 178, 179, 180, 182, 184, 185, 186, 187, 189, 190, 191
Stupin, General, 500
Stürmer, M., 428, 563
Suczawa, 485, 496, 497, 498, 501
Sukha, 183, 184, 187, 189
Sukhomlin, General, 347, 435, 492, 499, 535
Sukhomlinov, General, Minister of War, 42, 45, 219, 220, 222, 277, 278, 331
Sukhomnin, General, 534
Sukhovnin, General, 593
Sukotin, 512
Sumenson, the spy, 658
Suvalki, 77, 167, 169, 239, 240, 244, 253
Suvorov, 148, 182, 186, 331, 462
Svir, 338
Svyatoi Nos, 356, 359, 360
Svyentsyani, 343, 397, 404, 505
Sweden, 278, 354
Switzerland, 574, 699
Syedlets, 215, 264, 265, 294, 295, 296, 309, 314
Syenno, 126, 130, 131
Syeradz, 212
Szczucin, 109

Tambov, 526
Tannenberg, B., 91, 204, 214, 241, 525
Tarné, M., 353, 354
Tarnobrzeg, 105, 285, 289
Tarnopol, 384, 434, 435, 440, 492, 640, 645, 665, 666
Tarnow, 282
Tartar, 233
Tashkent, 43, 498
Tauride, Palace, 557, 563, 575
Tekinski Regiment, 445
Teliache, 640
Tereshchenko, M., 528, 529, 553, 554, 563, 572, 612, 616, 617, 621, 624, 661, 663, 667, 673, 674, 676, 698, 702, 703, 704, 709
Termez, 424
Text of Emperor's abdication, 570
Thomas, M. Albert, 354, 362, 417, 418, 419, 421
Thorn, 76, 151, 164, 179, 202, 214, 253
Thornhill, Major, 429, 430, 579, 580, 588, 612, 658, 661, 662, 729
Tilli, Captain, 468
Tilsit, 55, 238
Times newspaper, 222
Tolmachev, 481
Tolpigo, General, 58

Tolstoi, 496, 580
Tomashov, 285
Torgovitsa, 440
Torklus, General, 63, 65, 93, 94, 610
  unbusinesslike methods, 66
Tornau, Baron, 162
Tornea, 424
Trans-Baikal Cossack, 490
Trans-Caspia, 287
Trans-Caucasia, 49
Trans-Vistula Front, 265, 292, 293, 307
Travnik, 304
Trentino, 437, 447, 550
Trepov, M., 418, 425, 427, 429, 495, 512, 514, 515, 522, 526
Tristen, 462, 466
Trotski, 655, 663, 691, 704, 715, 720, 724, 726, 727, 728, 730, 733, 739, 740
Trubetskoi, Prince, 345
Tsarevich, 570, 692
Tsarskoe Selo, 277, 429, 430, 468, 514, 517, 563, 668, 692, 717
  Palace, 571, 578, 582
Tseplev, 130
Tseretelli, the Socialist, 621, 651, 672
Tsurikov, General, 536
Tsyekhanov, 71, 198, 241, 294, 310, 311
Tuchow, 282
Tugan-Baranovski, Colonel, 685
Tukhum, 325
Tula, 526
Tumanov, Colonel Prince, 616, 654, 669, 670, 671, 685, 703, 714
  General Prince, 186, 212, 346, 514, 654, 670,
Turbin, General, 198, 295
Turkey, 491
Turkistan, 49, 544
Turov, 739
Tushin, 206
Tver, 697

Ukraine, 720, 727
Ulster, 38, 104, 678
Ural Cossacks, 126, 151
Urals, 309, 323, 526, 528, 598, 624
Usdau, 66, 68, 69, 85
Ushakov, Captain, 176
Ussuri Cavalry Division, 245
Uzsok Pass, 236

Vagneux, Captain, 642
Vakhrushev, General, 534
Valk, 594
Van der Fliet, General, 43, 737
Vannovski, General, 258
Vansovich, Lieutenant, 161
Varta River, 203, 204, 214
Vartenov, General, 458

Index 759

Vasiliev, General, 208, 355, 688
Vasilovski, 664
Vaslin-Ocna, 485
Vasnev, 124, 125, 126, 131
Velichko, 631
Velitsk, 467, 469
Velyarshev, General, 435, 501
Velyun, 179, 185, 204, 214
Verdun, 446, 478, 550
Verjbolovo, 239, 278
Verkhovski, General, 689, 695, 696, 698, 701, 703, 719, 720
Vernander, General, 222
Veselovski, Count, 112
Viborg, 93, 689
    Island, 560
Vickers, Messrs., 218, 257, 273, 275
Vienna, 100, 167, 284, 489
Vigonovskoe Lake, 446, 450
Vilapolski, Marquis of, 171
Vileika, 338, 342, 343
    -Smorgoni Line, 339
Vileisk, 336
Vilhaminov, General, 587
Viliya, 338
Vilkomir-Dvinsk Road, 337
Vilkovishki, 237
Vilna, 47, 205, 240, 321, 324, 325, 327, 328, 341, 342, 344, 459, 505, 536, 538, 595, 665
    -Dvinsk Railway, 557
    -Grodna-Warsaw Line, 264
Virjbnik, 166
Vironovski, General, 536
Virubova, Madame, 514, 521
Vishkov, 312, 313
Vislitza, 110
Vitonej, 462, 463, 465, 466, 467, 473
Vistula River, 56, 77, 91, 97, 99, 101, 102, 105, 106, 108, 109, 135, 140, 141, 142, 285, 288, 289, 292, 328, 343, 508, 550, 95, 117, 127, 130, 133, 134, 143, 144, 146, 147, 149, 150, 151, 155, 157, 158, 160, 165, 168, 171, 172, 175, 177, 181, 184, 185, 186, 187, 190, 198, 200, 202, 203, 204, 214, 218, 219, 222, 224, 243, 245, 253, 280, 281, 283, 293, 294, 297, 298, 310, 311, 313, 314, 317, 321, 322
Vitebsk, 43, 335
Viviani, M., 417
Vizna, 241, 242, 256, 257
Vladikavkaz, 707
Vladimir Volinski, 293, 460, 467, 483, 485, 487, 507
Vladivostok, 105, 222, 352, 424, 425, 426, 703
Vlodava, 296, 307, 308, 314
Vloshchova, 116, 117, 191

Vlotslavsk, 179, 203
Vogack, General, 520
Voislavitse, 298
Volbrom, 183, 184, 185, 195
Volga River, 238, 386, 510, 598
Volhiniya, 231, 459, 464
Volinski Regiment, 553
Volkovisk, 309
Volochisk, 51, 383, 404, 432, 433, 435
Volodchenko, 689
Vologda, 355
Volya-Penkoshevskaya, 231
    Tsirusova, 208, 209
Von Bothmer, General, 434, 440, 445
Von der Brincken, General, 500
Von Linsingen, General, 434
Voronej, 400
Voronov, 500
Vrotslavsk, 41
Vselojski, General, 525
Vyeprj River, 304
Vygnanka, 441

WALTHER, GENERAL, 410
Wardrop, Mr., 708, 711
Warsaw, 57, 61, 71, 75, 76, 77, 88, 97, 98, 99, 100, 102, 114, 118, 127, 135, 136, 137, 142, 143, 144, 146, 147, 148, 149, 150, 151, 155, 156, 164, 166, 167, 169, 170, 177, 178, 195, 196, 197, 198; 199, 200, 207, 213, 214, 224, 225, 226, 227, 231, 234, 235, 237, 238, 259, 266, 276, 285, 292, 293, 295, 296, 309, 310, 311, 312, 313, 324, 325, 331, 401, 550, 580
    -Chenstokhov Railway, 168
    -Ivangorod Line, 151
    -Mlava Railway third line added, 61
    -Mlava Railway, 91
    -Novo-Alexandriya Line, 169
Webel, General, 236
Wehlau, 90
Wenden, 345, 433
Westphalen, Colonel, 107, 128, 137
Willenberg, 56, 57, 69, 74, 75, 79, 81, 82, 244, 311
William the Chasseur, 658
Williams, Harold, Dr., 562, 572, 577
    General Sir John Hanbury, 40, 44, 55, 167, 223, 275, 496,
Wilson, Sir Henry, 365, 366, 516, 517, 519, 522
Windau, 325
Winter Palace, 656, 672, 682, 687, 706, 708, 723, 738
Wistoka, R., 101, 139, 171, 172, 174, 179, 244
Woodhouse, Consul-General, 728

Index

Woyrsch, General, 95, 96, 284
Wrangel, 137

YABLONNA, 297, 310, 313
Yakovlev, General, 491, 500
Yakubovich, Colonel, 616, 617, 624, 653, 671
Yalu, 329
Yangrot, 178, 180, 184, 187
Yanov, 57, 87, 126, 131, 326
Yanovets, 152, 158
Yanovka, 469, 471
Yanushkevich, General, 42, 43, 45, 218, 270, 274, 330, 331, 332, 493, 536
Yasenn, 115, 116, 117
Yasinga Pass, 236
Yedvabno, 250, 251, 254
Yegerski Regiment, 180, 246, 470
Yelcha, 193, 194, 196
Yepanchin, General, 240
Yermolintse, 384
Yermolyaev, 596
Yoffe, the Bolshevik, 731, 732, 733, 734, 736
Yudenich, General, 593
Yukanskie Islands, 360
Yunakov, General, 347, 536

Yusupov, Prince, 512, 513, 514
Yuzefov, 127, 134, 142

ZADROJE, 189
Zaionchkovski, General, 479, 483, 484, 486, 501, 533
Zambrov, 297, 313, 315
Zamostie, 96, 169, 286, 289
—Krasnostav-Kholm, 294
Zankevich, General, 471, 557
Zapolski, General, 640
Zarembi, 79, 243
Zavikhost, 102, 127, 140, 142, 147
Zavoiko, 681, 682
Zegelov, General, 52, 53, 54
Zegrj, 314
Zemstvo Alliance, 334
Zeppelin, 309
  brought down, 73
Zinoviev, the Bolshevik, 656
Zloczow, 299, 665
Zlota, 110, 112
  Lipa, 477, 639
Zolbnev, 103, 106, 134
Zolkiew, 292
Zvolen, 131, 132, 133, 134, 152, 158, 159, 161, 162

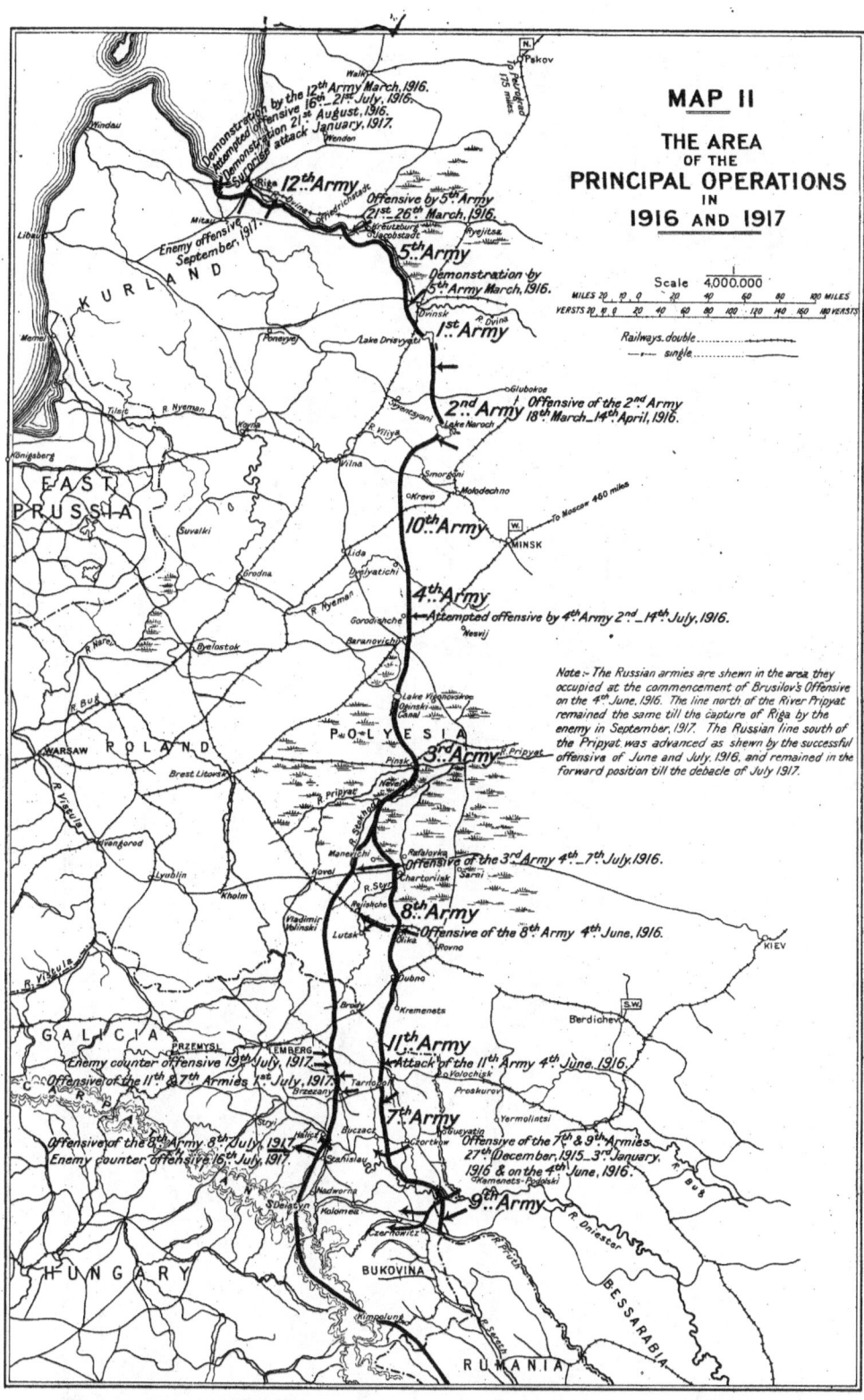

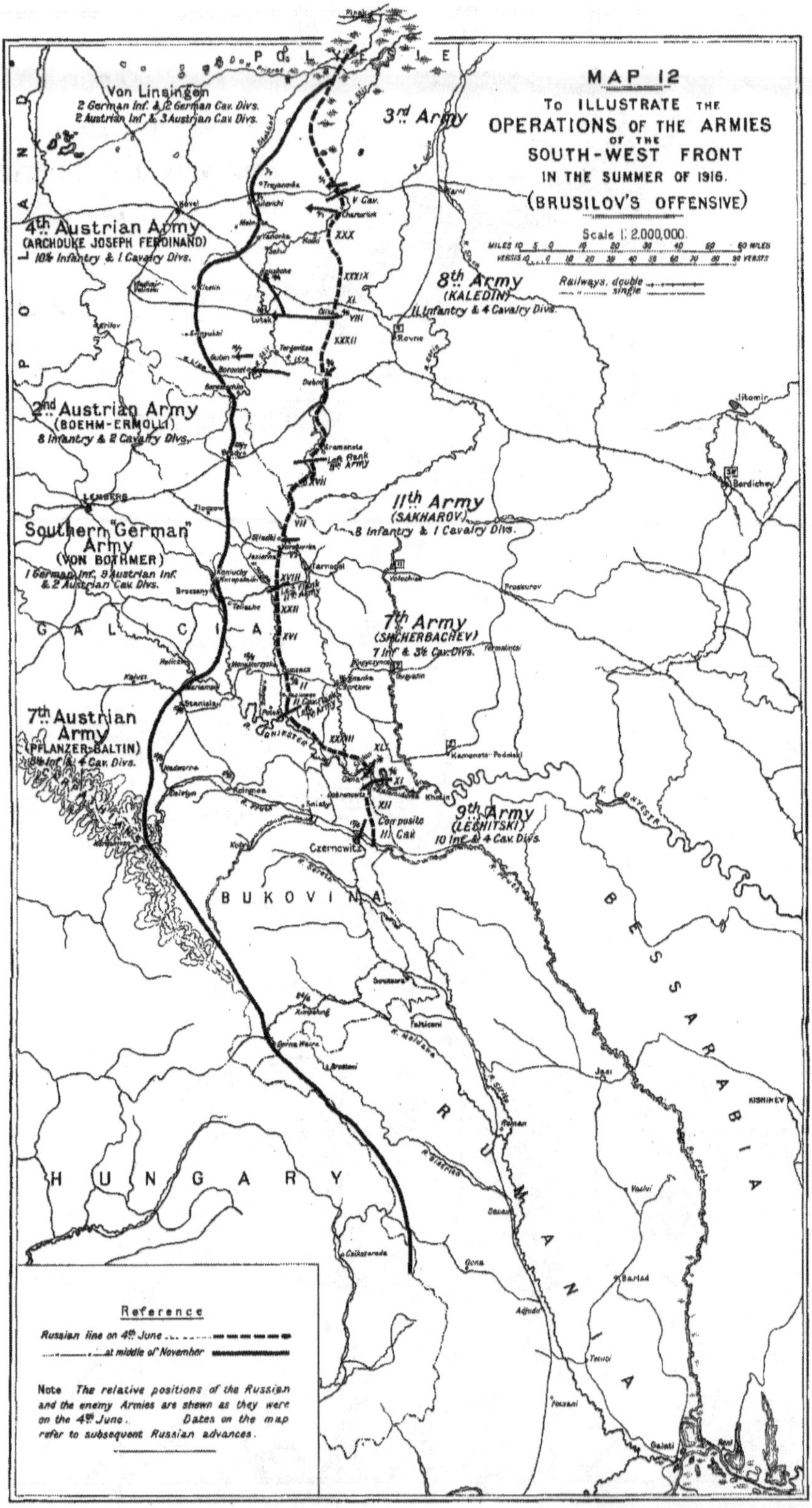
MAP 12
To ILLUSTRATE THE
OPERATIONS OF THE ARMIES
OF THE
SOUTH-WEST FRONT
IN THE SUMMER OF 1916.
(BRUSILOV'S OFFENSIVE)
Scale 1: 2,000,000.
Railways, double
single
POLESIE
Von Linsingen
2 German Inf. & 12 German Cav. Divs.
2 Austrian Inf. & 3 Austrian Cav. Divs.
3rd Army
4th Austrian Army
(ARCHDUKE JOSEPH FERDINAND)
10½ Infantry & 1 Cavalry Divs.
8th Army
(KALEDIN)
11 Infantry & 4 Cavalry Divs.
2nd Austrian Army
(BOEHM-ERMOLLI)
8 Infantry & 2 Cavalry Divs.
11th Army
(SAKHAROV)
8 Infantry & 1 Cavalry Divs.
Southern "German" Army
(VON BOTHMER)
1 German Inf, 5 Austrian Inf. & 2 Austrian Cav. Divs.
7th Army
(SHCHERBACHEV)
7 Inf. & 3½ Cav. Divs.
7th Austrian Army
(PFLANZER-BALTIN)
8½ Inf. & 4 Cav. Divs.
9th Army
(LECHITSKI)
10 Inf. & 4 Cav. Divs.
POLAND
GALICIA
BUKOVINA
BESSARABIA
HUNGARY
RUMANIA
Kovel
Lutsk
Rovno
Dubno
Lemberg
Tarnopol
Czernowitz
Kamenets-Podolsk
Berdichev
Proskurov
Jasi
Kishinev
Galati
Reni
Reference
Russian line on 4th June
" " at middle of November
Note The relative positions of the Russian and the enemy Armies are shown as they were on the 4th June. Dates on the map refer to subsequent Russian advances.

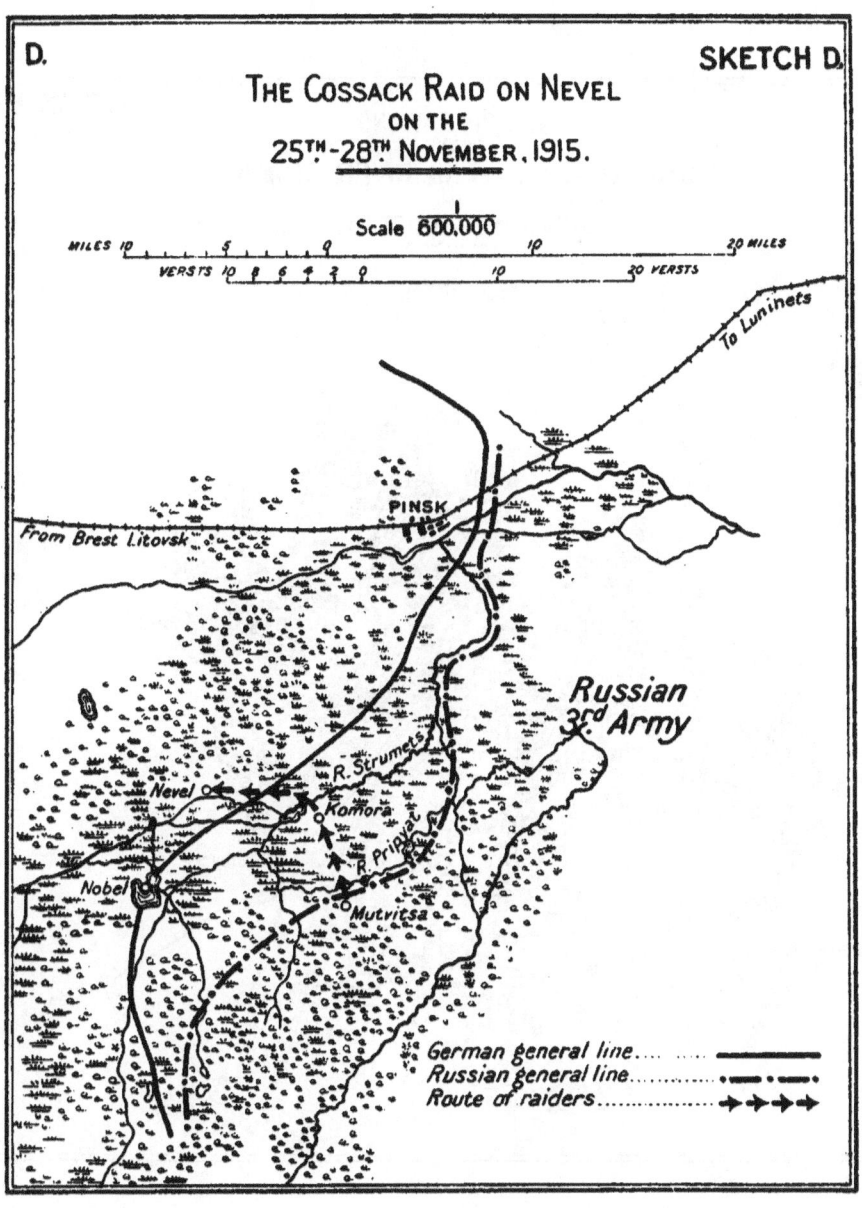

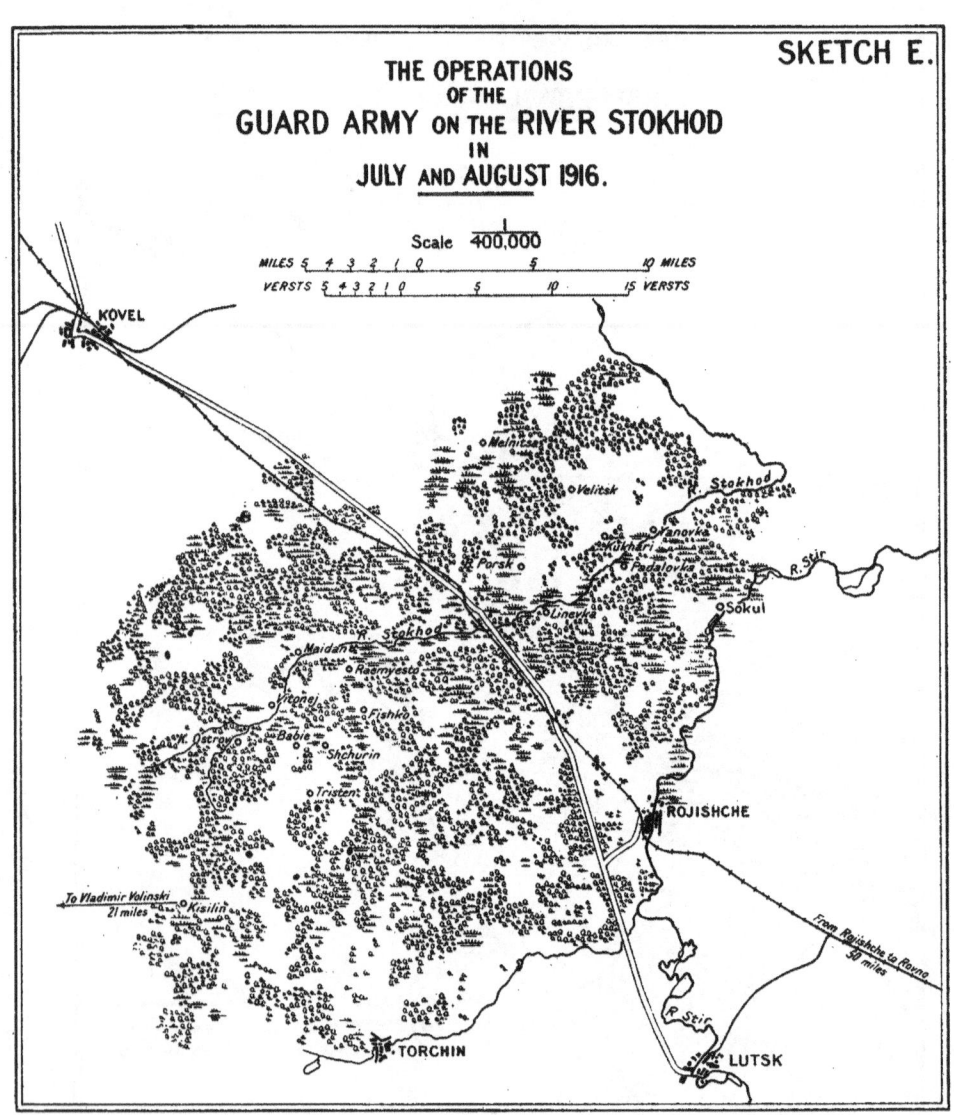

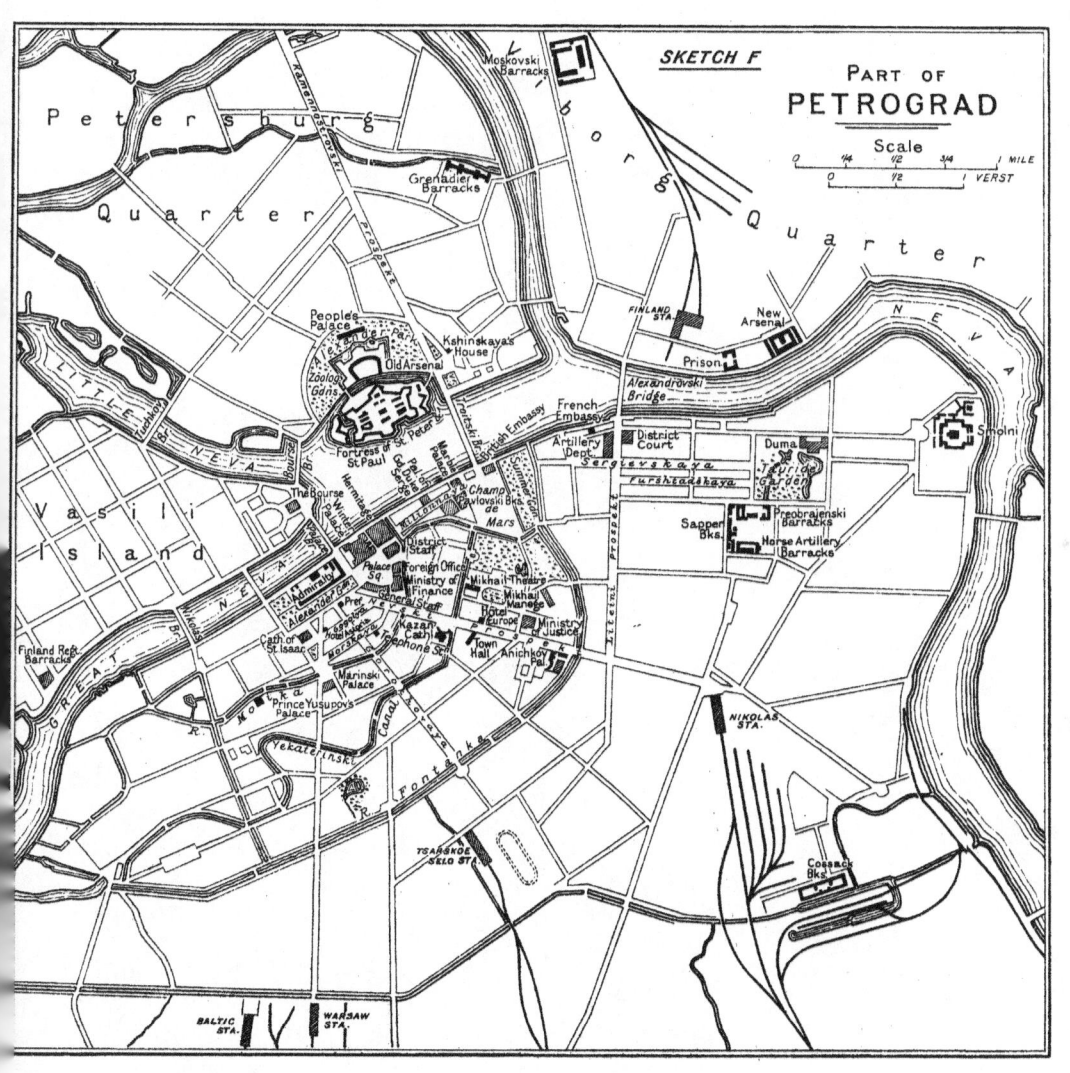

www.ingramcontent.com/pod-product-compliance
Lightning Source LLC
Chambersburg PA
CBHW021148230426
43667CB00006B/301